Churchill, the Liberal Reformer

Churchill, the Liberal Reformer

The Struggle for a Modern Home Office

Duncan Marlor

First published in Great Britain in 2024 by
Pen & Sword History
An imprint of Pen & Sword Books Limited
Yorkshire – Philadelphia

Copyright © Duncan Marlor 2024

ISBN 978 1 39905 132 3

The right of Duncan Marlor to be identified as
Author of this Work has been asserted by him in accordance
with the Copyright, Designs and Patents Act 1988.

A CIP catalogue record for this book is
available from the British Library

All rights reserved. No part of this book may be reproduced or
transmitted in any form or by any means, electronic or mechanical
including photocopying, recording or by any information storage and
retrieval system, without permission from the Publisher in writing.

Typeset by Mac Style
Printed in the UK by CPI Group (UK) Ltd, Croydon, CR0 4YY.

Pen & Sword Books Limited incorporates the imprints of After
the Battle, Atlas, Archaeology, Aviation, Discovery, Family History,
Fiction, History, Maritime, Military, Military Classics, Politics,
Select, Transport, True Crime, Air World, Frontline Publishing, Leo
Cooper, Remember When, Seaforth Publishing, The Praetorian Press,
Wharncliffe Local History, Wharncliffe Transport, Wharncliffe True
Crime and White Owl.

For a complete list of Pen & Sword titles please contact

PEN & SWORD BOOKS LIMITED
47 Church Street, Barnsley, South Yorkshire, S70 2AS, England
E-mail: enquiries@pen-and-sword.co.uk
Website: www.pen-and-sword.co.uk
or
PEN AND SWORD BOOKS
1950 Lawrence Rd, Havertown, PA 19083, USA
E-mail: Uspen-and-sword@casematepublishers.com
Website: www.penandswordbooks.com

In memory of my grandfather Fred Harwood Marlor, from Denton, Manchester, a Home Guard corporal in the 1899–1900 defence of Boer-besieged Ladysmith, who was close to starvation when he and his fellow-defenders were rescued by Winston Churchill and his comrades.

Contents

Abbreviations		vii
Acknowledgements		viii
Introduction		ix
Chapter 1	Arrival	1
Chapter 2	Prison at the Theatre	7
Chapter 3	Minister's Mercy	11
Chapter 4	'A Very Curious Morning'	28
Chapter 5	'The Noblest Utterance'	39
Chapter 6	Bracelets and Hangmen	47
Chapter 7	Curing Criminals?	63
Chapter 8	Churchill and Eugenics	70
Chapter 9	Infamy 1: Tonypandy	77
Chapter 10	Infamy 2: Black Friday	81
Chapter 11	Identity	86
Chapter 12	The Significant Spectator	96
Chapter 13	Sentiment and Doubt	107
Chapter 14	Aliens	115
Chapter 15	The Dartmoor Shepherd	123
Chapter 16	A Day in Court	133
Chapter 17	Peasants and Pheasants	137
Chapter 18	Reforming the Reformatories	142
Chapter 19	Never to be Prime Minister?	147

Chapter 20	Saving Mr Polly?	159
Chapter 21	'Exactly Like Daisy Lord'	167
Chapter 22	The Cad and the King	177
Chapter 23	'Brilliant Lions'	181
Chapter 24	Lorna Doone and a Cup of Tea	186
Chapter 25	The Panther and the Mansion House	194
Chapter 26	'The Modern Nero'	199
Chapter 27	'The Brink of Civil War'	205
Chapter 28	Saving the Jews	214
Chapter 29	A Walk with Violet	219
Chapter 30	Civilization?	231

Notes 241
Bibliography 260
Index 266

Abbreviations

HO: National Archives, Kew, Home Office Papers
CHAR: Churchill College, Cambridge, Chartwell Trust Papers, 1874–1945
LMD: Cadbury Research Library, Birmingham University: CFGM/29/2/2/2, Lucy Masterman Diaries (This is a series of dated extended accounts rather than a day-by-day diary.)
CFG: Lucy Masterman, *C.F.G. Masterman*
Hansard: House of Commons Parliamentary Debates, Fifth Series except where stated (numbered by volumes and columns)
YS: Randolph S. Churchill, *Winston S. Churchill, Volume II, Young Statesman 1901–1914*
CV: Randolph S. Churchill, *Winston S. Churchill Companion Volume II, Parts 1,2 and 3*
HCS: Robert Rhodes James, *Winston S. Churchill His Complete Speeches, Volume II, 1908–1913*
SFT: *Speaking for Themselves: The Personal Letters of Winston and Clementine Churchill*, edited by their daughter Mary Soames
HF: Paul Addison, *Churchill on the Home Front, 1900–1955*
R and H: Leon Radzinowicz and Roger Hood, *The Emergence of Penal Policy in Victorian and Edwardian England*
H and B: *English Prisons Today: Being the Report of the Prison System Enquiry Committee*, Stephen Hobhouse and Fenner Brockway
TUC: Trade Union Congress
CID: Committee of Imperial Defence
WSPU: Women's Social and Political Union

Acknowledgements

Thanks are due to many people in the genesis, writing and production of this book.

I thank Douglas Newton, formerly History Professor at the University of West Sydney, author of a number of books on the period in question for kindly reading my drafts and giving his valuable advice and help; also, David Kynaston for his encouragement and inspiration, the book *Engines of Privilege* that he co-authored providing a key piece in the jigsaw of understanding regarding Churchill and his times.

I am indebted to many archive curators and librarians for their help. I should mention especially Alison A. Vinnicome, Archivist, Registrar and Fellow at Lucy Cavendish College, Cambridge for kindly digitising for me the political notes of Lucy Masterman at a time when travel was not easy. In thanking her I thank them all.

I thank Eleanor Pepper and her sisters for their permission to quote the diaries, papers, books and press articles of Lucy Masterman, who was their grandmother and, as the wife of Charles Masterman, Winston Churchill's parliamentary under-secretary at the Home Office, has left a wealth of information and insights.

I thank Kate and Ian Russell for their kind hospitality at Shulbrede Priory, Sussex, when I was researching the diaries of Arthur Ponsonby, Catherine's grandfather, and for permission to quote these.

I should mention that the book contains public sector and parliamentary information licensed under the Open Government licence v3.0.

Special thanks are due to Lester Crook, my distinguished commissioning editor at Pen & Sword for his judicious steering of the book and to Pen & Sword production editor Harriet Fielding and her colleagues for their excellent work.

Introduction

In his lifetime, Winston Churchill's social and political identity was wrapped in mystery and paradox. That is still so, despite regular reappraisals. This book looks at a neglected aspect of Churchill. He was Home Secretary for twenty months during the years 1910–1911. He declared a penal philosophy that arguably has a message for today. It is far removed from the present era's governmental and popular media approaches.

Most people of a certain age will have personal Winston Churchill memories. In 1965 I was a first-year college student. To me, Churchill was the legend of the generation before mine, in the present day an occasional television or newspaper image, an elderly, frail figure, framed in a window or a doorway. 24 January was a Sunday. There had been news that Churchill was gravely ill. In my room that day, around breakfast time, I switched on my transistor radio, expecting to hear the familiar BBC Home Service news and chatter. Instead, there was solemn music. It could only mean that Churchill was gone.

Memories move forward to 1982 and a group-holiday in Crete, with a Knossos and the Minoans theme. I was lucky enough to become friendly with a fellow party member, sprightly in his mid-90s, who recalled being at school at Rugby with Rupert Brooke. He turned out to be a retired military man, a very senior one. He had known Winston Churchill. On his return, General Sir James Marshall-Cornwall wrote a compelling memoir, *Wars and Rumours of Wars*. One chapter is called 'Mad Hatter's Dinner Party'. The date was 27 July 1940. The venue was Chequers. The Mad Hatter was Winston Churchill.

In 2004 I read the diaries of my late mother, May Smith, including her account of 1940. She was a Derbyshire teacher. On May 29 the diarist reports, 'My father says we'll have a bottle of champagne when West Street [where they lived] is re-taken.' Her family was expecting Britain to fall to the Nazis. 31 May has: 'All signposts are being taken down – in preparation for the expected German invasion.' I looked further into the drama in the course of editing a book of extracts from the diary (*These Wonderful Rumours!* Virago). The entries resonated the more when I read, in the Hansard record of Parliament, Winston Churchill's speech to the House of Commons on 28 May 1940, in which he declared his determination that Britain should fight on.

Most personal for me was the discovery, in Churchill research for this book, that in 1900 Winston and his military comrades achieved something but for which I might not have come into the world. My grandfather, Manchester hat-manufacturer Fred Harwood Marlor, took his share in the family business and emigrated to South Africa, to try the hotel trade. He found himself in Boer-besieged Ladysmith, where he became a corporal in the Home Guard. I remember my grandmother's account of Fred's poor physical condition at the end of the siege, a doctor telling him that if he could recover sufficient strength to carry his gun, he would pull through. Winston Churchill was among the British soldiers who rode into Ladysmith on 9 March 1900 to relieve the town. They found 'tattered men, cheering feebly, some crying, ghastly pale and thin' (Winston S. Churchill, *The Boer War*, p. 186). These will have included my grandfather.

Churchill had earlier escaped from a Boer prison camp. He never forgot the experience of imprisonment. When he became Home Secretary a decade later, with responsibility for the jails, he was the first with a personal history of having been locked up. He was convinced that there were better ways of dealing with offenders than mass incarceration. He thought that the rehabilitation of as many as possible was both more rational and more humane. His speech to Parliament on 20 July 1910 was called by two prison reform activists 'the noblest official utterance in our generation'. What Churchill said and what he did is a moving story. It has been largely passed over.

In 1966 then Home Secretary Roy Jenkins, who was pushing through nation-changing liberal reform, addressed Oxford University's Labour Club. I was in the audience. I had no idea then that what he was doing made him a second Home Office Winston Churchill.

This look at Winston Churchill as Home Secretary, with new research, addresses major neglect. When penal administration and the jails are an acknowledged scandal, Churchill's philosophy and approach speak to our here-and-now.

Chapter 1
Arrival

On 15 February 1910 *The Times* readers learned that in the reshuffle after the recent General Election a descendant of the Dukes of Marlborough had landed the senior cabinet post of Home Secretary in the Liberal government – one of the top three. He was Winston Leonard Spencer-Churchill, who styled himself Winston S. Churchill.

This was the modern age, changed out of recognition by the last hundred years. In that span's early decades, the quickest a human being could travel was the speed of a horse. Now the advance of communication in all departments was bringing a new kind of world. In the governmental area of which Churchill now took charge, a murderer fleeing across the ocean would be intercepted by the technology of radio waves.

In tradition-versus-change, Winston Churchill was a modernizer. At 35, he was the youngest holder of his post since Peel. He loved to be in the public view. A fortnight earlier, when he was still President of the Board of Trade, pressmen had followed his progress, with his wife Clementine, around London in a motor, as eighty 'labour exchanges' opened their doors for the first time, his creations.[1]

Before Trade, Churchill had been parliamentary under-secretary to Lord Elgin at the Colonial Office. He told his colleagues he aimed to be prime minister by his early 40s. Winston's bumptious self-advertisement grated with some. He rounded off a file minute on colonial policy with, 'These are my views. W.S.C.' 'But not mine. E.', annotated Elgin laconically. Churchill's hide was tough. There were early signs of an attractive side to him. In his administration of colonial affairs, he made penal interventions demonstrating fairness and humanity. When twenty-five Zulu activists were deported to St Helena by the government of Natal, Winston discovered that they were being given sub-standard food and put to work on stone-breaking. He instructed the Governor of St Helena to ensure that the deportees had a decent diet and plots for vegetable-growing, and the chance to earn money by manufacturing baskets and shoes.[2]

Promotion to the cabinet came in 1908 when H.H. (Henry) Asquith became prime minister. Churchill now turned into one of the socially-interventionist 'New Liberals', driving government into new territory: social insurance for the less privileged, state commitment to 'a minimum standard'. Whatever cause Winston adopted, he threw himself at it hard, his imagination supplying the rhetoric, an area of his performance which drew attention. He was a champion of the common people, though sometimes upper-class paternalism peeped through.

2 Churchill, the Liberal Reformer

Whilst he cared passionately for the interests of the poorer classes, the demos had to be kept in its place. And yet (Churchill's story is full of and-yets), he thought of himself as an outsider.[3]

The Home Office was not a leap into the unknown for Churchill since the Board of Trade worked with the Home Department, but he would be treading fresh territory, most especially responsibility for His Majesty's Prisons in England and Wales.[4]

He would later recall his upward career jump. He told readers of the *News of the World* in the spring of 1939 that Prime Minister Asquith, 'in a courtly letter suggested to me that the Irish office might form the best outlet for my efforts.' His article went on:

> I had a very clear view in the negative sense. It was thought that I had played a part in the election which entitled me to advance in the political hierarchy.[5]

Churchill made his case successfully. His salary shot up from £2,000 per annum to £5,000. This will have been welcome. Winston's means were chronically short of his lavish lifestyle – even with a considerable income from books and articles.[6]

The January 1910 General Election had robbed the Liberals of their overall majority. But the party, though now near-dead-heated with the Conservatives, could still rule, thanks to alliance with the Irish Nationalists and the forty MPs of the working-class Labour Party. Churchill had certainly been a key player for the government at the hustings. He had been on tour from Cornwall to his own constituency of Dundee, piston arms swinging as he delivered digs and jibes against the opposition Tories, spicing his performances with well-practised topical jokes.

Physically, he was distinctive rather than impressive: quite short; hair reddish and receding; trademark baby-face. He was good platform value. With hecklers, a confidential aside with his audience turned an interrupter into a third party. The wit was neat. A man in the gallery who shouted 'Rot!' at one of the minister's gigs was, said Churchill, 'expressing what is on his mind'. Newspaper reports carried regular interpolations of '(laughter)'. Some who never got to see the touring orator heard his speaking-voice on a recent gramophone record. The vowels are not entirely as expected: 'thorse', 'imporse', for example. The famous lisp which troubled the politician in his earlier days is there, but controlled. The voice that 1910 knew is higher-pitched and lighter than that familiar to later years, lacking the gravelly gravitas, but there are some Churchillian cadences.[7]

He was an author: the spinner of page-turner tales of military adventure in far-off lands, featuring himself. In the genre of British forces outwitting and overpowering their enemies, Winston S. Churchill books were good value. He had taken part in what readers of soldier literature drooled over – a *cavalry charge*: he had been with General Kitchener at the Battle of Omdurman in the Sudan. Readers thrilled to the author-hero escaping over the wall of a Transvaal prison, throwing himself on the coupling of a freight train and hiding among empty coal sacks, on his hair-raising way (with a price on his head) to join up with the British Army. Churchill also brought to the public his experiences on the Indian North-West Frontier (with Afghanistan) and in South Africa. Politically, he had written a biography promoting the career of his late father, Lord Randolph Churchill, a Conservative Chancellor of the Exchequer whose career had soared and crashed. 'Written' is figurative. Churchill's output was largely dictated: 'mouth to hand', he chuckled.[8]

The young minister's celebrity had been boosted by his 1908 Westminster wedding to Clementine Hozier. Clementine's independent spirit had been forged out of a childhood of family quarrels. Winston was captivated by her vivacious charm. The marriage was successful, but with Winston came his territory. Clemmie did not care for her husband's opinionated close chum, the Tory MP F.E. Smith, nor for her husband's heavy gambling on cards and at the casino, a magnet to him on his foreign travel. Winston lived far beyond his means and his debts worried his wife. But shared interests – golf being one – helped to cement the partnership. Frictions were managed.[9]

Since entering Parliament as a Conservative, Churchill had recast himself as a progressive Liberal, tilting against the privileges wielded by the House of Lords with its power of veto, which regularly wrecked the socially progressive legislation of the other place. He was a peace-promoting 'economist', calling for the battleship expenditure to be trimmed. He was closely associated with Chancellor of the Exchequer, David Lloyd George, taxer of the rich, whose 'People's Budget' of 1909 the Lords had vetoed, in defiance of convention since it was a money measure. That storm had triggered the election. It was remarkable that Churchill, cousin of a Duke, was George's close political comrade. The Welsh radical was loathed by many a great-house dweller. Once Churchill had dismissed LG as 'a vulgar, chattering little cad'. Now the pair were inseparable.[10]

One of Churchill's Liberal colleagues, Llewellyn Atherley-Jones, called him 'a soldier of fortune'. It was a common charge but Churchill could always convince himself that what he was doing was full-square with his principles. He was devoted to the political memory of his father. Randolph had by no means been a regular Conservative. He had promoted 'Tory Democracy', and had backed an expansion of the electorate and made reduction of military expenditure a special issue. There was plenty that his son could appreciate in the programmes of the Liberal Party. And anyway, Winston was never a well-behaved party man.[11]

Like Lloyd George, Churchill was a hell-raiser at election time. After the election, he was summoned to Downing Street by Asquith's wife. H.H. was on a rest-cure in Cannes. Margot was doing some politicking on her own account. She gave Winston a dressing-down: he was being damaged by being bracketed with Lloyd George and his 'violent speeches'. She exhorted him:

Why alienate *every* one – why not turn over a completely new leaf and make everyone love you and respect you?[12]

Churchill's reply was guarded, ('putting tea in his sugar', Margot satirized): 'Well I'm not sure [Lloyd George] didn't win as many seats as he lost, but he certainly said a good many cheap things. I was not going to compete.' Margot had been upset that H.H. had been prevented from delivering an election victory speech in his Fife constituency by suffragettes up lampposts who yelled, 'Votes for Women!'. Here was a mighty issue on which Churchill needed to make his position clear. He himself had been troubled by the women.[13]

The first meeting of the new cabinet prompted a *Punch* arrivals skit, in which the humourist reports Lloyd George descending on a parachute, whilst Churchill has relegated the chauffeur of his motor to the back seat whilst he himself takes the wheel. A cartoon in the magazine has Churchill in his new Whitehall office. By the window we see a shifty-looking character, whose clothing appears to have poacher's pockets. It is Lloyd George. The Chancellor muses on his friend's rise: 'I suppose you're going to settle down now?' WSC offers some comfort: 'If you find yourself in trouble, I'll see if I can't get you a reprieve.' Here is an allusion to a function of the Home Secretary of which Churchill would later speak in his newspaper reminiscence:

> Just when I was so pleased to have this move up in the world, one of my colleagues said to me: 'I gather they've got a bad murder case waiting for you.' Then I began to realise the painful duties which the Home Secretary has to discharge. Upon the Minister's table stands a card upon which are inscribed the names of all persons lying under sentence of death. These are duly crossed off as they are executed or have their sentences commuted to penal servitude for life.[14]

Churchill's *News of the World* article discusses the function of the Home Secretary: 'He is <u>the</u> Secretary of State, for most of the other offices have budded out of this function.' Churchill's new department touched most aspects of the nation's organized life. A sketch of its breadth is to be found in a letter of Churchill's predecessor Herbert Gladstone (son of Prime Minister Gladstone) to his sister:

> Answerable for the safety, health and working conditions of 7,000,000 people in factories and workshops, for a million in the mines, for the personal rights of all persons under police jurisdiction, for public decency, for the dark corners of police cells and prisons, the Home Secretary stands closest to the lives of the multitude.

Gladstone compared himself to 'a cab horse held up by the reins and shafts and bound to go on'.[15]

The Home Secretary's responsibility for jails covered just England and Wales because there was a Secretary of State for Scotland and one for Ireland. The average daily prison population was about twenty thousand. Gladstone had overseen progress making the penal system more humane. The landmark year of 1908 had seen: the Probation of Offenders Act (court status for probation officers); the Prevention of Crime Act ('borstal' training made available for young people between 16 and 21); and the Children Act (juvenile courts and a ban on jail sentences for offenders under 16). If Churchill was going to be a reformer, he had something to build on.

Herbert Gladstone had been quiet in cabinet. Not so Churchill. Financial Secretary to the Treasury, Charles Hobhouse, remarked that Winston's arrival in 1908 had resulted in the disappearance of harmony: 'the whole Cabinet atmosphere has been upset by Churchill.' Liberal Chief Whip Alick Murray (Master of Elibank) grumbled in his diary:

Churchill talks too much at the Cabinets and too loudly.[16]

Gladstone, now a viscount, was off to South Africa as Governor General, but not yet. He sent his Home Office successor some notes on the staff and the work. The backroom chief, Sir Edward Troup is fulsomely praised. Troup had steered the Home Office through finger-printing, photography, anthropometric data, and other modern-fangled innovations. Under his aegis, British compilation of judicial statistics had gone from amateur incompetence to European leadership. He interpreted law, constitution and practice, and most especially precedence. His work included framing answers for the Home Secretary and his junior minister at parliamentary question time. The Home Office had to field many representations, including from a body containing, in Troup's view, 'the crankiest people in the world'. That was the Humanitarian League, which campaigned against avoidable human and animal suffering, and had a particular interest in prisons. The League was watching with interest the new arrival at the Home Office.[17]

Troup is recalled in the memoirs of Harold Scott who entered the Home Office as a nervous junior in 1911. Scott speaks of Sir Edward's formidable 'code of accuracy, finish and integrity which permeated the whole department', calling him 'a rather silent, heavy Scot, with little sense of humour.' The H. O's culture of buff folders had not many moments of levity.[18]

If Churchill took a reforming line, he would have to work hard to carry his staff. As one historian puts it, 'Home Office officials tended to be particularly aware of reasons why changes should not be made.' That rationale would still be there in the BBC's 1960s/1970s radio comedy *The Men from the Ministry*, about civil servants in a Home Office-type department whose chief concern was to avert trouble. For a proactive young minister with a drive for change, this culture was likely to be a problem. Winston was going to need strength of personality, combined with diplomacy.[19]

Churchill's parliamentary under-secretary, Charles Masterman, one year older, had been with him at the Board of Trade, piloting through the House of Commons the Eight Hours Bill, which reduced the length of coalminers' working day. Charles, according to his wife Lucy, was dismayed when he first learned that he would be Churchill's junior minister. The self-impressed Winston could be a pain. A.G. Gardiner, editor of the leading Liberal newspaper, the *Daily News*, commented that Churchill was, 'so absorbed in himself that he does not pay others the compliment of even being aware of them.' The unstoppable WSC outpourings produced an Asquith comment, 'Winston thinks with his mouth.' Lucy Masterman wrote of Churchill 'pouring out undigested ideas'.[20]

Among the congratulatory notes received by Churchill was one from Sir Francis Hopwood, who had been his Permanent Under-Secretary of State at the Colonial Office. Hopwood wrote:

> Keep an eye on the sentences passed by fat-headed people and reduce them fearlessly. If you feel such interest in the 'prisoner' as you felt in the wrongs of the 'personal case' when with us you have a most beneficent period of service before you.[21]

Winston carried goodwill as he took on the challenge of the Home Office.

Chapter 2

Prison at the Theatre

Winston Churchill loved the theatre. At Harrow he twice narrowly missed the Shakespeare prize. He once dreamed of being a playwright: his mother talked him out of writing a play set in South Africa during the Boer War (with Herbert Beerbohm Tree, no less, to be producer). Jennie, daughter of an American financier, was a famed beauty. She had been one of King Edward's many lovers in his Prince of Wales days. It was the future King who introduced her to Randolph. She was her son's confidante and mentor, pulling every string to assist his career. Shortly after taking on his new office, Churchill was at the first night of *Justice*, at the Duke of York's. The play was from the pen of John Galsworthy, known for social commentary novels and cutting-edge drama. Galsworthy put prison cruelty under the spotlight. The Home Secretary was accompanied by the Chairman of the Prison Commission for England and Wales, Sir Evelyn Ruggles-Brise. Churchill was Galsworthy's perfect audience. After his Boer War confinement, he reflected on 'the hateful degradation of imprisonment.' The story was of a solicitor's clerk jailed for misappropriating his employers' money. Theatre-goers saw the young man broken by solitary confinement.[1]

Churchill saw *Justice* more than once. The drama presented the prison system officially called 'separate confinement', which inmates had to undergo in the first part of their sentence. In the three-minute 'cell scene' no word is uttered. A prisoner beats helplessly on his door. Stage notes call for: 'a whitewashed space, thirteen feet by seven, nine feet high; a floor of shiny blackened bricks; a barred window, a ventilator.' Winston, with his active brain, will have understood the torture of deprivation of stimulation. One moment haunted theatre patrons. The directions were:

> Falder moves slowly towards the window tracing his way with his finger along the top line of the distemper that runs round the walls.[2]

John Masefield lay awake all night after seeing it. The poet wrote to John Galsworthy that *Justice* could 'have an immense result upon our national attitude to crime'. What Galsworthy conveyed is captured in the memoirs of Fenner Brockway, who had the 'separate' treatment whilst serving time for military service refusal during the First World War: 'Sometimes I wanted to break windows and storm the door. I wondered if I would remain sane…'[3]

Solitary confinement dated from early Victorian times. Previously jails had chiefly held prisoners awaiting trial, and debtors. Then, the deterrence of crime was the 'Bloody Code', with over 200 offences carrying the death penalty and about ten per cent of those condemned being executed. When it was dropped, and with the end of transportation to Australia, the lead deterrent became imprisonment, including 'penal servitude' (sentences of three years or more). There was a fear that putting convicts together would breed crime. Separate confinement aimed to suppress 'contamination'. With the Separate System went the Silent System (the latter applying throughout sentences): 'prohibition of all intercourse by word of mouth among the prisoners'. Prisoners found ingenious ways round it: tic-tac, signs, morse on pipes and ventilators, and the singing of messages in the prison chapel to the tune of hymns. But the regime was remorseless. One governor called it 'harmful and evil', with its psychological damage to inmates who were naturally gregarious.[4]

A friend and confidant of Churchill, Wilfrid Scawen Blunt, poet and essayist, had done two months in prison in 1888 for Irish nationalistic activism. Through Blunt, Churchill had the benefit of the prisoner's-eye view. In 1909 he told Wilfrid: 'I am dead against the present system and if I am ever at the Home Office, I will make a clean sweep of it.' Now that he was, Blunt promised a paper. It arrived on 25 February 1910, with a plea: 'Don't leave it too long in your pigeon holes'. Wilfrid called for the end of solitary confinement, 'mind starvation of an enduringly pernicious kind', also of the prisoners' 'garb of infamy', meaning the drab-yellow uniform with its garishly ugly 'broad arrows' (technically a symbol of state property). Blunt also did not see why 'the prison warder should deny [an inmate] a cheerful word or look upon him sourly'.[5]

Blunt had reason to hope. By April it was being reported that Churchill was drastically shaking up the Home Office. An early WSC statement will have raised eyebrows. The new Home Secretary declared that it was necessary 'to arrange matters so that next year there will be 50,000 fewer people sent to prison than this year.' In 1909 there were 200,000 committals to prison, the majority on short sentences.[6]

Churchill would have to work with the Prison Commission and its chairman. Sir Evelyn Ruggles-Brise's celebrity (twenty-five years in post) had recently won the accolade of a *Vanity Fair* cartoon. Sharp, engaging eyes, neat moustache, well-tailored coat, and spare figure mark out a busy and successful man. Like Churchill, Brise was an aristocrat excluded from family inheritance by the primogeniture rule of eldest male son succession. Sir Evelyn would not be inheriting Spains Hall in Essex. Like Churchill, whose late father was only the third son of the Duke of Marlborough, Brise had to make his way in the world. Like Churchill, Brise needed earnings to keep up his lifestyle. The parallels between the two ran deep. Both were reformers. Both wanted their careers to make a mark.[7]

Brise hated *Justice*. Eye-witnesses reported that, whilst Churchill viewed with sympathy, the Prison Commission chief watched with 'his eyes starting out of his head'. Separate confinement was a cardinal principle for Sir Evelyn. He saw it as properly monitored by the professionals: governors, prison doctors, and chaplains ensured that prisoners did not suffer unduly. To Brise and his colleagues, Galsworthy was a nuisance, giving people wrong ideas, but they did allow him to interview prisoners.[8]

1910's jail population, though small in comparison with today, was a sizeable chunk of British humanity. The number who had a taste of prison was much larger than the daily average figure suggests. Most sentences were short. Sixty-one per cent of those imprisoned received two weeks or less, typical offences being default of fine payment (more than half), drunkenness, and breach of municipal by-laws. Jails, it should be mentioned, were entirely state-run. A hundred years earlier the idea of prisons for private profit had been debated and rejected. It would not re-emerge until the 1980s.[9]

In July 1910 the *Daily News* carried an editorial on prisons:

> The British system ranks decidedly low. It is much above the level of most of the United States, but it is far less scientific and, on the whole, less merciful than those of the leading Continental states.[10]

The paper mentioned low pay and poor conditions of service for prison officers. And there was the suffering of inmates in their cells:

> The only window is near to the ceiling, and not even the sky can be seen out of it. There are many countries which we think are backward, which have discarded [this arrangement].'

The *News* pointed to the lack of any women on the Prison Commission and to judges 'without the slightest familiarity with the science of penology'. In 1910 Britain was emerging from the shadow of harsh mid-Victorian acts rushed through Parliament in a climate of panic caused by 'garrotting' robberies in London. The Penal Servitude Act extended imprisonment and the Garrotters Act reintroduced corporal punishment for armed or violent robbery.[11]

Humane reform had made progress. In 1894 Asquith as Home Secretary set up a committee, chaired by Herbert Gladstone. The then Chairman of the Prison Commission was ex-soldier Sir Edmund Du Cane. Much of what went on in jail was intrinsically futile. The tread-wheel had inmates doing six thousand feet daily. The 'crank' handle had to be turned thousands of times a day. It could be tightened by the warders ('the screws'). Shot-drill had cannon-balls passed along a line. Failure to meet the standards incurred loss of remission. Prison was about the complete control by the state of the bodies and minds of the inmates, symbolized by the observation holes in the cell doors. The Gladstone

Committee went some way to recalibrate the raison d'être. The tread-wheel-type rigmarole now disappeared. Previously, prisoners had been, to quote its report, 'treated too much as "a hopeless or worthless element of the community".' Now, reformation and deterrence became 'concurrent objects'. The committee wanted solitary confinement reconsidered. If Churchill was going to be a penal reformer, the tide was with him. There was plenty of scope. Much of the deliberately spartan Victorian regime remained. An example was the sanitary arrangements, Du Cane having had cell plumbing ripped out.[12]

The length of separate confinement was determined by classification. 'Star Class' (first offenders) did three months; other persons without serious convictions ('intermediates') did six; habitual offenders ('recidivists') did nine. John Galsworthy was informed by Gladstone that henceforth separate confinement was to be three months for all classes. This was set to come in on 1 April 1910. Penal enlightenment was the direction. A manifestation was shorter imprisonment tariffs and more alternatives to custodial sentences. The process was termed the 'Abatement of Imprisonment'. What brought it about is disputed. One viewpoint puts it down to the 'positivist criminology' in vogue on the continent: punishment to fit the criminal rather than the crime. Cesare Lombroso's 1876 *L'Uomo Delinquente* identified offenders of different types and looked to deal with them appropriately in order to reform them. (Unfortunately, the Lombroso school was tied up with eugenics and breeding theory.) A British example of the new approach was the Inebriates Act of 1898, by which habitual drunkards could be sent to specialist reformatories. The extent of the influence of penal positivism in Britain has been contested by the claim that British reforms owed much to radical humanitarianism. The Humanitarian League was about to be pleased by the advent of Winston Churchill.[13]

Chapter 3
Minister's Mercy

The Home Office's permanent under-secretary was a believer in the social quarantining of prisoners. Sir Edward Troup had told Herbert Gladstone that, with the exit of the tread-wheel and the crank, separate confinement was vitally needed for deterrence. If Churchill tried to remove it, he faced trouble. The scorn of prison mandarin Ruggles-Brise for John Galsworthy hisses in the Prisons Commission Report for the year ending 31 March 1910: 'the alleged horrors of separate confinement as portrayed in a dramatic representation omitted the explanations which would have enabled the public to grasp its meaning and purpose'.[1]

With Churchill on Galsworthy's side, a battle was on the cards. Those days were recalled in the memoirs of young Whitehall staffer Harold Butler:

> The old hands were rather dismayed by the temerity with which Mr Churchill challenged principles which had remained sacrosanct for many years, and by his appalling energy.[2]

Since Churchill was heretical, strategy was required. He asked Brise to put together the arguments *against* total abolition of separate confinement. By 25 February the Home Secretary had in his hands a compendium of beloved arguments. For the Commissioners, it was axiomatic that the criminal classes would strengthen each other's propensities if they mixed. The 'Silent' system had the same rationale. Conversation was permitted only as a privilege at exercise (marching round in circles) in regulated pairs for certain prisoners deemed to have earned it.[3]

In mid-March Winston Churchill received a letter about solitary confinement from pioneer investigative journalist and ex-prisoner, William Stead, writing two years to the day before he would perish on the *Titanic*, gathering material for an article on the wonder ship. Stead's career, which prefigured the modern tabloids, was erratic and wild, but it brought about the major reform of the raising of the age of consent from thirteen to sixteen. Stead broke the law in the course of his probes and tasted jail. Currently editor of *Review of Reviews*, he lamented the 'constant tendency on the part of all prison officials to forget that they are dealing with human beings'. He had common ground with Churchill:

> You, fortunately, have been in gaol, although only as a prisoner-of-war, but still you must have something of the feeling which binds us all in a bond of brotherhood.[4]

The extraordinary story of this Winston Churchill believer (WSC brushed off his association attempts), and occult delver, is beyond the scope of this account, but one curiosity may be mentioned: In December 1911 he wrote to Churchill to inform him that he had psychic information that in the beyond his father Randolph was fretting about his son's insufficient rest and sleep.[5]

Troup and Brise had to be brought on side. On 7 March the Home Secretary assured Sir Edward that he acknowledged 'the importance of making the first period of prison life a severe disciplinary course, interposing a hiatus between the world which the convict has left and the public works gang which he is to join'. The work squads were at the convict jails, where longer-term prisoners went after their initial separate confinement. WSC knew that upsetting his staff would endanger future reform – and would not be good for his political ambitions. He kept his tussles with Ruggles-Brise polite. It became clear that there would have to be compromise. In late May it was announced that separate confinement was to be cut to one month for first offenders and intermediates (still three for recidivists). Troup, on a circulating file on 10 June, called this 'retrograde'.[6]

The Prison Commissioners' Annual Report was required reading for the Humanitarian League. A columnist on its journal took vigorous issue with the report's claim that separate confinement was 'nothing like medieval cells and baronial dungeons, but the recognized basis of every prison system in every country'. *Humanitarian* saw 'whitewash'. The magazine was following Churchill's activity at the Home Office with rising hopes.[7]

Herbert Gladstone left departure notes for his successor. He thought that on prisons: 'it won't be a bad thing to give a harassed department some rest.' The impression was that the incoming minister just needed to keep things on the tracks. That was to miss the Churchill dynamic. Tinkering was no good. Winston's career was powered by action and publicity. His ambition required the making of a big mark at all stages. The obvious scope for major change at the Home Office was in criminal justice and in the penal institutions for which the department carried responsibility.[8]

Churchill set his staff to delve into the sentencing files. The results staggered him. He remarked in a memorandum on the 'gigantic' annual incarceration of minor offenders: 'pernicious', he called it. Offenders committing repeat trifling crimes were given long-term incarceration. He found: seven years' penal servitude for stealing a hen; ten years for a garden fork; twelve years for a piece of canvas. Keeping petty offenders out of jail was a central aspiration of the new Home Secretary.[9]

He applied his multi-directional energy and his imagination to a series of Abatement of Imprisonment projects. One idea was for unruly young offenders. 'Defaulters' Drill' would enable youths between 16 and 21 to stay out of prison by attending a course of tough physical workouts. Churchill had in mind minor assaults, larcenies, and public nuisance such as disorder with footballs.

The equivalent 'boisterous and exuberant moments' indulged in by the socially privileged at Oxford and Cambridge would, he said, never engage the risk of a prison cell. He spoke as one who was not among the 302 university educated MPs elected in January 1910 (213 having attended Oxford or Cambridge). When Churchill first entered Parliament, he reflected that his difficulty in being extempore in speech-making came from his lack of the university debating experience that many had. He did not have the oratorical assurance of those whose performance had been honed by student societies. He had to pre-work his speeches heavily.[10]

Under Defaulters' Drill, magistrates would have the power to award up to twenty-eight days' attendance:

> ...physical extension motions, Swedish gymnastics with or without dumbbells. The boys should not be exhausted, but the training should be severe and rigorous.

It would be administered by the police at the police station. Chief Constables were sounded. Yorkshire West Riding's chief did not like policing being mixed up with punishment. He would rather that errant boys had compulsory schooling or training in market-gardening. Birmingham's head policeman told the Home Office that working-class boys were underfed and physically weak. The workouts would be tough for them.[11]

A supportive letter (to *The Times*) came from the women's suffrage campaigner Sylvia Pankhurst. She wanted girls to get the benefit (if such it was) of the short-sharp-shock. Winston Churchill had tangled with Sylvia four years previously in Manchester during the 1906 General Election. The suffragettes of the Women's Social and Political Union systematically harassed Liberal MPs, despite the party being on balance pro-female suffrage. Churchill was a special target, perhaps because his manner was annoying. He was not against votes for women, but he did not include it in his campaigning. It is doubtful whether Churchill gave serious thought to extending Defaulters' Drill to females. His worlds – boys' schools, military academy, army, and Parliament – were male.[12]

Churchill was concerned at what he saw as an increasing tendency for courts to impose three-year borstal sentences for offences that would not have incurred more than six months under general prison-sentencing. Borstal training for young offenders was the crown-jewel of the Prison Commissioners, especially of Maurice Waller, who headed the day-to-day arrangements. Churchill took as an example of excessive sentences the case of a first-offender youth who had been given three years' borstal for stealing some brass fittings. He called Borstal: 'within limits desirable as a beneficial and humane refinement on the ordinary Prison System …a beneficial discipline for poor lads…analogous to the old system of apprenticeship', but he added that it was 'bad in itself'. Brise (who had founded the borstal system) was scandalized by the patronization: borstal had turned lives around. He invited Waller to write a memorandum. He wrote his own (long) paper for Sir Edward Troup, and attached Waller's to it.[13]

Waller was outspoken:

> The Secretary of State appears to be under some misapprehension as to the nature and intentions of the Borstal system…You do not play cricket and football in a prison. You do not associate in a common room with newspapers and weekly magazines in a prison. I venture that it might be desirable that he should acquaint himself with the system before issuing any general directions to alter the principles of commitment.

Brise backed Waller. He saw no increasing tendency to give three-year borstal sentences.[14]

Churchill was preparing to address Parliament on the subject of prisons and penal policy in the annual Home Office debate. He will have been aware that the attitude to prison inmates of his permanent under-secretary was a world away from his own. Sir Edward Troup's feelings are manifested in a note on criminal statistics:

> A large part of the prison population consists of persons of the habitual-criminal and vagrant classes, and most of these are constitutionally lazy. In prison, they have good clothing, sufficient food, warmth and comfort: they work for short hours and are not pressed. No doubt they miss tobacco, beer and female society, but otherwise they are much more comfortable than tramping in the cold and wet or standing outside public houses. Their general sentiment about a sentence of a fortnight or a month is, 'I can do that on my head.'[15]

He wanted discipline sharpened up. Troup's attitude was shared by other senior staff.

If the Prison Commission was basking in the laurels of the reforms of recent years, that complacency will have been encouraged by a series of articles in *The Times* in 1910. Later published as a book, *Our Prisons*, it invested jails with a rosy glow. Arthur Paterson thought that inmates being allowed to exchange 'a word now and then' was the mark of a humane system.[16].

A very different picture of the jails of this time is given in an account of a visit to Dartmoor by a future Prison Commission Chairman:

> [The inmates'] drab uniforms were plastered with broad arrows, their heads closely shaven…Not even a safety razor was allowed, so that their faces were covered with a sort of dirty moss…The prison regime had succeeded in making a large number of human beings into objects of ugliness and contempt…As they saw us coming, each man ran to the nearest wall and put his face closely against it, remaining in this servile position till we

had passed. This was a strictly ordered procedure. The men looked cowed and listless.[17]

Dehumanization was built into the culture. After a decade-and-a-half of reform the system of breaking spirits was still embedded. It was epitomized in the loss to inmates of their names. Warders barked out numbers.

Any attempt to assess prisoner experience in the jails is fraught with difficulty. There is the 1921 *English Prison System* by Ruggles-Brise; *The English Convict* by Charles Buckman Goring (1913); Arthur Paterson's cheer-leading for the authorities; the laudatory biography of Ruggles-Brise by Shane Leslie; and the convict memoirs. The period when Churchill took office was seeing the entry into the jails of members of the Women's Social and Political Union. The literature of suffragette prison experience is moving and revelatory but it is political. The most comprehensive picture of prison life in the early years of the twentieth century is to be found in the hefty tome *English Prisons Today*, published in 1922. Packed with statistics and testimony, it looks like an official report. It was not, but it was immensely influential. Its two chief authors, Stephen Hobhouse and Fenner Brockway, were ex-convicts, having been imprisoned for anti-war activity. Is the Hobhouse/Brockway report any less tendentious than the prison 'torture' accounts by suffragette ex-inmates? It seems to be. The Brockway committee little mentions the war. Its account looks in close detail at prisons. Most of the subjects of the research are the usual sorts of jailbird, from the unfortunate to the unsavoury.

Whatever reforms Churchill set in train would take years to work through. Thus, one may say that the Hobhouse/Brockway report offers insights into conditions that prevailed in 1910. On the treatment of prisoners by officers, the authors quote an ex-inmate who considered that the 'bullying manner [was] in most cases superficial.' Sarcasm is mentioned as a common warder feature. A theme is degradation of prison staff by their jobs. One warder admitted that, generally speaking, members of his profession were 'brutes', but added that, 'A warder loses or tends to lose his personality: he is merely a victim of the general surroundings in which he is placed.'[18]

Winston Churchill as Home Secretary had discretionary powers regarding sentences. Formal petitions were made. Sometimes an MP would make an approach on behalf of someone to the Home Secretary. Thus, in September 1910 a newspaper reported that Churchill had cut a jail term recently imposed on the ex-treasurer of a Chester-Le-Street Miners' Association Lodge for misappropriation of funds. This followed representation by a Labour Member on behalf of the Lodge. Stephen Smith, who was serving six months, was returned home. Winston's tender side, we may think, will have been engaged: a respectable man brought down by financial difficulties, or greed, but forgiven by his mining friends?[19]

Often newspaper stories prompted questions in Parliament. In April 1910 the *Daily Express* reported a magistrates' court case at Haywards Heath, Sussex: 'AMAZING SENTENCE ON A BOY OF TWELVE: SEVEN YEARS FOR 5d [2p]'. The paper saw 'an astonishing illustration of the English method of making criminals'. Twelve-years-old Charles Bulbeck was sentenced to six strokes of the birch rod and seven years reformatory confinement for the theft of a lump of coal. The *Express* told readers:

> The boy's father burst into tears and told the magistrates that he thought that they were 'a bit hard'. The magistrates laughed and the Clerk to the Justices said: 'You should look after your boy better'.[20]

The case was raised in Parliament by Irish Nationalist John Muldoon, a Dublin barrister. Churchill told him that he had telegraphed Haywards Heath but did not know whether his telegram would arrive in time to stop the birching. Muldoon was a prominent champion of Irish causes. As a Dublin barrister, he knew the courts. Winston Churchill was an active, even belligerent, advocate of Irish Home Rule. Lucy Masterman, wife of Churchill's parliamentary under-secretary, thought that Churchill was 'more deeply a Home Ruler' than he was a free trader.[21]

The Home Office file has a cutting from the radical newspaper the *Morning Leader* with the headline: 'BENCH'S HARSH VIEW OF A TRIFLING OFFENCE'. Coal and wood had been disappearing from a farmyard and a police constable had caught the boy taking a lump of coal. An editorial expressed the hope that the sentence would receive attention from the Home Secretary.[22]

Churchill's telegram was too late. The justices' clerk telegraphed back: 'The boy was whipped on Monday morning'. Home Office enquiries ascertained that the boy had been placed in Portslade Industrial School, Brighton. Industrial schools were for vagrant or ill-cared for children. The distinction between these and reformatories was spurious. A draft Home Office letter to the justices includes the comment: 'The S. of S. [Secretary of State] does not understand how [Bulbeck] could be committed to an Ind school.'[23]

The Liberal *Daily News* was in campaigning mode. Its pen picture of the family spared no cliché. The father, Alfred, was, '…the type of village blacksmith whose praises Longfellow sang.…' The boy was 'always a bright winning lad'. The mother was 'pleasant-looking, buxom, in the clean and trimly kept cottage near the smithy displaying with pride the books which Charlie had won for good conduct at school…' The parents said that the boy was asked by his mother to take a pram to buy coal and, worried about being late for school, went to the farm instead. An idyllic village family was being persecuted, with the Liberal Home Secretary to the rescue.[24]

Responses to Winston Churchill's enquiries were arriving. The Chief Constable of East Sussex wrote:

The father spends a good deal of his time and money in the evenings at the Public House, and the mother does not bear a good character, although nothing definite can be brought against her.[25]

Independent Irish Nationalist MP Laurence Ginnell, a barrister, wanted the Lord Chancellor to sack the magistrates. Other MPs raised their concern. Churchill told them that he thought that the birching was 'adequate punishment', adding: 'I have given telegraphic instructions for [Bulbeck's] discharge and for his being returned to his parents this afternoon.'[26]

The public excitement did not go down well with Home Office staff. A secretary commented on a circulating document: '[Bulbeck] is confessedly a thief and yet he receives chocolates and is cheered at railway stations.'[27]

The *Daily News* had another spread, including the boy's own account: he was '…very frightened in the dock, and after the terrible birching blood ran all down my legs.' Then there was the homecoming:

> …Out of a cottage doorway rushed a white-faced woman …'My boy! My boy!'…The blacksmith sped up the village street faster than he had ever done before…[28]

Readers who did not find this too cloying could celebrate the knight-in-shining-armour, the young Home Secretary. Accompanying the boy home had been the school's superintendent, who reported the Home Office telegram, which read:

> Home Secretary will make statement in House this afternoon that boy Bulbeck will be released today. Please send boy home today.

A memorandum by Winston Churchill called the telegram 'not happily worded': there was no need to refer to any statement to be made in the Commons. He was unhappy that the boy had been interviewed at the school: no more correspondents or photographers should be allowed in. He did not like the comments by Home Office staff in the minutes. These seemed to reflect the attitude of the property-owning establishment to the lower orders. He called the boy's offence 'no worse than robbing an orchard'. As a result of his intervention, the child remained with his family and would shortly be starting a job with a local dog-breeder. Churchill received a personal note:

> Dear Mr Winston Churchill,
> I want to thank you for sending me back home to my Mother and Father and I will always be a good boy and never take any coal or anything else again.
> I remain, Yours respectfully
> CHARLES BULBECK[29]

Not all the press was cheering. *Punch*, picking up a question of Labour's Will Thorne about whether birching boys made them 'any better', ran an unflattering cartoon of the portly member, entitled 'ONE OF THE GREAT UNCHASTENED'. It derided voluble Labour MPs as 'intractable little scions of the Proletariat who are turned out with such engaging manners and so much self-control by the Elementary Schools'. The property-conscious middle-class magazine thought that they showed the signs of not having been birched as boys, as in the public schools.[30]

Most prison inmates came from the poorer classes. Poverty was a major causal factor in crime. However, there were some prisoners from comfortable homes. A few had connections in high places. Early in Winston Churchill's Home Office term, a petition came to him from senior officers in the Royal Navy regarding a prisoner in Maidstone Jail. This prison's wall was hewn out of quarry-stone. Its intimidating entrance would be used in the 1970s as a scene-setter for the BBC television sit-com *Porridge*. First-time serious offenders were sent here, including middle-class embezzlers and fraudsters. Forty-nine-years-old former naval paymaster Edward Leveson was serving five years' penal servitude for fraudulent conversion of property. Naval friends presented a petition on his behalf in February 1910. They were willing to provide him with money to start a new life in Mexico. Leveson was well short of being considered for release yet, even with full remission for good conduct (a quarter of the sentence).[31]

Churchill examined the case. The first two items in the file have been destroyed. Presumably one was the actual petition. A clue is provided by a Churchill instruction to write to a Vice Admiral. The Home Office secretaries began their procedures. A letter went to the Director of Public Prosecutions, Sir Charles Matthews, who had personally conducted the prosecution. Sir Charles saw no merit in the petition. He remarked that 'the persons defrauded were not wild speculators, but solid and in some cases poor investors, whose securities were appropriated by the defendants in a heartless and wholesale way'. He thought that the £4,000 haul of Leveson and his accomplice Cooke was probably the tip of an iceberg. They could have made £100,000. He was not opposing sentence reduction but he thought that Cooke, who presumably did not have influential friends, should be included in any leniency.

Sir Edward Troup and the Home Office's legal expert, Ernley Blackwell felt that Leveson should remain in jail. The sentences were 'by no means excessive', said Blackwell: solicitors committing similar offences usually got seven years. Churchill remarked that penal servitude, 'for educated men like Leveson and Cooke must amount to agony.' He thought that mercy would not injure other convicts. He saw Leveson's Mexico opening as in his favour. He instructed Troup: 'Make me a proposal to release both prisoners at once upon licence.' Sir Edward was aghast. This would 'shatter trust in the fairness of sentences'. It would get about that convicts with high-place friends could get sentences reduced. He urged the Home Secretary to consult the judge.

WSC obliged. Sir Forrest Fulton, Recorder of the City of London, did not object to Leveson being released but thought that Cooke should also receive the benefit. The release campaign was home and dry. Troup hated the springing of Leveson. It was blatant special treatment for a socially advantaged person. He wrote: 'I still think release is not in the public interest.' But he did not press his dissent. The Home Office staff were there to administer the decisions of the Secretary of State, subject to these being legally possible. This intervention does not look good for Churchill: help for an upper orders jail sufferer seems to have edged out intrinsic fairness.

A Home Secretary had to sign many documents. Churchill made it clear to his department that a routine signature was not to be taken for granted. This was demonstrated when a document arrived on his desk regarding a Birmingham gem-setter Henry Wilkins, sentenced to ten years' penal servitude in January 1910 for receiving stolen goods, his second such sentence. Wilkins' goods had been removed to determine which were stolen, and so that legal expenses could be defrayed. The Home Secretary's formal assent was needed. Rather than just signing, WSC asked his staff: 'Is this not a very severe sentence?'[32]

The task of writing a report on the case fell to H.B. (Harry) Simpson, 49, barrister-qualified, who was the department's crime analyst. Simpson's inky minutes loop across many a file page. Educated at Winchester and Magdalen College, Oxford, he had been at the Home Office for twenty-seven years. A penal traditionalist, he remarked in 1896 on 'the growing disinclination to give long sentences of penal servitude for "trifling" offences'. He favoured long sentences for repeat petty offenders. He lamented the demise of the tread-wheel and the crank: 'characteristic symbols' to distinguish law-breaking convicts from paupers who, under the Poor Law, were given hard manual labour such as stone-breaking in return for subsistence not much better than in prison. Simpson agreed that Wilkins's sentence was 'very severe', but explained to his chief that severe punishment of receivers of stolen goods was usual, since:

> Without the 'fences' there would be little professional crime. Moreover the business is extremely lucrative and difficult to detect.[33]

Henry Wilkins had run a large receiving enterprise. Birmingham, with its jewellery quarter, was in Simpson's words, 'specially easy for thieves to reap a rich harvest'. Troup backed Simpson: 'Professional receivers are not merely criminals but the cause of crime.' His advice was 'No interference'.[34]

Churchill had an idea. At the Board of Trade, he had assisted with the passage through Parliament of the 1908 Prevention of Crime Act. This empowered courts to add an indeterminate sentence to that of persons sentenced to three years or more of penal servitude who had been convicted three times or more before. 'Preventive detention' would be more comfortable than regular jail. The new sentence had to be served first. There was confusion and opposition. Judges did not like it. The government had been pushed into a partial retreat. Detention during His Majesty's pleasure had been abandoned in favour of court powers to award preventive detention of between five and ten years. The definition of the 'less rigorous regime' had not been published. None of those sentenced were yet through their preliminary penal servitude. It would have to be resolved by 1911 when preventive detention prisoners would be entering a specially built prison, Camp Hill, on the Isle of Wight.[35]

To Churchill, Henry Wilkins looked the very person for the new regime. In red ink he wrote: 'Is this not a case for preventive detention after 5 years P[enal] S[ervitude]?' Troup applied a damper: 'S[ecretary] of S[tate] has no power to commute until convict has served 3 years.' He wanted the decision left until Wilkins had served 5 years. Churchill was not going to be overruled. He came back: 'I still think the sentence excessive. Advise me how it can be mitigated.' Troup played another card. He asked Churchill to consult the judge who passed the sentence: 'Often he knows circumstances which we do not.' WSC conceded. He wrote to the judge, the Recorder of Birmingham, John Dugdale.

The Recorder's reply will have afforded private satisfaction to Simpson and Troup. He could find no points for leniency:

> It is the very worst case I have had to deal with in 32 years. Considering the enormous amount of mischief he must already have done in turning honest men into rogues, I felt that his sentence must be unusually severe.

He sent his case notebook. This revealed that a locked box belonging to an accomplice of Wilkins was found to contain the proceeds of over 40 robberies. Illicit goods were valued at £700, and there was £500 of freshly molten gold and silver, along with crucibles and moulds. Dugdale sketched some context on receiving: among those involved were jewellery business employees, often honest persons corrupted. Simpson and Troup had won. The Home Secretary confirmed it on 6 June 1910: 'Yes, there is no case for interference after the Recorder's letter.'

There was of course a famous receiver in the pages of Charles Dickens. Fagin made children into criminals. Did that depiction tell against Henry Wilkins? The Home Office crime figures for 1908 have 354 convictions for receiving; the daily average prison population of receivers was thirty-nine. This suggests that most sentences for receiving were far lighter than that given to Wilkins; and that conviction of 'fences' was perhaps not quite as rare as suggested.

The home secretary had pressed a concern. Meanwhile he was looking at 'Prisoner Calendars', these being lists of offenders, offences, and sentences, compiled from law-court sessions. They enabled Churchill to drill down into some actual cases. He later explained to Parliament that he looked at Calendars 'in order to view the whole stream of our criminal punishments'. He was having grave doubts about preventive detention. One case was Thomas Lane, who received five years' penal servitude plus five years' preventive detention for stealing a horse.

Convicted at Northampton and with three previous convictions, Lane was seen by the magistrates as an 'habitual criminal'. The Home Secretary thought that the horse-stealer should be given hope of getting out earlier. He wrote:

> S of S wishes Dept to consider whether [Lane's] sentence should be commuted to 3 years p[enal] s[ervitude] and 7 years preventive detention.[36]

That still adds up to ten, but preventive detention was adjustable, the intention being for most recipients to serve far less than the tariff.

Harry Simpson resisted:

> The sentence of PS cannot be converted to PD till convict has served 3 years. Something will then turn on how the new PD prison is going on and also upon the convict's conduct in prison.

Troup backed him. Churchill resisted them:

> I have considered the sentence again. It may be reduced as follows: the PS is to be reduced from 5 to 3 years: the PD from 5 to 4. The convict is to be informed tomorrow.

Telling the prisoner meant the decision could not be changed. Back came Troup, to remind Churchill that five years was fixed by statute as the minimum tariff for preventive detention. Churchill had had enough of procedural argument. He wrote:

> Reduce the PS from 5 to 3. Leave PD unaltered. Inform convict forthwith.

He prevailed, with a nod to the rules.

After initialling, the home secretary wrote further:

> I have serious misgivings lest the institution of PD should lead to a reversion to the ferocious sentences of the last generation. After all, PD is PS in all essentials: but it soothes the consciences of judges and of the public. There is a grave danger that the administration of the law should under softer names resume in fact a more severe character.

Churchill's minutes were sometimes read by his parliamentary under-secretary's wife. Lucy Masterman found in them 'a tendency towards the rhetorical'. She was intrigued by WSC's exchanges with some bishops about suicide, which was illegal. In 1908 there were eighty convictions for attempted suicide. Under *felo de se*, the suicide's property became forfeit to the state and burial in consecrated ground was barred, but this could be got round by a verdict that 'the balance of the mind was disturbed'. The bishops did not like that. Lucy's diary records:

> Winston drafted what Charlie [Masterman] thought was a most injudicious reply, saying that he thought if religious fears did not deter suicide, he did not think a coroner's verdict would.[37]

Churchill was not religious, except for faith in an undefined providence. He frustrated the bishops, though *felo de se* stayed on the statute book until 1961.

The Prisoner Calendar digging produced one Alfred Prinscep, who came up at Wolverhampton Quarter Sessions on 29 April 1910 for stealing three pairs of boots. Prinscep had served previous time for similar. The new sentence was eighteen months with hard labour. (The term 'hard labour', which often appears, had been fairly meaningless since the abolition of the tread-wheel and the crank.) Churchill saw an anomaly in the Prinscep sentence. He scribbled across the calendar: 'On what principle was he not charged as a habitual?' He compared Prinscep with eight other sentences – of three, four or five years' penal servitude plus five years' preventive detention. Why was Prinscep not given PS + PD?: 'Quite indistinguishable from other cases which have been punished by 5PS + 5PD'.[38]

The case seemed to Churchill to illustrate the haphazard nature of preventive detention sentencing. Harry Simpson differed. He thought that the Home Secretary's list of preventive detention sentences showed *how well* PD was working: 'very striking uniformity in sentences instead of the previous bewildering diversity and inconsistency'. He wanted *more* preventive detention – 'for men who live by preying on society'. Winston replied:

> Mr Simpson's argument is Draconic. A universal death penalty would equally remove all the disparities that exist between sentences, and compared with punitive detention would be cheaper and far more efficacious.

The sarcasm was lost on Simpson, who came back with a laboured distinction between burglars who killed and those who did not.

The Home Secretary had no wish to give Prinscep a stiffer sentence. He did not like habituals getting preventive detention. He was trying to show that it was unfair because it was arbitrary. He wanted to hear from Wolverhampton police why Prinscep was not charged as an habitual. A letter from Edward Troup went to Chief Constable Burnett, who replied:

> The question of indicting this man as an habitual criminal under the Prevention of Crimes Act, 1908 was not considered…being inadvertently overlooked by me, which I regret.

This was just what Churchill was looking for. In the file minute we hear his voice:

> He forgot! It slipped his memory. It was an accident: the mere caprice of fortune…Lucky Prinscep. If his crimes were heinous, he redeemed them by his genius for electing to fall beneath a Chief Constable who "inadvertently overlooked" the powers he possessed.

The explorations unearthed food-pilferer, James Wright, 25, convicted at Southampton for: 'feloniously stealing cheese, one tin, one jam-roll pudding, cooked ham and cooked beef, and for being a habitual criminal'. Wright's sentence was three years' penal servitude plus five years' preventive detention. The home secretary scribbled across the calendar:

> Surely an excessive sentence. There is a great difference between stealing food to <u>eat</u> and property to sell. Special report.[39]

He added:

> Certainly a hateful sentence – on which I propose to take action. 3 months would have been quite enough.

He saw an individual deep in poverty, struggling for bare subsistence, tempted by food, and perhaps hunger, to steal. Cruel sentences like this swelled the convict population. Churchill had no revolutionary belief in breaking unfair law but he did think that everyone was entitled to a reasonable welfare safety net, including the right to food. The state was failing the likes of James Wright. A Home Office investigation began. Wright's convictions went back to 1897. He had enlisted in the army and deserted, after which he started 'a career of crime'. He had been taken back by his father several times but each time had robbed him or those doing business with him.

Ernley Blackwell arranged for the Director of Public Prosecutions to assess Wright. Sir Charles Matthews identified:

> …not a hungry man stealing food to satisfy his hunger, but a systematic thief, stealing food wherever he knew it to be stored, and keeping it in a larder.

Wright had spent most of the last decade in jail. The DPP thought that the only hope for reform was preventive detention: 'an opportunity which would be denied him if, by a series of short sentences, he remained amongst his criminal companions and surroundings.'

Heartily endorsing, Blackwell saw:

> the futility and cruelty of imposing a series of short sentences on a man of this kind…. Possibly he is a fit subject for a labour colony of some kind. He will certainly be better off in p. s. + p. d. than leading [a criminal life] varied at short intervals by a few months in a local prison.

Troup concurred. Churchill rejected the negativity:

> No doubt it is annoying that people should be guilty of a succession of petty thefts: but the injury to society is not serious – the thefts are punished one by one as they occur. It is natural that these punishments should increase in length. But the appalling leap to 8 years of Prison, for an offence which – even where committed by a man of bad character – is normally met by a few weeks, cannot be reconciled with any system of sedate and dispassionate

justice. The Calendars show me scores of cases exactly similar or worse where 6 months or less is inflicted. It was a mere fluke that this man fell under the sledge-hammer of prosecution as an "habitual".

To Churchill, the operation of preventive detention, by imposing many years of imprisonment for a fairly minor offence, went against natural justice. Troup, Blackwell and Simpson simply saw nuisances to society needing to be safely locked up. Blackwell's 'labour colony' idea did have some appeal to Churchill – if somewhere there was 'a good island for these pilferers under conditions not offensive to human nature'.

Blackwell and Troup requested the Home Secretary to ask the Recorder of Southampton his reasons for the sentence. Temple Cooke reported that the police had given Wright a 'very bad character', and that he had failed to earn any remission in prison. Churchill did not change his decision. His instruction was that the prisoner should be released on licence after 18 months. This was 'ticket-of-leave', the final stage of longer sentences, when a prisoner would be released under a police-supervised licence and could be returned to prison in the event of a breach of its terms. Wright's subsequent history would be of further convictions for housebreaking, burglary and larceny, and eventual classification as a 'pauper lunatic'. Whilst this was not one of Churchill's happier interventions, his grave doubts about the operation of preventive detention, which found echo on the humane progressive wing of Liberalism, look well based.[40]

Another case at which Churchill looked was thirty-six-years-old Ernest Gill, sentenced at Derby to six years' penal servitude. The Prisoner Calendar records that Gill 'feloniously did steal three billiard balls.' It was the sentencing judge who raised this case: Sir Charles Darling, wrote to the Home Office to say that he had had no alternative on the sentence, given Gill's previous record, but that he would like it to be changed to three years' penal servitude plus three years' preventive detention.[41]

Billiard balls had undone Gill before. In 1905 he was sent down for three years for stealing three, along with an overcoat. Churchill was happy to oblige the judge. Simpson and Blackwell did not want the sentence changed: Gill was a pest requiring lengthy imprisonment. They tried to deflect their chief by pointing to the rules: the convict should serve three years and *then* the remaining three could be commuted to preventive detention. WSC was not having this. He wrote in red ink, on 4 April 1910:

> After 3 years of his sentence have been served in PS he is to be sent – unless his conduct is bad – to Preventive Detention.

The governor of the prison was instructed to tell the prisoner immediately. The sentence was still too long for Churchill. He wrote on the file, 'I have been reflecting on this case at intervals and I have come to the conclusion that the sentence is excessive.' Churchill knew Darling socially and wrote to him privately. Darling had sent his congratulations to Churchill on his appointment, offering to give him legal help. He had no problems with Churchill simply shortening the penal servitude term. He shared with the Home Secretary his thoughts:

> I am sure any mitigation of Gill's sentence which you advise will be for the best but we have yet ourselves to resolve a problem so difficult that our ancestors, in despair as I think, invented the gibbet and died contented – which I shan't do.

He was speaking of the 'Bloody Code' deterrence days when public execution was followed by the dangling of the body on a gibbet for passers-by to view.[42]

Sir Charles reflected:

> I am afraid that our system does not yet provide means for finding honest employment for such persons as Gill.

As the file went on its Home Office rounds, the margin at this point gathered two violently pencilled question-marks.

The judge's reflections continued:

> You will I hope hold your present office long enough to be able to establish something like the labour colonies which I am told in some countries have been found to give good results, and even to pay their way – if ever you should go to investigate these personally, I should like to go with you – Holland I believe has the best.

The best-known labour colony in Europe was Merxplas in Belgium (previously Holland).[43]

Harry Simpson was stung by the judge's agreement with Winston Churchill. He wrote:

> The question is whether society is justified in preventing criminals committing crime by physically restraining them for a term of years when it fails to prevent them by deterrence or reformation. By passing the Prevention of Crime Act, Parliament in 1908 answered the question in the affirmative.

Ernley Blackwell was with Simpson. He predicted that Gill would be reconvicted six months after release.

Churchill gave his decision on 19 June:

> Let the sentence be treated as one of 3 years P.S. & the convict informed.

The grumbling secretaries had to accept it.[44]

During mid-1910 the name Annie Connolly started to appear on Home Office minutes. Annie, 37, lived in Royton, near Manchester. Winston Churchill, having been a Manchester MP, will have known the harsh mill-working environment. Whilst electioneering in 1906, he left his hotel with his secretary Edward Marsh to take a stroll, reflecting: 'Fancy living in one of these streets, never seeing anything beautiful, never eating anything savoury, never saying anything *clever!*' In April 1910 a strange incident brought local resident Annie Connolly before the magistrates. The woman had thrown pepper in the face of a baby. She had a previous conviction for drunkenness.[45]

Home Office involvement may be traced to Churchill's perusal of a Salford Assize Courts Prisoner Calendar. Annie was, 'ordered to enter her own recognizances in the sum of £5 to keep the peace and to be of good behaviour for 6 months and to come up for judgement if called up.' Churchill wrote: 'Inadequate. Special report.' Home Office officials were against intervention. Edward Troup agreed that the sentence looked insufficient but thought that, 'we can do or say nothing'. Harry Simpson, uncharacteristically on the side of gentleness, thought that the lenient treatment might 'have the effect of promoting better relations.' In his case resumé, Ernley Blackwell sketched Annie getting into a drunken rage over a small boy of the neighbouring Clayton family throwing stones at her window; Annie marching up to the Clayton residence armed with pepper; Mr and Mrs Clayton, the latter with a baby in her arms, coming to the door; Annie throwing pepper; the baby suffering acute eye inflammation (but no lasting damage). Churchill would have liked Connolly returned to court and jailed. That could not be, but he wanted local chief magistrate James Beardoe-Grundy sacked unless he could account for the lightness of the sentence.[46]

It was not so easy. The sentence was a collective magistrate decision. Troup doubted whether the Lord Chancellor would ever remove a magistrate on the grounds of Home Office disapproval of his leniency. Churchill fired off an angry memorandum:

> The magistrate is unfit to hold his position. The awful disparity between the punishments inflicted for the most trivial offences against property and the gravest offences against the person was never more strikingly illustrated.

He surely had in mind the boy Bulbeck. He called for 'a report on the record and character of this Magistrate'. Nothing helpful to Churchill was found. If Grundy could not be removed, Churchill would have to settle for a stiff reprimand. If so, he wanted publication. Troup advised caution: 'the independence of the judiciary from the control of the executive is one of the cardinal principles of the constitution.'

On 23 July a Home Office letter informed Beardoe-Grundy that 'Mr Churchill would be much obliged for information as to the reasons which led the court to treat the offender with such marked leniency.' The magistrate, apparently oblivious of being in trouble, wrote back:

...If you had <u>seen</u> and <u>heard</u> the witnesses you would have approved of the sentence.

Troup noted 'a most inadequate reply'. Simpson tried to think himself into the courtroom scene. He was the author of an 1888 book of essays entitled *Cross Lights*, including 'Shakespeare on the Stage'. Did he use his theatrical imagination when he suggested that perhaps the magistrates were 'moved by a profusion of tears and expressions of contrition' from Annie? Gladstone had called Simpson 'a man of brilliancy but occasionally flighty judgement'. Harold Scott in his autobiography called Simpson 'capricious: quite capable of deciding a matter in contrary senses on successive days'.[47]

Churchill still wanted action. A letter was dispatched to the magistrate:

...Mr Churchill considers that this mode of dealing with the offender constitutes a lamentable failure of justice in respect of such a hateful and inhuman assault, and he desires to express his regret that the magistrates should by discharging the prisoner without sentence have allowed themselves to appear as condoning such an offence.

Grundy was hurt: 'a censure which I scarcely think I deserve', he wrote back. He cited his curriculum vitae: he was 'well-known to the Prison Commissioners at Whitehall'. But he still gave no explanation for the sentence, except to say, 'I have not and would not knowingly condone such an offence.' If Churchill's rebuke of Grundy aimed to publicize the bias of courts in favour of property over person, it failed since communications between the Home Office and magistrates were by convention private.

Could there have been a personal factor in Churchill's ferocity? His baby daughter was approaching her first birthday. Was Winston thinking of little Diana when he so furiously pursued this magistrate?

Chapter 4
'A Very Curious Morning'

Churchill faced his first questions about suffragettes within a fortnight of taking office. Why had Selina Martin, in Liverpool's Walton Jail, been 'put in irons, frog-marched and forcibly fed?', asked Irish Nationalist William Redmond. Martin and another woman had confronted the prime minister as he was getting out of a motor-car. On receiving two months with hard labour, they went on hunger strike and refused to wear prison dress. Friends reported that they were in straightjackets. Churchill replied that Martin had been 'very violent and destructive' and needed to be restrained. Force-feeding required the insertion of a twenty-inch tube up the nose. Churchill's predecessor had tried it out, finding it no more than 'rather unpleasant'. There was no suggestion of Winston following up.[1]

Suffragette disruption of public life very much included Churchill's meetings and travel. A militant had flown at him with a horsewhip at Bristol's Colston Hall in the previous November, yelling of 'the insulted women of England'. In December, at Southport's Empire Hall, at a Churchill General Election meeting, a suffragette climbed through the roof: as he was saying that the House of Commons represented the will of the people, a female voice rang out from high up: 'But it does not represent the women, Mr Churchill.' The theatrical effect was intense. It was Dora Marsden, an activist regularly in trouble (later editor of the *Freewoman* magazine). Churchill told the gathering: 'The authors must be punished. If they are women they must be restrained with great gentleness, and if they are men they must be punished with great severity.' Chivalry to women, WSC's regular stance in the suffrage conflict, will not have helped him.[2]

The prison authorities were in a quandary over how to process socially respectable suffragettes. There were three prison divisions. Under the first (hardly ever granted) relative luxury was available for those who could afford it. The second had a small population. Its regime was little different from that of the third. The distinction, as explained by Edward Troup, was that the second was for prisoners 'of good antecedents', the third for those of 'bad or doubtful character'. In practice it was class distinction. Female suffrage militants were split between the second and the third.[3]

'Society' was tightly interconnected. Tories and Liberals bayed at each other across the floor of the House of Commons, but gathered at weekends at each other's great houses, hunting-and-shooting, socializing, and philandering. The 'season' ran from February to early August. As well as sporting events – Ascot,

Henley, Goodwood, Eton v Harrow cricket, and so on – there were the grand balls at which young women 'came out' after being presented at court. Winston Churchill belonged to this top social layer. So did some of the suffragettes coming to the attention of the Home Office. Winston knew that small-world was likely to catch up with him.

And so it did. An early Churchill romantic interest had been Pamela Plowden, who married Victor, Earl of Lytton, a Conservative. Winston and Victor were friends. A sister of Victor, Lady Constance, was a suffragette. She devised a scheme. To show that the authorities were rougher with working-class suffragettes than with those of her own class, she dressed the part of Jane Warton, a poor seamstress. She threw a protest stone at Walton Jail. The result was a fortnight inside Walton, in the Third Division. When she had previously been imprisoned as Lady Constance, she went on hunger strike and when medical tests showed that, despite her statement of good health, she had a weak heart, she was released instead of being force-fed. 'Jane Warton's statement of good health was simply accepted. She had the feeding tubes, and was slapped on the cheek by the doctor. Constance had her class discrimination evidence. Her brother was a campaigner for female suffrage. Churchill was about to find personal awkwardness.[4]

'Jane Warton', having aroused suspicion, was released on medical grounds on 23 January 1910, shortly before Churchill became Home Secretary. The follow-up began. Constance wrote to *Votes for Women* newspaper and *The Times*. She arranged for a medical report, which noted 'grave risk to health and life' from force-feeding. Churchill wrote an internal Home Office memorandum. The prison officials should be backed: the charges were 'trivial' and 'imaginary'; Lady Constance was 'an unruly and hysterical woman'. However, staff composing the reply to Earl Lytton's representations should 'endeavour to couch it throughout in a manner which will safeguard our position whilst showing consideration'. Churchill did not however just affirm the status quo. He instructed that in future:

> Before forcible feeding is resorted to, a written and formal certificate must be given by the medical officer, showing that he has thoroughly examined the prisoner and that he considers that no harm can result.[5]

The Women's Social and Political Union had declared a temporary truce, since a cross-party move was set to be made in Parliament. A pro-women's suffrage Conciliation Committee had been formed, with Lord Lytton as its president. Its secretary was Liberal journalist H.N. Brailsford. Fifty-four MPs were associated (twenty-five Liberal, seventeen Conservative, six Labour, six Irish Nationalist). The group was preparing a bill. If successful, it would at last enfranchise some women. The expectation was that Winston Churchill, as a progressive, would back it. In his soldiering days he had called Votes for Women 'this ridiculous movement' but now as a Liberal politician he was open to female enfranchisement.[6]

Churchill acted early on the status of suffragettes in prison. On 28 February he wrote a minute proposing a code of regulations regarding 'the treatment of political prisoners in His Majesty's Prisons'. These would be for persons who had 'committed an offence, involving no moral turpitude, with a distinct political object'. Suffragettes were the obvious application. For those in this division:

> ... Food might be obtained from outside on payment; the prisoner should wear his [sic] own clothes; no compulsory work should be executed; no cutting of hair or any unnecessary interference with usual habits should be practised.

Such prisoners 'should be allowed access to all books which are found in a good public library, and without restriction to number, subject only to reasonable convenience'. However, they should not be permitted to receive daily or weekly newspapers, or contemporary publications dealing with political affairs. Sir Edward Troup and Sir Evelyn Ruggles-Brise were strongly opposed: what about political murders? Churchill took this point. His made his wording vaguer. He followed a formula that Herbert Gladstone had been considering.[7]

The change was announced by way of a reply to a planted parliamentary question. On 15 March 1910 veteran Irish Nationalist, John O'Connor (imprisoned in his youth for Fenian activity) asked about political prisoner status for women's suffrage campaigners when they came into conflict with the law. The Home Secretary said that:

> I feel, as did my predecessor, that prison rules which are suitable to criminals guilty of dishonesty or cruelty, or other crimes implying moral turpitude, should not be applied inflexibly to those whose general character is good and whose offences, however reprehensible, do not involve personal dishonour.[8]

The proposed rule would pass into the criminal code if not objected to. Suffragettes were the obvious application.

About this time Churchill heard from Wilfrid Blunt. His friend liked to set up persons of interest for him when he came down to Sussex. He had an idea:

> I suppose you would be afraid to meet Conny Lytton and hear her prison experiences? She is not dangerous. She writes approving your prison reforms with certain qualifications which she wishes to discuss with me. If she came, I would ask her brother Victor too.[9]

Churchill's response to this idea, we may imagine, will have been fruity. Constance's memoirs mention Winston visiting her brother at 'his country place' (Knebworth House, Hertfordshire), in April 1910:

> Mr Churchill read through the whole [prison] case, until he came to the report of the letter [by herself] to my mother written on the slate. 'Twould

be hopeless', he said, 'to bring forward any complaint with this letter in the background'.[10]

Prison regulations regarding the writing and receipt of letters were often remarked on for the meagreness of permission: no writing to anyone by a third division prisoner for eight weeks after the commencement of a sentence; receipt of a letter allowed only once a month. Constance's slate-composed letter showed that she was aiming to communicate deviously in order to keep from her mother where she was and to preserve the Jane Warton identity. This will have helped Churchill duck out of intervention.[11]

Herbert Gladstone saw Churchill's announcement. He wrote a pointed letter. He was glad that his successor was 'acting on my proposals as regards prison rules', but 'rather more than surprised' at the form of his announcement:

> Two deductions will initially be made – first that you initiated the changes and I did not; secondly that you have done the obviously right thing and that I from foolishness and inhumanity did not. Whereas as you know I asked Brise a long time ago to draw up proposals for consideration.[12]

The barb did not fluster WSC. He blamed the newspapers. He would repair the credit omission by way of answer to a question in Parliament. But the new rule was his own decision:

> I decided to make a special code for political offenders as soon as I was appointed Home Secretary, and I dictated a memorandum in the first two or three days. It was not until the matter had reached its final stage that I learned with pleasure from the official files how nearly we were in accord.

He cheekily advised his predecessor not to get perturbed: he, Churchill, had often found that his 'laboriously quarried out' work at the Colonial Office was used with advantage by his successors. He was 'always very glad'. He implied that, unlike Gladstone, he did not brood. Gladstone's indignation was further stoked. He wrote back that Churchill, having been strongly in favour originally of a 'political offender' category, was now excluding political motive as grounds for special prison conditions: Churchill's alterations, he said, 'follow my minutes in details… based on the same principles.'[13]

Gladstone was not the only one chafing at WSC's credit-scooping. Alick Murray, the Liberal Chief Whip, had suffered from it. He remarked in his diary: 'This is Winston all over. In mining parlance, if he can jump another man's claim, you can trust him to do it.' Why was Churchill so concerned about his place in history? It seems to go back to his relationship with his late father. On Winston's side, there was admiration, awe indeed, of the parent who commanded the political scene before falling out with his party and resigning as Chancellor of Exchequer, dying (perhaps of syphilis) at 45. Lord Randolph (courtesy title as a son of the Duke of Marlborough) had only scorn for his son. After his death, Winston had a mission to prove his worth to his father's spirit. He helped the process by the employment of spin.[14]

Churchill set up the obliging John O'Connor to ask another question, to which he replied:

> ...I have noticed with considerable regret that my action has been commented on in some of the newspapers as if it were a reflection upon the humanity and good sense of my Noble Friend Viscount Gladstone. I was careful to state that my views were in full harmony with his, and I have every reason to believe, that he would have taken this or some similar step had he been so fortunate as to remain at the Home Office during the piping times of peace.[15]

More Churchill mischief twinkles. It sounds as if Gladstone had been removed to make way for a better man, Winston. What about the 'piping times of peace'? It may have looked so in the spring of 1910, but the lull in the industrial strife of recent times would not last much longer – and the following year would bring the threat of European war.

The Conciliation Bill was introduced by David Shackleton, a Trades Union Congress leader, a big man with a heavy, dark beard. He was repaying a debt to the women's movement. His return at a 1902 Lancashire by-election (one of the earliest Labour MPs) was as the representative of the mostly female weavers' union.[16]

The Conciliation Committee's bill had its main (second reading) debate on 11 and 12 July 1910. The proposal was that the parliamentary vote should be extended to women already eligible to vote in local government elections as householders or owners of business premises. All female householders would receive the vote, even if they only occupied part of a house. Some working women would be included. Most married women would be excluded since a woman would need to be an occupier in her own right.

As well as being able to vote in local government elections, women could be elected as councillors on the same basis as men. Women were in office, Poor Law commissioners for example. They were on the civil service lists but the Home Office was still a male preserve. Harold Scott's memoirs recall that:

> Our typing was done by boys fresh from school, who tapped out their work with one finger until they gradually mastered their machines – which had obvious effects upon efficiency. Letters frequently had to be typed five times.[17]

This was the Home Office environment: conservative resistance to the advance of women. But even the H. O. had lady inspectors on its lists. Everywhere women were breaking through. Parliamentary voting remained a glaring exception.

Whitaker has a list of persons *not* eligible to vote in parliamentary elections: 'Aliens, minors, lunatics, peers, judges, women…' The Conciliation Bill offered a chance to make a start on putting that injustice right. Churchill's voice could be important on an historic day.[18]

Lucy Masterman's diary tells us that Churchill ('in a rather tepid manner a suffragist', she called him) intended to vote for the bill. On Churchill's attitude to female suffrage, we may note what he said at an election meeting at Manchester's Free Trade Hall:

> (Churchill)…The House of Commons is elected by millions of the people. – (A man in the audience: "but only by one sex.") True, only one sex at present votes – (hear, hear) – but the other sex has great influence – (cheers), – might easily have a greater, and will someday have direct influence.[19]

His position was support for female enfranchisement for parliamentary elections, but 'someday' suggests no keenness on its arrival any time soon.

Hopes that Churchill would be on the side of the bill were spurred by his new Prison Rule. Henry Brailsford obtained a private interview. The Home Secretary allowed the campaigner to quote him as being a supporter *in principle* of the Conciliation Committee. Churchill sent the bill to the Liberal Whips to look at. They bristled at Conservative electoral benefit, but did not oppose. The measure would be a start on female enfranchisement, which the majority of Liberal MPs wanted. What line would Churchill take in Parliament? Many would be watching.[20]

Sometime shortly before the Conciliation Bill debate, Churchill had a session with his parliamentary under-secretary. Charles Masterman had a deeply moral social perspective. His soul was upset by vulgar flaunting of wealth. He disliked the nouveau riche (as did some Conservatives). He was committed to improving the lot of the poorest of society. He worked well with Churchill on the New Liberal agenda but the outlooks of the two ministers diverged vastly. This is well brought out in an exchange between Charles and Winston, preserved by Lucy Masterman:

> Charlie said: 'I have a great admiration for [Keir] Hardie. He is not a great politician, but he will be in Heaven before either you or me, Winston!' 'If Heaven is going to be full of people like Hardie', Winston replied, 'well the Almighty can have them to himself'.

Churchill was not concerned with the moral condition of people's souls. Nor was he troubled by the nouveau riche. On money, his chief concern was not having enough of it. On the Conciliation Bill's aim to enfranchise some women, he was just about onside. Charles Masterman was negative. He got to work on Churchill.[21]

Lucy Masterman's diary says of what turned out to be a crucial session between the Home Secretary and his parliamentary deputy: 'Winston and Charlie had a very curious morning':

> Charlie began to put to him the points against Shackleton's Bill – its undemocratic nature, and especially particular points such as that John Burns's "fallen women" friends would have the vote but not the mother of a family and other rhetorical points.[22]

John Burns, once a Labour parliamentary pioneer, was local government minister in the Liberal government. He was known for his earthy conversation: he had jested recently that he had in common with the legendary William Gladstone (a heavy moralist), that they both liked the company of fallen women. (Winston Churchill could also be earthy: he flicked his register between refined and crude.) The Masterman journal continues:

> Winston began to see the opportunity for a speech on these lines, and as he paced up and down the room, began to roll off long phrases. By the end of the morning he was convinced that he had always been hostile to the Bill and that he had already thought of these points himself.[23]

Lucy used the diary passage in her biography of her husband, adding a further piece of imagery, that Winston 'snatched at Charlie's arguments as a wild animal snatches at its food.' (p. 166)

The cabinet fudged. The bill could have its second reading debate but the government would not provide any more time after that. That meant that it could not pass into law. The prospective block to further progress did not negate the importance of Churchill's speech and his vote. It would be noted, especially by the WSPU.

In the two-day debate, the rejection of the bill was moved by Churchill's close friend on the Conservative benches F. E. Smith. A 38-years-old lawyer, F.E. was a well-practised debater. He was a cut-and-thrust jouster, a dark-haired 'swell', exuding arrogance as he lounged on the green benches. He was a Tory democrat. Churchill appreciated that, as well as the brio. In one official parliamentary report to the King, he described an F.E. speech as 'masterly'.[24]

Smith said that women were 'sexual specialists': men were political debaters – in their workplaces, in the pub, in the street. He warned MPs of the logical consequences of giving votes to even a few women: another bill would follow, removing women's disability from entering Parliament. He felt sure there was no majority for having female MPs and cabinet ministers. It was not, he said, that women were inferior, but… Then came an infamous peroration:

> The sum total of human happiness, knowledge, and achievement would have been almost unaffected if Joan of Arc had never fought, if Siddons had never played and if George Eliot had never written.[25]

Margot Asquith once commented on Smith: 'His brains go to his head.' G.K. Chesterton said: 'Chuck it, Smith!' For Churchill, closeness to this male chauvinist swaggerer did not help his stance as a New Liberal reformer.

Churchill spoke on the second day. He was preceded by Conservative John Butcher, who spoke of Finland (part of the Russian Empire). The Tory had alarming tales of women elected to the Finnish Diet (devolved assembly): 'discontented socialist spinsters', who were liquor prohibitionists, anti-tobacco and in favour of 'enforcing morality by legislation'. MPs could imagine viragos storming into Parliament, closing the bars, and confiscating their cigars. (WSC, as well as being fairly violently against socialism, liked a drink and a cigar.) When the Home Secretary rose to speak, he declared that he could not support the bill. He was not against votes for women:

> I believe that there is a proportion of women capable of exercising the Parliamentary franchise...in every class throughout the community.

But Churchill's direction of argument was ominous. When he claimed that women had benefitted from the social legislation of the male Parliament, a 'mirthless laugh' (as Churchill himself described it) rose from a member of the Conciliation Committee, Labour's Philip Snowden. The home secretary's position, here stated, on votes for women was that it should be either for 'a comparatively small number of women of all classes...the strongest, most capable and most responsible', or votes for everyone, male or female, over twenty-five years old. (This produced an 'Oh!' from twenty-seven-years-old Tory Lord Winterton).

Churchill then launched into the line on which Charles Masterman had coached him:

> A young, inexperienced girl of twenty-one would have a vote, and the mother of seven or eight children, who for twenty-five years has directed the policy and economy of a family, would be refused the vote.

With General Election polling spread over several weeks, some people could cast more than one vote in different constituencies – for residence, business premises, and as graduates voting in university divisions. The bill, Churchill argued, would provide various opportunities for multiple voting. A man could give his wife a vote as the occupier of their premises whilst he himself voted where he had his business; if he had a town property and a house in the country, he could make a daughter the occupier of one of these whilst he voted in the other. Warming to his theme, he considered stables: a man could put his wife down as the occupier of their residence and call himself the occupier of the equestrian facility. Presumably the premise of these sketches was that a woman had no political mind of her own and would be deployed to vote as her husband or father instructed her.

Now came Churchill's pièce de résistance: morals and female voting:

It would be possible for a woman to have a vote while living in a state of prostitution; if she married and became an honest woman she would lose that vote, but she could regain it through divorce.

Divorce was disreputable: Churchill floated the appalling vision of a divorced woman *voting*.

There were women in the House of Commons: high up above the chamber in the Ladies' Gallery. Their view was partly obscured by a metal grille in front of them. It had been there since Parliament was rebuilt after the fire of 1834, apparently to ensure that the male legislators were not distracted by glimpses of females. In 1908 two suffragettes had chained themselves to it. Among the women behind the grille today was Lady Laura McClaren, distinguished horticulturalist and owner of the famous Bodnant Gardens in North Wales, a passionate campaigner for female suffrage. Lucy Masterman records that when Churchill spoke, 'Lady McClaren wept in the gallery.' Why did the speech so upset her? The reason was not WSC's absurd sophistry, but the fact that he as Home Secretary was casting his weight against the bill, thereby dooming women to go on waiting for the vote.[26]

Lloyd George's intimations of opposing the bill were confirmed when he said of Churchill's speech: 'I agree with almost every word.' The debate ended at 10 o clock and the electric bells jangled for the allotted two minutes. In the procession through the Noes lobby, Churchill had with him Prime Minister Asquith. In the Ayes lobby was the Conservative leader Arthur Balfour, former prime minister. The Ayes had 299; the Noes 190. The triumph for female suffrage was hollow. A further vote assigned the bill to a Committee of the Whole House. This meant that the committee stage would be in the debating chamber, rather than MPs of a Grand Committee going over it upstairs. Since the government had decided against sanctioning the necessary time for a Whole House stage, the measure faced oblivion.

Sooner or later women were going to be admitted to the parliamentary process. Churchill, supposed man of modernity, was out of step with the great change which was surely on the way. The Labour MPs were out in force for it. Keir Hardie, Philip Snowden, and Ramsay MacDonald, the leading names of the party, were in the Ayes lobby. Churchill and Lloyd George had the company of just two Labour men. Where did this leave the progressive credentials of this supposed pair of people's champions? The debate left some of their supporters wondering.

The dynamics of the Conciliation Bill outcome are depicted in a *Punch* cartoon. The scene is the cabinet table. A smug-looking prime minister is standing up to shelve (literally) the scroll containing the bill. In the foreground are Sir Edward Grey, Foreign Secretary, Lord Haldane, War Minister, and Augustine Birrell, Secretary of State for Ireland. These were prominent supporters of votes for women. Asquith is saying: 'Well, gentlemen, now that your individual consciences have had their fling, let's get to work again.' With the prime minister being anti-women's suffrage, it probably was as cynical as that. But in the process Winston Churchill's progressive credentials had been damaged.[27]

For Churchill, the repercussions were personal, including a deeply cutting breach with Victor Lytton, with a rancorous exchange of messages. Edward Marsh told Winston:

> I couldn't help writing to Victor – and I think I ought to show you what I have written. I am broken hearted about this quarrel.

Back came a note: 'You are a good little boy; & I am vy fond of you.'[28]

Marsh was 33 when Churchill took him on as his secretary at the Colonial Office. He stayed with Winston through a succession of ministries. He was good value. He had a parallel career as a translator and as a patron of poets and artists. He was the scribe of much of Churchill's vast outpouring – governmental, political, and literary. It would be wrong to imagine Eddie as a ghost-writer, turning WSC's stream-of-consciousness into articles and books. Churchill, a future Nobel Prize in Literature winner, was more than capable. We may think however that Marsh assisted the finished structure. He was Churchill's muse, making introductions on the writing and artistic side. He was not over-bothered with politics. Socially snobbish, he adored 'smart set' country-house gossip and anecdotes. These did not much stimulate Winston, who commented to his wife on one lavish country-house party: '…[I] survey how much more power and great business are to me, than this kind of thing.' But he did put in appearances on the great houses circuit. Ettie, Lady Desborough, recorded Winston as 'one of the faithful' at her Taplow Court, Buckinghamshire gatherings. Winston did love an audience and there was plenty of scope there for that. Ettie told Arthur Balfour that Churchill would 'address himself in the looking-glass – a sympathetic and admiring audience'.[29]

The Home Secretary's attitude to female suffrage was given extensive coverage in his Dundee constituency press in December when he met several women's deputations. One of Dundee Women Liberals, a Miss Scotland, was sharp. She asked for a vote 'as a business woman, a householder and an employer of labour': 'Those I employ have a vote: I have none.' When Churchill met the Secretary of the Women's Freedom League, Lila Clunas (a schoolteacher who had once been jailed for three weeks for taking a swipe at Asquith whilst presenting a petition: she was released after hunger-striking), Clunas called Churchill's attitude to the Conciliation Bill 'a great disappointment':

Miss Clunas: You said a chick of 21 would qualify under the Bill.
Mr Churchill: I never used such an expression.
Miss Clunas: Then a girl of 21. You declared that a girl of 21 could qualify under the Bill, whilst a mother of seven or eight children

would not. I have never met a girl of 21 who is a householder but I know many mothers with families of seven or eight – poor women – who under this Bill would qualify.

Mr Churchill: You won't get that.[30]

The demise of David Shackleton's bill did not inhibit a rapprochement with Winston Churchill. The two men had got to know each other in Churchill's Trade Ministry period. Shackleton led a delegation to Germany to investigate state labour exchanges and health insurance. Rumours that Churchill was about to offer the MP a job in the Home Office proved correct. The projected post was 'Labour Adviser'. A deal was worked out. Why did Churchill pluck Shackleton? The answer perhaps was WSC's middle-ground politics. Shackleton was more trade unionist than Labour. He was a virtual Lib-Lab. At his last Trades Union Congress event, at Sheffield, antagonism between the militancy of the rising new Labour generation and old-fashioned trade unionism came to a head. Dockers' leader Ben Tillett told Shackleton that he had to choose between 'the employing class' and his own. The word 'traitor' was heard. The friction between Shackleton's Liberal-friendly outlook and those in the Labour movement who saw the Liberal Government as foes of the workers crackled. Tillett called the directing of workers through labour exchanges 'the greatest evil that has befallen us'. Shackleton in vain defended the system that he had helped bring into being. Whether his arrival in the Home Office would be a bridge between government and workers was doubtful. Meanwhile the distance between Churchill and the women suffragists was widening.[31]

Chapter 5
'The Noblest Utterance'

Winston Churchill had a duty of writing parliamentary diary letters for the King. He composed elegant digests liberally laced with his own commentary, as he sat on the front bench. At 68, the well-padded Edward VII was the nation's figurehead. The government needed his acquiescence in creating, if required, a block of new peers to vote out of existence the Lords' power of veto. If Irish Home Rule failed because the Lords rejected it, Irish Nationalist support and the governmental majority could be lost. The monarch's health was not good. A chill turned to pneumonia. At 11.40 pm on 6 May 1910, Edward's reign, a year short of a decade, was over. Twenty minutes later Churchill was performing his duty as Home Secretary of announcing to the Lord Mayor of London that the King was dead.[1]

Now would come the black clothing, crepe bands, and the muting of public excitement. The previously expected new General Election to try to resolve the constitutional crisis, would not be happening in the next six months. Instead of preparing for a national electioneering tour, Churchill could concentrate on Home Office policy. In particular he could work towards his prospective major speech in Parliament on penal administration. He presented Sir Evelyn Ruggles-Brise with a point-by-point letter, instructing him to produce 'in austere and precise official language, paragraph by paragraph', proposed changes as discussed between them. Since penal policy was not regarded as party-political, it would not be affected by the mourning inhibitions.[2]

Reforms needed money. The Treasury's bean-counter Charles Hobhouse, the Financial Secretary, thought that the Home Secretary was over-spending. He wrote to Churchill intimating that the proposals for a new system of assistance for convicts on release could not be afforded. He lamented the 'remarkable' increase in money going on prisons, for 'victualling', 'clothing', 'escort' and 'new buildings': the prisons department should be tightening its belt. Churchill asked Brise to put together a rebuttal of the extravagance charge. This was swiftly forthcoming, including that prison industries enabled money to be returned the Treasury. The *English Prisons Today* report lists thirty prison occupations. Leading by far is mailbag makers (2736), followed by 'knitters and repairs' (235) and 'pickers and sorters' (228). These days prison work had a productive purpose of a sort, though Hobhouse and Brockway found that prisoners had little proper training. Prison labour aimed at occupying inmates. Money earned by the prison and returned to the Treasury was a spin-off rather than labour exploitation of prisoners. However, some of it at least seems to have been deliberately arduous and tedious (like the unpicking of old ropes). Here was an area to which Churchill might turn his reforming energies if he stayed long enough at the Home Office.[3]

Aid to discharged convicts was a central plank of Winston Churchill's penal reform programme. He and Brise saw eye-to-eye here. Churchill's passion to break the cycle of ex-convicts returning to crime shines out of his correspondence with Charles Hobhouse:

> ...the hopeless regularity with which convicts return to penal servitude. I have discovered that out of the convicts discharged during the years 1903–1905 three out of every four are already back in penal servitude ...A supervision more individualised, more intimate, more carefully considered, more philanthropically inspired is necessary.[4]

The Churchill-Brise planning envisaged a central council, with a committee on which were representatives of five leading charitable societies and of central government. Previously, the gratuity in respect of merit marks built up by prisoners was paid to them on release by the police to whom they had to report. Now it would come from the societies. The Home Secretary's efforts culminated in a conference, held on 19 July 1910 and attended by Masterman, Troup, Brise, Wemyss Grant-Wilson, head of the Borstal Association, and representatives of religious and charitable organizations. Churchill in a rousing speech declared that the new association could cut back hard on recidivism. The council's office went live at the start of 1911, with Brise as chairman and Grant-Wilson as his deputy. Arrangements were built in to transfer ex-prisoners who abused the system to police supervision.[5]

Finance was one of a multitude of constraints on a reforming Home Secretary. Time pressure was another. The Home Office dealt with everything from roller-skating nuisance to the Anglican Book of Common Prayer. The devotional item featured in Churchill's written parliamentary replies of 7 July 1910. Lord Hugh Cecil was fretting about a missing comma in the Lord's Prayer. The accountability of the government for Anglican prayer-books went back to the 1530s and the Breach with Rome. Hugh was a High Church stickler. Winston will have been well briefed by his civil servants:

> ...In deciding the punctuation of the petition 'Thy will be done on earth as it is in heaven', I presume that the University presses consider they have adopted that which represents the structure of the Greek original. I am in full agreement with the Noble Lord, and I am glad that we have found a common ground to stand on, though it be only the breadth of a comma; but I have no power to issue any instructions as to the punctuation of the Prayer Book.[6]

His answer to Cecil continued playfully that the missing comma could be rectified by an Act of Parliament but that the pressure of government business made this unlikely. Lord Hugh, known as 'Linky', had been best man at Churchill's wedding. With his fluting voice, he was one of Parliament's best orators. A.G. Gardiner wrote of the awe that he inspired in Churchill: 'He speaks of him as one who dwells within the Palace of the King, whilst he stands without the gate.'[7]

Commas were a diversion from Churchill's preparation for his big parliamentary speech on penal policy. The challenges facing a reforming Home Secretary were enormous, but if anyone had the necessary energy, Winston did. A. G. Gardiner once evoked the fizzing young minister thus:

> [For Churchill] life is a succession of splendid sensations, of thrilling experiences. He rushes from booth to booth with the delight of a boy at a fair. He must shoot at every gallery, shy at every cocoa-nut, see every bearded woman and two-headed man. He is reckless of his life and his money. All that matters is this magic world of which he has become the momentary possessor, and which he must devour ere the curtain is rung down on the drama and the dream.... "Keep your eye on Churchill" should be the watchword.[8]

The 'Prisons Vote' debate, on 20 July 1910, was part of Parliament's regular vetting of the money it granted to government departments. Before setting out his vision, the Home Secretary answered points. He admitted that the Prison Commission had no woman. He would arrange to involve the lady inspector in female prisoner matters. He would do what he could to improve technical instruction opportunities for women in prison. For most prisoners, said Churchill, their stay was not long enough for anything to be achieved. On the 1909–1910 daily average, of 3,000 to 4,000 convicts (meaning serving three years or more), just 131 were female. The general daily prison average for women was about three thousand, most doing short sentences in local jails.[9]

The Home Secretary gave further information about his new category of prisoners 'not guilty of any acts involving moral turpitude'. They would not have to wear prison clothing; the regulation prison bath would not be compulsory; they would be permitted to obtain food from outside, to exercise freely, to converse with other prisoners when taking exercise, and 'to have at their own expense such books, not dealing with current events, and such literature as is in accordance with the public interests'. Rule 243A, the 'Churchill Rule', was applied to 508 prisoners during 1910–1912. Hobhouse and Brockway state that the provisions most valued were own-choice exercise companions and books from outside.[10]

The debate heard from William Byles, Liberal, a North of England newspaper proprietor and veteran social reformist. Byles shared with the Commons a letter from a visiting justice who had been into Manchester's Strangeways where he encountered a fifteen-year-old boy in prison clothing. The lad had lost his job in a coalmine because he could not pay for a broken mining-lamp. He and his mother had been evicted from their accommodation. He was found by a policeman sleeping in a closet. He was in prison, said Byles, by reason of poverty. He was keenly anticipating the speech of 'a very enlightened Home Secretary'. Under the law, those without shelter had to go to a workhouse. Home Office statistics for 1908 record 6,592 convictions for sleeping out. The daily average prison population for this offence was 261.[11]

Winston Churchill's central theme was his aspiration to keep offenders out of prison as far as possible. In the previous year ninety thousand had been jailed in default of payment of fines. Many could have produced the money, if they had been given time. He gave examples from Wandsworth Prison of young men who were in there as a result of being unable to pay fines on the spot for minor offences – such as obscene language and breach of the Pedlars' Act. The result of instant imprisonment was that:

> The State loses its fine, and the man goes to prison, perhaps for the first time – a shocking event. He goes through the formalities for a four, or five, days' sentence, and the State has to pay for it all. More than half of committals to prison in default of paying fines are for offences of drunkenness…When the sentence of seven or fourteen days is over, release is very often celebrated by the prisoner, but a fine effectively enforced means a period of temperance and of saving, and it achieves the very purpose which the court and the country had in view.

A first offender, Churchill explained, could easily fall into a cycle of imprisonment. There were many ways in which an innocuous member of the working class might be loaded into a police van: drunkenness and 'loitering' were regular examples.

The Home Secretary thought that probation should be used more. After praising the 'admirable' recent Children Act, which had practically abolished imprisonment for those under 16, he turned to jailed youths between 16 and 21:

> An old prison visitor told me that often they cry the first time, but not on subsequent occasions…It is an evil which falls only on the sons of the working classes.

He said that undergraduates at Oxford University who had 'boisterous and exuberant moments' were not put in prison. Working-class youngsters were jailed even when no injury was inflicted on anyone. He declared that: 'In my opinion no boy should go to prison unless he is incorrigible or has committed some serious offence.' Churchill had rid from his brain the popular myth that impoverishment arose out of bad character when he read Seebohm Rowntree's 1901 *Poverty: A Study of Town Life*.[12]

Defaulters' drill had an airing: it could save 5,000 lads from prison, said the Home Secretary. He pressed his theme of keeping youths off the slippery slope of jail sentences. A special opportunity had arisen with the accession of King George V. Usually, a new reign was marked by the release of some prisoners. Churchill tweaked the tradition into what he called 'a general pro rata reduction of sentences over the whole prison population'. 11,000 prisoners were involved. At a stroke 500 years of imprisonment and penal servitude were taken off. The Home Secretary assured the House that: 'No evil results of any kind have followed.' It worked out at two-and-a-third weeks per prisoner.

Then came the reduction of solitary confinement. The change would not apply to 'convicts who return again and again to penal servitude.' Churchill drew mirth when he said that separate confinement would be an option for those who wanted it, since some prisoners 'shrink from association with the prison gang, and prefer to remain in their cells'. He was assuredly correct. Scope for bullying and intimidation in the prisons of 1910 was limited, with severely restricted association, but of course it existed.

Churchill brought to Parliament his disquiet over sentences of three or more years penal servitude plus five years or more preventive detention. He reported his findings on the arbitrary nature of preventive detention. Currently 174 prisoners classified as habituals were serving sentences that included preventive detention. Echoing his comments on the Home Office files, he warned:

> There is a great danger of using smooth words for ugly things. Preventive detention is penal servitude in all its aspects.

It was inherently unjust, he thought, whatever the benefits for society, that a person should receive a sentence far longer than the normal tariff for their offence. Preventive detention had to be closely watched and had to be within the ambit of 'a great effort to rehabilitate'.

The speech included Churchill's radical revolution in ticket-of-leave. Under the new system, the only object for the body coordinating the work of the charitable societies among whom released persons would be distributed, would be 'to do the best for the convict'. When prisoners emerged through the prison-gates they would have nothing more to do with the police. He did however add the wide qualification of 'except in the case of refractory persons'. Those who were non-cooperative or continued to show criminal tendencies would have police surveillance.

Churchill unveiled his ideas for 'brain food' in prison. Prisoners needed mental and cultural stimulation. The Home Secretary's plan was for lectures and musical events. These would be:

> the means of supplying persons in prison with food for thought, and in regard to music a certain solace. A few months ago, the Somerset Light Infantry had their band in Dartmoor Prison and played to the convicts. The effect on all these poor people was amazing…

This caused a Conservative, former judge in Egypt Sir Bertram Falle, to giggle at the thought that, 'The music will be an added punishment to some.' Churchill brushed his interrupter aside and moved into his peroration:

> We must not forget that when every material improvement has been effected in prisons, when the temperature has been rightly adjusted, when the proper food to maintain health and strength has been given, when the doctors, chaplains, and prison visitors have come and gone, the convict stands deprived of everything that a free man calls life. We must not forget that all the improvements, which are sometimes salves to our consciences, do not change that position. The mood and temper of the public in regard to the treatment of crime and criminals is one of the most unfailing tests of the civilisation of any country. A calm and dispassionate recognition of the rights of the accused against the State, and even of convicted criminals against the State, a constant heart-searching by all charged with the duty of punishment, a desire and eagerness to rehabilitate in the world of industry all those who have paid their dues in the hard coinage of punishment, tireless efforts towards the discovery of curative and regenerating processes, and an unfaltering faith that there is a treasure, if you can only find it, in the heart of every man – these are the symbols which in the treatment of crime and criminals mark and measure the stored-up strength of a nation, and are the sign and proof of the living virtue in it.

These words have been called by Leon Radzinowicz and Roger Hood in *The Emergence of Penal Policy in Victorian and Edwardian England* 'eloquent identification of the balance of considerations which should guide the penal system of a progressive country'.[13]

The speech delighted social reformers. York's Liberal MP Arnold Rowntree, Quaker manufacturer of chocolate, urged his wife to read it:

> It was most refreshing, showing what a progressive mind Winston has.[14]

The Hobhouse/Brockway report called the speech 'the noblest official utterance of the kind in our generation'. The general reception was warm. Churchill received a supportive letter from the editor of the popular *Daily Express*. Ralph Blumenfeld, a Conservative, saw prison reform as a 'non-partisan' issue. He wrote, 'I am glad to have been able to pay you a little tribute for your humanitarian attitude.' Cross-party support came in a letter of commendation from John Heaton, Conservative MP for Canterbury, who was taking a health-cure in Germany and read Churchill's speech in *The Times*: 'a scheme marked by a rare combination of good sense and imagination'. Heaton, a former journalist, funded a pamphlet. He pronounced it a success: well-received 'in thoughtful circles' (including by governors of gaols).[15]

The glow included a favourable article in the big circulation *Daily Mail*, and enthusiasm in the *Daily News*: 'Prison reform may expect from Mr Churchill a considerable impetus.' The *Nation* hailed 'Mr Churchill's brilliant speech'. The influential Liberal magazine saw a 'change of tone and direction', and the resumption of 'an old and pregnant Radical tradition'. It noted approvingly that Churchill was 'no indiscriminate friend of the Indeterminate Sentence Act'.[16]

The speech was music to penal reform organizations. Thomas Hudson, Secretary of the Howard Association, found many points for which his organization had been pressing for years.[17]

Humanitarian magazine saluted Churchill:

Humanitarians throughout the kingdom will rejoice that Prison Reform is engaging the serious attention of the Home Secretary. His speech marks the commencement of a new era in dealing with crime...[18]

Its editorial declared:

Every one of the points which Mr Churchill has emphasised: the cruelty of solitary confinement and of the death-like monotony in prisoners' lives; the mischievous effects of police supervision after release; the need of [reform regarding imprisonment for non-payment of fines], of keeping youths out of prison, and of exempting 'political prisoners' from all unnecessary degradation, has been urged again and again by humanitarians during the past twenty years.

The Humanitarian League in its two decades had seen some progress on penal reform. With Churchill at the Home Office, hopes quickened. Its magazine however remarked on the continuing shyness of the English about using the word 'humane' as a compliment. John Galsworthy in writing to *The Times* had felt it necessary to say that, 'these reforms are not humanitarian...merely sensible.' *Humanitarian* predicted that when hanging, flogging, and stag-hunting were abolished, it would be declared to be a triumph 'not of humaneness but common-sense'.[19]

Applause for Churchill was not universal. 'Our arch-sentimentalist', jeered *Blackwood's Magazine*, 'has found a new pet in the criminal.' This journal, popular in middle-class households, viewed the Home Secretary as soft on the criminals who robbed of their rewards those who practised thrift and enterprise. Churchill, said *Blackwood's*, was 'succumbing to unthinking love of democracy'. The magazine had scorn for music and lectures in prison:

Are [prisoners] to be wooed softly with music and nurtured on lectures and magic-lanterns? Shall no thought of pity be harboured for the bruised head of their victim?[20]

It wanted not compassion but retribution. The Home Secretary's speech roused no enthusiasm in *Punch*, with a similar readership. Its 'Essence of Parliament' page, a forerunner of the 'sketch'-type commentary of today, omitted that day completely.

Churchill did not wait for reaction to settle. The day after the debate, he wrote a minute for his staff:

> It is important that departmental action should follow hot foot upon the Parliamentary announcement made last night.[21]

He put his action requirements into six categories: 1. Defaulters' drill ('I want a detailed memorandum…'); 2. Grace for fines; 3. Youthful offenders; 4. Detention in police cells in lieu of prison (this being a Churchill idea for very short non-prison sentences to avoid the jail environment); 5. Preventive detention; 6. Aid on discharge ('let us proceed at once to form the central agency'). At the foot of the document is a note from Troup to Ruggles-Brise setting out how Churchill's instructions were to be carried out. Categories 1 and 3 would have a committee to look at them; 2, 4, and 5 would be dealt with at the Home Office; 6 would be for the Prison Commissioners. The Home Secretary's staff were jumping to attention.

Chapter 6

Bracelets and Hangmen

The 1910 parliamentary summer recess began on 3 August. Winston Churchill left the country that evening. Ahead of him was a Mediterranean trip with friends aboard the yacht of Baron de Forest, a rich man with Liberal political aspirations. A press release (Churchill's movements seldom went unadvertised) mentioned a cruise and 'a shooting expedition in Asia Minor'. The party, as well as Winston's wife, included F.E. Smith – 'the Home Secretary's political foe', said one paper, but this was doubtful.[1]

There was presently a newspaper feeding-frenzy around the discovery of dissected body pieces under the cellar of a semi-detached North London house, the residence of medical practitioner Hawley Crippen. The gruesome remains were believed to be Mrs Cora Crippen. Hawley had fled with his lover Ethel Le Neve following an interview at his home by Metropolitan Inspector Dew, concerns having been raised about where his wife was. *Illustrated Police News* shrieked: 'COLD, BLOODY AND GHASTLY CRIME....FLIGHT OF DR CRIPPEN AND HIS PRETTY LADY TYPIST'. A national manhunt got under way, with a police reward of £250 offered. It had 'converted the country into a pack of bloodhounds', lamented the *Nation*. Churchill presumably had to approve the bounty, the Metropolitan Police being his responsibility. It will have been personal to him that the absconding pair were run down. News of their arrest on board an Atlantic ship out of Antwerp, on its arrival in Canada, broke just before Churchill left on his holiday. TRIUMPH OF WIRELESS proclaimed the *Daily News*.[2]

During Churchill's absence from the country some of his powers had to be formally transferred to a colleague. These included his discretion in the matter of persons condemned to death. For murder, judges had no alternative to passing a death sentence. However, if the Home Secretary signed a 'respite', the effect was the cancellation of the scheduled execution, 'until the King's pleasure is known'. He then advised the monarch to grant a conditional pardon. This advice was invariably accepted and a reprieve was issued, substituting a life sentence (the actual time served to be determined later).[3]

A week into his Home Office tenure, Winston Churchill was dining with friends. A fellow guest, Jean Hamilton, recorded a moment in 'the feast' when Churchill turned theatrically to her:

> We make too much of death…I have had to sign a death warrant for the first time today and it weighed on me. 'Whose?' I said. 'For what?' 'A man

who took a little child up a side-street and brutally slit her throat...Think', he said rather savagely, 'of a Society that forces a man to do that.'[4]

Attention-seizing remarks were a WSC stock-in-trade. Actually, there had been no 'death-warrant' in Britain since before Queen Victoria's day. There *was* an approaching execution but the previous Home Secretary had already decided against reprieve. Churchill, in his neat, functional handwriting, added his input:

> I have given an independent consideration to this case. I concur in Mr Gladstone's decision that there are no grounds for interference with the due course of the law.[5]

At Manchester prison, 24-years-old ex-Royal Navy stoker, Joseph Wren, was remorseful. He had been depressed because, being out of work, he could not marry his girlfriend and provide a home for their baby. He said that he had intended to kill the baby to save the woman 'from disgrace'. Unable to get to the child, he instead cut the throat of a miner's child (actually a boy). He said: 'I was not in my right senses.' He had attempted suicide several times. Murder followed by suicide or attempted suicide was a recurring pattern in crime files. A meeting under the auspices of the local Social Democratic Party sent a mercy plea to the King: 'Many of our unemployed here know the pangs of hunger, trials and privation suffered by this poor boy.' The letter will have struck a chord with Winston Churchill. Talking to Jean Hamilton, he was thinking of the chasm between the feasting well-to-do and those at the bottom of the social heap like Wren, who lost his mind and killed.[6]

Churchill sent the King a case analysis:

> ...No doubt the harsh conditions of his life and the hopelessness of his outlook roused him, and prompted him to commit a terrible act as an expression of his spite and hatred with which suffering had filled his heart, and as a ferocious demonstration similar in its character to anarchistic crimes against Society in general.[7]

We have noted Churchill's newspaper mention of a card tracking forthcoming executions. Harold Scott's eyes fell on this beside the clock on Churchill's office mantelpiece, whilst he was waiting to be introduced. The five cards of Churchill's Home Office time have survived among his papers. Each is divided into columns, the far right being RESULT. These days, all death sentences were for murder. In Britain, the incidence of recorded murders was one of the lowest in the world: between 129 and 163 per annum between 1862 and 1906. Most murders were committed by men. Often drink was a factor. Most victims were women, about half being wives, mistresses, and girlfriends.[8]

Two days after the dinner, Churchill wrote a minute on another condemned prisoner's file. This time it was his own decision. Twenty-seven-year-old ex-soldier George Perry had stabbed to death his girlfriend, who was going to leave him. Perry had been convicted at the Central Criminal Court (CCC), the Old Bailey. With its dome topped by a female figure holding a sword and scales of justice, the CCC was next to where the old Newgate Jail had stood, 200 yards north-west of St Paul's Cathedral. Perry's defence had been 'impulsive insanity'. The case was looked at by Home Office secretary Ernley Blackwell. Forty-two years old, the Scot was an ex-barrister. Herbert Gladstone wrote of him:

> He is devoted to his work, and you can implicitly rely on his accuracy and the soundness of his law.[9]

Blackwell was unusual for a first division civil servant in not being a university graduate. He was the senior legal under-secretary. The others in the top legal group around Churchill were Sir Edward Troup, Sir Henry Cunynghame, legal under-secretary of state (another ex-barrister) and William Byrne (also barrister-trained), of whom Gladstone wrote: 'he has a good deal of the Irishman in him… an excellent official.' And there was the Home Office's crime statistician, Harry Simpson. In capital cases, Churchill's primary advisers were Blackwell and Troup. A reprieve petition for Perry pleaded that his brain had been affected by fevers during service in India. Blackwell found nothing in his medical history. Churchill penned a brisk 'Let the law take its course.'[10]

Executioners and their assistants were paid per-job. Prime Minister Asquith had a boyhood memory of seeing outside Newgate Prison the dangling corpses of five executed men, with white caps over their heads. That was four years before the 1868 end of public hanging, since when executions had been within prison walls. Any problems had to be reported. There was one during Churchill's tenure.[11]

Chief executioner Henry (Harry) Pierrepoint had an assignment at Chelmsford Jail on 14 July 1910 to hang ex-soldier Frederick Foreman. (Pierrepoint's nephew Albert would be a famous hangman.) The part-time occupation attracted applications every week, many from cranks. The word 'hangman' was not used in official parlance. Harry Pierrepoint was known for his unpleasant habit of putting the noose around the prisoner's neck before the hood (still white) went on. He duly presented himself the afternoon before his scheduled business.[12]

Foreman, 45, had been convicted of the murder of his girlfriend after a drunken row. He was illiterate, his petition for mercy being written for him at the jail by a local schoolmaster. Frederick addressed a plea personally to Winston Churchill: 'I beg for mercy and a chance to lead a better life.' Ernley Blackwell saw 'a particularly cruel murder: I can suggest no reason for interference.' A regular practice was for the sentencing judge in a capital case to send his notes to the Home Office, frequently giving his view on whether the execution should go ahead. The Foreman judge thought that it should. So did Churchill, who wrote tersely, 'No interference.' So it was that Pierrepoint came to Chelmsford.

It was in the prison gatehouse on his arrival with his assistant, John Ellis, that an incident occurred which was brought to Churchill's attention.[13]

Hanging was scientific. 'Died hard' was no more, death apparently being near-instantaneous. The expertise was about measuring the depth of the required 'drop' – sufficient (but not excessive) for a neck-breaking jolt. Pierrepoint first had to make a note of the prisoner's age, height, and weight. He turned up inebriated and merry. When he saw his assistant recording the details, he flew into a swearing rage and struck Ellis behind the ear.[14]

The outcome was, as Blackwell informed the High Sheriff of Essex:

> Mr Churchill would be glad if you would note that Pierrepoint should not be employed on any future occasion as Executioner.[15]

Sheriffs, drawn from the upper social ranks, performed a role part-administrative and part-ceremonial (such as declaring parliamentary election results). When a death sentence was passed in their district, they had to appoint an executioner and an assistant from the Prison Commission's list. They had to be present at the hanging. Unsurprisingly, a sheriff would sometimes pass gallows attendance to his deputy.

The sacked Pierrepoint wrote a rambling letter to Winston Churchill, protesting that in all his executions there had been 'not a single hitch'. He accused Ellis of 'undermining' him. He was disabused of hope of reappointment. Ellis became chief executioner. Another heavy drinker, he would ultimately commit suicide. Alcohol abuse seems to have been a common denominator of murderers and hangmen. It might seem surprising that Churchill as a progressive Home Secretary never for a moment questioned hanging. On this, he was a conventionalist.[16]

On his holiday, Churchill left behind several death sentences. Boer War veteran Edward Woodcock, 40s, had killed the woman with whom he was living, cutting her throat with a razor when both were the worse for drink. She was already on crutches after a kick from him on a previous occasion. The prisoner was sentenced on 21 July by Lord Coleridge, with the ritual assumption of the 'black cap', with the regular words intoned: '…hanged by the neck until you are dead'. Judges were celebrities. Coleridge, once a Liberal MP, was drawn by *Vanity Fair*. He sent in his observations to the Home Office, as did the Leeds Chief Constable, who described Woodcock as, 'an idle and dissolute man, greatly addicted to drink'. Ernley Blackwell's report stressed the heavy force that must have been applied. His view was that, whilst 'no doubt the man had some immediate provocation from a nagging, drunken woman…it is at least probable that he treated her very badly.' He advised 'no interference'. Edward Troup agreed. So did the judge.[17]

Winston Churchill looked at various documents, including a letter from Woodcock to a friend:

...I knew that I had no one else to blame only myself for been [sic] so silly as I let my temper get the best of me....

It concludes with eight kisses: 'these is for our little Annie.'

The Home Secretary's memorandum assessed that Woodcock had a 'very bad record of petty and serious crime', but that he had been better behaved since his return from the army. A key factor for Churchill was that 'it seems unlikely there was any premeditation.' His decision was that:

> Having regard to the circumstances, and also to his bearing afterwards – which shows him not devoid of good – the sentence of death shall in the King's mercy be commuted to Penal Servitude for life.[18]

He signed a respite and wrote a letter for the King. This would be decisive. No monarch had refused to sanction the government's will since Queen Anne in 1708. Before leaving, Churchill gave the Foreign Secretary, Sir Edward Grey, who was standing in for him, the details of current death sentences: there was no need for him to review the Woodcock case since the reprieve was settled except for the formalities.[19]

Ernley Blackwell was dragging his feet. On 5 August, four days before Woodcock's still standing execution date, he telegraphed to Churchill a long memorandum. The Home Secretary was currently at Monte Carlo, Monaco. He was enjoying life, writing to Edward Marsh: 'You will be glad to hear that I visited the gambling hell on four occasions and took away upwards of £160.' Winston loved Monte Carlo. Over the years he lost much money there, but presently the roulette wheel was being kind to him. Blackwell had received the concerns of the trial judge. Lord Coleridge believed that Woodcock had premeditated the killing: so long as the death penalty existed, the murder of defenceless women should be punished with it, in the absence of solid ground for mercy. The judge's letter spoke of 'a similar horrible murder', which must be John Coulson, a Bradford foundry worker who killed his wife and son. Coleridge, who sentenced the two men on consecutive days, could not see why the Home Secretary was making a distinction.[20]

Coulson had drink and assault convictions. When his mill-weaver wife took out a summons against him, he cut her throat and that of their five-year-old boy. Blackwell and Troup advised that, 'the law must take its course.' Churchill concurred. He told Sir Edward Grey that if he agreed with his decision:

> Only new facts would require to be adjudicated in the brief interval between my departure and the date of the execution.[21]

Coulson and Woodcock were set to be dispatched together at Armley Jail, Leeds. The senior Home Office staff and the judge wanted that event to go ahead.[22]

Coulson would not have company on the gallows. The Home Secretary cabled Blackwell that whilst he valued the judge's opinion, his own conclusion was 'definite' and for 'mercy'. He instructed the senior legal secretary to submit the respite to the King and to commute Woodcock's sentence. Blackwell had to do as he was told. Woodcock was reprieved.[23]

Churchill reprieved two young women this summer. Each had killed a new-born 'illegitimate' baby. Italian-born Margherita Garibaldi, 22, lived with her aunt and uncle in Hanley, Staffordshire, helping with the family tea rooms and ice-cream stall. Her child died as a result of pressure to the windpipe. The defence argued accidental death when the woman was in 'a state of delirium'. 'The real culprit', said her barrister, 'is the coward who even now has not owned that he is the father of the child.' The jury in delivering a guilty verdict, strongly recommended mercy. The judge delivered the sentence 'amid an oppressive silence'. Execution was scheduled for Stafford Prison. Churchill moved swiftly. Two days after the sentence he signed a respite and wrote to the King. Customarily, a reprieve did not happen until days from the execution date several weeks later. Churchill cut convention. The importance of his speed of action is shown in the Hobhouse/Brockway report, regarding an unnamed woman who was almost certainly an infanticide convict:

> The reprieve did not come till the woman had been weighed to see what drop was needed and till within two days of the execution. Matron was absolutely ill with suspense, and the feeling among the officers and the other prisoners – not to mention the poor thing herself – was intense. It was torture.[24]

The authors explained that, 'the kindliest of officials dare not forestall the prerogative of mercy by holding out any assurance that the sentence will not be executed.'

The Home Office received notice that Stoke-on-Trent Labour MP John Ward had put down a question regarding reprieve for Garibaldi. Blackwell's advice was that it would be 'contrary to well established practice for S. of S. to say what advice it will be his duty to give H.M. with regard to a capital case'. Troup agreed that the question was 'improper'. The pair suggested that Ward should be told privately about the reprieve and asked to withdraw. Churchill did not oblige:

> I do not see why the fact should not be stated that the prisoner has been respited. There is much public feeling.

The question went ahead. The Home Secretary phrased his answer tactfully with a view to the backroom seniors:

> I could not have answered this question if I had not already given my advice to His Majesty. I advised him that the prerogative of mercy should be exercised and the capital sentence respited. The prisoner was at once informed.[25]

Margherita wanted to return to Italy. Seventeen thousand North Staffordshire residents signed a petition to Churchill asking for her release. Her solicitor was informed that Churchill was 'unable to advise at present any further interference with the sentence'. Margherita would have to do some penal servitude before release could be considered.

Another infanticide death sentence was passed on 20 July, in Liverpool. Mary Ellen Moore, 24, an out-of-work domestic servant, was charged with killing her recently born baby, which had apparently died from suffocation. It was reported that 'the prisoner was led from the dock in a collapsed condition.' Winston Churchill was written to on the day of the trial by the Governor of Liverpool Prison, John Dillon, to inform him that he had received Moore into his custody 'under sentence of death but with a strong recommendation [from the jury] to mercy'. Mary Ellen's defence had applied for an appeal. Normally the question of reprieve would not arise until after this was heard. But Churchill wanted the execution cancelled before he went on holiday. Writing to the King, he expressed his disquiet about death sentences on young women who had disposed of babies with which they could not cope:

> I wish some means could be devised to respite and commute in these cases at the same time that the sentence is pronounced.

The press announced the reprieve with the appeal still a fortnight away.[26]

Churchill's reprieves during this summer included 31-years-old carter Alfred Derrick, sentenced at Chester. Derrick had strangled his girlfriend and then stabbed himself in the neck. He appeared in court with his throat swathed in a large white scarf, and speaking with difficulty. An unusual reprieve issue was in play. A medical report, which arrived several days before the scheduled execution date, stated that Derrick's wound had 'hardly healed'. Hanging would most likely tear it open again.

Blackwell gave his advice:

> Respite and commute on ground that owing to the condition of prisoner's neck the execution could not be carried out without great risk of a revolting spectacle.

Consideration was thus given to the psychological welfare of those attending the execution. Given the oft-reported mental suffering of the personnel around a condemned prisoner, one might think that this issue brought into question hanging generally. Some thought it did. They did not include Churchill.

Troup concurred with Blackwell: 'it is in accordance with precedent to respite on this ground.' Churchill's decision was:

> Respite and commute: but mainly on the ground of the condition of his throat. This fact should be made public if necessary.

In the minute, 'mainly' replaces a squiggled out 'only'.[27]

One of Churchill's reprieves had an unhappy sequel. A month after being spared, Edward Woodcock was found hanged by his own hand in his cell. He had contrived a rope out of cotton remnants which his work had been to pick free from spinning tubes. He had attached it to the ventilator. He left a letter on his slate for his sister and brother:

> ... I think I had rather be dead than be in gaol for life...If I get out with 15 years I should be 61. Where could I find work at that age?...Your poor unfortunate brother, E. Woodcock.[28]

Edward Troup took grim satisfaction:

> In such cases the death penalty is more merciful than penal servitude, as well as far more effective as a deterrent to others.

Winston Churchill saw vindicated his view that 'the prisoner was not a common scoundrel.' He instructed efforts to be made to give effect to Woodcock's wish as to burial: a grave in his family's cemetery. Executed persons were by law buried in the grounds of the prison where they had been 'last confined'. WSC wanted to avert this for Woodcock. He called for a report on the outcome.

Nearly forty years later, Churchill as Leader of the Opposition spoke in a parliamentary debate on hanging. He was clearly thinking of the Woodcock case:

> ...After the crime [Woodcock] walked downstairs where a number of little children to whom he used to give sweets awaited him. He took all his money out of his pocket and gave it to them saying, 'I shall not want this anymore.' He then walked to the police station and gave himself up. I was moved by the whole story. The judge advised that the sentence should be carried out. The officials at the Home Office, with their very great experience, suggested no interference with the course of the law. But I had my own view, and I was unfettered in action in this respect.[29]

The detail of Woodcock and the children will have engaged the tender side of Winston. Harold Butler recalled 'a softness of heart with which [Churchill] is not always credited, but which is one of his most endearing characteristics'.[30]

In the 1948 debate, Churchill shared with MPs his thoughts about being Home Secretary: 'There is no post that I was more glad to leave.'

One of the capital cases in the summer of 1910 involved a railway killing. The train, like many, was without corridors. On a March morning at the end of the Newcastle to Alnmouth run, a body was discovered squashed under a seat. The man had been shot. The deceased, John Nisbet a colliery clerk, had been on his fortnightly trip to deliver a colliery's wages. The money bag with its £370 in coins was missing. It turned up at the bottom of a mining air-shaft minus the gold and silver. Police arrested a 45-years-old sometime mining commission agent, John Dickman, who was also a bookmaker and a gambler, apparently in recent financial difficulties. The gun was never found, nor the missing money. The man had an unusual quantity of sovereigns on his person when arrested. The case ran its course. The detectives investigated; the court sat; the jury found Dickman guilty; the Court of Criminal Appeal confirmed. The evidence was plentiful but circumstantial. The Home Office was the backstop regarding doubt in capital cases. Perhaps there was some here. Churchill turned Sherlock Holmes.[31]

He posed questions. Nisbet was alive in his compartment at Stannington station. By the next stop, Morpeth, he was not visible, nor did he emerge. Here Dickman handed in his ticket and an excess fare of two-and-a-half pence. He claimed to have been carried on as a result of being engrossed in the *Sporting Chronicle* (it being Grand National day). Churchill asked various questions, including how long was the journey between Stannington and Morpeth. The answer was six minutes. He asked: 'About how many people left the train at Morpeth?' The answer was twelve or so. Could the killer have thrown the money bag out of the train-window and later recovered it? Winston considered this hypothesis, finding it 'very improbable'.

The crux was identification. The evidence from three witnesses at Newcastle station was cumulatively suggestive against Dickman but none individually identified both Dickman and Nisbet as compartment companions. Part of the evidence was tainted. It transpired that one identification witness had been given previous sight of the accused through a half-open door. A Home Office investigation found police malpractice. Churchill had arranged for this to go before the Appeal Court.

The Home Secretary looked at another identification issue. At the preliminary court hearing the wife of the deceased fainted as she was leaving the witness box. She claimed that seeing the prisoner from a certain angle made her realize that she had glimpsed him on the train with her husband when she waved from a station by their home. Churchill was sceptical. He called this testimony 'sensational'. But he thought that the other pieces of identification were collectively strong enough without it. He remarked on the convoluted nature of Dickman's account of what he was doing during the crucial two hours after he left Morpeth Station: he claimed that he was ill and went into a field, where he rested. His story was that the purpose of his trip was to meet a contractor at a colliery near Stannington station to discuss business possibilities. This man gave evidence: he had no Dickman arrangement and he was not at the colliery that day, but Dickman had made visits there before without an appointment, including on the previous miners' payday. Churchill thought that, for the prisoner, this 'cut both ways, deeper against him'.[32]

He wrote a memorandum. This has Churchill's inventiveness of vocabulary, including the phrase 'bracelet of evidence', meaning the interlocking of the identification evidence against Dickman with the suspicious features of his story of his movements. WSC summed up:

> How incredible is it that the man who was the victim of such an extraordinary series of accidents should be the same who, by quite another set of occurrences, should be able to give such an untrustworthy account of his actions after leaving Morpeth Station?

Churchill asked Troup and Blackwell to check his points of fact. He came well out of the marking. The only error was a train-timing two minutes out.

Troup and Blackwell both advised 'no interference'. The Home Secretary made his decision:

> The execution of the sentence follows on this necessarily. The murder was one of the most cold-blooded, deliberately planned and brutally executed crimes for sordid ends that can be cited. The law must take its course.

John Dickman's execution was set for 9 August, at Newcastle prison, the same day as John Coulson at Leeds. The last-word responsibility for these two condemned men was sitting uncomfortably on the shoulders of Sir Edward Grey, as he would later tell Churchill. Grey's grandfather, Sir George Grey, had been a mid-Victorian Home Secretary. Churchill included in his *News of the World* reminiscences Sir Edward telling him that his grandfather 'found one morning, coming out of a church in the country, twenty people kneeling among the tombstones praying for mercy for a man doomed to die, an impression which had dwelt with him all his life.'[33]

Representations to the Home Office included one from the trial's shorthand writer, C.H. Norman, who wrote to Churchill that he was worried about bias against Dickman, including aggressive treatment by the judge and the prosecution. He praised Churchill's prison reforms but his tone changed in a later communication: 'to execute a man on suspicion [is] a principle so immoral and horrible that it could only emanate from the minds of Home Office staff.' There is a margin annotation: 'Abuse of Home Office staff'.[34]

The left-of-centre political and arts journal the *New Age* ran a leader on Dickman. That week's issue would have 'certainly examined Mr Churchill's proposed prison reforms with some care', but for the case taking precedence. It called capital punishment 'public murder added to the crime of private murder'. The writer had doubts about Dickman's guilt. The magazine was passed by Blackwell to Grey, with the information that Churchill had seen it.[35]

Newspaper letters showed that Winston Churchill was known for his 'love of humane justice'. Writers hoped for a reprieve in what was seen as 'an enlightened age'. Mary Bell of Carlisle wanted an end to death sentences on circumstantial evidence. On the other hand, an anonymous correspondent hoped that, 'the Home

Secretary will turn a deaf ear to the whining sentimentalists.' Blackwell kept Grey up to date: 'the case against the prisoner remains the same.' Sir Edward was twitchy. He wrote to Churchill later that 'the constant stream of letters pointing out the weak points of the evidence was very uncomfortable.'[36]

There was public indignation about the reported treatment of Dickman's wife and his children, Kitty, 17 and Harry, 14. When Annie Dickman arrived at Newcastle prison, she asked for a separate room for a meeting with her husband. The governor, H.J. Hellier, refused. The *Daily Mail* had: 'DICKMAN AND HIS CHILDREN: REFUSAL OF A LAST GOODBYE'. It ran an editorial: 'Inhumanity in Prisons'. A correspondent called the final visit arrangements 'barbarism...the torture this must have inflicted on this unhappy man.' Reminding readers of the paper's recent articles on 'the points of sensible and humane changes which Mr Churchill has now set afoot', the *Mail* called the treatment of Dickman 'the old perverted views of vengeance'. For Churchill, this was damaging.[37]

What happened at the final meeting? On the day before the execution Annie and the children were permitted half-an-hour's audience. A metal grille kept them apart. When Dickman was led away they could only wave goodbye. The governor, writing to the Prison Commissioners, claimed to have had knowledge of 'a diabolical scheme, cunning and daring'. Presumably he meant the passing of poison. When Winston Churchill learned what had happened, he penned a report:

> ...It was an error of judgement to refuse this request. The proper course would have been to allow the prisoner's wife and children to take a personal farewell, provided that they were willing to be thoroughly searched before being admitted to go within reach of the prisoner. The incident leaves an unpleasant impression, and taken in conjunction with the improprieties which occurred at the time of the prisoner's identification, and of the presence of promiscuous newspaper reporters in the jail, does not create a very good impression upon my mind.[38]

The visit was apparently conducted under regular arrangements – described in the Hobhouse/Brockway Report as 'the meat safe' and 'the cage', the former being 'two small compartments partitioned from each other by two screens of thick wire gauze about a foot apart'. The cage was recalled by the wife of a prisoner: 'I shall never thoroughly get over the shock which I had when I saw my husband through the bars...I felt that I was looking through the dim light at some fierce, uncouth animal at the zoo.' The fact that he was unshaven and dirty worsened the woman's experience.

The *Newcastle Illustrated Chronicle* ran a day-by-day diary by Annie Dickman, a former teacher. It is perhaps of significance that, whilst protesting against unfairness in the trial and her husband's treatment, she nowhere actually maintains his innocence. The press coverage confirms the admission of reporters to the prison. The Hobhouse/Brockway report speaks of a 'recent occasion when two Press men were permitted to attend an execution'. Those present at the gallows could reach double figures. They included the chaplain and a doctor. The *Chronicle* had macabre titbits for its readers, including that just before 8 a.m. 'the under-sheriff made the usual formal demand to the governor for the body of Dickman for execution.' Then there was 'the procession' from the prisoner's cell to the gallows. This would be the last execution at Newcastle Jail. The Prison Commission was having building work done to site gallows inside prisons next to the condemned cell (the function of a connecting door being kept from the prisoner until the last moment). For Dickman, it was still the march to the shed. A crowd of fifteen-hundred gathered outside the jail, hearing a 'dull thud' at one minute past eight. Half-a-century later, Lucy Masterman remembered that residents close to one jail were troubled on hanging days:

> It appeared that people in the neighbourhood were able to see some of the circumstances attendant on an execution from their windows and wrote to [Churchill] to demand a greater measure of concealment. Winston was scornful: 'They don't ask that these unfortunate people should be spared, only that they mayn't be obliged to see it. I won't do a thing about it.'[39]

Among the *Chronicle*'s post-execution headlines was: 'NO CONFESSION'. The paper reported that John Dickman 'walked as erect as a soldier on parade and did not blanch when the open doors of the execution-house and the suspended rope came in view.' Meanwhile it was reported that in Leeds John Coulson 'walked steadily to the scaffold.' If he and Dickman were calm, Edward Grey was not. The Foreign Secretary told Churchill later:

> I think this part of your job is beastly and on the night before the men were hung I kept meditating upon the sort of night they were having, till I felt as if I ought not to let them hang unless I went to be hung too.[40]

Churchill will have understood Grey's bad night. He had them. Lucy Masterman recalled that he told her husband that he 'often lay awake all night before an execution, only finding sleep when the clock struck eight and he knew it was over and no more was to be done.' Given that he had to go through this on average twice a month, his relief when he moved on is scarcely surprising.[41]

This was a summer of sensational murder cases. During the earlier stages of the Crippen case, Winston Churchill let his imagination run. Lucy Masterman's diary has:

> [Churchill] advanced a new theory of the Crippen murder: that it was Le Neve who was the culprit, and that Crippen merely cut up the body in order to shelter her, and is now standing the racket with the same motive. He

worked out this idea with much fervour and nearly convinced himself that it was the case, though he would not admit more than that this view did not contradict any of the established facts of the case.[42]

The Home Office liked to have one of its own in court for major trials. When Hawley Crippen appeared at the Old Bailey, it was Harold Butler on duty. Butler (Eton and Balliol), 27, later recalled 'the demeanour of the little doctor as he listened keenly but impassively, blinking placidly through his spectacles'. Crippen was found guilty on 21 October and sentenced to death.

Churchill wrote in his 1939 *News of the World* retrospective:

> I cannot remember the House of Commons ever having attempted to sway the decision of the Home Secretary in a capital case. Nor is the Home Secretary compelled to grant painful interviews to relations of the condemned. In other countries a different custom rules.[43]

The evidence against Crippen was collectively strong. There were his financial difficulties; his mistress's use of his wife's property; his flight with the mistress; the body pieces being wrapped in a pyjama jacket matching Crippen's nightwear; a scar on a piece of skin tallying with a known abdominal mark of Mrs Crippen. In addition, large quantities of a lethal agent were found in the remains: Crippen had made a purchase of the drug in question from a local chemist. For Ernley Blackwell, the evidence was 'overwhelming'.

The Crippen trial was followed swiftly by another, of one day, to determine whether his mistress was his accomplice. Ethel Le Neve was defended by F.E. Smith. As the Lord Chief Justice, Lord Alverstone, was beginning his summing up, a figure slipped into the courtroom. The press reported: 'MR WINSTON CHURCHILL IN COURT'.[44]

Smith won his case, his line being that Ethel was unaware that her lover was murderous. She was discharged and thus became available to comfort Crippen with daily visits. Petitions and representations had arrived on the prisoner's behalf. Churchill wrote on his file that they added nothing significant. His decision was, 'Let the law take its course.' He was however content for the doctor's wait for execution to be eased by visits from Le Neve. A Home Office official called attention to a rule that 'the grant of visits to prisoners under sentence of death rests with the V[isiting] C[ommittee].' Churchill's file minute was sharp: 'The permission is not under any circumstances to be refused subject to the necessary regulations.' After the first visit, police had to make a way for Ethel and her sister to get back to their cab through a crowd of five hundred, of 'hostile demeanour', as a note put it. Churchill instructed, 'Let good arrangements be made to rescue her from molestation.'[45]

The visits (which inspired Ernest Raymond's 1935 best-selling novel *We the Accused*) sparked a protest on behalf of 'over seven thousand London working men', members of the Metropolitan Workmen's Council. This found 'the most extraordinary contrast' between John Dickman, barred from a farewell embrace of his wife and children, and Hawley Crippen granted togetherness with his mistress:

Ernley Blackwell fielded this, Churchill initialling:

> The prisoner sees Le Neve in the V. C. Room – a long table separates them and an officer sits at each side. This is the usual arrangement at Pentonville in the case of condemned prisoners.[46]

The Workmen's Council saw Dickman as Newcastle working class, Crippen as a middle-class London doctor. This was misconceived. Churchill's permission for the meetings included vigilance: 'the Governor should be warned to take all possible precautions against poison being conveyed to the prisoner.' It would be embarrassing for him in Parliament if Crippen 'cheated the rope'. The medical man did try. He broke off one of the metal arms of his spectacles with a view to using it to cut an artery. The plan was foiled.[47]

Shortly before the Crippen trial, Churchill was at a house party hosted by Wilfrid Blunt, whose diary records him stepping from his motor: 'fur-collared jacket, tight leggings and gaiters and a little round hat…his 'half-mischievous face'. Presumably the bird-shooting that is mentioned accounts for the attire. With Crippen in the news, the chat between Churchill and Blunt touched on executions:

> [Churchill] is in favour of capital punishment but, while thinking executions cannot be made a spectacle for hooligans, will see to it that relations and friends shall be allowed to be present.[48]

He presumably meant friends and relations of the person being hanged. This is perhaps not as impossible an idea as it might sound. The Capital Punishment Act of 1868 allowed for 'such relatives of the prisoner or other persons as it seems to the sheriff or the visiting justices of the prison proper to admit' to be present at an execution. In practice, no relations or friends seem ever to have attended on the morning of a hanging. There would scarcely be room. Oscar Wilde's *Ballad of Reading Jail* calls the party which entered the cell of the condemned person before execution 'dread figures thong[ing] his room'. There was no question of Le Neve being there for Crippen.[49]

Churchill never questioned the institution of capital punishment. He said to Edward Grey: 'To most men – including all the best – a life sentence is worse than a death sentence.' He later summarized his capital case impressions for Wilfrid Blunt:

> Nearly all of the cases of murder are a combination of love and drink, young fellows who on a sudden impulse kill their sweethearts, sometimes in the

most barbarous fashion yet with the excuse of temporary rage amounting to madness.

'Nearly all' is rhetoric, but the Home Office files do have a number of such cases.[50]

No woman had been executed since 1907, nor were any whilst Winston Churchill was at the Home Office. In 1910 Churchill intervened regarding a British woman who had narrowly escaped execution in Japan. The British Consular Court, which until 1900 had jurisdiction over British citizens in Japan, condemned Edith Carew in 1896 for the arsenic poisoning of her husband. It happened that the Mikado granted some sentence reductions for Japanese prisoners and out of diplomatic courtesy Edith's sentence was commuted to penal servitude. She was serving it in Britain, at Aylesbury. In the spring of 1910, a petition for Carew's release came to Harold Butler. He favoured the application:

> She might properly have been hanged, but as she is neither brutal, criminal nor dangerous by instinct, society does not need to be protected and she is herself unlikely to benefit by a few years more in prison.[51]

He put his tiny initials under the typed minute. Harry Simpson counter-signed with his big florid ones. The file then went up higher. Next month it came back to Butler: 'a fat file...faded newspaper cuttings and yellowing documents'. It had gathered negative minutes. Edward Troup reiterated the 'deliberate poisoning' and recalled that Edith had tried to put the guilt on a governess. However, beneath Troup's input was a question from the Home Secretary:

> Has she anywhere to go, or friends or means?

An answer came from Simpson:

> Yes, she belongs to a good family. Her father Mr J.A. Porch is a J.P. for Somerset living near Glastonbury.

The Porches were in *Burke's Landed Gentry*. They owned the ruins of Glastonbury Abbey. Eight years later a cousin of Edith Carew, Montague Porch, at 41 would become WSC's stepfather. Tight indeed was the world of society. Simpson thought that Carew would 'lead a quiet, useful and honourable life'. To Ernley Blackwell, gentle birth and an available home were irrelevant:

> Her crime was murder of the worst sort and she escaped hanging by an accident. Her petitions show no sign of penitence.[52]

Troup agreed.

The most recent page of the file had Churchill's decision, dated 30 April 1910:

> I have come to the conclusion that mercy may be extended in this case. Let the convict be released on licence when she has served as for a sentence of

20 years, i.e., as I calculate it, after serving 13 years and 4 months. Inform her friends accordingly.[53]

Since women could gain sentence remission of up to one-third, this implied that Edith was being treated as if she had gained maximum remission, which does not seem to have been the case.

Carew emerged from prison on licence on 26 October. She was readmitted to the dinner-party circuit. Her coarse hands (she had worked in the prison kitchen) were noted. Was Churchill rescuing one of his own? In his interventions, Winston sometimes nodded to the establishment to which he belonged.[54]

Chapter 7

Curing Criminals?

Sir Evelyn Ruggles-Brise was a close follower of international penal developments. He was chairman from 1910 of the five-yearly International Penal and Penitentiary Congress. He was keen on the application of science to penology, especially the differentiation of prisoners into categories. Successive Home Secretaries and their staff were not enamoured of modern-fangled sociology and psychology. Then in February 1910 came the appointment of a Home Secretary whom a historian of the Prison Commission has called 'the most remarkable exception to the rule of Home Office caution and restraint'. Winston Churchill quickly picked up the doctrine of segregation of offenders into treatment categories. He set about refining it. On his summer cruise-boat he worked out a grand scheme of principles, which he embodied in a memorandum. He sent it to London to be read by Troup, Ruggles-Brise, Blackwell and Masterman.[1]

Churchill wanted to make penal detention increasingly 'one complete series of specialisations':

> The general mixed prison should go with the general mixed workhouse into extinction…Instead of having a lot of prisons of substantially the same type and reproducing the same features, scattered about all over the country, we should have a regular series of scientifically graded institutions which would gradually and increasingly become adapted to the treatment of every variety of human weakness.[2]

He set out five general aims:

1. To abolish all imprisonment for periods of less than one month;
2. To reduce by one-third the annual committals to prison;
3. To reduce by between 10 and 15% the average daily prison population;
4. To classify this reduced prison population in 20 or more main categories;
5. To distribute these different categories for specialised treatment throughout the prisons of the country according to administrative convenience.

He also wanted imprisonment for debt abolished. 10,000 people were jailed in 1909 as a result of County Court judgements, mostly, in Churchill's view, owing to 'a genuine deficiency of means'.[3]

Ruggles-Brise's reaction reached Churchill by way of an Edward Marsh letter:

> Ruggles's breath was rather taken away and he burst into Homeric laughter when he read that it would be easy for the P. Commrs to classify into 20 groups. But on the whole he was enthusiastic; he said that your grasp of the subject was marvellous, and that *if* you were to be here for the next five years, it could be done.[4]

Ernley Blackwell was sceptical. He pointed to the logistical problems of shunting large numbers of prisoners around the country. Quite coincidentally, the issue of convict transfer was raised next year with Churchill in Parliament by London Liberal MP Edward Pickersgill, who asked:

> whether it was with [Churchill's] knowledge and sanction that convicts being conveyed from one prison to another were unnecessarily exposed to the public gaze?[5]

Pickersgill asked if the Home Secretary knew of the experience of 'a famous man of letters when a convict' on a platform at Clapham Junction. Oscar Wilde was abused by members of the public when being transported under warder-escort from Wandsworth to Reading in 1895. A plaque marks the spot.

A Home Office document from Churchill's period sheds light on the problems of prisoner transportation. The writer mentions amalgamation of prisoner journeys, for example gathering together convicts from Manchester, Shrewsbury, and Worcester for transport to Portland on the Isle of Wight. Long distance meant rail:

> By pulling down the blinds of third-class saloon carriages, these are converted into prison vans. It is to be remembered that full fares are charged by the railway company, and that all escorts, entailing as they do a return for the officer, are enormously expensive.[6]

Apart from the organizational problems of specialization, Ernley Blackwell thought that detailed generic classification would be impossible in practice short of putting together prisoners who had committed specific types of crime. There was also the loss of emotional support for prisoners by reason of distance. Visits to prisoners by friends would be more difficult. Admittedly, because of the humiliating arrangements for visits and their shortness – (half an hour), many prisoners preferred to do without them, but one ex-inmate told the Hobhouse/Brockway inquiry that: 'The visit of a wife or a mother or a sweetheart had a wonderfully refining and beautifying influence.' The geography of specialization would reduce the opportunities. At remote Dartmoor, only about five per cent of convicts had visits.[7]

The Home Secretary's proposals included a revising-board to bring about uniformity in sentences. Edward Marsh reported a Blackwell head-shake: 'He thinks the Courts would strike, as they are very jealous of the interference of the Executive.'⁸

We have seen that Churchill's attitude to borstal upset the Prison Commission. Edward Troup wrote to the holidaying Home Secretary urging him to read the memoranda of Brise and Waller, with which he said he was in substantial agreement. He thought that Brise's view on a scale of punishments was not so different from Churchill's (except on Defaulters' Drill). Churchill annotated airily: 'Read. We have got on rather beyond this now.' A month after Churchill's return, Wilfrid Blunt's diary records:

> Winston is going on energetically about prison reform, and will push it much beyond what he has already announced publicly.⁹

On 26 September 1910 Churchill presented to the prime minister his projected Home Office timetable for the next year. A bill for improving safety regulations in the coal-mining industry (to follow the Miners' Eight Hours Day legislation of 1908, which Churchill and Masterman put through Parliament) led but did not excite WSC. His projected legislation to reshape the penal system did:

> The second Bill will deal with the punishment of offenders, and will perhaps be more interesting and certainly more extensive than its companion.¹⁰

The Home Secretary called his proposed measures 'scientific and benevolent'. The key statistic was the 125 thousand people committed to prison for a fortnight or less in the previous year. Churchill told Asquith that he hoped to reduce that number drastically. The starting point would be suspension of all custodial sentences of less than a month, except for violence, crueltyn or wilful destruction of property. It was to be no soft touch, since repeat offenders would serve their original sentence and more. 'Habitual drunkards, rogues and vagabonds' would get severe doses of training. Central to the vision was classification: 'the essence of penology'. It already existed to a degree: Parkhurst for the physically and mentally infirm; Broadmoor for the criminally insane; Aylesbury for female convicts; Maidstone for middle-class and younger convicts. Churchill visualised much more categorization. He rolled off a list of types of establishment which he said were 'coming *disconnectedly* into view'. 'Homes for inebriates' existed; 'detention prisons for recidivist convicts' were on the way; 'institutions for the criminal weak-minded' were so far in Churchill's mind only, likewise 'labour colonies like Merxplas for loafers and vagrants'.¹¹

The central idea was that 'no occasional offender ought to be sent to prison for a single trivial offence.' The corollary was that those with a criminal *habit* should be sent to a specialist institution dealing with that type of behaviour. The Home Secretary saw his proposals as analogous to the recommendations of the 1905 Royal Commission on the Poor Law for specialized institutions for those who were not coping. These included, in place of the general workhouse: long-stay hospitals for the chronically sick; asylums for the mentally weak; homes for children; labour colonies for vagrants and the incorrigibly unemployed. The recommendations had yet to be adopted. The Commission's Majority Report emphasized charity and voluntary organizations. It wanted to keep the Poor Law but with its agencies more specialized. The Minority Report (Beatrice and Sidney Webb) wanted state-run social security, with unemployment insurance, to replace the Poor Law. Not many Liberals supported it. Churchill did. Whilst the majority report edged towards confinement of those who, through physical infirmity, disease, or mental incapacity were a danger to themselves or a nuisance to the public, the minority report definitely called for this. Churchill was with the latter. He favoured governmental control of problem groups. He saw, as in a blinding flash, Poor Law and Prisons as two sides of the same coin.[12]

Prominent in Churchill's document was his drive for sentencing uniformity:

> The courts are so numerous and diverse that it is impossible to work any scientific system through them by means of Home Office circulars.

A central unified sentencing system was going to tread on the toes of the judges and magistrates. Troup and Blackwell fretted. Ruggles-Brise thought that Churchill's twenty categories of prisoner in tailored institutions around the country was not in the real world. We may imagine the muttering and more in Whitehall as Churchill's schemes rolled in. It was happening. Maurice Waller had once been Herbert Gladstone's private secretary. He regularly corresponded with the ex-Home Secretary. In an 18 August 1910 letter he was caustic about Churchill: 'He does not know enough about these subjects yet and sometimes does not seem to take care to learn. He is exercising other Branches of the Home Office too, greatly.' He told Gladstone: 'I'm sorry to say that W.C. does not regard Preventive Detention with favour.' He commented that, 'His point of view quite ignores the fact that PD will be no more and no less than he chooses to make it.'[13]

Churchill put his proposals into a cabinet paper, dated 25 October 1910, entitled 'Abatement of Imprisonment'. He saw Poor Law and penal administration together as the management of the weak, the poor, the deviant, and the dangerous, for the betterment of themselves and society. David Garland's analysis of British penal history reminds of the part played by decision-making individuals. Winston Churchill was one such. He was no Victorian-values proponent, nor was he into character-building. He was a governmental interventionist.[14]

Whilst Trade Minister, Winston Churchill had been introduced to one who would have a major influence on his thinking on social security. Future architect of the welfare state, William Beveridge, who devised Churchill's labour exchanges system, had some views fashionable in progressive circles before the wars, but which now seem surprising to say the least. Churchill followed Beveridge in discerning a category of unfortunates who would have to be dependants of the state, as incapable of efficiency and unemployable. Such persons would be maintained adequately in public institutions but, as Beveridge put it in 1906, would forfeit 'not only the franchise, but civil freedom and fatherhood'. Churchill thought that now that there were labour exchanges, the unemployed who could not secure a subsistence through earnings should be 'curatively' treated, exactly as if they were hospital patients.[15]

With his chaotically creative energy, Churchill once he was in the flow of anything, strove to lead it. His prisons chief, advanced in categorization theory though he was, struggled with Churchill's twenty types of jail project. However, Ruggles-Brise and Churchill were much in agreement on general principles, and their working relationship for the most part ran smoothly. Of the occasional bumps, one was over two prison officers.

On 3 June 1910 Churchill received from Ruggles-Brise a recommendation that two warders, Robert Page and Edward Lowdell, of Warwick Prison, be dismissed for 'scandalous conduct'. The officers several times, whilst escorting a prisoner to court, 'made a detour and went to a Public House and drank with him.' Brise will have expected Churchill's approval as a formality. The Home Secretary wanted the warders to be retained:

> This conduct was grossly improper. Still there is a great distinction between it and any offence like cruelty to a prisoner, false evidence, corruption or open insubordination. Could not a less severe punishment be imposed?[16]

The Brise jaw dropped. He further justified sacking: the landlord had given the warders a piece of his mind about letting an escorted prisoner buy them drinks; the hostelry was not on the way to the court: the diversion had made the party late; the man was an habitual drunkard and violent, awaiting trial on a charge of unlawful wounding and larceny. It was part of standing orders, said Brise, that prison officers must not frequent public houses or be 'unduly familiar with prisoners'. The Commissioners had to maintain strict standards: 'they feel sure that the S of S will support them in this view of their duty.'

Edward Troup endorsed.

Churchill was irritated: what was the use of submitting the case to him when 'action appears to have been taken already?' Brise pointed to precedent: there was no case on record of a Home Secretary declining his consent for disciplinary action. Troup took the prisons chief's side: it would be a 'serious hindrance to administration' if the Commissioners had to get retrospectively the sanction of the Secretary of State to the numerous appointments, promotions etc among subordinate officers. Churchill retorted that his agreement could be taken as read for 'reprimand, suspension, deprivation of pay' etc, but in the matter of discharge from the service he should have an opportunity of considering the case. Dismissal could be challenged in Parliament. He thought that suspension and a severe reprimand, possibly with reduction to a lower rank, would have been sufficient. However, he confirmed the action taken.

The matter could not end like that. As Secretary of State, Churchill outranked any civil servant. From the Prison Commission lower floor in the Whitehall building came a letter expressing the 'great regret' of Sir Evelyn that the Home Secretary was 'not able to support the Commissioners' decision in this case', along with a reminder that, 'Misbehaviour on escort…is always dealt with in the Army and Navy with great severity.' But the message concluded:

> However, as the S of S is not able to agree with the action taken, the Commissioners feel that they have no alternative but to reinstate these officers with other punishment in lieu, and action has been taken accordingly.

WSC's acknowledgement was matter of fact:

I am obliged to the Commrs for the course they have adopted.

Was Churchill capriciously displaying his authority, or was it reasonable correction of an over-severe punishment? The behaviour of Page and Lowdell looks outrageous. On the other hand, the life of warders was tough. J.E. Thomas' history of prison officers sees an unenviable role, as the jails started to become less harsh whilst they themselves were increasingly tightly controlled by their superiors. In the saving of the jobs of two officers who relaxed in an irresponsible manner on a day out of their workplace, we may perhaps see Churchill's sentiment. As a child, he was taken long walks by the husband of his beloved nurse Mrs Everest. The man had served thirty years as a prison warder. He would tell the young Winston of mutinies in the jails and how he himself several times had been attacked and injured. Now Churchill had the power to help two warders.[17]

J. E. Thomas considers that 'Churchill's reformative enthusiasm on behalf of prisoners had no counterpart in his handling of staff affairs.' He looks at the Home Secretary's replies in Parliament to questions on the treatment of prison-officers. Staffs of different prisons had been communicating with a view to having a general federation, as with postal workers. The Prison Commissioners were hostile. An inter-prison warders' meeting planned for a London hotel had been forbidden. Several Labour MPs raised the matter with Churchill. Philip Snowden wanted to know, 'why the freedom enjoyed by other branches of the public service is denied to these men?' Churchill closed ranks with the Commissioners. Saving the jobs of a couple of the warders was one thing, trade union-type aspiration another:

> Disciplined forces must be governed by special regulations. It would not be possible to allow a trade union to be formed among prison warders any more than among policemen or soldiers and sailors.[18]

The top of the prison service attracted ex-army officers. Prison governor correspondence with the Home Office bristles with military rank. Any suggestion of even the mildest step in the direction of trade unionism among warders was absolutely to be suppressed as far as the Commissioners and Churchill were concerned. But with the advance of trade unionism, and a sizeable block of Labour members in Parliament, the aspiration for a prison officer representative body was not so easily squashed. The *Prison Officers' Magazine* was carefully moderate in tone, but the nickname of 'the red un' was not just about print colour. Churchill, a man of military background himself, was for keeping warders in their place. His efforts to improve life for jail inmates had no counterpart in respect of the working conditions of prison staff. The limits to Churchill's social radicalism were shown at the Home Office.[19]

Chapter 8
Churchill and Eugenics

In December 1910 Winston Churchill updated his legislation proposals for the prime minister. There was a new item. The preamble was:

> I am convinced that the multiplication of the feeble-minded, which is proceeding now at an artificial rate, is a very terrible danger to the race.

He had an alarming tale:

> The feeble-minded girls and young women are the easy prey of vice and hand on their own insanity with unerring and unfailing fertility. Runciman [Education Minister] tells me that he has now got 12,000 feeble-minded and defective children in the special schools…The girls come out by the thousand at 16, are the mothers of imbeciles at 17, and thereafter frequent our workhouse lying-in wards year by year. The males contribute an ever-broadening streak to the insane or half-insane crime which darkens the life of our towns and fills the convict prisons…

He proposed:

> …to keep all the feeble-minded children of both sexes who require custodial care, now in the hands of the education authorities or in other public institutions, segregated from the world and from the opposite sex.

This would be 'a first instalment…a mere stopgap':

> The day will of course come when the acquiescence of the feeble-minded person in a sterilising operation will enable a considerable proportion of these people to obtain a larger liberty than is possible at present. But it will be time to think about the conditions under which they may be let out when we have obtained the power to make sure that they are effectively shut up.[1]

Winston Churchill was talking eugenics. He had suddenly become a zealot. The crusade had swept along so many in recent years that its principles had turned into orthodoxy, though with a few passionate opponents. Churchill wanted to use the (pseudo-) science, though not in the way attributed to him in a supposed quotation which gets repeated. He did not propose that '100,000 degenerate Britons should be forcibly sterilised.' This is source-free mythology. Churchill wanted voluntary sterilization as a means of allowing some of those confined in institutions to gain their freedom.

The Home Secretary looked at another social control issue. The biography by his son Randolph states, in an account that has been followed, that in the House of Commons on 10 February 1911 he said that 'tramps and wastrels' needed to be dispatched to labour colonies. That day the Labour Party initiated a 'Right to Work' debate. Churchill did not speak in it but in his parliamentary report to the King, he added views of his own:

> As for tramps and wastrels there ought to be proper Labour Colonies where they could be sent for considerable periods and made to realise their duty to the State. Such institutions are now being considered at the Home Office. It must not however be forgotten that there are idlers and wastrels at both ends of the social scale.

'Wastrel' was a word deep in the Winston psyche. His father once warned him that he would end up as 'a mere social wastrel'. Churchill's 'wastrel' remarks got him, not for the first time, into hot water with the Palace. King George's Secretary, Lord Knollys, conveyed to his opposite number with the prime minister, the monarch's alarm at the Home Secretary's 'very socialistic views'. Asquith passed the letter to Churchill. The result was a letter from a mortified WSC to the King: the previous sovereign had been happy with parliamentary accounts 'frequently of a discursive character and containing expressions of personal opinion upon the subjects under discussion'. Winston went on (in the third person):

> Mr Churchill cannot understand why [his remarks] should be thought to be Socialistic. The Govt contemplates measures to deal with vagrancy and the punishment and reform of tramps and incorrigible loafers by means of labour colonies on the continental system and the H.O. is already studying the subject with a view to drafting a bill...Even-handed justice would require that all persons should render some Service to the State, whether rich or poor. This is not to attack the wealthy classes, but only to point to those particular persons whose idle and frivolous conduct brings a reproach to the meritorious class to which they belong.

Churchill was digging himself into a deeper hole, but, as ever, he was exhilarated by his verbal composition, with that risqué edge that he could not resist when talking to the Palace. A perplexed Lord Knollys commented that, 'He means it to be conciliatory, I imagine, but he is rather like 'A Bull in a China Shop'. When the King took further offence, Knollys hopefully suggested that Churchill could learn from the parliamentary letters of greats like 'Lord Palmerston, Lord Beaconsfield and Mr Gladstone, which are bound up in my room'. The reform project was a lost cause. Winston, whilst sprinkling 'humbles' in his correspondence with the Palace, evidently had no intention of practising this mode. He offered to stand himself down from parliamentary letters, but the King asked him to continue his 'always interesting' letters. His Majesty's incorrigible subject was happy to oblige.[2]

If there was planning at the Home Office for a bill to round-up tramps and put them in labour camps, fortunately it never saw the light of day.

Churchill had read an American pamphlet by a Dr Sharp, formerly physician at the Indiana Reformatory. Its subject was a state law prescribing sterilization for persons in state custody who were judged mentally unfit. Mental incapacity had a scale (on both sides of the Atlantic): 'idiots' (persons incapable of looking after themselves); 'imbeciles' (capable of looking after themselves but not of earning a living); 'feeble-minded' (capable of earning a living under favourable circumstances but not with normal prudence). The Indiana Act aimed 'to prevent procreation of confirmed criminals, idiots, imbeciles, and rapists.'

Winston devoured Dr Sharp's tract, marking sections with a thick blue pencil. He wrote a memorandum: 'I am drawn to this subject...Of course it is bound to come someday.' He admitted that there were 'many Party misgivings'. There was indeed strong Liberal opposition to medical interference with people who happened to be a social nuisance. For Churchill, sterilization was a possible way of keeping down the number of people locked up. He set in train a departmental discussion on what the arrangements would be. He himself, as he indicated on a number of occasions, favoured voluntary sterilization. He forwarded Dr Sharp's booklet to the Medical Adviser to the Prison Commission, Sir Bryan Donkin.[3]

Sir Bryan – medically distinguished and politically radical – had been to America, where he heard about social sterilization. He called the Indiana law 'Gilbertian... the arrogation of scientific knowledge by persons who had no claim to it'. Edward Troup was not so dismissive but he did go along with Donkin's warning that the medical profession would be strongly against any such law in Britain. The Royal Commission on the Feeble-minded, in its report two years previously, had recommended that the mentally 'inadequate' should be detained in institutions. As things stood, detention applied only to the criminally insane. Herbert Gladstone had made no move. On 13 June 1910 there was a parliamentary question for John Burns, the local government minister, on whether the government was going to carry out the Royal Commission's recommendations. The Poor Law administration for which Burns was responsible included the workhouses where many of the 'feeble-minded' were housed. He passed the question over to Winston Churchill. The Home Secretary answered:

> ...The Government are fully alive to the importance of this matter, and a draft Bill is already in preparation, though legislation this Session is, I fear, not practicable.[4]

On 15 July, the prime minister and Winston Churchill received a deputation led by Montague Crackanthorpe, President of the Eugenics Society. Crackanthorpe wanted segregation of the feeble-minded and cited laws in some USA states prohibiting marriage between the mentally weak. Churchill had to be careful in his response, since Asquith was not so starry-eyed about eugenics. The Home

Secretary pointed to 'immense difficulties: some people may feel that [eugenics-based government action] belongs more to the politics of the future'. But he went on:

> There are 120,000 or 130,000 feeble-minded persons at large in our midst. These unhappy beings deserve our care and assistance. But let it end there if possible. If by any arrangement we are able to segregate these people under proper conditions, so that their curse dies with them and is not transmitted to future generations, we shall have taken upon our shoulders a work for which those who come after us will owe us a debt of gratitude.[5]

Eugenics posed an alternative to the familiar political party debates. With its genetic strengthening aims, it linked into the imperial campaign to boost the British stock.[6]

Churchill's interest in the possibility of voluntary sterilization of the weak-minded drew him to the case of a youth convicted at Beverley Quarter Sessions of attempted bestiality with a mare. Alfred Oxtoby was found to be insane and ordered to be 'detained in custody till His Majesty's Pleasure be known'. The Home Office received a report from Hull Prison's Chief Medical Officer. Oxtoby had admitted to committing the same offence previously. His educational attainment was 'lowly'. The doctor's opinion was that he was 'likely to prove a source of danger to others if he is allowed at large'. Oxtoby 'had got into trouble with females [presumably animals] on previous occasions.' The family had applied for him to be released to their care. Home Office opinion was that release would be 'very risky'. A further report was called for: had he shown any sign of being dangerous to women or children?[7]

On 9 October 1910 Churchill wrote a memorandum on weak-mindedness and the possibility of sterilization. He contested what he saw as Dr Donkin's underestimation of the power of heredity in 'defects physical, mental and moral'. He could not agree that, 'virtue and vice, honesty and dishonesty are concrete virtues acquired by the individual.' If breeding by the feeble-minded could be prevented, 'a considerable class of the latter could be allowed to live outside special institutions':

> I think it is cruel to shut up numbers of people in institutions...little better than prisons, for their whole lives, if by a simple surgical operation, they could be permitted to live freely in the world without causing inconvenience to others. I certainly do not look forward to that millennium for which some scientists appear to hanker when the majority of the human race will be permanently confined within the walls of state-maintained institutions, attended by numerous doctors and guarded by legions of warders.[8]

If Churchill pursued sterilization, a Liberal backbench backlash could be expected. One week after his pronouncement on the Indiana law, there was a put-down from his own parliamentary under-secretary. Charles Masterman gave his opinion of the pamphlet:

> I feel inclined to suggest minuting this: 'Bring up again on Jan 1st 1950'.

That meant bury it. Masterman derided the supposed science. He felt sure that it was beyond the scope of British legislation. It would have to be justified as being 'necessary for the welfare of the present generation, as well as for the protection of the future' – in other words not just for strengthening British stock for future imperial contests.

Alfred Oxtoby was sent to Broadmoor Asylum. A January 1911 letter from a doctor there, John Baker, considered that Oxtoby had the characteristics of 'a low-grade imbecile…a typical example of the village fool, with dangerous sexual tendencies'. Home Office minutes show Churchill keeping an eye on the young man. Dr Baker dismissed Churchill's hopes that an operation might provide a 'cure', allowing release:

> …There does not appear to be any prospect of cure by sterilization. Certainly the procreative power would cease, but its effect in lessening the sexual appetite is extremely problematical – probably it would have no effect at all.

He said that in any case Oxtoby would not be able to give his consent to an operation. Such surgery would be impossible at Broadmoor: patients subject to hallucinations would allege that the medical staff were mutilating inmates.

Related to eugenics was 'psychometrics', the notion that body-shape, the head especially, revealed personality, including crime-propensity. A request came to the Home Office in August 1910 from persons who wanted to run their instruments over the skull of John Dickman after his execution, presumably to look for homicidal contours. They got short shrift. There was to be no return to the days when the gallows supplied the anatomists.[9]

Churchill's eugenicist bible was a pamphlet of a talk given in May 1909 at London's Mansion House to the National Association for the Welfare of the Feeble-Minded, by Dr A.F. Tredgold, who had been one of the advisers to the Royal Commission. Towards the end of 1910, the Home Secretary circulated it around the cabinet, with a covering memorandum:

> …This address gives a concise and I am informed not exaggerated statement of the serious problem to be faced. The Government is pledged to legislation, and a bill is being drafted to carry out the recommendations of the Royal Commission.[10]

Tredgold had a bizarre census of British mental deficiency, as on 1 January 1906: 8,654 idiots, 25,096 imbeciles and 104,779 feeble-minded. He saw the mentally infirm as threatening the British stock. He viewed mental weakness as part of a wider malady, encompassing epilepsy, consumption and alcoholism; and 'degeneracy' as genetic, degenerate families breeding at a faster rate than healthy ones and the infirm spreading weakness by interbreeding with the sound. Linked to this was social failure: 'criminals, prostitutes, paupers and ne'er-do-wells'; there was a 'close relationship between criminals and the feeble-minded'. 'National progress', maintained Tredgold, 'can only take place when means to improve the fit are accompanied by methods to prevent the increase of the unfit.' He wanted farms and industrial colonies, in which the mentally weak could be supervised, where they would be happier with each other than in the outside world, and would contribute to their own support. Underlying this pseudo-medicine was the imperial advancement drive:

> We must each one of us, as intelligent citizens of a great Empire, bestir ourselves to see that this tide of degeneracy is stemmed'[11]

Churchill wanted the government to back Tredgold with legislation. He was long conversant with racial stock theory. In 1899 he said to his cousin Ivor Guest, 'The improvement of the British breed is my aim in life.'[12]

Lucy Masterman sheds some light on eugenicist legislation plans at the Home Office:

> [Churchill] appealed to Charlie [Masterman], 'If we could only get [the House of Lords question] shunted, think of all we could do. Boy prisoners, Truck, feeble-minded.' This last was a sop to Charlie, for he has handed over the Bill to him to draft and see through.[13]

('Truck' was the deduction of money from workers' wages, to pay for equipment or clothing or workplace fines, a considerable abuse.) Masterman apparently was set to pilot a eugenics-based bill, if it got onto the government programme. He seems to have come round to the project. He wrote to Churchill early in January 1911, from a continental holiday, to urge that the bill should be pressed forward, 'if you can get L.G. to sanction expenses.'[14]

The Home Secretary fielded questions from MPs wanting legislation on the feeble-minded. Liberal Sir James Yoxall reeled off a catalogue of woes related he said to mental infirmity: weakened physique, crime, immorality, unemployment. Conservative Robert Houston wanted totals for feeble-minded women giving birth in homes and asylums; for unmarried mentally weak mothers; and for children born to ex-prisoners. Churchill will have disappointed the statistics enthusiast with the news that there were no such figures. It was becoming clear that there was no room for a bill on the government's timetable. When, on 31 May 1911, Conservative barrister Sir Clement Kinloch-Cooke asked Churchill, 'whether he can give a date for the introduction of the measure he proposes for the care and control of the feeble-minded', the Home Secretary had to reply: 'I regret that I cannot give any date.' The Churchill/Masterman bill never emerged.[15]

Churchill's eugenics zest continued after he left the Home Office. In October 1912, Wilfrid Blunt's diary has:

> Winston told us he had himself drafted the Bill which is to give the power of shutting up people of weak intellect and so prevent their breeding. He thought it might be arranged to sterilize them. He thought that if shut up with no prospect of release, many would ask to be sterilized as a condition of having their liberty restored.[16]

The then pending legislation was the Mental Deficiency Bill, which aimed to confine indefinitely a large number of people classified as mentally defective, supposedly for their own good as well as to prevent them from breeding. There was overwhelming parliamentary support, but the tenacity of the opposition at the committee stage led to the bill being dropped. In 1913 the government introduced a new version. The provision for 'feeble-minded' persons to be placed in institutions to stop them breeding was gone, as was the ban on marriage with the mentally weak, but the bill still had sweeping provisions. It legislated for putting into institutions a wide range of persons. It amounted to the arbitrary removal of the personal rights of many individuals.[17]

Did Winston Churchill draft the Mental Deficiency Bill? Radzinowicz and Hood state that, 'We looked in vain for evidence to support the contention.' The bill passed with just a handful of MPs against. Churchill was sometimes in the Ayes lobby but he did not speak in the debates. The Mental Deficiency Act became law on 1 April 1914. It would remain in effect until 1959.[18]

Lucy Masterman quoted her husband on the Churchill brain process:

> In nearly every case an *idea* enters his head from outside. It rolls round the hollows of his brain, collecting strength like a snowball. *Then*, after whirlwinds of *rhetoric*, he becomes convinced that it is *right*; and denounces everyone who criticises it...He sets his ideas to rhetoric, as musicians set theirs to music. He can convince himself of almost any truth if it is once allowed thus to start on its wild career through his rhetorical machinery.[19]

Churchill was not quite an original thinker but his development of ideas was highly imaginative. His phrases were his engine. Prison reform was a largely happy product of the drive; eugenics was one that could have been disastrous.

Chapter 9
Infamy 1: Tonypandy

For Winston Churchill, a major diversion from penal reform was increasing industrial strife. The public peace was under novel stress. The movement known as syndicalism was growing in strength. It aimed to improve the lives of the working classes by grabbing power in the workplaces. In the coalfields of South Wales and the dockyards of the Clyde, syndicalists and anarchists saw strikes, sometimes with violence, as the direct route (as opposed to the parliamentary one) to redistribution of wealth. Revolutionary syndicalism aimed at class war and a general strike. The old order was under attack.[1]

The first violent disorder on Winston Churchill's Home Office watch was at Newport docks in May 1910. The Empire Transport Company was trying to break a strike of stevedores by bringing in men from London. It complained to the Home Office of assaults and intimidation. Riots developed. Newport magistrates requested 300 Metropolitan Police and that the War Office should hold troops in readiness. Churchill was anxious to avoid soldiers being used. He did however advise that any troops should be mounted, as more effective and with less risk of loss of life. In the event, soldiers were not required.[2]

This dispute was settled through Board of Trade machinery. In Randolph Churchill's biography of his father, Newport reads like a Winston success. But credit may be due elsewhere. Sir Almeric Fitzroy, Clerk to the Privy Council, describes in his diary having to go to London at short notice to hold a meeting of the Privy Council to pass an Order in Council confirming the new King's promotion of himself to Admiral of the Fleet. He needed to raise a quorum. In town he found War Minister Lord Haldane unexpectedly available:

> [Haldane] accounted for his being in London by having had to undertake the charge of the Home Office, as Winston Churchill insisted that he needed a holiday, assuring his colleague that he left a clean slate behind him and there would be practically no work to do. As a matter of fact, Haldane said that the business of the Home Office had been three times as heavy as that of the War Office as he found a labour war on the verge of breaking out at Newport, which only appears to have been averted by the promptitude with which he was able to act.[3]

Sir Edward Troup's book on the Home Office sheds some light. He states that Haldane 'forbade the unloading of a ship at Newport because of the certainty that it would lead to a riot which the police force was too small to cope with.'[4]

Churchill had left England on 20 May for Switzerland and Venice. Forwarding addresses included the Hotel du Palais, Lucerne, and the Grand Hotel, Goeschenen. Winston was no follower of the all work and no play school. His continental vacationing could not be disturbed even when an industrial crisis with Home Office implications was brewing.

Summer and autumn brought a rash of unofficial strikes. Some unions were seeing a contest for supremacy between the older Lib-Lab moderates and a younger generation fired up by the spirit of revolution. The industrial strife was called first 'The Unrest', then 'The Great Unrest'. The employer side hit back against the workers. The Shipbuilding Employers' Federation imposed a national lock out, aimed at the Boilermakers' Union, whose leaders had been unable to stop 'wild cat' strikes on the Clyde and the Tyne. In South Wales thirty thousand miners were out. The colliery owners were balancing output reduction resulting from the Eight Hours Act with low wages. The dispute centred on the collieries known as the Cambrian Combine. It was angry and it spread fast. A hotspot was the Glamorgan colliery of Llwynypia close to the town of Tonypandy in the Rhondda valley. Appeals were made to Churchill by the two sides.[5]

How Churchill reacted would give rise to an enduring debate. Left-wing orthodoxy has it that an upper-class minister on the side of the coal-owners sent in the army. Thirty-eight years later, Parliament heard an exchange between Labour Prime Minister James Callaghan and another Winston Churchill, the Conservative MP grandson of WSC. Winston junior was complaining that a large pay increase for miners was not justified. The response of Callaghan, a South Wales MP, was the purest acid:

> ...I hope that the hon. Gentleman will not pursue the vendetta of his family against the miners – [Interruption.] – at Tonypandy for the third generation.[6]

Jim Callaghan was invoking the socialist tradition that in 1910 enemy of the workers Churchill dispatched strike-breaking troops to South Wales.

What happened? The Glamorgan Chief Constable requested from the military authorities two companies of infantry and two hundred cavalry. Churchill and War Minster Haldane decided to halt the infantry at Swindon and the cavalry at Cardiff. Meanwhile, on Churchill's instructions as an alternative to using the army, a detachment of several hundred Metropolitan Police arrived at Tonypandy. The Home Secretary sent a personal message to the striking miners, which was read to a mass meeting on 8 November. The tone was one of friendly respect. The Board of Trade's conciliator, George Askwith, wished to meet union representatives, said Churchill: the miners should 'get fair treatment', but the rioting 'must cease at once.'

Churchill was trying hard for a peaceful resolution. His appeal for calm failed. On the night following the meeting there was more heavy rioting, with shops looted, plate glass windows smashed, and crowds out of hand, as women and children joined in. A mob tried to flood the Glamorgan colliery, in what a *Times* reporter called 'an orgy of naked anarchy'. In the battle between strikers and management agents, who were trying to protect the mines from harm, 320 horses were trapped underground. The King conveyed to Churchill his worry about these.[7]

Churchill now permitted substantial forces of infantry to enter the colliery district, whilst detachments of cavalry were stationed at Pontypridd. However, he instructed that the troops should be kept strictly in reserve. The front line was still the police. Writing to the King, the Home Secretary reported that these had beaten off assaults on the colliery by the rioters. He said that soldiers would not have deterred the attacks on the shops: 'there appears to be no reason at present why the policy of keeping the military out of direct contact with the rioters should be departed from.'[8]

Liberal Chief Whip Alick Murray thought that at this precarious time Churchill needed some reassurance. He informed him that 'the principal Liberal papers in the country' were with him in his policy of keeping troops out of the front line on the coalfields and using Metropolitan Police instead. Murray sent the Home Secretary favourable leading articles. The *Morning Leader* called Churchill's approach 'humane and bold'. The *Daily News* said that, 'Mr Churchill has preferred a wiser and more humane, if less sensational, mode of restoring order.' *The Manchester Guardian* thought that Churchill's decision to hold back the troops had taken 'some courage: it in all probability saved many lives.' The reaction of the Conservative press was diametrically opposite. The *Daily Express* slammed 'the last word in a policy of poltroonery which may cost the country dear'. *The Times* declared that, 'the rosewater of conciliation is all very well in its place, but not in the face of a wild mob drunk with the desire of destruction.' The Tory papers saw a weak Liberal do-gooder, when what was needed was the smack of firm action to deal with a grave breakdown of law and order.[9]

The violence escalated. Strikers fought to prevent strike-breakers from entering the pits. One man had a fractured skull. An attempt was made to blow up a colliery manager's house. Railway signalling equipment was seized by the strikers; trains were halted and searched for 'blackleg' labour. Rioting became widespread.[10]

Churchill justified his policy in his reminiscences of the Home Office:

> I was preoccupied with every kind of scheme to avoid soldiers firing upon strikers. All my plans were to prevent this blot and stain…At Tonypandy an expeditionary force of Metropolitan Police dispersed a dangerous crowd by swinging their rolled-up mackintoshes.[11]

The picture is quaint, but there was a less charming side to the mobile Metropolitans. There were outraged reports of thuggery. Parliament would hear about it at length from Keir Hardie. Still, Churchill's claim that he strove to keep troops and strikers apart, to avoid bullets ripping into crowds, is backed up by the history of the 1910 Tonypandy dispute. The fury of the Conservative press against him for weakness and timidity is telling testimony against the legend of a trigger-happy interventionist.

However, that was not the end of the story. As the troubles worsened, troops patrolled the Rhondda, along with the Metropolitan Police. After locals threw stones at the police, the infantry was in action with fixed bayonets. Soldiers were in the valleys for nearly a year, amid bubbling resentment. The strike would last until August of the next year, with the men eventually starved back to work, having to accept an offer that was no better than that of a year previously. There were many incidents and injuries on both sides. At the Home Office, Edward Troup saw 'socialistic ideas now prevalent in South Wales' and 'a readiness to damage property, e.g., to destroy mines by flooding, which has never been known before in any strike in the mining industry'. Troup was not concerned with social unfairness as a factor in the breakdown of public order and a decline in respect for property.[12]

With cost-of-living rising and working-class remuneration failing to keep pace, the unrest had plenty of fuel. George Askwith quoted in his memoir an end of 1910 review by the Labour MP Philip Snowden. Whilst apportioning blame on both sides, Snowden assessed that:

> It is the duty of statesmanship to acknowledge the justice of the desire of the workers for a more human and cultured life, and to satisfy this unrest by concessions of reform. If employers and politicians are so unwise as to ignore the demands of labour, then what might be done by safe and constitutional methods will, by great suffering and loss, be accomplished by industrial strife and through social anarchy.[13]

Like Snowden, Churchill looked to fairness to improve the quality of life for the common people and was committed to the constitutional route to reform. Had he embraced Snowden's industrial vision, there could perhaps have been more prospect of a solution. He could have told his governmental colleagues that the coal-owners needed to be leaned on to share their profits more fairly with their workers and that the forces of law and order should not be used to prop up injustice. The Head of Cambrian Coal, D.A. Thomas (the future Lord Rhondda), a Liberal MP, said that the management would 'in no circumstances concede the principle of a minimum wage'. Churchill provided the protection for Thomas's mines. Arguably, he could have promoted social justice in this dispute without compromising his role as Home Secretary. Churchill backed the institution of trade unions. In 1908 he called them 'the most respectable and most powerful element in the Labour world…the bulwarks of our industrial system'. But his failure to align himself clearly with the cause of social justice in the South Wales coalfields put his identity as a radical progressive in doubt. Churchill's imagination was bold, but it was lacking in the matter of industrial relations.[14]

Chapter 10
Infamy 2: Black Friday

On 17 October, the Chancellor of the Exchequer was booked to address a meeting in Holborn, not far from the centre of London. As he stepped from his motor-car, a young man darted from the crowd and grabbed his coat, yelling 'Lloyd George, you're a traitor'. As police moved in, another man hit a sergeant on the chest. The assailants were Victor Duval, Organizing Secretary of the Men's Political Union for Women's Enfranchisement, and suffragist George Jacobs. Winston Churchill wanted an exemplary sentence. He had been bothered by Duval at a Bristol meeting and on a train. He instructed Edward Troup to write to the Metropolitan Police Commissioner, demanding to know why Lloyd George had not been given adequate police protection. He seems to have been spooked by the incident. His memorandum had a touch of melodrama: 'An assassination with a Knife could easily have taken place.' He thought that 'gangs of paid ruffians' were being hired to attack ministers. He wanted Duval and Jacobs 'treated with the extreme rigour of the law', with the City Solicitor leading the prosecution.[1]

The Metropolitan Police Commissioners set the Criminal Investigation Department to see whether the pair were indeed hired hit-men. The findings were negative: 'fanatical believers in Women's Suffrage [but] not hired to commit special outrages'. Assistant Commissioner Bremner thought that bringing in the City Solicitor 'would give an exaggerated importance to the case.' Churchill conceded that Duval and Jacobs were not mercenaries, but still wanted the offence 'severely dealt with.' He was unsettled by the ambush on his political comrade.[2]

The City Solicitor did not appear at the Guildhall when Duval and Jacobs came up, but his deputy did. The men each received a forty shillings (£2) fine. Both refused to pay and were sent to Pentonville for seven days in the second division. The Home Secretary received a reminder about his new rule from secretary of the Men's Political Union for Women's Enfranchisement, Frank Rutter. Also writing was women's rights activist Katharine Gatty. She called on Churchill to rectify the 'serious blunder' of the second division and appealed to his 'open-mindedness on prison administration'. She pointed to Irish Nationalist MP Laurence Ginnell getting the first division when he was sentenced for 'cattle-driving' in the land-rights campaign in Ireland: there was 'much less violent incitement from women's suffrage activists than from Irish cattle-drivers'. She enclosed a card of upcoming Humanitarian League meetings. Next week's was 'The Home Secretary's Prison Reforms'. Duval and Jacobs got the Churchill Rule.[3]

Parliament reassembled on 15 November. The WSPU announced a demonstration for 18 November, which would become known as Black Friday. On that day as the militant suffragists gathered at Caxton Hall, Westminster, news filtered through from the Commons that the prime minister had announced that the constitutional conference attempting to resolve Peers versus People had broken down and that Parliament would be prorogued on 28 November prior to dissolution. In what time remained government business would take precedence. There was no mention of the Conciliation Bill. The WSPU unleashed their planned action. Three hundred women, in twenty-five detachments, marched on Parliament.[4]

Churchill had a plan ready. His instructions to the Metropolitan Police Commissioner were that full-scale battle should be averted by the immediate arrest of suffragettes as soon as they breached the law. Large numbers would be taken into custody but this would be temporary. There were to be no prosecutions except for serious offences. The strategy was to defuse.

It did not work. Parliament Square was the scene of bedlam. Usually, the police who dealt with suffragette demonstrations, being familiar with the women, were sympathetic and tactful. Not this time. It was a different force. When the suffragettes tried to push their way past, they were dealt with brutally, sometimes lasciviously. They were kicked and punched, arms were twisted, breasts were grabbed, as the constables roughed the women up. The police, imported from the East End, were used to dealing with poor and uneducated people, whom they knocked about with impunity. The presence on the demonstration of ladies of the upper ranks of society provided opportunity for licence. So it was that, according to the women's subsequent testimony, there was 'language beyond description', as with the constable who 'gripped me by the thigh and said, "Oh my old dear, I can grip you wherever I like today"'. Churchill wrote sharply to Police Commissioner Sir Edward Henry. Replying, Henry said that the instruction for early arrests reached him too late, since police were already out.[5]

On 22 and 23 November there were further marches, in what became known as the Battle of Downing Street. Windows were smashed at the Home and Colonial Offices. Of 177 suffragette arrests, nearly half produced charges. On 25 November the WSPU formally resumed militancy. For its leadership, the Black Friday miscreant was Winston Churchill. Emmeline Pankhurst later wrote:

> ...We had a new Home Secretary, and there appeared to be new orders given to the police, because they showed a kind of ferocity in dealing with the women that they had never done before.[6]

There is no evidence of any Churchill complicity with or approval of what happened. It would have been entirely against his attitude and his character. A Churchill phrase in Parliament, 'that copious fountain of mendacity the Women's Social and Political Union', was not entirely unjustified in this case. It was in a reply to a question from Conservative MP Lord Henry Bentinck on 11 March 1911 about Black Friday. Churchill said that:

> I have given explicit instructions that in the future, with a view to the avoidance of disagreeable scenes, for which no one is responsible but the disorderly women themselves, police officers shall be told to make arrests as soon as there is lawful occasion.[7]

The phrase 'disorderly women' was used by Winston more than once. He also spoke of the 'high state of hysteria' of suffragettes, the regular charge used by those who maintained that women were emotionally unsuited to politics.

At the Battle of Downing Street, one of the demonstrators was Anne Cobden-Sanderson, daughter of Victorian radical Richard Cobden. After the crowd dispersed, she was observed by Winston Churchill, who according to Sylvia Pankhurst's account, summoned a policeman and shouted, 'Drive that woman away.' Anne was considerably shocked, since as Sylvia put it, 'she had often been his hostess and was on intimate terms with his wife's family.' The often-self-absorbed Churchill probably did not make the connection. Afterwards the suffragette reported her experience to a male supporter, Hugh Franklin (a nephew of Postmaster-General Herbert Samuel), who vowed, 'I will whip him for this.'[8]

Franklin was at a Churchill Liberal election meeting on 26 November at Bradford. After heckles, he and his friends were ejected, Churchill calling their interruptions 'money-fed'. The Home Secretary took an early evening train back to London. So did Franklin, with a dog-whip. With Churchill were two plain-clothes police bodyguards, a sergeant, and an inspector. As the train left, the two policemen went through the carriages. Franklin was sitting in a third-class compartment, with a woman whom the sergeant recognized as a suffragette. To reach the dining-carriage, Churchill would have to pass through Franklin's compartment. The sergeant took a seat by the suffragette, facing Franklin. When Franklin saw Churchill approaching, he jumped up and drew the whip from his pocket, shouting, 'Take that, you dirty cur!' The policemen suppressed his attack. At the subsequent Bow Street police court proceedings Churchill gave evidence in person. Franklin received six weeks. Churchill's wife told Winston's regular golfing companion, newspaper proprietor Sir George Riddell, that the suffragettes disturbed the sleep of her husband and herself on boats and trains, and that on one occasion when a male suffragist forced his way into their train compartment, 'Winston threatened to smash his face.'[9]

There was a further Franklin ripple. Before his imprisonment, the suffragist had written in *Votes for Women* newspaper:

> When Mr Churchill as the chief policeman orders his thousands of trained entrants to become a set of real hooligans, no one is left to act as protectors of law and order.

Churchill was stung. He wanted action in the courts. The Solicitor-General, Sir John Simon, was against this, arguing that it was 'very rare' for a ministerial intervention in the courts over an injurious statement to be advisable: 'for the Home Secretary personally to pursue a creature who has already been sentenced for an assault on him would be most unwise.' Winston was persuaded.[10]

A victim of the Battle of Downing Street was Augustine Birrell, who twisted his leg as he tried to flee suffragettes who were jostling ministers. The hapless Birrell was traumatized. He poured out his story to C.P. Scott: the women had stroked his face and knocked his hat off and mangled it, telling him, 'You must be a wicked man not to help us.' Birrell was told by the Director of Public Prosecutions that two of his assailants had been identified and that charges were being contemplated. Winston Churchill was keen to see prosecution. His attitude to the suffragettes had turned litigious. But Birrell told him that he did not want charges pressed, though he urged Churchill, 'Please keep your eye on the hags in question.'[11]

Winston was also after votes-for-women activist Emmeline Pethick-Lawrence. She had called him an 'oppressor'. Director of Public Prosecutions, Sir Charles Matthews, advised that whilst the language was probably criminally punishable, prosecution would involve Churchill appearing in court and that the fine available would not be worth the trouble. Winston returned to the prosecution question when *The Times*, on 2 March 1911, reported Christabel Pankhurst as saying that:

> The women who went to Westminster in November 1910 were brutally and in many cases indecently ill-treated by the police acting under the orders of the Home Secretary.[12]

On behalf of Churchill, Edward Troup wrote to Matthews to enquire 'whether you think Miss Christabel Pankhurst or *The Times* could be prosecuted criminally for libel'. Again, Churchill was dissuaded, but he was riled by the persistence of the WSPU accusations. In Parliament, he commended the Metropolitan Police for behaving on 18 November with 'forbearance and humanity'. There was plentiful testimony otherwise. Mary Frances Earl, who had a bloodied nose and twisted thumbs, said that the police 'deliberately tore my undergarments, using the most foul language, seized me by the hair and forced me up the steps on my knees.' Mary was one of over a hundred who made statements about police brutality. On 3 March *The Times* carried the accusation of suffragette Mrs Saul Solomon that the methods of the police were 'those used to fell the burglar, to maim the hooligan'. She called the constabulary 'the obedient tools of the government'.

Churchill refused a request by the Conciliation Committee for a public inquiry. The personal animus between him and the suffragettes was a serious problem. The untrue story that he gave orders to the police to rough up female demonstrators did not go away. It lingers today in certain presentations of the votes-for-women story. With Black Friday and the Battle of Downing Street, as with the Tonypandy Riots, we see Churchill looking narrowly at public order. The Home Secretary's reputation as a progressive politician wanting to make society fairer, could have been strengthened had he shown concern about police behaviour in London and South Wales and set up inquiries to investigate it. Instead, he brushed complaints aside, and hostages to fortune were taken. The young minister, whose tenure as Home Secretary had begun brightly, was raising some questions in the eyes of the reform-minded.[13]

Chapter 11

Identity

The quicksilver of Churchill's political identity cannot be pinned. One thing should not be forgotten: he was a soldier before becoming a politician. The army served as a springboard for his election to Parliament. The taste for khaki lingered. In 1902 he took a commission as a reservist Imperial Yeomanry captain in the Oxfordshire Hussars; in 1905 he was promoted major. Every summer he joined the Yeomanry at their camp in Blenheim Park. Each year Winston was a keen spectator of military exercises somewhere, including France and Germany. In September 1910 he watched the annual set-piece army manoeuvres on Salisbury Plain. He was not the only cabinet minister watching the contests between the Reds and the Blues, but he was probably the one most in his natural environment. No one was startled by the sight of the Home Secretary on horseback in military uniform. It was known that this was his other persona.[1]

Holidays were another Churchill identity-marker. The major one in 1910 was the summer cruise to Turkey. *The Manchester Guardian* was given the reporting access, its material being syndicated. The country followed Churchill's progress. The boat's owner, Baron Maurice de Forest (an Austrian title), was the orphaned son of a circus performer, adopted by an Austrian-born philanthropist. Inheritor of a fortune, versatile and intrepid, Tootie did motor-racing, aeronautics, and skiing. Churchill backed him as Liberal candidate for Southport in January 1910. De Forest was defeated but he would be successful at a by-election in July 1911. Winston spent much time on his boat. Tootie was the sort of person Churchill liked: a social outlier, colourful, risk-taking, and rich. Lucy Masterman thought that de Forest was: 'definitely one of the people who [are] a bad influence on Winston'. Churchill was not bothered by raised eyebrows.[2]

The papers ran sketches of the boyish hi-jinks of Churchill, de Forest, F.E. Smith and others, as they rode the railway through the Meander valley, Winston and F.E. perched on a seat above the 'cow-catcher':

> ...At the next station Mr Churchill might have been standing under the tank hose enjoying a shower bath. British officials seemed astonished. The Turks were scarcely surprised. Are not all Englishmen mad?[3]

Churchill had a special interest in Turkey. He was attracted to the Islamic world. (He liked the monotheism of Muslims and disliked the polytheism of Hindus.) He was keen on the Young Turks reform movement. He enjoyed a meeting with several of its leaders. He also had an audience with the Sultan, finding him, said

Wilfrid Blunt, 'Uninteresting, indeed gaga'. The trip was, in the way of Churchill, full of risk. There is a grainy snapshot of Winston riding with the Ottoman guards as they escorted the train through brigand country. He did not emerge from his Turkish adventure without mishap. It was reported from Smyrna that he was slightly wounded in the leg by an errant hunting gun. An operation was required.[4]

The joint trip of Winston Churchill and F.E. Smith to Turkey caused curiosity. A *Punch* cartoon made allusion to it a few weeks after the return of the travellers. Churchill and Smith are sitting together thumbing through a book. It is the new official *The Life of Benjamin Disraeli* by W.F. Monypenny. Smith notes: 'Master of epigram – like me!' A wide-eyed Churchill exclaims: 'Wrote a novel in his youth – like me!' Then both say:

Travelled in the East like us. How does it end?

There was no need for the magazine to spell out to readers the prime ministerial aspirations of the pair.[5]

WSC's holidaying with F.E. Smith was not new. Smith, with his middle-class origin and parvenu status, was a type whose company Winston liked. F. E.'s conceited wit appealed to him. The pair shared an aspiration for political alliance between the upper and the working classes as a vehicle for reform. Friendship with F.E. had a particular potential for Churchill at this time. There was cross-party plotting, with Smith as a Tory-Liberal go-between. With the constitutional conference deadlocked, Lloyd George launched an under-cover proposal to cut the Gordian knot: a Liberal-Conservative coalition. It should here be stressed that Lloyd George and Churchill, despite their regular political coordination, were not soul-mates. Lucy Masterman's diary records a defining conversation:

> …At one point Winston said, 'I am all for the social order.' George sat up in his chair and said: 'No! I'm against it. Listen. There were 600 men turned off by the G.W. Works last week. These men had to go out into the street to starve. There is not a man in that works who does not live in terror of the day when his turn will come to go. Well, I'm against a social order that admits of that kind of thing.' And he made a kind of ['menacing' crossed out] beckoning gesture I have seen him use once or twice. 'Yeth, yeth', said Winston hurriedly, subdued for a moment…[6]

The two however had plenty in common politically and easily worked together as prime-movers of the government's programme. A key plank was National Insurance, which faced the hostility of the insurance societies, a major political interest since agents visited nearly every working-class house. A coalition of the Liberals and the Conservatives could overpower this formidable obstacle. The two big parties would be able together to legislate moderate social welfare reform without having to humour the Labour Party, the Irish Nationalists, and their own radical wings. Juicy bones could be on offer to the Tories in the shape of compulsory military training, a stronger navy – maybe even tariff reform. The Liberals would get a referendum in Wales on disestablishment of the Welsh Church; the Irish Home Rule question could be settled.[7]

Lloyd George put his idea to Churchill in late September, on a North Wales golf course. Winston and Clementine were staying with him and his wife. Churchill was a good golfer, an MP memoir commenting that, 'Bonar Law, Churchill, Lloyd George and others are great at driving and putting.' Churchill did jest about 'chasing a quinine pill round a pasture with weapons ill-designed for the purpose', but the combination of sport and chatter engaged him pleasantly enough. Lloyd George later told George Riddell about the conversation during this round:

> I said to Winston, 'I have two alternatives to propose – the first to form a coalition, settle the old outstanding questions, and govern the country on middle lines which will be acceptable to both parties but providing measures of moderate social reform. The other, to formulate and carry through an advanced land and social reform policy.' Mrs Winston said, 'I am for the second.' Winston replied, 'I am for the first!'[8]

The reactions are instructive. Clemmie, a radical Liberal, definitely favoured land tax. WSC had needed to be dragged round to support of it. The social reform that would come with a coalition was not resource redistribution through land tax. It was the less radical establishment of a social safety net: Churchill's politics. WSC was greatly taken with the Liberal-Conservative government idea. He 'forgot all about the game and he has never forgotten our conversation', said Riddell.

Writing to Lloyd George, Churchill confirmed his backing for the coalition idea, but tentatively:

> My opinion has not departed from our conversations…If we stood together, we ought to be strong enough either to impart a progressive character to policy, or by withdrawal to terminate an administration which had failed in its purpose.[9]

The qualification suggests insecurity on Churchill's part. It is confirmed by what Lucy Masterman described as 'a rather comic scene' between the pair. Lloyd George asked for Churchill's opinion of the coalition project 'from the point of view of the person left out of it'. This looks like putting tactfully to Churchill that the Tories might block Churchill, the floor-crossing ratter. Conservative animus against Winston was still brisk. The penny dropped instantly. Churchill, as Mrs Masterman relates, 'worked himself up into an astonishing state of indignation, pouring forth rhetorical denunciation of the whole affair.'[10]

Churchill and Lloyd George were dubbed 'the two Romeos', but the alliance was based on political calculation. The two were seen as the leaders of radical opinion. Beatrice Webb remarks in her diary of 30 November 1910: 'Lloyd George and Winston Churchill have practically taken the *limelight*, not merely from their own colleagues, but from the Labour Party. They stand out as the most advanced politicians.' But a cross-party government would be unknown territory. Churchill was not yet an equal of Lloyd George in their relationship, even though the Chancellor admitted to chafing at his friend's bagging of kudos.[11]

Churchill continued to be keen on coalition. Mrs Masterman's diary preserves a WSC exchange with her husband on the subject:

> Winston keeps on discussing it with Charlie and meets all Charlie's objections to it by the complaint: 'Oh, you are in one of your soup-kitchen moods!'

There is a frank pen addition by Lucy to the typescript:

> He got more and more passionate in favour of it, praising government by aristocracy and revealing the aboriginal and unchangeable Tory in him.[12]

Is the real Churchill uncovered here? A.J.P. Taylor well put it that:

> There was something odd about a Radical who denounced dukes during the week and spent his weekends at Blenheim.[13]

Lucy Masterman has an account of a dinner at Churchill's house on a Saturday during the time of the People's Budget debates:

> Lloyd George and my husband began a somewhat wild chaff about the revolutionary Tumbrils and a guillotine in Trafalgar Square, partly to tease Winston Churchill, who was liable to be rather easily horrified by such talk. When Lloyd George suggested he might become the Napoleon of such a revolution, he began to think 'there might be something in it.'[14]

Lloyd George thought that it was 'extraordinary that anyone could have so little humour'. But Winston was not amused about aristocrats on guillotines. They were his class. However, the mention of Napoleon put a different angle on the matter. Napoleon, who like his own father rose and crashed (on a bigger scale), was his hero. Churchill installed a bronze bust of the Corsican on his desk at the Colonial Office in 1905, the start of what Edward Marsh called 'the Napoleon period'. WSC himself as a new Napoleon was a notion that did not come amiss. As for Lloyd George, Lucy Masterman has an LG quotation suggesting that there was, as she put it, 'a certain seriousness' behind his badinage about guillotines and tumbrils:

> All down history nine-tenths of mankind has been grinding the corn for the remaining tenth; and have been paid with the husks and bidden to thank God they had the husks.[15]

On the proposed coalition we may imagine Charles Masterman trying to cool Churchill's zest by pointing out that, though coalition might make for an easier social legislation route, in the longer term it could damage working-class hopes if power had to be shared with a party favouring the interests of landowners and industrialists. Masterman also thought that a coalition fixed in backrooms would scarcely be democratic. That does not seem to have worried Winston.[16]

Churchill and Masterman had a good working relationship, Charlie taking in his stride the WSC self-promotion and bombast. Lucy Masterman commented on Winston as:

> ...rather attractive. He is an extraordinary transparent creature. Many of my friends have complained of his intriguing in his early days. I never heard or saw any attempt at intrigue by him that could have taken in a kitten; and his very vanity is somehow childish and disarming.[17]

Liberal Arthur Ponsonby saw a different Churchill. A May 1911 Ponsonby diary listing of disagreeable things has 'Winston Churchill's intrigues'. But one may see where Lucy Masterman's notion of WSC transparency came from. Churchill was carried along by a child-like belief in himself and his causes. The tributes on his death would include a Clement Atlee description of 'the most protean person I ever came into contact with'. The shape-changing Greek sea-god is an apt metaphor. Winston would seize on a cause and throw himself at it, with himself as chief prophet. But the duration of a Churchill zeal was uncertain.[18]

The mainspring of the coalition plotting seems to have been a Lloyd George/Balfour mutual admiration society. Balfour had progressive leanings. He had delivered the landmark 1902 Education Act. A Liberal-Conservative arrangement would suit Winston Churchill's centrism. Reportedly, Churchill was pencilled in as War Minister. It all became academic when Tory backbenchers gave the scheme the thumbs-down, wanting red-meat Toryism, not common ground with the Liberals.[19]

With the House of Lords imbroglio persisting well into 1911, where was Winston Churchill in the arguments? All over the place it would seem. At the January 1910 General Election, he delivered rousing veto-riddance speeches. He sounded radical. He told Asquith in a 14 February 1910 memorandum that he thought: 'The time has come for the total abolition of the House of Lords.' But he added that if that failed, he was in favour of reshaping the Lords on a democratic basis. Given that the chance of abolition of the House of Lords was practically nil, that put Churchill in the Reform camp. Lucy Masterman's notes state that:

> ...So many people knew that Churchill disliked the abolition of the Veto and preferred a programme of House of Lords reform.[20]

Churchill did not want the constitution changed. He belonged by birth to the aristocracy and he was for the social order. That meant not interfering with the share that the Lords (including his cousin the Duke of Marlborough) had in legislation. At one point he pronounced: 'We cannot defend intellectually our position on Veto.' This put him at odds with Lloyd George. The Chancellor reported to Charles Masterman a Winston rage:

> He began to fume and kick up the hearth rug, and became very offensive, saying: 'You can go to Hell your own way, I won't interfere. I'll have nothing to do with your __ policy', and was almost threatening, until at last I had to remind him that no man can rat twice. Oh, he'll come to heel alright. He always does when he sees which way the wind is blowing.[21]

Churchill meanwhile was yelling at Charles Masterman: 'No, no, no; I *won't* follow George if he goes back to that d-d Veto [abolition].'

Charles' wife is interesting on Churchill and democracy:

> Winston of course is not a democrat, or at least he is a Tory democrat. 'I am in favour of government of the people, for the people, but not by the people', he said to Charlie once. At this time he was certainly playing rather a double part.[22]

After slithers in the government, Lloyd George found his resolve: if it did not go for scrapping the Lords' Veto, he would resign. Asquith now also declared for veto abolition. The cabinet united: if necessary, five hundred new peerages would be created. Churchill's temper subsided and he was back on side, honing his rhetoric against the Upper House. Lucy Masterman had a wicked reflection:

> Probably it was oratorical impulse that won. It was a great deal easier to make good speeches against the House of Lords than in their favour.[23]

The way that Churchill's rhetoric led him was noticed by Edward Grey. In 1908 Grey said (recorded in the diary of Lord Esher, Liberal politician and royal courtier): 'Phrases master him rather than he them.'[24]

Yo-yoing on a great issue did not help Churchill's credibility. Lucy Masterman declared:

> I now make this prophecy concerning Winston: It is that if he ever does rise to the leadership of the party, he won't lead it for long or successfully. The function of a leader is to lead public opinion. Winston follows it – often a little late; and very often does not know his own mind.[25]

She added (in a sentence omitted from the quotation from her diary in her 1939 biography of her husband): '[Churchill's] absolute insincerity on this whole matter [veto] sickened George very much.'

The collapse of the constitutional conference's attempts to resolve the issue of the House of Lords' Veto power produced a *Punch* cartoon of Asquith and Lloyd George loading a guillotine-bound tumbril with aristocrats (including Arthur Balfour). The actual outcome, more prosaically, was the new General Election. The government managed to obtain an undertaking from King Edward's successor George that if they won again at the polls and if the House of Lords still resisted the removal of veto, he would create 500 new peers. It was time for the 1910 Parliament's obsequies. Before the short-lived assembly passed into history, an adjournment debate produced a raw confrontation between Keir Hardie and Winston Churchill.[26]

The Labour veteran was angry about the Metropolitan Police at Tonypandy. He wanted an inquiry. The differences yawned between Hardie and Churchill. Both were international travellers but whilst Churchill had been an imperial soldier, Hardie had journeyed to learn about workers' lives and conditions. Whilst Hardie proclaimed the equal rights of all races, Churchill saw indigenous peoples as loyal subjects of the British Empire. There were some areas in common. As a boy colliery-worker, Hardie had operated an air-supply door: Churchill at the Board of Trade and the Home Office got to know much about such working details. One of Hardie's campaigning slogans was the eight-hours day for miners: Churchill brought it about. But shared outlook was in short supply. There was no sign of a meeting of minds when the white-bearded Hardie (of aged appearance in his mid-fifties) and Churchill (who always looked like a baby) squared up in Parliament over the South Wales conflict.

Hardie read out testimonies of brutality and misbehaviour by the imported Metropolitans. Churchill retorted that only the police stood between the strikers and the military. Hardie shouted back 'Nonsense'. Churchill rounded on him:

> What is the use of the hon. Gentleman's coming here with the pretence that nothing is going on, when there is in reality a savage war between the two forces?[27]

The Home Secretary had a list of injuries to policemen. The confrontation, as recorded in Hansard, got brisker:

> Mr KEIR HARDIE: There is no love lost between us.
> Mr CHURCHILL: I know perfectly well, from every act and speech of his, his life is directed to injuring and assailing the party to which I belong. As he justly says, there is no love lost between us, though I entirely respect the consistency of his career.

On mayhem wreaked by strikers, Hardie said that the reports were exaggerated, whilst Churchill praised the Metropolitans and ignored the credible reports of violent and offensive behaviour by them. The Home Secretary was not helped by Welsh Liberal Sir John Rees (soon to floor-cross to the Conservatives) rising to denounce the 'disastrous results' of the Eight Hours Act: 'These riots are immediately due to the interference with private rights and the proper freedom of employer and employed.' Churchill intervened: 'I certainly do not at all regret the passage of the bill.' Glasgow MP George Barnes, whose short tenure of the Labour leadership was coming to an end, backed Hardie's call for a public inquiry into the conduct of the police. Churchill resisted. His attitude was pushing him in the direction of conflict with the Labour movement.

The General Election of December 1910 would be the last with polling-days spread over several weeks. There was no goodwill for the Liberal government's re-election from the suffragette movement. *Votes for Women* found points in favour of a Conservative victory: it 'would mean the loss – hardly to be regretted – of "friends" of the type of Mr Lloyd George and Mr Winston Churchill.'[28]

On the stump, Churchill's modern New Liberal identity was powerfully engaged. In January 1910, as the results of that election came in, he had declared:

> The Conservative gains have been made in residential centres or in small cathedral and county towns which do not contribute to the great manufacturing strength on which the well-being and prosperity of the country depend.[29]

He identified with a vibrant Britain of industrial muscle. Churchill liked power more than pretty scenes. Now he criss-crossed the country again to rally Liberal support. On 7 December it was the eve-of-poll in his Dundee constituency. In the two-member seat, Churchill and Labour's Alexander Wilkie were tacit running-mates. Given Churchill's hostility to socialism, this might seem surprising, but Wilkie was soft-Labour. In January, Churchill and Wilkie had easily beaten the Conservative duo. Now Churchill told his audience in the city famous for its jute mills but scarred with unemployment and poverty:

> The end is not political change. The end is social amelioration (cheers), an endeavour to secure if we can a better, a more even, and more suitable condition of society for the great mass of the labouring classes of this country. (Cheers.)[30]

The remark that he did not want 'political change' is revelatory. Likewise, the vocabulary: '*we* can secure *for* the labouring classes.' During the course of this evening Winston Churchill fulfilled a challenge that he had accepted from one of his two Conservative opponents, Seymour Lloyd, to debate with him. The event passed without anything notable, though Churchill produced a trademark epigram when referendum was raised as a possible solution to the constitutional impasse. The idea should be 'put in a bag', he declared, along with the Tory referendum proposal regarding tariff reform: 'like the Kilkenny cats'. The delivery of the phrase may be imagined. WSC and Wilkie were comfortably re-elected, though with reduced majorities. Churchill proclaimed that Liberal victory in the General Election was on the way: 'the white flag hangs over the Tory club, over many a noble residence and public house.' The latter reference played to the temperance gallery (important to Liberals). Churchill was anything but temperance, but he was not of the class that needed to use pubs.[31]

His zig-zags were not finished. The day after his own result he was at the Drill Hall, Swindon, where the Conservatives were defending a 635 majority in the North Wiltshire division. He declared that 'the absolute veto of the House of Lords is doomed.' 'Loud cheers' rang out, but the qualification of veto abolition is interesting. It is clear from newspaper reporting that Churchill roused his election audiences. The Conservatives, as mentioned, were floating the idea of a referendum on tariff reform. Churchill told Swindon that this was a Tory ploy to get the votes of both tariff reformers *and* free-traders, the latter being able to vote Conservative at the General Election and then, if the Conservatives won, against tariffs at the referendum. He said:

> Such a policy of trying to have it both ways always leads to having it neither way. (Cheers.) Let them take their discredited and discarded trash where they got it from – to Birmingham. (Cheers.)[32]

Birmingham meant the Chamberlain political dynasty, which led the tariffs campaign. In Swindon, the Liberal candidate Richard Lambert, a barrister making his fourth attempt to enter Parliament, took the seat by 128 votes. Lambert's letter of thanks for a 'magnificent speech', lights up the Churchill effect:

> It was your speech which mainly brought about our success. I have personally come across several Tories who were influenced by it, and eventually voted for me, and yesterday I heard of one of the managers in the Swindon [railway] works, who told a Liberal friend that he had to leave halfway through your speech, because, if he had stayed, he would have had to vote Liberal.[33]

Churchill's election value is described by Lucy Masterman: 'Winston works like a tiger to get his men in in different constituencies.' She states that in January 1910 all but one of Churchill's band got in. The day after the Swindon speech an artist drew him declaiming at Dartford skating rink. The eyes are piercing and we see an intensity as he points the index finger of his right hand whilst extending the palm of his left. His man here, Jimmy Rowlands, a working-class Lib-Labber, overturned a Conservative majority, taking the seat by 234.[34]

At the Dartford meeting, Churchill addressed the audience as 'gentlemen'. Were they all male? Or did he ignore female presence? By law, parliamentary elections were men's business and therefore there was no reason for females to attend (unless they were wives of candidates). These days many women had other ideas. One way or another, the political voice of women was being heard. A newspaper report has:

A male voice: "How did you treat Mrs Sanderson?" The interrupter was hustled out of the building.
[Churchill]: Mrs Cobden-Sanderson came to Downing Street to break the Prime Minister's windows and I told the police to move her down the steps into the Green Park (Hear, hear.) And I hope that if your meeting is disturbed by these interrupters who go about from place to place making it a regular profession to break up public meetings, you will just move them a little further (laughter) – always taking care not to hurt them.[35]

The overall outcome of the December 1910 General Election was practically identical to that of January: a virtual dead-heat between Liberals and Conservatives, but with the Liberals able to rule thanks to the Irish Nationalists and the Labour members. The scene was now set for the showdown on the Lords' veto. Churchill told his Swindon meeting that the government favoured a five-year rather than, as at present, a seven-year maximum length for a Parliament. Legislation would bring that about in the coming year. What no one knew was that the December 1910 Parliament would, as a result of war, have to be repeatedly extended, becoming history's second Long Parliament.

Chapter 12
The Significant Spectator

Harold Scott started work at the Home Office in early 1911. He was taken on his first day to Winston Churchill's room. His meeting with the Home Secretary made a deep impression:

> ...It was a lofty room, lined with bookcases, and in a wide stone fireplace blazed a cheerful fire. Sitting at a massive desk with his back to the fire was Mr Churchill.

'Why did you choose a sheltered profession like the civil service?', Churchill asked Scott. The young man made a no doubt carefully rehearsed statement: 'it seemed to me that the work of the higher civil servant was varied, interesting and worthwhile.' Scott's memoir continues:

> 'Indeed it is' said Mr Churchill, thrusting out his chin, and he began to talk warmly and eloquently about some of the problems which the Home Office had to face. I listened spellbound as he discussed the need for reforming our criminal law and penal system...Still expatiating on the art of administration, the Home Secretary got up and went into an alcove, reappearing in a few minutes with a towel. Vigorously polishing his face with it, he continued to talk, until he announced that he was ready to go to lunch and rang the bell for Edward Marsh...'Eddy', he said jovially, 'you know more about these young men from the university than I do. Take charge of Mr Scott and look after him.'[1]

One of only two non-public school members of the administrative class of the Home Office, Scott had won a scholarship to Cambridge. Churchill made a point of meeting all those starting at the Home Office. He aimed to change the conservative mindset of the place from the bottom-up.[2]

Where did Churchill go home to? He lived at 33 Eccleston Square, Pimlico, a tall, white-stuccoed residence, close to that of F.E. Smith. Always juggling his money, he had relinquished two telephone extensions to save £3 a year – a bad move Eddie Marsh thought since it meant Winston having to come down to the hall to take calls. Churchill's finances were precarious. There was his addiction to gambling; there were risky investments; and there were the demands of his lifestyle. His bank borrowing topped £2,000 by early 1910. Bills were hefty and overdue: books, wine, and cigars. His publishing helped. In 1909 he received advances of £150 and £100 from Hodder and Stoughton for his speech collections *Liberalism and the Social Problem* and *The People's Rights Defended*. But cost-cutting was required. Panelling in the front room and the library of the rented house had recently been completed but several of the servants' rooms had to make do with cheap linoleum.³

The Churchill household, as recorded by the census of 2 April 1911, comprised Winston, Clementine and Diana and eight servants, including nurse and lady's maid. All the Churchill servants were female except the hall-boy. The domestic staff have practically no visibility in the biographies. The census has the information that the cook was Elizabeth Jackson, single, 43, Lancashire-born. On 3 January 1911, after a presumably Jackson-prepared breakfast, Churchill was taking a bath, an enjoyed routine. He was disturbed, as he later recalled, by an urgent knocking at the door. It was 10 a.m. He was wanted on the telephone by his office on an 'absolutely immediate' matter. He took the call draped in a towel and dripping wet.⁴

A gunfight was happening on a London street. Its origins lay in a shocking mid-December event. An armed gang of Russian Empire émigrés had shot dead three policemen whilst raiding a Houndsditch jeweller's shop. They were Latvian 'anarchists' (anti-Tsarist revolutionaries). Now two members of the gang had been cornered in a house on Sidney Street, Stepney. They had automatic pistols. Churchill's authority was requested for troops to assist the police. He gave his permission and hastened over to the Home Office.⁵

There, at 11 a.m., Ernley Blackwell signed a report:

> The War Office telephoned that the City Police had asked for an armed guard of 20 soldiers...The men Fritz & 'Peter the Painter' have been located. 700 Police have surrounded the buildings. There has been a lot of shooting...⁶

Winston Churchill decided immediately to go to the scene. On a day of fierce winds with flecks of snow, he and Edward Marsh travelled by motor-car, taking Blackwell. Here was some unexpected stimulation for Churchill. Harold Butler's memoirs comment that, 'it must have been hard to prevent him from taking a shot at the gunmen himself.' The away-day was poorly viewed in the Home Office but Blackwell and Marsh had to go with their chief.⁷

A drab East End street had acquired an assemblage of police, soldiers' and officials and, behind a cordon, a large crowd. A combined operation of City of London Police (Houndsditch being in the city) and Metropolitans (Stepney being in the Metropolitan area) was in progress. The press was present in numbers. Churchill was in public view, holding conferences with police inspectors. Divisional Superintendent Mulvaney's operational log (which does not mention Churchill) explained the strategic calculations. An attack on the front door of the house was ruled out: it would result in great loss of life. The soldiers (from the Tower of London) had taken up vantage points and were returning the fire of the anarchists. They were a lieutenant, two non-commissioned officers, and seventeen men of the Scots Guards. Not many years from now some of them would be facing bullets on the continent of Europe – as would the Home Secretary. If one person at what became known as the Siege of Sidney Street, epitomized the pre-echo of war of which this episode reeks, it was Philip Gibbs, *Daily Chronicle* star reporter. Gibbs was in military correspondent mode:

> …Most terrible and deadly in sound was the rapid fire of the Scots Guards… followed by a silence, intense and strange, after the ear-splitting din…[8]

Four years hence he would be reporting from France and Belgium.

In a 1932 *Thoughts and Adventures* reminiscence Churchill recalled finding 'a regular fusillade' when he arrived. An intermittent hail of bullets was coming from the besieged house and from the police and soldiers opposite in requisitioned houses. Churchill was recognized by the sightseers – and booed by Tories among them. He was used to this.[9]

The newspapers had no doubt that the Home Secretary was in charge. The *Daily Mail* was categorical: 'Mr Churchill at once took command. He called his generals round him in consultation…' The *Chronicle* concurred:

> Mr Churchill stood out in the street, although the bullets were flying wildly up and down. He motioned the line backward, and took four or five of the Scots Guards a few yards nearer the house and directed their fire.

The *Illustrated London News* had a full front-page drawing based on photographs of Churchill at the scene. The sensational story was:

> THE HOME SECRETARY AS DIRECTOR OF THE 'BATTLE' OF THE EAST END
> Mr Winston Churchill arrived on the scene of the extraordinary "battle" soon after half-past eleven, and at once took active part in the direction of operations, arranging the tactics in consultation with the officers. The Home Secretary was by no means unwilling to take risks of being hit…[10]

The *Chronicle*'s reporter noticed WSC lighting of a cigar:

> Now and then he would give an order, telling this line to advance or that to retire. Noticing the side-door of our yard to be open, he shouted, "Close that door, or you will be shot".[11]

The yard, across the road from the besieged building, had a tall gateway, from which Churchill kept a reconnaissance. The prowling Winston alternated between the yard and the corner of the street. The police cordon was 200-strong, with large numbers of other constables outside it managing the mass of watchers. The multitude, Churchill wrote, looked 'alarmed and angry'. He heard 'several cries of, "Oo let 'em in?"', blaming him as Home Secretary for not bringing in immigration restrictions.[12]

Almeric Fitzroy called the press accounts of the Home Secretary as incident commander 'nonsense, largely swallowed by the palpable credulity of the public'. But WSC, who loved to be the centre of any show, did give the impression of being more than an important spectator. And he was. *The Times* said that he was 'full of resourceful suggestion'. Winston's own account tells that he had an idea that the soldiers should make:

> …a direct advance up the staircase behind a steel plate or shield. Search was made in the foundries of the neighbourhood for one of a suitable size.[13]

It was reported that the Home Secretary had to be coaxed to a more sheltered spot. Eighteen months earlier Winston had written to Clementine from a Yeomanry camp on the Thames:

> I would greatly like to have some practice in the handling of large forces. I have much confidence in my judgement on things, when I see clearly, but on nothing do I seem to feel the truth more than in tactical combinations…but never, I fear, in this state of existence will it have a chance of flowering – in bright red blossom.[14]

Charles Masterman, on vacation in France, saw lurid drawings of Sidney Street. On his return, bursting into Churchill's room, he spluttered: 'What the hell have you been doing now, Winston?' 'Now, Charlie, don't be croth. It was such fun,' lisped the Home Secretary. Churchill was back in military action. In a letter that evening to Asquith, he described:

> …firing from every window, bullets chipping the brickwork, police and Scots Guards armed with loaded weapons, artillery jingling up.[15]

By 1 p.m. the building was on fire. The shooting from inside continued. Meanwhile a fire brigade arrived. Churchill would later give evidence to an inquest on two bodies which were subsequently found. Under cross-examination, he stated that he confirmed to the firemen the instructions from the police that they were not to put out the fire at present, since so doing would have meant loss of life for fire-brigade officers.[16]

It has been regularly stated that the Home Secretary directed the fire brigade to let the house burn down. This interpretation appears supported by Churchill's letter to Asquith:

> I thought it better to let the house burn down rather than spend good British lives in rescuing these ferocious rascals.[17]

That was Churchill bombast. In his retrospective, he describes what seems to have been (give or take colouring) the sequence of events. The fire-officer, he said, was angrily determined to do his job: 'anarchists, automatic pistols, danger zones, nothing of this sort is mentioned in the regulations of the London Fire Brigade.' Churchill moved in to tell the fire-fighters, 'on my authority as Home Secretary', that the house was to be left to burn down. He did use his ministerial authority, but only to confirm the instructions of the police. He had personal knowledge of how lethal were the rapid-fire Mauser pistols that the besieged gunmen were firing. In the 1898 cavalry charge at Omdurman, he had a semiautomatic Mauser. With it he killed several spear-wielding Sudanese attackers.[18]

The *Daily Chronicle* gives Churchill in the thick of the battle:

> ...Smoke had begun to come out of the second-floor window, and the officers tightened their hold on their revolvers: 'The house is on fire; they will bolt now'. Seeing this Mr Churchill sent two of the policemen with shot-guns and these took careful aim at the windows on the ground floor [producing] a crash of glass.[19]

Remarkably, the battle was viewed on the bioscope on the very day by patrons of the music-halls. A four-minute British Pathé film shows the Sidney Street house to be the end-section of a block. Smoke and flames issue from its windows. There is a sea of watching faces. Another newsreel pans over the crowd heaving behind the cordon. Various chiefs may be seen conferring and directing gun-clutching police and soldiers. Winston Churchill, top-hatted, stick in hand, and clad in a fur-lined coat with an astrakhan collar, gives every appearance of strategy-making as he edges along at the head of a troop of police, watchful and purposeful, waving his hand urgently at one point.[20]

Sidney Street the Movie went onscreen at the Coliseum at 5.30 p.m. It was advertised as the Home Secretary 'directing operations in the danger zone'. Edward Marsh, in his correspondence with Lady Gladstone, gushed:

> I'm on the biograph, where I make a most gratifying appearance as almost the central figure of 'Mr Churchill directing the operations', at the Palace [Theatre], which is nightly received with unanimous boos and shouts of 'shoot him' from the gallery...[21]

Marsh and Churchill on Sidney Street were a conspicuous pair of top-hats. The film was silent of course, though no doubt with sound added in the theatre. There was plenty of opportunity for gallery shouters. Some clue on Churchill's reception is provided by Marsh:

> Why are London music-hall audiences so uniformly and bigotedly Tory? You would have thought a stray Liberal must occasionally find his way in by accident – but it seems not.[22]

The conflagration in the building had to bring a conclusion. The *Chronicle* related:

The house was a roaring mass of flame...'Let us make a rush', said one of the plain-clothes men. 'No', said the Home Secretary. 'We want no more loss of life.' He gave orders to open wide the doors of the yard, so that those inside could take uninterrupted aim should there be a bolt down the street. At this time a Maxim gun from the Tower came up but Mr Churchill ordered it out of action.[23]

Churchill's deposition for the Coroner's Court states: 'I never directed anyone to send for a Maxim gun.' A machine-gun could fire 500 rounds a minute. The invention had helped Europeans to suppress and rule African peoples. Soon the European nations would be turning this instrument of mass death against each other.[24]

The Home Secretary left about mid-afternoon, when the house had burned down and the shooting had ended. The ruins disclosed the two charred bodies which would be the subject of the coroner's inquest, one having been shot, the other apparently suffocated by smoke. Churchill's account relates:

> These were established to be the corpses of Fritz Svaars and Jacob Vogel [Fogel], both members of Peter the Painter's Anarchist gang, and both certainly concerned in the police murders.[25]

Peter the Painter had escaped abroad.

Churchill later admitted that he should have 'remained quietly in my office'. In *Thoughts*, he mused on the anomalies of a government minister at a quasi-military operation:

> ...It was no part of my duty to take personal control or to give executive decisions. From my chair in the Home Office I could have sent any order and it would have been immediately acted on, but it was not for me to interfere with those in charge on the spot. Yet, on the other hand, my position of authority, far above them all, attracted inevitably to itself direct responsibility.[26]

Winston was compulsively drawn to the spotlight. This increasingly marked aspect of his personality was noticed by Charles Masterman, whose wife wrote in her diary:

> This is a very odd weakness for such a big man, as he is in some ways. He cannot resist the limelight in any form; he cannot relinquish any opportunity of standing forward in a sentimental position and being cheered for it.[27]

The new House of Commons was not due to assemble until the first week of February, but Sidney Street was drawing much press comment. *The Times* thought that the military-style operation was wrong-headed. Capture, not killing, should have been the aim: 'on a sober review, we are not sure that the outcome redounds very much to our credit.' The paper hosted a lively letters debate. To the fore was a pertinent question: what was a cabinet minister doing at a gun-battle? Lawyer Sir Harry Poland thought that Churchill had compromised his office. The correspondence was joined by Edward Pickersgill, who thought that Churchill had acted 'very foolishly', given that the Metropolitan Police were his responsibility.[28]

Liberal MP and press proprietor Sir Henry Dalziel sent to Churchill complaints that came in to his popular *Reynold's Newspaper*. He sent them to Churchill, along with a covering letter supporting him. If he hoped to get a reaction for his paper, he was not disappointed. WSC in his reply, commented:

> I share your surprise that a section of our fellow countrymen should be so ready to join in the carping and sneering criticisms of the ill-informed Continental Press. There are, and there ought to be, other ways of dealing with beasts of prey than by choking them in British blood.[29]

Dalziel published Churchill's letter. There seems to have been a mutual publicity relationship between the newspaperman and the cabinet minister. A photograph of Churchill in electioneering action shows prominently a *Reynold's Newspaper* poster. The two men played golf together. Dalziel would later build up a massive circulation for his *News of the World*, in which, as we have noted, Churchill wrote. A feature of the paper was sober but detail-specific coverage of divorce cases.[30]

On 12 January the Home Secretary issued a statement in *The Times*:

> ...I did not assume the direction of events. I did not interfere in any way with the dispositions made by the police authorities on the spot. I never overrode them...I did not send for the Artillery.

He blamed 'sensational reports' and 'spiteful comments' in the newspapers. Churchill must have been, we may think, exquisitely torn: whilst enjoying the commander kudos, he had to insist to critics that he had been a watcher only.[31]

On 19 January *The Times* delivered a further rebuke:

> ...The presence of a high officer of State, who is the official superior of the police, is not desirable on such occasions, and especially in such a conspicuous fashion...Criticism of them becomes criticism of him, and it is at once made a party question.[32]

One could add to the Sidney Street debate. What if the anarchists had been captured and convicted of murder? Their files would have crossed the Home Secretary's desk. He and his chief adviser on reprieve would have had their objectivity compromised by having been at the scene where the criminals were apprehended.

Winston Churchill appeared in person at the inquest on 'Two Unknown Men', on 18 January. His deposition stated: 'I am Privy Councillor and Principal

Secretary of State for the Home Department.' During the proceedings there was an exchange between one of the lawyers, a Mr Godfray, and Churchill. The *Daily News* had:

[Godfray] May I ask you what you mean by 'the highest covering authority'?
[Churchill] I mean the highest covering police authority.
[Godfray] You were not speaking of yourself?
[Churchill] I think I am the highest police authority.
[Godfray] I quite bow to that. But you are not speaking of yourself in that sense now?
[Churchill] Yes, I was.

Churchill could be snippy if his status was sold short. However, he stuck to his line that he was simply giving the police any assistance they might require.[33]

He wrote a private letter to the coroner. One detail seems to raise the whole question of his presence at Sidney Street:

…I made it my business to go round the back of the premises and satisfy myself that there was no chance of the criminals effecting their escape through the intricate area of walls and small houses at the back of no. 100 Sidney Street.[34]

The information that the Home Secretary carried out in person an on-the-ground check reads oddly.

The new Parliament opened on 6 February 1911. After the King's Speech in the House of Lords, MPs returned to their own chamber for the traditional multi-day Debate on the Address. The Conservative leader Arthur Balfour was disappointed that the Foreign Secretary was not in his place. But another ripe target was. Sitting next to Asquith was the ambitious and self-pleased Home Secretary. Balfour was known for his languid comportment and dead-pan wit. Winston Churchill was in awe of him. He once remarked that he would 'pay £10 to dine with Balfour any night'. The ex-prime minister was known for well-mannered viciousness. Churchill once said of him: 'Had he lived in the French Revolution, he would have consigned a dangerous enemy of his government or party, or even an erring colleague, to the guillotine with much complacency, but in a thoroughly polite manner.' Today Balfour reflected on the Home Office – and its incumbent:

That office has not usually been a perpetual source of interest and surprise, but much turns upon the personality of the holder of the office, and the right hon. Gentleman has in various ways succeeded in attracting the gaze of the civilised world….

The teasing with menace had Churchill's attention. The Home Secretary's hands were thrust deep into his pockets. The Tory grandee began with Churchill's handling of the South Wales industrial trouble:

> ...most deplorable disturbances...accompanied by much destruction of property and attacks upon the person. The right hon. Gentleman might have avoided a great many of these occurrences had he not, at a critical moment, refused to carry out decisively and effectively the measures which he contemplated.[35]

Would Sidney Street get a mention? Of course, it did:

> I am not quite clear as to his position with regard to an incident which attracted a great deal of attention in London not very many weeks ago.

Everyone knew where this one was going. An elegantly fashioned barb whistled over:

> ...a very remarkable combination of the blackest tragedy and something which almost looked like comedy. Troops were assembled in large numbers, policemen were assembled in overwhelming numbers, and guns were brought to the scene of action, and from that scene of action the right hon. Gentleman was not absent.

We may imagine Balfour's delivery of 'not absent'. He continued:

> I understand that he did not call out the troops or assemble the police, and that he had nothing to do with the massing of artillery. He was there in – well, I do not know the position he was in.

The repeated 'he', and the pregnant pause, will have delighted those whom Churchill irritated. The Conservative leader went on:

> He was, I understand, in what is known as the zone of fire...I understand what the photographer was doing, but what was the right hon. Gentleman doing? I should have thought that anything more embarrassing to those responsible for the operations than to have the head of the office who is over them all present with the photographer as irresponsible spectators, could not be imagined.[36]

Churchill well remembered the speech in his later recall. He conceded 'a not altogether unjust reflection'. It will have stung, but being selected as a Balfour target on Parliament's big day could be seen as a compliment. Such was the line that the prime minister took when he replied to the debate, saying that it was 'flattering to be singled out'. Asquith observed:

My right hon. Friend suffers from the dangerous endowment of an interesting personality.[37]

Everyone knew Churchill's 'interesting personality'.

The toughest parliamentary questioning of Churchill came from Viscount Wolmer, a newly elected Lancashire Tory. Wolmer, 23, just down from Oxford University, was associated with the group of titled young Tories who sat below the Opposition gangway. His politics looked for alliance between the aristocracy and the working class. He wanted to know about the lack of refreshment for the police during the very long day on Sidney Street. A clergyman, Lionel Lewis, had seen constables being got up without breakfast at 4.30 a.m. They were not fed all day. Lewis, writing to *The Times*, called this 'stupid and cruel'. Churchill was on the back foot: A few policemen 'got overlooked in the turmoil'. He admitted that the police shift was 'perhaps twelve or thirteen hours'. He had a report of 'a cart full of provisions supplied by a benevolent lady'. Wolmer did some research of his own, telling Parliament that the constables had gone without food for between twelve and twenty-one hours. Churchill's response was that, 'It may very often happen that the police in times of emergency or soldiers in battle may be kept working rather beyond the ordinary hours.' It was an unimpressive defence of what looked like lack of care by the authorities for the police constables. Behind the Sidney Street feeding issue lay deep-rooted grievance inside the Metropolitan Police: low pay, difficulty in supporting families, even malnutrition. The authoritarian, semi-military structure of the force was not conducive to decent status and working conditions for its rank and file. Churchill was finding that he had to give attention not just to what the police were employed to do but to how they were looked after.[38]

Winston had been energized by the Battle of Stepney. A.G. Gardiner would paint him in a 1913 essay:

He sees himself moving through the smoke of battle – triumphant, terrible, his brow clothed with thunder, his legions looking to him for victory, and not looking in vain. He thinks of Napoleon; he thinks of his great ancestor…[39]

In 1897, whilst serving with the Malakand Field Force, Churchill wrote to his mother about his fearlessness in the field, riding whilst others took cover. He explained: 'I play for high stakes and given an audience there is nothing too daring or too noble. Without the gallery, things are different.' At Sidney Street the gallery was there. Two months earlier George Riddell wrote in his diary about Churchill and war. The newspaper proprietor played golf with Winston one or two days most weeks. Sir George gained close insights. A November 1910 entry describes WSC as 'very fond of discussing military subjects…he has often told me there is nothing like war…complete detachment from the history of the world and the absence of thought for the morrow.' His journal has a remarkable Churchill declaration:

> [Churchill] said that if the country were engaged in a land war, he would throw up his position as Home Secretary and go to the front.[40]

'Land war' meant the predicted European war.

Sidney Street had provided Churchill with a battle. Towards the end of the month, he was reminded of a different sort of conflict. The *Daily News* reported that when the Home Secretary's motor-cab turned into Downing Street, taking him to a morning cabinet meeting, it was chased by a woman carrying a long pole topped with a broad arrow and a banner asking, 'Should Winston Churchill go to prison?' The *News* told readers that the pursuer:

> ...made a dash for the Home Secretary, and running behind the car, nearly knocked his hat off with the pole. Mr Churchill smiled at the tall lady as she failed to keep up with the cab.[41]

The suffragettes were back.

Chapter 13

Sentiment and Doubt

On 11 December 1910 on the intervening day between his election rally at Dartford and one at Poole, Winston Churchill overruled the advice of his chief legal adviser and refused a reprieve. This does not fit the merciful Home Secretary picture. The condemned man was one of three whom Sir Charles Darling condemned on successive days at the Old Bailey. The other two won reprieves, Churchill agreeing with his advisers: both were in the category of knife or razor attacks by young men on female partners, homicide familiar to the Home Office files. About London barber's assistant, ex-soldier Oliver Smith, who quarrelled with the woman with whom he lived and slashed her throat, Churchill wrote:

> …He did not mean to kill her when they sat down to breakfast. It was a mad impulse.

For Churchill, Smith's military service in India probably boosted his worth. Ex-soldiers (imperial service and Second Boer War) are a heavy thread in the files.[1]

Darling, once a Conservative MP, was reckoned to be a good summer-up but a judge whose dignity was compromised by his habit of laughing with and at witnesses. He disliked modern sociology and psychology, calling it 'Ruggles-Brisia'. An unappealing nugget of this talkative justice is that he allowed himself to be painted wearing the death-cap in the act of sentencing. He did not send in trial notes to the Home Office, as did most judges.[2]

The third of Darling's mid-November 1910 death sentences was on a German-Jewish bookbinder. Noah Woolf, 59, had lived at the Hebrew Home for Christians in London's Upper Holloway, until he was evicted after upsetting other residents with his religious arguments. He had a hostility to Russian-Polish Jews. On a return visit to the home, he used a butcher's knife to murder Andrew Simon, a Polish Jew against whom he harboured a grudge over Simon's complaints to the management about him. The jury recommended mercy. Pentonville Prison's Medical Officer was inclined to think that at the time of the killing, Woolf was 'not responsible for his actions'. Ernley Blackwell, favouring reprieve, noted that, 'the man was undoubtedly labouring under a heavy sense of injury.'[3]

Petitions arrived from religious organizations and elsewhere. Woolf's barrister spoke of 'an old man with no money, no solicitor advising him and few friends'. He reminded the Home Secretary of the jury's mercy recommendation. The scheduled Pentonville double-execution of Woolf and Smith was averted by

Smith's reprieve, but John Ellis was still required for Woolf. Winston Churchill saw 'a premeditated and deliberate murder'. The knife had been sharpened; Woolf had been carrying it about. 'There can be no doubt', Churchill wrote on the file, 'that he had resolved and planned, with malice aforethought, to murder'. Churchill's refusal of a reprieve was in stark language:

> It is this rage and lust for vengeance that the law punishes with death…Not to punish it with death would be contrary to the spirit and intention of the law. I cannot find it within my duty to interfere with the sentence, which must be executed in the usual course.[4]

This suggested the classical school of the punishment fitting the crime.

As the results of the General Election were being digested, there was another capital case disagreement between Churchill and his advisers. George Newton, 19 years old, an East End gasworks labourer, was sentenced at the Old Bailey on 14 January 1911 for the murder of his fiancée. Ada Roker had told him that she was leaving him. After Newton visited the factory worker at her mother's house, Ada was found dead, her throat having been cut with the razor that he had brought with him. He had strapped the woman's arms to her sides. Newton gave himself up immediately, saying on the way to the police station, 'It was done quick, and I was copped quick.' The defence was insanity: that the prisoner had not been aware of what he was doing. The jury recommended mercy on account of Newton's youth.[5]

In his notes for the Home Office, the sentencing judge, Sir William Grantham, saw the motive as jealousy: 'if she would not marry him, no one else would.' He disagreed with the jury on clemency. He did not think that youth was always an excuse. A number of recent murders had been committed by youths: they should know that they could not be sure of mercy. Troup and Blackwell leaned towards reprieve. A petition signed by 72,000 and was forwarded by the Mayor of West Ham. The execution of a teenager was rare. The young man had no previous convictions. At Chelmsford prison, Newton's behaviour greatly puzzled Governor Marriott, as he informed Winston Churchill. The prisoner seemed to be unaware of his situation. He was writing to people that he was 'happy as a sandboy'. The chaplain thought that Newton was not of sound mind. On prisoner correspondence, it may be noted that so heavy was the censorship by the authorities that one former jail inmate told the Hobhouse/Brockway inquiry: 'It is practically impossible for a prisoner to write anything but a cheerful letter.' Grumpiness about conditions or treatment was liable to result in a prisoner having to re-wite a letter. Could this explain the strange remarks by Newton? Churchill arranged a mental examination by two doctors.[6]

On the official 'Petition for Reduction of Sentence' form, Newton wrote a personal plea to Winston Churchill. He said that his mind was 'a total blank when the awful event occurred…I beg and pray that you Honourable Sir will reconsider this my final appeal to seek mercy from His Most Gracious Majesty.'

The examination by the doctors determined Churchill's decision. A Home Office telegram was sent to the Governor:

> S of S has carefully considered the petition of the convict George Newton. Regrets that he must adhere to his decision that the law must take its course. Inform convict.

Churchill's sentiment cut this time against the murderer, with the victim in mind. He confirmed the noose for a young man who apparently had anticipated escaping it. A doctor wrote to the Home Office: 'it is a reversion to a blood-thirsty idea of justice to send a youth of 19 to the gallows.' In a memorandum on a different matter, Sir Evelyn Ruggles-Brise pointed out that, 'in the eye of criminal law, as of civil law, a person cannot be regarded as fully responsible before the age of 21.' Churchill had no qualms about declining to halt the execution of a teenager. Here we see one of the limits to his progressive humanity.[7]

New Year's Day 1911 brought sensation. A police constable patrolling Clapham Common came upon a corpse in the gorse bushes. The dead man, Leon Beron, was a Russian-Jewish community landlord. He had been stabbed and beaten to death. His gold watch-and-chain with five-guinea-piece attachment was gone. A letter – so it was reported – was cut into each cheek of the dead man. Conspiracy speculation got busy. S for Spy, it was claimed. Had Beron betrayed the Houndsditch gang? The police soon had a man in custody, also Russian-Jewish. Stinie (or Steinie) Morrison turned out to be an alias for Alexander Petropavloff. A professional burglar, he had spent most of the last decade in prison. With Sidney Street bursting onto the news, there was speculation that the murder could be another of the doings of foreign anarchists. The call to tighten 'aliens' legislation had new ammunition.[8]

Stinie Morrison came up at the Old Bailey before Justice Darling in the middle of March. At six feet three, he was a man with a presence. Harold Butler, who was sent to the court by the Home Office, remembered 'his coarse, handsome face and his passionate assertions of innocence'. Improper police behaviour was alleged. Police statements were contradictory. Had Morrison been fitted up? The matter was raised in Parliament. Winston Churchill organized an inquiry, conducted by Conservative lawyer MP (and future Home Secretary) George Cave. As a result, Constable George Greaves, whose evidence differed from that of other police in Morrison's favour, was disciplined. Labour MP Will Thorne called this unfair. He protested about Greaves' transfer to Pinner, which he said would be detrimental to the policeman's career. Churchill said that Greaves had been found not to be a reliable witness in court. He had been sent to 'a particularly healthy district' and could still qualify for promotion. Thorne was not soothed. Greaves, prior to his transfer, he said, had been attending Yiddish classes with a view to becoming a police interpreter. There was no opening at Pinner. He wanted him returned to his former division. Churchill declined to intervene. Thorne asked:

> Is the right hon. Gentleman aware that in the locality there is discontent on account of the bad treatment this constable has received?[9]

Churchill was not aware of discontent. The Home Secretary's attitude of supporting the police chiefs matched that of the conservative-minded department that he headed.[10]

At Stine Morrison's trial, the judge, Charles Darling, was supercilious about a London immigrant community, remarking to the jury:

> …those Brodskys are foreigners, apparently Polish or Russian Jews…Do you not know that it is very common among people of certain classes and certain nationalities if they have got a good case not to rest upon that case? If you have talked to anybody who has administered justice in India you will know that there…in order to overthrow perjured evidence they themselves procure perjured evidence.[11]

He doubted whether the evidence was sufficiently conclusive to convict. He was nudging the jury towards not guilty. The evidence and testimony were full of clashes: Morrison's money sources; cabs and trams; a claim that he was watching Harry Lauder at the Shoreditch Empire at the time in question but theatre detail contradicting this; and story-changes by witnesses. Identification was questionable, with a suggestion that witnesses had previously seen a photograph of Morrison. Before the discovery of the body, Morrison had dined with the victim at a Polish restaurant in Whitechapel; the two subsequently took a cab together. It was suspicious, but short of damning. The judge reminded the jury that there was no 'non-proven' verdict, as in Scotland. They must be reasonably certain before finding the prisoner guilty. The jurymen did not linger over their deliberations. They breezed back swiftly with a guilty verdict. Darling had no option but to pass sentence of death. When he added the usual words, 'May the Lord have mercy on your soul,' Morrison shouted back, 'I decline such mercy; I don't believe there is a God either.' The Appeal Court confirmed the conviction. Then it was Winston Churchill's turn to look at the case.

According to Harold Butler's memoirs, neither the Home Office staff nor Churchill doubted that Morrison was at least a party to the crime, but they were not sure that he acted alone. Years later the inkling of a second party was apparently confirmed when a woman revealed that her husband, an associate of Morrison, had been with him on the night of the crime and had returned home bloodied. In English law, Morrison would still have been guilty of murder, since there would have been common purpose even if he himself had not struck the fatal blow, but the presence of such a person would be a factor in the consideration of clemency.[12]

Winston Churchill announced a reprieve for Stinie Morrison over a week before the execution date. There was surprise and curiosity. The murder was appalling, premeditated, and in the course of theft – and the perpetrator had a shocking record. Why was he spared? Presumably it was because of doubt about the safety of the verdict? In Parliament Henry Dalziel asked the Home Secretary if he had any objection to stating his reasons. Churchill replied that statements about the reasons for granting or refusing a reprieve were not usual practice. However:

> I may state that my decision was taken after full consultation with the judge and with the Lord Chief Justice; and that it does not imply doubt as to the guilt of the prisoner or question the Tightness of the verdict given by the jury.[13]

One would expect Morrison's Home Office file to have the comments of Blackwell, Troup, and Churchill. They are missing. There is however indication elsewhere of why Churchill reprieved Morrison. The 1938 biographer of Charles Darling, Derek Walker-Smith, then a young Conservative MP, consulted Darling about the Morrison case. His book states that:

> The grounds given [by Churchill to the King] for this decision were that other evidence might turn up leading to his acquittal; in other words there was reasonable doubt of the proof of his guilt.[14]

Darling explained to Walker-Smith why he thought that the jury's verdict was the wrong one. He personally did not doubt that Morrison was guilty of murder, *but*:

> The view I took was that, had I been a juryman, the evidence that I had heard was not sufficient to prove to me beyond all reasonable doubt that Morrison had committed murder.[15]

Darling presumably told Churchill that he thought that the verdict was the wrong one. In Churchill's parliamentary answer to Dalziel, we see his careful deployment of vocabulary. He could not give publicly his reason for reprieve, but his description of the jury's verdict as 'tight' *implies* the reasoning: they were right to convict *on the evidence*, but since the evidence was beset with flaws, further items might turn up to contradict it. Also, whilst he said that his intervention did not imply doubt as to Morrison's guilt, he did not say that it did not imply *doubt as to the required level of proof* of the man's guilt. It did so imply.

The Morrison file includes a pasted extract from Hansard in which Churchill answers a Conservative MP about the judge's observations during the trial on the subject of 'photographic snapshots in court'. Surreptitious picture-taking had been prompted by the Crippen proceedings, hats being used ingeniously. There is a press photograph of Crippen and Le Neve at their Bow Street committal proceedings and there is an angled snap of Crippen in the dock at the Old Bailey. (There is also a photograph of Churchill giving evidence at the post-Sidney Street inquest.) Photography was forbidden – as was sketching in court. Eleven years later a furtive snapper would capture the delivery of a death sentence. The judge, Sir Horace Avory, known as Acid Drop – presumably not just for the sharpness of his comments – was the hanging judge of his era. He sent Churchill ten death sentences.[16]

The Stinie Morrison case prompted a *Humanitarian* comment on the illogicality of the death penalty: the guardians of the law in cases like this where the evidence was circumstantial and not necessarily reliable, were 'unable, on the one hand, to carry the sentence into effect, or on the other, to release the prisoner whom they dare not hang'. With John Dickman, Winston Churchill by declining to intervene took a chance, safely in his view, on the 'bracelet' of circumstantial evidence being secure. With Morrison, safety was lacking and he reprieved.[17]

In his 1939 *News of the World* reminiscences, Winston Churchill makes what looks like a reference to the Morrison case. He speaks of the Home Secretary's severe burden in having to decide, after the passing of a death sentence, 'without any legal training and upon the case as presented, whether in fact [the person] had done the deed': even if the minister was 'advised by austere, patient, just-minded officials, who had years of experience behind them, it was an invidious responsibility.' Quite bizarrely, in his article he states that there was no Criminal Appeal Court 'in my time', even though it was established in 1907 and during his Home Office tenure recourse to it was commonplace. He says, in mentioning that he was 'extremely glad' about the reform, that 'I did not myself benefit from its operation.' Leaving aside the excision of an inconvenient fact, the point about the agony of the Home Secretary over a death sentence arising from circumstantial evidence is well made. The Court of Criminal Appeal could not re-run a case. It was restricted to legal issues and new evidence. Churchill plainly suffered personally where there was doubt about guilt in death sentence cases.[18]

Stinie Morrison made a nuisance of himself in Parkhurst as he continued to protest about his conviction. Churchill's successors at the Home Office had to field four petitions from the prisoner asking for the original hanging sentence to be carried out. Morrison's health was damaged by hunger strikes. He died in jail in 1922. He was WSC's most troublesome capital case. It demonstrated, one might think, the unanswerable case against the death penalty. Churchill never for a moment had such a thought.

We have noted Constable George Greaves, a campaigner viewed by the police authorities as a troublemaker. There was another such of higher rank, prominent in the Churchill archives without engaging any historian attention. Inspector John Syme crusaded for better conditions and improved pay for ordinary police officers and for ending the scandal of police families having to turn to charity. When Syme supported two men who he thought had been disciplined over-harshly for a mistaken arrest, he was reduced to the rank of sergeant and then sacked. Thus began a long campaign for his reinstatement and against what some saw as tyranny in the police authority. The controversy was still alive in 1948, when an MP who reviewed its history remarked that a great number of people 'in high places' were involved, one of whom was 'the Home Secretary of 1910, now the Leader of the Opposition'. He added that, 'it seems to do them little credit'. What happened? Winston Churchill granted Syme an interview on 22 April 1910 to discuss his grievances. Churchill wanted compromise, since Police Commissioner Sir Edward Henry would see himself as undermined were Syme to be restored. He did offer to reinstate the policeman but on the lower rank of station sergeant. Syme refused. There was vigorous lobbying for Syme. The *Westminster Express* called for a full and independent inquiry. Edward Troup, who had been written to by Syme, warned about the consequences if the ex-inspector were to be put back. There were echoes of the George Greaves affair – and indeed Syme wrote to Churchill about the 'persecution' of the police constable. Syme and Greaves had previously worked together at Scotland Yard. At their different rank levels, each saw himself as a victim of unjust disciplinary action as a result of raising the issue of faulty or unfair police procedures.[19]

Syme's struggles seem to have unbalanced him. On 17 June 1911 he found himself before the chief magistrate at Bow Street. He had addressed a letter to Ramsay MacDonald, containing a threat 'to make an attack in public on the person of the Right Hon. Winston Spencer Churchill, MP'. Syme asked MacDonald, 'Must I kill my opponent with my own hand?' He wrote another letter threatening to kill an Inspector Reed of the Metropolitan Police. The authorities seem to have regarded these utterances as attention-seeking rather than representing any serious menace.[20]

Syme faced trial at the Old Bailey before Justice Darling. Winston Churchill, as he wrote to Clementine on 3 July 1911, considered the ex-inspector's menaces to be the product of psychological disturbance. He thought that he would 'probably get 12 months, during which his mind will either get better or worse.' He was sympathetic. At the trial, only the threat against Inspector Reed was prosecuted. The jury found Syme guilty, but with the rider that his utterances were 'bluff and made in order to call attention to his grievances'. Darling handed Syme six months, lighter than expected. Winston told Clemmie:

> Darling of course could not resist a chance of being funny. [Syme's] friends are going to try to get him out of the country; and this, if possible, I shall facilitate.[21]

It is hard to imagine that Syme would want to go. Churchill was personally gracious over the wild threats against him by the ex-policeman, but he does not seem to have had much interest in his campaigning. He was content for the police to be the servants of the public and the government, without negotiating clout and dependent on others for their wages and conditions. He was a top-down politician and administrator.

Syme would go to prison on a number of occasions, hunger-striking and at one time being sent to Broadmoor. He won two official enquiries. The second largely supported him and granted him a backdated medical pension. In 1913 he founded the National Union of Police and Prison Officers. Banned by the Police Commissioners, it continued with a secret membership. Festering police discontent would culminate in the national strikes of 1918 and 1919. Police were no longer prepared to be the bodyguard of the propertied classes, taking the pay and conditions deemed suitable for them. Out of the strikes would emerge the Police Federation, not a trade union but some way towards it, and representing an improvement in the status of the rank and file. To a significant degree, the case that John Syme made to Winston Churchill was conceded. It was not a cause that resonated with Churchill. During 1910 and 1911 he was moving away from progressive radicalism.

Chapter 14
Aliens

Until the early years of the twentieth century Britain had no restriction on immigration. It was a place of refuge, especially for the persecuted Jews of the Russian Empire. Open door was seen as a badge of strength. Some viewed the near-unique tolerance as soft. On 16 March *The Times* saw the Stinie Morrison trial as confirming that:

> ...the East End of London counts among its population a large number of very dangerous, very reckless, and very noxious people, chiefly immigrants from the Eastern and South-Eastern countries of Europe.[1]

In April 1904, the Conservative government introduced an Aliens Bill. With a rise in xenophobic and anti-Semitic feeling, and resentment over 'sweated labour' undercutting wages in tailoring, it was clear that one aim was to control Jewish immigration. The bill brought disquiet to Jewish communities. Churchill, in transit to the Liberals, needed a new constituency. He cultivated Manchester North-West, whose electorate was a third Jewish. He supported Jewish causes, championing immigrant rights. There was an obvious element of expediency, but his new cause was fired by passion. He wrote a public letter to Manchester cotton merchant Nathan Laski declaring that anti-Semitism, 'which has darkened recent Continental history', did not appeal to the English working classes: they would 'resent a measure which besmirches those ancient traditions of freedom and hospitality for which Britain has been so long renowned.'[2]

Churchill led a line-by-line assault in committee on the bill. The government had to abandon it. Winston's new zeal was not contrived. He had close Jewish friends, including Maurice de Forest. A revised Aliens Bill was passed in August 1905. It required immigrants to prove financial resources and to be without criminal record, evidence of insanity, and contagious disease. Churchill opposed the change of direction. At the 1906 General Election he was returned for Manchester North West with a mandate to watch the working of the act. In 1908 he had to face his electors in the constitutionally compulsory by-election on his elevation to the cabinet. He made promises to the Jewish community. He lost the seat, but he was quickly returned at another by-election, for Dundee. His friendship with the Manchester Jewish community continued. He did not completely abandon his pledges. The establishment of receiving houses at ports to deal fairly with entry requests, was begun in 1909, with the Port of London added in May 1910.[3]

Immigration came under Winston Churchill's Home Office responsibility. The clamour continued for tightening the Aliens Act. Churchill's ear was bent by King George, whose secretary wrote to him on 5 January 1911:

> His Majesty is sorry to hear a bad account of the injured fireman [in the collapse of a wall after the fire in the Sidney Street building]. He hopes that these recent outrages by foreigners will lead you to consider whether the Aliens Act could not be amended so as to prevent London from being infested with men and women whose presence would not be tolerated in any other country.[4]

Damage was done to tolerance by terror incidents, but the King's picture of London being 'infested' by terrorists was a wild misrepresentation. However, terrorism in London was serious. The Houndsditch triple police murder which gave rise to the Sidney Street Siege was the worst since the 1867 Clerkenwell Outrage when a Fenian bomb killed 12. The year before Houndsditch there had been the Tottenham Outrage, when two Jewish Latvian anarchists tried to intercept a vehicle carrying factory wages. The fleeing raiders commandeered a tram, before being trapped and shooting themselves. A policeman and a boy were killed and twenty-one people injured. The Latvian background was the aftermath of the 1905 uprising against Russian imperial rule, when government troops killed 73 demonstrators in Riga, and two thousand people were executed without trial. The mother of one of the Tottenham anarchists lived in Riga. In that city there had recently been a Sidney Street-type siege, with Mauser-equipped revolutionaries penned in a flat and soldiers outside the window. There was an offer of assistance from Riga regarding the Houndsditch murders. The British Consul there informed the Foreign Office that the local Detective Department chief was willing to come to London to assist in searching for the wanted men. Churchill instructed that this should be politely declined. Questions from Labour and left-wing Liberal MPs on what Tsarist police were doing in London, would have been uncomfortable. Churchill remarked to the King on 'this particular tribe of miscreants from the Baltic provinces'. Members of the 'Flame' movement of Latvian revolutionaries behaved in Britain as if they were in the Russian Empire carrying out 'expropriations'.[5]

The administration of the Aliens Act was raised in Parliament in July 1910 by Aretas Akers-Douglas, a lawyer who as Home Secretary in the Balfour government was its author. Churchill will probably not have been aware that Akers-Douglas, in a 1905 parliamentary letter to King Edward, had quoted his comment on the decorative gear of military staff: 'those gorgeous and gilded functionaries with brass hats and ornamental duties who multiply so luxuriously on the plains of Aldershot and Salisbury'. The King harumphed in the margin at the presumption of 'a recent subaltern of Hussars'.[6]

Akers-Douglas called Churchill's failure to produce a scheduled report on the administration of the Aliens Act 'unaccountable'. He was perturbed that expelled

Winston Churchill and Clementine Hozier engagement 1908. (*Chronicle/Alamy*)

Churchill electioneering in 1910, with ballot-box prop. (*Granger/Alamy*)

Ministers Sir Edward Grey, Winston Churchill and Lord Crewe leave a cabinet meeting after the Liberal General Election victory in January 1910. (*Alamy*)

Churchill in 1911. (*Granger/Alamy*)

Churchill at the 'Siege of Sidney Street'. To the right is Edward Marsh. (*Alamy*)

Sidney Street: Churchill in conversation with a fireman. (*Alamy*)

Churchill giving evidence at the inquest following the discovery of two bodies the burnt-down besieged house in Sidney Street. (*Alamy*)

'Dartmoor Morality' satirical postcard on the 'Dartmoor Shepherd'. The convict, between Churchill and Lloyd George, is in a shepherd's smock and prison uniform trousers. The two politicians have robbed a henhouse and are making off with birds (which have critical messages about Liberal policies and campaigns). (*Alamy*)

Stinie (or Steinie) Morrison at the Old Bailey on 6 March 1911, the first day of his trial for the murder of Leon Beron. The snapshot has been taken surreptitiously. (*Trinity Mirror/Mirrorpix/Alamy*)

Winston Churchill and Reginald McKenna, 1909 (*Fremantle/Alamy*)

Winston Churchill at his desk at the Admiralty, 1914. The arrangement could easily be the Home Office. Churchill's bust of Napoleon has moved over with him. (*Alamy*)

Strangeways Prison, Manchester. (*Redharc Images/Alamy*)

Lincoln Prison chapel: the only survival of the 'separate' system within a chapel. Inmates part-sat, part-stood, within a coffin-like cubicle, from which they could only see the preacher. (*Maurice Savage/Alamy*)

Winston Churchill and his wife Clementine with General Bruce Hamilton at Aldershot in 1910, watching Army manoeuvres. (*Alamy*)

Winston Churchill and F.E. Smith as imagined by *Punch*, 2 November 1910. The ambitious 'students' are reading a new biography of Benjamin Disraeli, which shows how to become Prime Minister. (Leonard Raven-Hill, *Punch*)

House of Commons, 1909: the debating chamber as viewed from the Speaker's Chair. The Government benches are on the right; Opposition on the left. Above are the viewing galleries. (Unknown photographer/Alamy)

The end of the female suffrage Conciliation Bill. In the foreground of the 20 July 1910 *Punch* cartoon (l. to r.) are supporters of the bill Edward Grey, Richard Haldane and Augustine Birrell. (Leonard Raven-Hill, *Punch*).

Charles Masterman and David Lloyd George in 1911 on the veranda of Lloyd George's house at Criccieth, North Wales. (Lucy Masterman, *History Today*, 1964).

Evelyn Ruggles-Brise (Lesley Ward, 'Spy', *Vanity Fair*)

alien criminals were returning by buying first-class tickets, one man excusing his days-later return on the grounds that, 'I like England very much better'.[7]

Churchill, after a fulsome apology for the report's delay, delivered himself of a metaphor:

> The right hon. Gentleman and I have always differed greatly on the Aliens Act. He was the parent of that measure. He produced one child, which did not long survive, and I am not sure I did not have some part in putting it out of the way. But afterwards he produced another and stronger infant, which has now grown up to manhood, and has taken its place in the legislative and administrative machinery of the country.

The sweetness-and-light with the Conservatives was fine for government-opposition relations but for some, Churchill's endorsement of Tory aliens legislation now that he was no longer dependent on Jewish votes did not bode well. The Jewish community was not reconciled to the act.[8]

Mentioning in his correspondence with Lady Gladstone the pressure for new aliens legislation, Edward Marsh took the Liberal view, hoping that Churchill would 'bring in a Pistol Bill, which seems a better way of dealing with the crux than trying to stiffen up the Aliens Act.' Actually, Churchill had already decided to toughen the Aliens Act. He wrote to the prime minister:

> I think I shall have to stiffen the Administration of the Aliens Act a little, and more effective measures must be taken by the police to supervise the dangerous classes of aliens in our midst.[9]

He was aware that new aliens legislation would meet Liberal resistance. He received a plea from radical Potteries MP Josiah Wedgwood:

> Please do not be rushed into exceptional laws against anarchists. It is fatally easy to justify them but they lower the whole character of a nation.[10]

Wedgwood feared 'the betrayal of English traditions'. He was 'frightened by *The Times*'. His letter is a reminder of the strength of radical Liberalism in the English political tradition, in which equality before the law and the right of asylum for the persecuted were bedrock principles. Churchill knew that if he were seen as infringing these, he would have trouble.

The Home Secretary informed the King that he was considering 'any useful and practical measures by which the hands of the police authorities may be strengthened in dealing with foreign criminals in this country'. He prepared an Aliens (Prevention of Crime) Bill for circulation in draft around the cabinet. He put to the prime minister that, whilst the right of asylum should not be abandoned, 'the principle of expulsion for abuse of hospitality is capable of more effective development.' He floated 'two naughty principles':

First, a deliberate differentiation between the alien, and especially the unassimilated alien, and a British subject, and second, that an alien may, in certain circumstances, be deported before he has committed any offence.[11]

He added a Liberal conscience soother:

If an alien has lived here for five years free from crime, he will, except in respect of bearing arms, suffer no disability or risk of expulsion.

The bill would make increased penalties available for 'criminal or undesirable aliens', including prison with hard labour for expelled aliens who returned. Possession of firearms by aliens would be restricted. The Home Secretary would have the power to expel a convicted alien regardless of whether or not the court recommended it. Courts would be able to require sureties of good behaviour. Ship-masters bringing in a banned alien would have to pay the state prosecution expenses and take back the alien (and any dependents), providing 'proper accommodation and maintenance during the passage'.

The new act was to work with the 1905 Aliens Act. Was Churchill changing politically, or was he moving with the flow? He will have seen the build-up in the press of attacks on himself and the government. The *Daily Telegraph* accused ministers of 'pretending not to know what Anarchism means and what sort of foreign riff-raff is being freely introduced into England'. The influential *Pall Mall Gazette* saw the arrival in Britain of Europe's 'most abandoned ruffians'. The *Daily Express* complained of 'the heart which bleeds for the misfortunes of every country but its own'. Ex-CID chief Sir Robert Anderson, in an article on 'The Problem of the Criminal Alien' in February's issue of *Nineteenth Century and After*, wrote of Britain having become 'a cesspool for the scum of creation'. Churchill wanted to counter the criticism. By aiming legislation plans at immigration from Eastern Europe, he was inevitably linking in with the anti-aliens campaign, which pitched to xenophobia and anti-Semitism. A mid-March 1911 article in *The Times* wailed:

...A new ghetto has absorbed the Mint, Whitechapel and Stepney, stretching out to Shoreditch, to Hackney and to Stratford, and even across the river. In many streets four out of six names are Polish, German or Russian....The overwhelming majority of the alien newcomers are Jewish, and from one half to two thirds are from Russia...A large proportion of them never learn more than, at the most, a smattering of English. They work for Yiddish employers, read Yiddish newspapers, buy in Yiddish shops and enjoy themselves in Yiddish clubs and theatres...[12]

Some of the immigrant community had arrived with the migration to Britain of about 200,000 Jews from the Russian Empire, mainly Poles, during the last half-century. It was driven by the desire to escape from persecution. Feelings against the immigrants were exacerbated by the distortion of statistics. The *Daily Mail*, on 'London's Aliens' on 6 January, gave the impression that huge numbers of East Europeans had poured into London between 1901 and 1908. Churchill set up an investigation. The task fell to John Pedder, the Home Office's demography expert (of whom Gladstone wrote: 'strong ability, somewhat dogmatic and aggressive, but his work is excellent'). Pedder found that the *Mail* writer had taken the decennial census figures for 1861 to 1901 as those of single years between 1904 and 1908: part of the article had jumped across to the *Telegraph* and other papers. Churchill wrote to Lord Northcliffe to point out the howler. Northcliffe blamed *London Citizens' Year Book 1910*.[13]

Churchill's proposed new Aliens Bill did not find a berth in the government's timetable. He decided to make use of the Ten Minutes Rule, a procedure mostly for backbenchers, named after the time allowed for presentation. Introducing his bill on 18 April 1911, he claimed that it did not raise party controversy, being solely concerned with 'alien crime'. In the previous July Charles Masterman had used the Ten Minutes Rule to bring in the Mines Rescue and Aid Bill. Charlie enjoyed, as his wife related, 'a pleasant reception', cheered by a good attendance as he walked up the House with his bill. Next day Churchill told Masterman: 'I am going to bring the Shops Bill in under the Ten Minutes Rule.' He did, though Charlie was down to pilot it. Winston bagged the limelight.[14]

Churchill's Aliens Bill, having had its permission-to-introduce First Reading, was scheduled to have its second reading (main debate) on 21 April. As a Ten Minutes Bill, it would face a hazard. To block such a bill an MP simply had to shout 'I Object!'. On its designated day the bill failed to appear. Presumably there were intimations. Churchill did not give up. He had an alternative route in mind.

Another Aliens Bill had appeared. Conservative Edward Goulding, a barrister, produced a 'Bill to Amend the Aliens Act 1905'. This was tougher than Churchill's. Every immigrant would have to register their residence, including changes of address. Churchill's margin notes on the Home Office copy indicate some degree of acceptance but with major alterations needed. The Liberal Party would not wear a requirement for address registration. Was there negotiation behind the scenes? This is unknown.[15]

On 28 April the Goulding and the Churchill bills were both up for second reading. The idea was that the two, having each been passed and committed to committee, would be looked at together and out of them would emerge a new Aliens Bill. For the Home Secretary, it was important that the Conservative bill, which was set to go first, was not voted down: if so, his own would be unlikely to make progress.

Opening the debate on his bill, Edward Goulding declared that London had become 'the sink of foreign human refuse'. Immigrants, he said, had practically monopolized tailoring, shoemaking, and cabinet-making, completely driving out British workers. He was at pains to deny anti-Semitism: 'I remember that one of the most brilliant leaders the Tory party ever had was a member of the Jewish race.' After the homage to Disraeli, Goulding berated the inadequacy of legal powers to expel criminal aliens. In a conclusion looking like dubious territory for the cooperation of a Liberal Home Secretary, he declared:

> If we continue to harbour every enemy of faith and patriotism, of public law and social peace, we shall allow a canker to grow and fester that will in time eat into the very heart of our country.[16]

Leading against the bill, Liberal Handel Booth, chairman of the Yorkshire Iron and Coal Company, disagreed with Goulding's claim that the spirit around it was not anti-Semitic. He was preparing the way for Churchill:

> ...If you strip this spirit from this Bill you will have very little left except what the Home Secretary is going to deal with in a much superior Bill.[17]

The speech of Charles Roberts seconding the rejection included a Liberal objection to the Goulding bill's clause requiring aliens not to be employed at less than the rate fixed by the Trade Board Act or the trade unions in the district:

> When it comes to platform speeches in the country, the air is rent with cries of the dangers of socialism, but you never see a Bill introduced from the Tory Benches which does not contain advanced socialistic propositions.[18]

What, one may wonder, would Liberals like Roberts think of some of Winston Churchill's dreams of state intervention?

The Parliamentary Labour Party now had a new leader. Ramsay MacDonald, a Scot who sat for Leicester, was often remarked on for his looks. He was slim, tallish, locks of greying hair with a quiff at the front, and a cartoon-friendly moustache. He was unequivocal about the Goulding Bill: 'we do not think that a single line of it will be of the least value.' However, he said that since the government was willing that it should go upstairs because it wanted to engraft its own bill on it, Labour MPs would be prepared, on that basis, 'to sit quietly whilst Mr Speaker puts the Question: That this Bill be now read a second time'. (If when the question was put, there was verbal assent and no shout against it, the bill would proceed to committee without a vote.) MacDonald then blasted the bill's proposed registration system:

> This colossal system of police registers, compelling law-abiding, decent aliens to go in hundreds to the nearest police stations to register their names, is a proposal absolutely alien to the most fundamental conceptions of English civic liberty.[19]

MacDonald was a great orator when he had Parliament's ear. Winston Churchill, speaking later in the debate, called him 'my honourable friend', an appellation certainly not applied by him to Keir Hardie. He spoke of MacDonald's 'controversial brilliance'. Was this qualified plaudit offered with a view to future joint working? JRM did like to cooperate with the Liberals, getting himself into trouble with some in his own party. However, this was long-term Labour strategy.

The Home Secretary dangled some concessions to the Conservatives, including lowering the number of aliens constituting an immigrant ship. He said:

> My predecessor used that power in regard to a line of steamers, which was regularly sending in a consignment of German gipsies, who were causing a great deal of inconvenience. I myself recently have lowered the number in regard to certain vessels which were bringing in a too persistent stream of Chinese. I think it very undesirable that a large Chinese population should grow up in this country – on every ground, moral, racial, social, industrial.[20]

After these casual racial swipes, and a mention of the new Port of London receiving house, Churchill went on:

> The Government Bill in one respect even goes beyond the proposal of the hon. Member. We propose to increase the penalties on persons who return to this country after they have been expelled.

He also mentioned a prospective Pistol Bill to restrict gun ownership. But he was against expelling immigrants to make more room. He called this department of the bill:

> …very harsh measures to take against some person who had long been living here, just because he is overcrowded through the landlord's fault, or the failure of the authorities to put into operation the Public Health Acts; to expel him in his old age to a country which to all intents and purposes has become to him a foreign country.

It had become clear that there were plenty of Liberals who would shout for a vote even if the Labour Party sat quietly – which they did not. The result was: 118 in favour; 84 against (including MacDonald). The stage was set for Churchill's bill to have its debate and presumably to be sent upstairs to join that of Goulding. It is regularly stated that the Churchill bill passed to the committee stage, where it ran out of time. That is not so. What happened is recorded in Hansard:

> … Question proposed, 'That the [Churchill] Bill be now read a second time.'
> Sir F. BANBURY
> I object.
> Mr CHURCHILL
> Surely the hon. Baronet is not going to object to this Bill after the other Bill has been read a second time?
> Sir F. BANBURY
> Certainly I am. I voted against the other Bill.
> Mr CHURCHILL
> Oh, very well.[21]

Sir Frederick Banbury had spoken in the Goulding debate, at some length. He thought that the Goulding bill's clause requiring trade-union rates of pay for alien workers had the smack of socialism. Banbury, sixty, Conservative MP for the City of London, was Chairman of the Great Northern Railway. Sharply moustached and of impeccable formal attire, this champion of the old school was a scourge of Ten Minutes Rule bills.[22]

Churchill's plans were in disarray. The following week, Liberal Joseph King asked when the Home Secretary intended to move the second reading of his Aliens Bill. King commented that many MPs who backed the Goulding bill would not have done so had they known that it was not going to be joined in committee by the Churchill bill.[23]

The day after the aliens debate a Liberal wrote to Winston Churchill to remind him that it was, 'entirely contrary to the practice of old-fashioned Liberalism to get into panics and manifest this hostility to foreigners.' Henry Wilson, 78 years old, a Sheffield industrialist, represented Holmfirth in the non-conformist heartland of Yorkshire's West Riding. His *Dod's Parliamentary Companion* entry declared that he was: 'A Radical, opposed to Aggressive Foreign Policy, Militarism, Protection etc'. His causes included temperance and the disestablishment of the Anglican Church. He was the full-ticket traditional Liberal. Churchill, who was supposed to be a banger of the drum for the traditions of the Liberal Party, had to respond. His return letter said:

> ...I am glad myself that the Bill has got a second reading, not because I agree with it and its clauses, but because I see a prospect of using it as a vehicle to carry the provisions of the Government Bill on the same subject into law.[24]

He said that he had no desire to show hostility to foreigners ('you do me an injustice'), but he thought that further measures were needed to deal with alien crime. He added:

> There are some aspects of the purely artificial and commercial form of alien immigration which undoubtedly need to be corrected.

That would give scope for going beyond 'alien crime' into Goulding territory, the restriction of immigration itself.

The Goulding Bill did not emerge from the committee. The Home Secretary abandoned his attempts to bring in legislation to amend the 1905 Aliens Act. What had been his motives? The titles of the clauses of his bill – 'Powers of expulsion and arrest'; 'Restriction of firearms'; and so on – stress its criminal-control nature. On the other hand, there is the phrase 'criminal *or undesirable* aliens'. There is the impression of the Home Secretary edging into the waters of immigrant control politics. His position was raising questions.

Chapter 15

The Dartmoor Shepherd

Winston Churchill's first prison visit, five weeks into office, was to Parkhurst, Isle of Wight. His inspection tour will have fixed in his head the standard thirteen-feet-by-seven cell, with its viewless, barred window. Parkhurst was one of the four male 'convict prisons' (the others being Portland, Dartmoor, and Maidstone). Here longer-term prisoners worked in gangs. Parkhurst took physically and mentally weak men. Churchill looked at its asylum and hospital. Then he went to Parkhurst Forest to look at Camp Hill, the preventive detention establishment under construction. Its sixteen ft high outer wall was complete.[1]

His next trip was to Pentonville. Opened in 1842, this North London prison was the archetype of cellular isolation, with its central hall and radiating wings each with cells on different levels. With surveillance from the centre, the arrangement epitomized Victorian penal control, physical and mental. Winston Churchill aimed to make the system more civilized. Clean-sweep change was impossible but he was determined to do what he could. These days, Pentonville was used mainly for short sentences arising out of Metropolitan court cases. A recent jail census recorded 1,174 (male) prisoners. Each cell contained a bed-board, wash-basin, sanitary pot, shelf for toilet articles, slate, and Bible. It was here where executioners were trained.[2]

Churchill's 28 September 1910 visit was part of his investigation into youth imprisonment. He arrived in the evening, 'quite unexpectedly', the press reported. Accompanied by Charles Masterman and a Prison Commissioner, he interviewed forty young prisoners. The politically unfriendly *Dundee Courier* spun the Home Office's press release:

> ...[Churchill] heard [the prisoners'] stories, and as they promised to amend their ways if their punishments were remitted, the Home Secretary, touched by their contrition, arranged for immediate remission of their sentences. That he has time, in the midst of his multifarious duties, to perform a little deed of kindness is to the credit of this rather erratic statesman. Mayhap he had in mind when he extracted promises from the unfortunate young men that they were, like some of his own promises, made to be broken.[3]

Lucy Masterman's diary preserves fragments of the conversations:

> They readily confessed their crimes, and never attempted to assert that they had not committed them, or that the police were down on them. "What

are you in for?", Winston asked of one. "Stealing £6 17s 4d, Sir". Winston asked the same question of another lad, and was told "Assault": "What sort of assault?". "Brutal assault, Sir," replied the prisoner cheerfully. Winston is very interested in the subject of boy prisoners, and their case, in spite of the Borstal systems and the [Children Act], is undoubtedly scandalous. A great number of boys were in prison merely for sleeping out, that is, having no homes; and more for what was put down as "obscene language", which in most cases was nothing more than putting out their tongues at the police.[4]

The Pentonville remissions sparked an adjournment debate in the Commons, on 21 February 1911. Lord Winterton accused Churchill of 'usurping the functions of the judiciary' and pursuing 'the humanitarianism of the crowd'. He thought he knew how the Home Secretary had made his selection:

Did the right hon. Gentleman simply ask for a list of prisoners and with the aid of a lead pencil and with closed eyes select certain names? Did he, as I have reason to believe, merely remit the sentences of those whom he happened to interview?[5]

Another Conservative, Alfred Lyttelton, saw in Churchill 'a Home Secretary who has had about three weeks' experience in criminal law, goes to the prison, makes a cursory investigation, and then advertises the fact in every newspaper in the country'. Churchill was on his feet to say: 'I never mentioned a word about it to any single human being outside the Home Office.' Lyttleton retracted (though presumably Churchill will have arranged or authorized the press release). The Home Secretary gave Parliament his own account:

I visited in order to see the prisoners of the juvenile division. I saw about forty. I found sixteen cases which appeared to me to merit investigation. After a prolonged process of sifting, both on the spot and subsequently with the magistrates who convicted and with the police authorities, I arrived at the decision that in seven cases certain reductions might be permitted. I wanted to draw the attention of the country to the terrible evil by which 7,000 or 8,000 lads of the poorer classes are sent to gaol every year for offences which, if the Noble Lord had committed them at college, he would not have been subjected to the slightest degree of inconvenience. The sentences appeared to be of a kind on which some remission might justifiably be made. Robert Hall, 18, was convicted in September for using obscene language-

Hansard here has:

Earl WINTERTON
Does the right hon. Gentleman suggest that that is a kind of crime which I would have committed at [New College, Oxford]?

Mr CHURCHILL
Nothing is further from my mind than to suggest that. Robert Hall was fined seven shillings [35p] with the option of seven days' imprisonment. I said he might be released, without consulting a magistrate but not until after inquiry of the police. There is no obligation whatever on the part of the Home Secretary to consult a magistrate in the exercise of the prerogative. The next case was that of a lad of 20 who was convicted for travelling on the railway without a ticket and sentenced to pay a fine of twenty shillings [£1] or go to prison for fourteen days. I found that he had been for fourteen miles by road in search of work. Very improperly he came back by train without a ticket. He had served seven days, and I thought that was sufficient: he had no previous convictions. In the cases of those who were undergoing very short sentences I did not consult a magistrate, but I did so with the longer sentences. The next was a youth of twenty convicted of loitering. His sentence was one month. I released him without consulting a magistrate. The next was a youth of seventeen, convicted for obscene language. Again I make no reference to the Noble Lord. The lad had been sentenced to fourteen days' imprisonment, and if he had belonged to the wealthier classes, he would have paid the fine without the slightest difficulty. The last case is one of one month passed upon a youth of twenty, for loitering outside a railway station, probably in the hope of getting a bag to carry. I saw all the young prisoners in Pentonville Prison. I earnestly hope to introduce legislation which will give us a different method of punishing these young boys who commit offences for which in no other walk of life would they receive the stigma of being classed with what the Noble Lord, with his loose mode of talking, calls the convicts of the country.

Rising from his bench was the bony frame of Lord Hugh Cecil. The member for Oxford University called the Home Secretary: 'the cheap actor playing to the gallery below the gangway…the language of the vulgarest demagogue'. Demagoguery was a charge sometimes levelled at Churchill and Lloyd George. It was put in a more friendly way by A.G. Gardiner:

> Mr Lloyd George and Mr Churchill are as popular as music-hall artists, men who love the platform and delight in intimate intercourse with the crowd, who draw their intercourse direct from the democracy…[6]

In late October 1910, Churchill headed west to the convict prison at Princetown, Devon, generally known as Dartmoor, where once Napoleonic War prisoners were held. The expedition was remembered by Harold Butler. He had anticipated an undisturbed office morning, calculating that the chief could not possibly be back until later in the day. He was wrong. Just after 11 a.m. he heard 'the furious buzzing of [Churchill's] bell [in his own room to summon him to Churchill's office]'. The

Home Secretary had returned: 'spruce and debonair in his grey frock-coat with a sheaf of minutes and directions dictated in the train, all on fire to translate the impressions of his trip into action'. The awed civil servant later looked up early-morning trains. Butler can be shown to have jumped to the wrong conclusion. *The Times* published an itinerary. Churchill, accompanied by Lloyd George and his wife, stayed at the Devonshire residence of Liberal MP George Lambert: the two ministers, having dined at the jail with its governor, returned to London the evening before Butler was startled. Churchill had presumably breakfasted at Eccleston Square. The show which fooled Butler made the intended impression.[7]

Why did Churchill take Lloyd George? Was the Home Secretary demonstrating to the Chancellor of the Exchequer the financial needs of the prison service? No doubt so, but there was another reason, relating to the forthcoming General Election. A month later Lloyd George was at Mile End in East London. This was hallowed ground: near here in July 1909 LG made his famous Limehouse Speech, denouncing the oppression of the poor by the ruling-classes and proclaiming his People's Budget. His oratory was magnetic. One who once experienced it and never forgot was Robert Graves (in 1916):

> The power of his rhetoric amazed me...I had to fight hard against abandoning myself with the rest of his audience.[8]

Now the Chancellor spoke of his Devon trip:

> My friend the Home Secretary and I paid a visit to Dartmoor. On that bleak mist-sodden upland I saw an old man of 65 in convict garb. He had been sentenced to thirteen years' penal servitude because, under the influence of drink, he had broken open a church poor-box and stolen 2s [10p]. The next time I am called a thief and a robber because I venture to propose a tax upon the wealthy and spare the poor, I will say, 'you are living well upon the proceeds of the church poor-box emptied by your ancestors.'[9]

The pathos was enhanced as more detail emerged. The prisoner worked as a shepherd. He loved his sheep. He knew them all. He was charming. His name was David Davies.

Parliament was not yet dissolved. Newspaper reports brought questions for the Home Secretary about the Dartmoor shepherd. Churchill told MPs that Davies had been convicted many times during the last 40 years; he had been sentenced at Shropshire Quarter Sessions last October to three years' penal servitude for the poor-box theft; on his pleading guilty to being an habitual criminal he had received a further ten years' preventive detention. 'The most serious and severe sentence ever imposed under the system of preventive detention', said the Home Secretary He said that he would use the Royal Prerogative to release the man in the course of the next few months; meanwhile endeavours were being made to secure him employment as a shepherd: he was 'the most skilful shepherd ever known at Dartmoor'.[10]

Davies was released on 6 January. *The Times* reported that a place had been found for him as a shepherd, with the stipulation that he could not leave within six months without Home Office permission. The paper added, not helpfully for Churchill and Lloyd George, that Davies was said to have been 'quite contented' at Dartmoor. The facilitator of his new job – at Ruthin, Denbighshire – was Lloyd George.[11]

The happy ending started to come unstuck. On 11 January *The Times* reported that 'the old shepherd of Dartmoor…left on Sunday [8 January] without permission and has not been heard of since.' A letter-writer in the paper asked whether the release was 'part of a settled policy of rendering nugatory the 1908 Prevention of Crime Act, just as the Aliens Act was emasculated by departmental rules?'[12]

As police hunted for the absentee herder, mockery was likely for Churchill and Lloyd George when the new Parliament assembled. The government could ride it out, provided that the Dartmoor Shepherd did not go back to thieving.

On 16 January a retired judge wrote to *The Times*. Sir Alfred Willis in 1895 had sentenced Oscar Wilde to two years' hard labour for 'acts of gross indecency with other male persons', a tariff (the maximum) that he called 'most inadequate'. The penal servitude enthusiast had provided assistance in 1907 to a person trying to enable Davies to emigrate to Texas when he was discharged. Willis gave his impressions of Davies:

> Once in prison he was quiet, docile and harmless – a model prisoner – but he had an incurable mania for theft, generally petty. When released he expected soon to be back again, and his expectations were always satisfied. He never committed any act of violence.

Willis thought that Davies was ideal for preventive detention:

> Even the rigours of penal servitude are not painful to him, and under the less rigorous discipline which the Home Secretary has it in his power to lay down for preventive detention he will probably pass a healthful and happy old age.

He asked, 'Is it not lamentable that two Cabinet Ministers should select such a case as this for the exercise of a useless and mischievous clemency?'[13]

On the other side of the argument was ex-chaplain of Wandsworth Prison, William Morrison, who thought that:

> One of the principal reasons this country is so free from serious crime is that our criminal law has in the main the great sanction of public opinion behind it. Invaluable assets of social order are thrown away every time a sentence is inflicted which violates the average sentiments of the community.[14]

With Willis in *The Times* disputation was correspondent Q.S., who thought that sympathy for criminals meant a lack of concern for victims. Also against Churchill was his serial critic Edward Pickersgill. A letter from the MP to *The Times* heaped praise on Willis as 'a just and merciful judge', a description which would have interested Oscar Wilde.[15]

Churchill now issued a statement, published by *The Times* on 27 January. David Davies, he said, was among cases presented for his perusal in his investigation of sentencing:

> In the whole list of about 120 persons convicted up till then as habitual, there was no crime so petty, and since the passing of the [1908 Prevention of Crime] Act there have been only two sentences so long.

He detailed Davies' convictions, dating back to 1870. Offences included larceny, burglary and sacrilege:

> The burglaries were not daring or professional, the criminal was not armed, the amounts were very small, and there was no crime of cruelty or violence. The convict had been a nuisance but not a danger to society…His last sentence of 13 years, for a man of 67, was to all intents and purposes a life-sentence. In his own words he would 'never see liberty again'.

He had found a Prisoner's Petition, dated 19 October 1909, begging for a reduction of sentence. Davies was sore: 'scores of people, even policemen, have asked me, "Whatever possessed the judge to pass such a sentence?"' The Home Secretary went on:

> Everything I learned confirmed me in my intention, and on my return to London I directed that the convict should be informed officially that he would presently be released on licence.

Churchill took issue with Sir Alfred Willis' notion of preventive detention providing a content old age. Accommodation was not 'a home of refuge from whose cloistered seclusion aged sinners may placidly, contentedly, healthfully and happily watch the sunset of life'. Jail was jail. The shepherd was not among the 'dangerous and brutal criminals whose passions of predatory violence or ferocious lust render them a peril and an affront to civilised society'.

Sir Alfred had another go. He was hurt by 'a very unfair perversion of my observation': he had been referring to David Davies alone, 'an exceptional person'. He thought that had Davies not qualified for preventive detention he would have had repeated ordinary sentences.[16]

Another legal eagle weighed in. Mr Justice Grantham remarked to Lancaster Assizes Grand Jury in February 1911:

> No doubt you will have heard of the celebrated individual who has obtained worldwide reputation because of the intervention of a gentleman very high in His Majesty's Government…

The former Conservative MP was known for upsetting groups (publicans, miners, fellow-judges) with his observations. At these assizes he had before him Margaret Kerrigan, sixty-two, charged with attempted suicide. Margaret had forty-seven previous convictions for drunkenness and small thefts. The judge saw a parallel with the Dartmoor Shepherd, both being individuals who could not take care of themselves, for whom extended detention was beneficial. He gave Kerrigan two years' penal servitude. On 2 May, Winston Churchill answered a question about the case from Liberal lawyer Harold Baker. He had news:

> I have been able, I am glad to say, to make arrangements for this woman's being, with her own consent, removed to an inebriate reformatory, a more suitable place for her than prison.[17]

Margaret was rescued from jail, but it is not known how happy the outcome was for her. The Inebriates Act of 1898 allowed for indeterminate detention of up to three years for drink-related offences, to be served after the sentence for the offence. Inebriate institutions were run on 'spiritual, moral and educational' lines, as a Prison Commission report put it. Sir Evelyn Ruggles-Brise's 1921 book speaks of 'disgrace and contamination' regarding the inmates. Winston Churchill's attitude was very different but his approach had contradictions. Prisoner classification on which he was so keen, had scope for indefinite detention. However, as Victor Bailey points out, Churchill was not prepared to depart too far from the classical nineteenth-century notion of punishment needing to be proportionate to the crime. His position was: 'I am opposed in principle to indeterminate detention except on purely medical grounds.'[18]

The shepherd affair, following on Sidney Street, was not conducive to the Home Secretary's dignity. Spoof letters from the runaway sheep-tender appeared in the *Penny Illustrated Paper*. Digs and snipes in the new Parliament kicked off in Arthur Balfour's previously mentioned speech in the Debate on the Address. The Conservative leader was careful not to seem to be opposing prison reform, saying that he did not want to return to 'the old indiscriminate methods of brutality which happily have long been abolished'. But he had some advice for the Home Secretary on use of the prerogative of mercy:

> It should be rigidly consistent and not deflected either to the right or to the left by any of those considerations of the interesting or the picturesque, which are apt perhaps to influence imaginative souls to an undue extent.[19]

The political advertising of a prisoner release at election time (Lloyd George's error rather than Churchill's) had badly misfired. The convention that penal administration should not be a party issue had been beneficial for recent prison reforms, and so far, Churchill's measures had been opposed only by a reactionary fringe. If the mainstream harmony were damaged by a rumpus, the Home Secretary might find his penal reform programme harder to put through.

A flurry of shepherd questions on 8 February looked like a Conservative ambush. Sir Henry Dalziel's attempt to help Churchill by asking 'whether the granting of freedom to this old man has done any harm', let in a Conservative to remark: 'it did a lot of good at election time.' The Tory Lords below the opposition gangway piled in, Viscount Wolmer wanting to know whether the owner of the farm would be 'supplied with another person'.

The chortles and the banter were embarrassing for the Home Secretary. On 20 February a new angle offered hope of relief. Churchill told MPs:

> In certain quarters of the district a strong suspicion is entertained that the man has been enticed away for some political purposes.[20]

Churchill saw a 'political dodge'. Was the flight of the shepherd a Tory plot? Now the Irish Nationalists entered the fun, William Redmond inquiring whether Davies had been 'engaged to lecture for Tariff Reform'. Churchill remarked wearily about 'satire'.

On 5 April, as reported in *The Times*, the shepherd story took another turn:

> David Davies…was brought up at Oswestry Police Court yesterday, charged with stealing four bottles of whisky.

Davies had become a media celebrity. A week later it was reported that:

> The prisoner, who came into court smiling, was represented by Mr Bowdler, instructed to defend by a London daily newspaper.[21]

On 19 April, a shepherd question from a Conservative was sharper than the regular ones. William Bridgeman, whose Oswestry constituency gave him an interest in the Davies case, and who one day would himself be Home Secretary, asked whether:

> … any representation was made to [Churchill] before the visit paid by him and the Chancellor of the Exchequer to Dartmoor, that the case of David Davies required revision?[22]

Churchill's reply was straightforward. Mentioning the convict's petition, he said:

> I decided to review the sentence more than four months before I visited Dartmoor with the Chancellor.

Lloyd George's quaint picture of two cabinet ministers bumping into the shepherd amid the Dartmoor mists, was misleading. The pre-arranged nature of the meeting with the prisoner is confirmed by a biography of the convict two years after his death. As Davies told an acquaintance, he was summoned to the Governor's office, where 'two very nice gentlemen' were waiting to see him. One of them told him: 'I am Mr Winston Churchill and this is Mr Lloyd George.' For a Home Secretary to meet in person a prisoner whose sentence he was reviewing was unheard of. There were the Churchill interviews with Pentonville prisoners but these were part of an investigation of youth imprisonment. Conservative charges that the Dartmoor Shepherd was used politically by the Liberals at election time had some basis. The scene of two cabinet ministers sitting in a prison office waiting to meet a convict must have been one of Dartmoor Jail's more remarkable moments. Lloyd George suffered with Churchill in the fall-out of the misfiring publicity wheeze. The Chancellor wrote to Charles Masterman on 3 February: 'The Tory press have behaved like cads.' According to a Clementine comment in later years, Winston was 'very angry and complained bitterly to Lloyd George.' It was an unhappy episode.[23]

What about the claimed Tory plot? Churchill soon had to discount it, telling the Commons:

> I am glad to say that nothing has come to my knowledge which confirms the opinion held in certain quarters that he was enticed away for a political purpose.

David Davies was sentenced on 5 July to nine months' imprisonment. He lived eighteen more years. He was found dead by a roadside in Montgomeryshire, having escaped from a workhouse, wearing slippers. His minor celebrity had continued during these years but also his inmate status, in one form or another – and he had made another attempt on a poor-box. What was the effect of Churchill's entry into Davies' life? The subject features in the autobiography of the Governor of Lewis Prison, Major Wallace Blake, whose memory of Churchill's administration drips with sarcasm:

> During my sojourn at Lewis, the country was favoured with the services of a most energetic and zealous Home Secretary; one moreover who knew more about prisons than all the Commissioners, Governors, warders and convicts put together…An example of the zeal of this Secretary of State was continually to chop and change the standing orders.[24]

Blake's entertaining pen is unfair on Churchill. With the logjams in the government's legislative programme, standing orders were the Home Secretary's chief means of putting through reforms. WSC stretched this administrative outlet. The major's version of the Dartmoor Shepherd was:

> …I remember in particular how he incurred the undying hatred of one old lag who was perfectly happy in tending flocks on Dartmoor, by giving him

both his undesired freedom and the trouble of having to rob a church in order to get back 'home' to his beloved sheep.

The mishmash is a travesty. Whether Blake had any knowledge of Davies subsequently hating Churchill is doubtful. It must be remembered that Davies himself had appealed to the Home Office for release.

By the summer of 1911 the shepherd row was fading, though inevitably the mishap would be paraded by the opposition in the yearly Home Office debate in June. By then there would be graver matters for Churchill's attention.

Chapter 16

A Day in Court

Winston Churchill knew about the inequity of the jury system. Juries (all male until 1920) were class-skewed. This was raised by a deputation to the Home Office of the Parliamentary Committee of the Trades Union Congress in mid-March 1911. Churchill's reported reply caused lawyer Conservative Reginald Neville to ask him in Parliament about his comment that:

> ...the jury system in this country has long departed from the thoroughly old-fashioned British democratic theory on which it has been based.

Neville wanted to know (in what spirit is not clear) whether the Home Secretary 'proposes to take any steps to deal with the matter?' Churchill's reply was guarded:

> The juries in the Superior Courts are almost entirely drawn from one or two special classes, and wage-earners are practically excluded. I think it will be desirable that before legislation is undertaken the whole question should be the subject of an inquiry.[1]

The TUC delegate who complained about juries wanted workmen on them, with adequate payment. His particular grievance was that:

> When we offend a large firm and some of our men are prosecuted, a special jury is called and some of its members may be the greatest shareholders in the company which is proceeding against the men.[2]

Churchill was supportive: qualification for special juries 'ought not to turn on the rateable value or the number of windows in a person's house'. On payment of jury members, he said:

> The present law engages the payment of a guinea per day to a special juryman and nothing at all to the common juror, who may be a poorer man. I am glad that the Trade Union Congress have brought the matter up.

Class weighting was blatant. In a Home Office file covering this period, a pasted extract from *Justice of the Peace* magazine outlines the qualification for special juries: 'esquires and persons of higher degree, bankers or merchants; persons occupying private dwelling houses rated at not less than...' Newspaper reports of the swearing-in of grand juries at the county assizes are full of gentry-suggestive addresses and titles.[3]

In his reply to the TUC delegation, Churchill sympathized with complaints about the utterances of judges about trade-unionists:

> It is true that on several occasions statements have been made from the Bench reflecting on trade unions in language which is extremely ignorant (hear, hear) and wholly out of touch with modern thought.[4]

Churchill explained that judges were the Lord Chancellor's territory. He gave no indication that he would be getting involved personally with trying to make the legal system more democratic.

Court bias was raised with the Home Secretary in Parliament by David Shackleton. An employer who summoned workmen to court might be a client of the legal clerk who advised the magistrates; if a factories or mines inspector were prosecuting an employer for mistreatment of workers, the same unfairness might apply. Churchill shared his concern but said that he had no power in the matter. A Conservative Member suggested that the Home Office could send a circular to magistrates. Churchill promised to look into the idea. It was an obvious one. He regularly used such circulars.[5]

Winston liked to get around. On Monday morning, 17 October 1910, a distinguished trio descended on Lambeth Police Court. Usually, it was the accused who were nervous. Today the magistrate, Arthur Hopkins, may have had butterflies as officials ushered to seats flanking him, Winston Churchill, Charles Masterman, and Ernley Blackwell. The press, pre-alerted no doubt, reported on the court's morning session:

> From time to time the Home Secretary made some whispered comment to [Hopkins] during the progress of the typical Monday morning cases of assault, disorderly conduct and the like, and his sympathetic attention was particularly noted while the mother of a poor boy who was charged with theft was giving her evidence.[6]

Next day it was the turn of the chief Metropolitan Police Court. Observing the Bow Street proceedings were Clementine Churchill and Edward Marsh. The two and Winston were of the same social provenance. At one of the Season's balls, as Eddie and Winston watched young ladies making their entrances, they assessed how many ships each woman would launch. In this take on Marlowe only Diana Manners and Clementine (then Hozier) scored the full thousand, First, Clementine was in the lower court, watching with close interest cases 'not of an exciting character'. Then she moved to the upper one, presided over by London's chief magistrate, Sir Albert de Rutzen, 80 years old, of part-German descent. Here she was 'accommodated with a seat at counsel's table', the reporter observed with fascination. These proceedings had more drama. There had been a police raid on a gaming-house in Bloomsbury High Street. Clemmie's thoughts may have strayed to her husband's penchant for the Monte Carlo roulette wheel.

Home Office crime statistics give some background on convictions for betting offences. There were different categories. In 1908, under the Vagrancy Acts there were 1,971 convictions for 'Gaming', whilst under 'Betting and Gaming (Gaming Houses, Lotteries etc)', there were 466. The resulting average prison populations were 156 and 62 respectively. Winston Churchill's social class meant that his gambling addiction had legal outlets.[7]

Clementine was seen around with her husband officially: at prisons, police events, now a magistrates' court. At election time she made speeches. To the public eye, she was a devoted supporter of Winston's politics. Differences were strictly out-of-sight. These were significant. The independent-minded Clemmie used to be a women's suffrage activist, often dressing in the movement's uniform of collar-and-tie.[8]

In the summer of 1911, there was unpleasantness on the London magistrate scene. Metropolitan magistrate Cecil Chapman, Arthur Hopkins's Lambeth colleague, outraged Police Commissioner Sir Edward Henry with a letter. Chapman was associated with the committee of the Men's League for Women's Suffrage. This was organizing 'a corps of witnesses', to monitor any repeat of Black Friday. The invitation to league members to sign up was enclosed. The Commissioner called the letter 'threatening'. He wrote to his opposite number at the Home Office, Sir Edward Troup.[9]

Troup shared Henry's indignation. The clash of interests for Cecil Chapman, as both magistrate and guardian of suffragettes, if cases came before him in the aftermath of violent confrontation at a demonstration, would be intolerable. Troup's suggestion was that the chief magistrate should point this out to Chapman and ask him to withdraw from participation in the work of any female suffrage society. The matter went to Winston Churchill. He had previously supported Chapman over a complaint from a Liberal MP. The magistrate apparently had fined a 15-year-old boy ten shillings (half £1) for loitering on the approach to London Bridge railway station: unable to pay, the boy had been given seven days' hard labour at Wandsworth Prison. Churchill put a different complexion on it: the boy had been charged three times recently with similar offences and had been treated leniently; the magistrate thought that he was over 16; he was out of the control of his parents; the sentence did not carry hard labour. The Home Secretary added however that he had sent a reminder to magistrates that under the 1908 act under-16s were not to be sent to prison.[10]

Churchill wanted Chapman dealt with. He put it bluntly to Troup:

> Failing a satisfactory explanation and immediate withdrawal, my intention is that he should be dismissed forthwith. Pray consider the steps.[11]

Troup wrote to the magistrate. Chapman confirmed that the signature under the appeal for a corps of witnesses was his. He seemed not to realize that he was in serious trouble. He assured Sir Edward that the surveillance was no reflection upon the police: his committee's 'gentlemen and ladies in the streets' were intended to be helpful to the authorities.

Troup urged caution upon Churchill. A police magistrate *could* be removed by the King on the recommendation of the Home Secretary, but this would be 'a grave step'. The permanent under-secretary suggested firstly a letter to the magistrate. This was drafted, with heavy re-working: strong words about suffragettes did not make it into the final version. The communication, sent by Troup on Churchill's behalf, called on Chapman for an immediate and unqualified withdrawal of his letter to the Police Commissioner and for him in future to 'abstain from all such conduct':

> Failing this [the Home Secretary] will be unable to consider your retention of your present position as being in accordance with the public interest.[12]

Chapman got the message. He wrote back: 'I have no hesitation in at once withdrawing [the letter] in an unqualified manner.' He would cease involvement with the Men's League. He followed up with a personal visit to the Home Office. A Troup minute stated that, 'Mr Chapman called this morning in a very humble state of mind.' The climb-down saved the magistrate. Troup advised Churchill, in view of Chapman's 'complete submission', that his withdrawal of his letter and his assurances for the future should be accepted. 'I agree', was Churchill's last file comment. Chapman will not have taken lightly the threat of expulsion from the list of the thirty Metropolitan Police Court magistrates. The distinguished office carried an annual salary of £1,500.

There may be more to this than meets the eye. Cecil Chapman is on *Whitaker's* Metropolitan Police Court lists for 1910 and 1911, but missing from 1912, only to return in 1913 (for Tower Bridge). There is no more of him in the Home Office files after 1911 – except for one intriguing item. Churchill was gone from the Home Office a couple of years when a cutting of a Chapman letter to the *Observer* was pasted into his file. Written from the Athenaeum Club, its date is a week before the end of the ominous month of July 1914. In it the magistrate who three years earlier had been humbled at the Home Office, is striking back. Chapman is appreciating a retiring colleague. We hear the voice of Cecil as in the convivial company of fellow magistrates ('we know each other as comrades'), a man well regarded in his circle. The tone sharpens when he speaks of the colleague not having been awarded any honours during his career:

> ...studiously ignored by the Home Office, as all Metropolitan magistrates are, it is not surprising that one who was gifted with a keen sense of humour should have offended the solemn nonentities who might control his destiny.[13]

The 'solemn nonentities' presumably included Troup and Churchill. Chapman should have known that history can spring surprises.

Chapter 17
Peasants and Pheasants

Poaching convictions engaged politics. In the December 1910 General Election, the sitting Conservative at Newmarket, Cambridgeshire, George Verrall, a horse-racing official, lost his seat to the Liberals. He alleged dirty tricks. He had been on the bench when a poacher was given a month's imprisonment. He believed that Churchill had deliberately orchestrated feeling for Liberal election benefit. He wrote to *The Times*:

> The Home Secretary saw a fine chance of advertising himself. Although he had received all the details from the justices, he waited six and a half days before he telegraphed to let the man go free.[1]

Presumably the Liberals were stirring feelings by presenting a poacher trying to feed his family and being persecuted by a bench of landowner-favouring Tory magistrates.

The social background to poaching cases was the subject of parliamentary debate in 1911. The countryside was the playground of the rich. Recreational shooting of specially bred birds, particularly pheasants, was at an all-time peak. Half of agricultural land was subordinate to the requirements of hunting, shooting, and fishing. Winston Churchill was occasionally to be found at shooting parties. In December 1910 he was at Warter Priory in Yorkshire, where Lord and Lady Nunburnholme hosted earls and lords aplenty, including WSC's uncle Lord Tweedmouth. Winston wrote to Clemmie: 'Tomorrow pheasants in thousands – the vy best wot was ever seen…I expect I will have a headache tomorrow night after firing so many cartridges.' His shooting-card records 2,947 dead birds on the first day; 2,034 on the second.[2]

Less than a quarter of Britain's population now lived on the land. For rural dwellers who did not belong to the well-to-do classes, economic survival was a challenge. With the Liberal government's aspiration to redistribute wealth by means of land-tax legislation, the woods, fields, and halls of the gentry were hot politics. On 27 February 1911, Arthur Ponsonby described in his diary annoyance that he felt whilst walking near his home in Sussex: 'A delicious walk in the woods spoilt by the usual appearance of gamekeepers…preserving these absurd pheasants, to be shot by [shooting parties]…'[3]

The land reform campaign fuelled ire below the opposition gangway, where courtesy-title aristocrats like Viscount Helmsley (heir to the Earl of Feversham) yelled against measures that might diminish the value of land. Part of Winston

Churchill's soul was with the aristocratic shouters. Lloyd George once remarked to Charles Masterman: 'If we put a special clause in the Budget exempting Sunny from taxation, Winston would let us do what we liked.' Sunny was Charles Spencer-Churchill, Duke of Marlborough, Winston's cousin. Clementine disliked him. On one occasion at Blenheim, as she was replying to a telegram from Lloyd George, the Duke remarked, 'Please, Clemmie, would you mind not writing to that horrible little man on Blenheim writing-paper?' Clementine thereupon packed. She would not be assuaged by an apology. The incident hurt her the more because her husband made light of it.[4]

The magistrates' courts were seen by many as pro-gentry. Before them appeared men who raided the woods to augment their income. It was not a clear-cut matter of peasants-versus-pheasants justice, but for many hard-pressed rural families, food (or cash) gained from poaching could make a big difference to their domestic economy. A poaching case in March 1911 had the interest of Frederick Kellaway, newly elected Liberal member for Bedford, a journalist. At Towcester, Northamptonshire, footwear industry worker, George Townsend, resident of nearby Pattishall, was found guilty of poaching. He had previous convictions.[5]

Townsend was charged with 'Breach of the Poaching Prevention Act'. This legislation gave rural police stop-and-search powers. The man was challenged by two constables on a country road early on a frosty morning. He had a mongrel collie dog, the court heard; he and a friend were pushing bicycles; his trousers were muddy. The police thought that he had been in the fields after game. In his coat pocket was the stock of a gun; tied onto his cycle were the other parts of it. It had recently been fired. Townsend denied having left the road. His statement was confirmed by his friend – who however had poaching convictions. The accused man had a gun licence. He used his gun, he said, for (legally) shooting pigeons. The magistrates fined him one-pound-ten-shillings (£1.50) and ordered his gun to be destroyed. Winston Churchill's time-to-pay facility for fines was awaiting a legislation opportunity, but grace was sometimes given: Townsend had a month. If he did not pay, he would go to prison for a month's hard labour.[6]

Townsend did not deny being a poacher, but he was aggrieved about being convicted on suspicion alone. He had a large family and was currently in financial difficulty as a result of a doctor's bill of £4 for two of his children. If he went to jail, his family would face a month of great hardship. The loss of the gun removed a means of assisting his domestic economy. He followed politics and thought that Frederick Kellaway might be interested in his conviction. He sent the MP the details. Kellaway put down a question for Winston Churchill. Meanwhile columnist 'S.L.H.' of the *Morning Leader* delivered some wry points of advice: 'not to look as if you had been in a field; to live as far from Towcester as possible; to order yourself lowly and reverently to all your betters.' Spencer L. Hughes was Liberal MP for Stockport.[7]

Kellaway's question concentrated on the gun licence and the witness. He thought that the Home Secretary should suggest to the Lord Chancellor that the magistrates were unfit for office. Churchill in reply stated that he had communicated with the justices but had not yet received a reply. He added that, 'I have telegraphed to expedite matters.' The local newspaper recorded 'Liberal cheers'.[8]

Kellaway had a communication from Townsend asking him to put his letter 'before Mr Churchill as I shall either have <u>to pay or go to prison as next Tuesday</u> is the time allowed.' He said: 'I have a large family and it comes hard.'

At the Home Office William Byrne considered it doubtful whether evidence of a gun having been fired at game was sufficient for a breach of the Poaching Act. Edward Troup, whilst agreeing that the evidence was 'thin, rather hard lines', thought that since Townsend was almost certainly coming away after poaching, interference should be rejected.

Churchill wrote his decision on the Home Office file:

> The evidence does not justify the conviction. The previous record of the defendant is bad: but that should not have weighed with the J.J. [magistrates] in deciding guilt or innocence.
>
> Free Pardon[9]

A free pardon was rare: 4 in 1909; 2 in 1910. Judicial interventions by Home Secretaries usually took the form of remission. A free pardon made it as if the sentence had never been given. Churchill here was with the backbench Liberals on the side of a poacher against magistrates accused of being in the pocket of the dukes.[10]

The decision did not hold. Churchill had to tell Kellaway at question time on 3 May that:

> I do not feel able upon any information at my disposal to confirm or reverse the decision to which the justices came. The prisoner had a right of appeal to quarter sessions, and his previous record comprises fifteen convictions.

Kellaway came back:

> Is the right of appeal any use to a man like this who is working for a wage of from 15s. to 16s. [75p to 80p] per week, and did he not pay the penalty of his previous convictions?

Labour's John Ward jumped in:

> Are we to take it that the fact of a man going along a road with dirty trousers and a dog, and that he has been previously convicted, is sufficient to convict him again?[11]

Where had Churchill's U-turn come from? The answer is provided by the Home Office file. Edward Troup had told him:

> The H.O. never deals with such cases on technical questions of evidence, but only looks at the substantial question: was the accused guilty or innocent? It seems to me clear that he was guilty. He does not even say that he is innocent.[12]

George Townsend now disappears from the public record. If he went to jail, he will have joined an average daily total of 154 in prison for offences under the Game Laws. (There were 1,151 convictions in 1908.) Probably however, we may guess, the shoe operative and sometime poacher will have managed with difficulty to pay the fine.[13]

The magistrates sent in their report to the Home Office, making the points that the Townsend gun had been fired, that the accused had chosen not to go into the witness box, and that his companion's alibi for him was vague. They received in reply, on Churchill's behalf, the comment that, 'the evidence against Townsend as reported in your letter appeared of such a character that it would have been more satisfactory if the charge under the Poaching Prevention Act had been dismissed.' It was a clear rebuke.

The next day was historic. It saw the launch in Parliament of a process which in its due course would ease the insecurities of families like that of George Townsend, and many more. After question time, Winston Churchill's political ally the Chancellor of the Exchequer stepped to the Dispatch Box:

> I ask leave to introduce a Bill 'To provide for insurance against loss of health, and for the prevention and cure of sickness, and for insurance against unemployment, and for purposes incidental thereto.'[14]

It was the first reading of the National Insurance Bill, the forerunner of the welfare state. The work on the unemployment insurance part of it had been mostly done by Winston Churchill, whilst he was Trade Minister, for trades like building and engineering, which were subject to cyclical unemployment, WSC conjuring the phrase 'the magic of averages'. Insurance would be compulsory and unemployment benefit unconditional, provided that workers registered with the labour exchanges. There was no German precedent for this, unlike with other Liberal government social legislation. It took Britain into what Churchill called 'the untrodden field in politics'. Churchill's work was Part Two of the National Insurance Bill. Though he was now Home Secretary, with that portfolio's vast range of responsibilities, WSC was still involved in the work on National Insurance. On 25 May 1911 he would declare In Parliament: 'There is no proposal in the field of politics that I care more about.' The government aimed to take the social revolution further, with its plans for taxation to redistribute, to an extent, the benefits of land-ownership. As we have seen, Churchill, cousin of a duke, was wobbly about that but he would be out and about at the next General Election, whenever that was to be, proclaiming the virtue of land taxation from the platforms, cheered to the echo no doubt by his Liberal supporters. History knows that did not happen. Three years on from 1911 a runaway train would derail New Liberalism, and much else.[15]

Chapter 18
Reforming the Reformatories

In the spring of 1911 Winston Churchill was asked in Parliament by Liberal George Greenwood, barrister, and Shakespearean scholar, about a deer pursued by the Berks and Bucks Staghounds which struggled and broke two of its legs on a fence, before having its throat cut. This hunt was notorious locally. Greenwood asked whether Churchill would consider amending the acts for the prevention of cruelty to animals to bring hunting within their operation. The Home Secretary agreed about 'painful and repulsive' incidents but said that, 'with every wish to put a stop to them, it is impossible for me to introduce legislation to this end in the near future.' He was an occasional hunter himself. His *My African Journey* account of his railway trip in 1907 as colonial under-secretary from the coast to Uganda includes an animal-shooting spree. With wild life, there were the Churchill contradictions. George Riddell in a 1911 diary entry mentions a worm wriggling on the ground during a golf round:

> Winston tenderly picked it up and placed it in the bracken saying, "Poor fellow! If I leave you here, you will be trampled upon by some ruthless boot!"[1]

On 17 July 1911 William Byles asked Churchill about a sentence at Derby on labourer Charles Lee, under the Vagrancy Act, of twelve strokes with the birch in addition to six months' imprisonment. Had Churchill received a memorial from the Humanitarian League calling for an end to floggings under the Vagrancy Act? The Home Secretary said that the sentence was for indecent exposure 'with intent to insult females on the highway': his sanction was not required. He had received the memorial. Byles came back:
> Does the right hon. Gentleman not think that it calls for a repeal of the Vagrancy Acts when we have brutalising conditions like these?

Churchill replied: 'I cannot admit that.'
A fortnight later Byles pursued Churchill again on the subject of birching. Was the Home Secretary aware of: 'the sentence by Mr Justice Scrutton at Leeds Assizes of twenty-four strokes with the cat, in addition to imprisonment with hard labour, passed upon two prisoners, Richardson and Conlon.' He asked:
> whether the division of the corporal punishment into two doses of twelve strokes each, with an interval of three months for the flesh to heal, is so

novel a refinement of this form of punishment that he will use his powers to prevent at least the second instalment of the flogging from being carried out?

The Home Secretary said that nothing could be done until the appeal was heard, but he indicated that he would intervene: 'In previous cases I have remitted a second instalment of a flogging for the same offence'.[2]

In late October the *Leeds Mercury* reported:

> The "Humanitarian" announces that the Home Secretary has remitted the second instalment of the "double-dose" sentence of flogging.[3]

This was about the time of Churchill's departure from the Home Office. If he had left, it may be taken that he will have ensured that the second instalments were not administered.

Birching was chiefly a punishment for boys, widely supported. Flogging sentences for adults – restricted to males since 1820 – were these days uncommon enough to be newsworthy. There had long been a campaign for complete abolition, but flogging was seen as a way of registering society's disgust at exceptionally depraved behaviour. Some favoured its use as a means of suppressing outbreaks of violent robbery. Churchill was not an advocate of exemplary beating, nor was he one of those who wanted to extend flogging, but he did support its retention.[4]

Flogging of juveniles was raised ten days after Churchill took office. Josiah Wedgwood wanted more magistrate attendance at birching, presumably to monitor abuses. Churchill was vaguely positive but he was not disposed to have Home Office circulars sent. Hansard records a supplementary question from William Byles: 'Could not the right hon. Gentleman put an end altogether to this barbarous method of punishing children?' Churchill replied:

> I do not think I should be able to give my hon. Friend an answer which would be satisfactory to him.[5]

On 19 April 1910 John Muldoon asked the Home Secretary about rules for flogging. Churchill told him that there were no Home Office regulations, nor did he have power to make any: 'I believe that when a boy is birched it is usual to divest of clothing that part of his body on which the birching is administered.' Apparently, the rod was applied to the buttocks, though in jails the prisoner took the blows to his back, facing an apparatus. Churchill was misleading in giving the impression that he could not influence the manner of beating. In the 1880s, after a flogger thrashed two boys of 12 and 13 in prison with a whip that he had soaked in pickle, boasting that they would not be able to sit down for a month, the then Home Secretary had a circular distributed to prevent repetition. Corporal punishment was commonplace in the public and preparatory schools. Churchill reminisced that at his preparatory school, St George's, Ascot, the clergyman headmaster's beatings 'exceeded in severity anything that would be tolerated in any of the Reformatories under the Home Office.' Beating children was in the fabric of British life. The Home Secretary saw nothing amiss with judicial corporal punishment for juveniles, and occasionally for adults. Birching would continue to be available until 1948.[6]

On punishment beating in jails, Churchill was asked on 23 November 1910 by George Greenwood about a photograph in the French magazine *L'Illustration*, which a number of MPs had viewed, of a warder at London's Wormwood Scrubs demonstrating the procedure. Greenwood wondered with the deepest sarcasm whether the Home Secretary would 'give facilities for English journalists to take similar photographs in prisons for cinematograph exhibitions or otherwise, in order to provide the public with an object-lesson in flogging by the cat as carried out at His Majesty's prisons.' Churchill was on the backfoot: the journalist should have submitted his proofs to the Prison Commissioners; he should not have been allowed to use a warder. William Byles wanted to know, 'if the instruments photographed are actually in use in His Majesty's prisons.' Churchill replied:

> I do not know. I have not seen the photograph. My hon. Friend is well aware that flogging is occasionally, though very rarely, used in His Majesty's prisons.[7]

Flogging in prison turns up in the correspondence of Sir Edward Grey with Winston Churchill when he stood in for him. Grey told Churchill that Home Office business sent to him included signing a warrant for 'a flogging of 12 lashes to an incorrigible tramp who misbehaved in prison and when being removed to a punishment cell bashed one warder in the face with a pair of loose handcuffs, hit a second, and pulled a third to the ground by the testicles.'[8]

A week after his 'double dose' question, William Byles again inquired about flogging. The Recorder of Liverpool had sentenced a young man to twenty-five strokes of the birch in addition to twelve months with hard labour, for being an 'incorrigible rogue', under the Vagrancy Act. Churchill called the sentence 'very proper and salutary'. The man had been convicted of living off the prostitution earnings of a girl of fifteen. Byles complained that the Home Secretary had been giving the impression lately that anyone objecting to flogging must be in sympathy with the crime for which it was the penalty. Churchill vigorously denied this.[9]

In March 1911 a bill to ban the judicial whipping of offenders of over sixteen years was presented by Hay Morgan, Liberal member for Truro. The Home Secretary wrote tersely on the file: 'Block.'[10]

In March 1911 the Humanitarian League petitioned Churchill:

> The time has come for the repeal of the Vagrancy Act of 1824, which gives magistrates the power of punishing so called 'incorrigible rogues' – often old tramps convicted of begging, or labourers out of work – with severe sentences of flogging.[11]

The League's magazine congratulated William Byles on his recent award of a knighthood. This was not for his campaigning against the birch. There seemed little prospect of abolition in the foreseeable future. Churchill did nothing to raise any hope.[12]

Flogging featured in a reformatory scandal in early 1911. *John Bull* magazine had: 'Reformatory Horrors: How boys at the "Akbar" School are tortured – Several deaths.' The *Akbar* reformatory had originally been a ship. After the inmates set fire to it, the school went ashore on the Wirral. It was now called the Heswall. Winston Churchill sent in an investigation team, headed by Charles Masterman and Ernley Blackwell. This was odd. With the Home Office having responsibility for reformatories, these investigators could hardly be independent. Masterman's report made recommendations but not for the dismissal of the superintendent, Captain Beuttler. As a result, on 23 February there was an adjournment debate in Parliament. Llewellyn Atherley-Jones, who called it, said that his motion was not aimed at Churchill personally: the Home Secretary was inspired by 'the highest spirit of humanity'. Charles Masterman spoke for the Home Office. The *John Bull* claims were shocking: 27 boys with permanent scars from the use of a heavy cane with a split end bound by a whipcord; mouths stuffed with blankets to stifle cries; a boy having died on the day he was due to be beaten. The centrepiece of the indictments was an occasion when the whole school was made to stand until 5 a.m. Churchill had confidence that his parliamentary under-secretary would carry the House. In his parliamentary letter to the King that night, he called Masterman 'an extremely able minister…remarkable for an unusual combination of being a strong churchman and an admired Radical'. Winston, as Lucy Masterman put it, was 'an absolutely loyal chief'.[13]

Charles Masterman argued that whilst the novel punishments were wrong, nevertheless Beuttler had done a good job. He produced various evidence. His speech swung the House. The clincher was that Masterman trailed a wide-reaching inquiry into reformatories and industrial schools. Crucially, William Byles backed Masterman and Churchill. In his own speech, Churchill made it clear that he was not going to let the reformatories be run like Dickens's Dotheboys Hall:

> There is a great deal more flogging going on in reformatory schools than is necessary or desirable…I have been carefully considering the issue of new regulations to restrict the use of corporal punishment.

Physical sanctions would now have to be in accordance with Home Office regulations, with 'instruments which are approved and of standard pattern'; beating must not take 'the undesirable and excessive forms revealed in this report'. Churchill then used the word that had been so much in his mind lately:

> We must consider the question of classification, which as in the treatment of crime and its attendant problems, is the first necessary step to be taken.

He announced that:

> I have decided to appoint a strong Departmental Committee to go into the whole question of the present methods of maintaining discipline in reformatory and industrial schools.[14]

Atherley-Jones rose to ask permission to withdraw his motion, in the light of 'the very full vindication by the under-secretary and the assurance by the secretary of state'. Some MPs shouted for the vote to proceed. The result was:

Ayes: 67; Noes: 244.

Atherley-Jones and his seconder voted against their own motion. Ramsay MacDonald and his Labour colleagues were with the Home Office, as were the Irish Nationalists.

We have a glimpse of Churchill in the thick of the Heswall row in an Edward Marsh to Lady Gladstone letter:

> Charlie Masterman, I and Winston spent an amusing afternoon birching each other with the 'sealed pattern' birches, to see if they hurt. They didn't! but it will be awful if there is a birching scandal at the H.O. 'Brutal cruelty of a Minister to his Private Secretary' – or vice versa.[15]

A century on, the merriment rings hollow. But Churchill's promises were usually carried out and so it was here. Lucy Masterman records that the reformatories committee found 'a much varying but in many ways disconcerting state of affairs'. Radical change was set in train – another example of real and substantial reform instigated by Churchill during his time at the Home Office.[16]

Chapter 19

Never to be Prime Minister?

By the spring of 1911 Winston Churchill was irritating the Conservatives a lot. His prime ministerial ambition was plain. He was asking to be taken down. There were some, especially the sparky young courtesy-title Lords below the Commons gangway, who jumped at any opportunity. Churchill had taken on the responsibility of standing in for the prime minister as Leader of the House when Asquith was away from the chamber. H. H. dined well: His enemies referred to him as 'Squiff'. His post-prandial disability was a Westminster scandal, kept from the public. On 9 March 1911 Asquith had gone to his bed and WSC was minding the shop as the Commons sat as a Committee of the Whole House. A Revenue Bill was making its glacial progress. The Conservatives were trying to slow it even more, a game that Churchill knew from his opposition days. His job was to keep things moving.

Before disappearing, Asquith had given the Commons what some Conservatives took as a promise that if proceedings went too deep into the nocturnal hours, the bill would be adjourned. By midnight, Winston Churchill had the company of just one other minister on the government front bench. So far, the atmosphere had been reasonable. Then it changed. With the consent of the presiding Deputy Speaker, Harry Whitley (a Liberal – and future Speaker), Churchill engaged a 'kangaroo closure' procedure, which enabled Whitley to be selective in which amendments got a debate and a vote. The calm was gone. Arthur Balfour remarked darkly: 'the fuel for a disturbance is evidently here.' The arguments about whether Asquith had or had not promised an adjournment were turning vicious. About 3.30 a.m., as the parliamentary correspondent of the *Daily News* put it, 'the storm broke'. Churchill found himself in the midst of fury, hubbub and comedy.[1]

Some Tories were out to get him. The *Daily News* observed:

> The more belligerent element on the Tory side thought this a favourable chance for paying off some old scores; accordingly, they interrupted and yelled whenever Mr Churchill spoke.

Churchill years later would call the House of Commons debating chamber 'this little room'. It could be very intimate. When a 'scene' was on, there could be very personal exchanges. It made it worthwhile for bleary-eyed reporters to linger through the small hours of a tedious revenue debate. The papers carried extensive coverage of the Commons in their broadsheet small type and when drama occurred it made good copy.[2]

One interlude featured Lord Hugh Cecil, highest of High Tories, and Jeremiah MacVeagh, a popular Irish Nationalist member. MacVeagh ridiculed Cecil for his superior manner, dubbing him, Lord Castlereagh, and Lord Helmsley (a Churchill relation), 'the noble triplets'. This trio was working up trouble for WSC. As the Home Secretary was explaining to the House that should the Revenue Bill be held up, last year's Budget would be 'treading upon the toes of the next one', Cecil called across the chamber: 'There is no good reason for breaking a Parliamentary undertaking.' Churchill retorted that Cecil, 'always deals in taunts and insults.' There followed what the *Daily Mirror*'s correspondent called 'a torrent of shouts'. For five minutes the Home Secretary was silenced by the yells: 'Mr Churchill, pale, heavy-eyed and rumple-haired, glared angrily at Lord Hugh.' The Conservatives did not succeed in halting proceedings. The *Daily News* reported 'a resolute Minister at the table'.

The debate continued. As the clock ticked towards 4 a.m., Cecil launched a full-on character-assassination, charging Churchill with:

> …promise-breaking. Such a proceeding, if it involved pecuniary matters, would lead to prison. If done in the ordinary course of private life and intercourse, it would drive [the person] from the society of gentlemen.[3]

Conservative Stanley Wilson mocked Churchill as 'the future Prime Minister of England'. Hansard missed that but it recorded a sting from Wilson:

> I would like to remind [Churchill] that this is his first endeavour to lead the House of Commons. I do not think this is an auspicious beginning.[4]

The *Daily News* commented that:

> The early hours witnessed some of the most tempestuous scenes of recent years, recalling save for actual violence the exciting days of the great Home Rule debates in 1893.

The Churchill-baiting Lords were stirring the pot, with Lord Winterton making interventions of mischievous righteousness. The atmosphere was getting combustible. A crowd of MPs had gathered at the Bar of the House, the boundary of the chamber where they could watch without being part of the proceedings. At one point, as the *Daily News* reported, when someone in 'the Cecil quarter' shouted something at someone standing at the bar, the person 'raised his foot and pointed the toe of a long boot'. The Commons clock ticked on towards breakfast time. Winston's stamina sustained him. His purpose of blasting the clauses through did not flinch. It was a battle, a parliamentary Sidney Street. At the same time, he was composing his daily report to King George:

...In the absence of the Prime Minister Mr Churchill has had charge of the business; which is advancing to its proper conclusion. There has been a certain amount of ill-feeling during this prolonged debate, but the temperature is again now normal and the discussion is good. Your Majesty's faithful servant dutifully submits the above.[5]

The faithful servant will have chuckled at his editing. There was more tumult before either the letter or the debate was completed. At around eight o'clock another attempt was made to halt proceedings, this time by senior Conservative Austen Chamberlain, who denounced 'an outrage on Parliamentary procedure, a gross breach of faith, unparalleled in the long traditions of this House': fantastic hyperbole.

A sub-plot was the by-play between the Irish Nationalists and the Ulster Unionists, whose Captain Craig jumped in with what the *Mirror* called 'a militant offer' to the presiding Whitley:

> On a Point of Order. If it is any assistance to you, Mr Chairman, I shall put the whole Nationalist Party out of the House.

'Pandemonium' erupted on the Irish benches.[6]

As morning broke, Lords Winterton and Castlereagh decided that the sport was good and now was the time to go in hard. Castlereagh loosed off withering scorn:

> [Churchill] will have little cause to look back to the first day on which he has led the House, with feelings of pride, and if his eye is fixed on the place where he is now sitting, his chance of gaining that place is more remote than ever it was.

That of course was the prime minister's seat. Castlereagh accused Churchill of 'prostituting the traditions of this House', predicting that he would lose the position of Leader of the House.

Churchill had intended that proceedings should continue until 11 a.m. But the marathon was running into a wall. The Home Secretary conceded with a brave face that there would have to be an adjournment. The House rose at five minutes before 10 a.m. For Winston Churchill, it had been a night of some exhilaration, but ultimately of frustration and defeat. His combative approach did not go with the tact required of a government business-manager. Bad blood had been generated. The young Tory Lords had made special trouble for him: Churchill, as a pushy radical minister, was red-rag-to-a bull. And yet Winston belonged to their class and, to a significant degree, shared their outlook. The contradiction was a repeating one.

Churchill did not brood. Appearing in the Commons dining-room, he may have startled Austen Chamberlain when he joined him for breakfast. Sharing eggs, sole, and bacon were two politicians aiming for the top. Austen had expectation around him as the son of the great Joseph; Winston thought that destiny was on his side. For WSC, the put-downs will have bruised, but he usually bounced back.[7]

26 June 1911 was Churchill's annual face-the-music day in the Commons: the Home Office Debate. With peers versus people coming to a head, the Tories were looking to land blows. Opening for them was Alfred Lyttelton, one of the House's illustrious sportsmen. Lyttelton had graced the cricket-field for Eton, Cambridge University, and England, whilst being no slouch at athletics and tennis. Twelfth child of a baron, he had been Balfour's Colonial Secretary. The Lytteltons illustrate the inexhaustible inter-connectedness of the establishment in this period. A Lyttelton brother, Edward, was Headmaster of Eton; another was General Sir Neville Lyttelton, commander in chief, Ireland. Neville had fought with Winston Churchill at Omdurman; with Grey and Balfour he had been one of the shapers of British foreign policy; and he was the father of Lucy Masterman. There is another angle on close-world: Lyttelton's private secretary when he was Colonial Secretary in the Conservative government, was Edward Marsh.[8]

In a previous parliamentary pot-shot at Churchill, Alfred Lyttelton had asked him:

> ...whether Sir E. Ruggles-Brise, K.C.B., attended the recent International Prison Congress held in Washington, representing the United Kingdom; and whether, in view of the wide public interest, he will lay the Report made by the British representative upon the Table?

Churchill confirmed Brise's American trip, adding that the report would be issued to members. Lyttelton's pointing up of the Prison Commission Chairman's international standing (and his gong) was not innocent. Brise, he insinuated, should be taking the credit for the recent prison reforms, not the self-advertising Home Secretary. Lyttelton, a barrister, depicted the Home Secretary as a meddling interventionist in criminal justice, who did not consult. He cited the cancellation of a sentence of fourteen days' hard labour for begging, about which the chairman of Guisborough magistrates, Sir Alfred Pease, was fuming. Lyttelton's charge-sheet mostly has the look of rehash, with the Pentonville remissions well up.[9]

Lyttelton's speech will have been read by the Home Office's Harry Simpson, whose latest criminal statistics publication earned praise:

> This gentleman says, 'In magazine and newspaper articles on crime and punishment the sentiment expressed towards the criminal is almost universally compassionate and even sympathetic. Some of the expressions might almost seem to indicate that the reading public is on the side of the

criminal.' He suggests that the steady increase of crime is largely due to the relaxation of public sentiment with regard to it.[10]

Simpson was a team-player at the Home Office, but we may guess that he will have been not displeased to see his commentary quoted in Parliament against a chief who often overruled him.

Lyttelton turned to Sidney Street. The MP presented two riots: Churchill dithering over Tonypandy; taking command at Stepney, but not being obeyed. It was a confused thrust. The Home Secretary poured scorn on the linking of Tonypandy and Sidney Street:

> What possible connection or comparison is there between a trade dispute carried on by Welsh miners and the action of two foreign criminals resisting arrest with lethal weapons in London?[11]

On himself as inappropriate star of the picture papers, Churchill said:

> It is the misfortune of a good many Members to encounter in our daily walks an increasing number of persons armed with cameras to take pictures for the illustrated Press which is so rapidly developing. I would remind him that his own Leader, when he risked his valuable life in a flying-machine was the victim of a similar publicity, but I certainly should not imitate the right hon. Gentleman by suggesting that he was himself concerned in procuring the attendance of a photographer to witness his daring feat.

Balfour had been a hundred feet up over Hendon airfield. Churchill, who in two years' time would be having flying lessons, was among the audience of 250 MPs and a thousand naval and military officers at an event concerned with the reliability of aeroplanes in war.[12]

Churchill was uncompromising as always on the powers of the holder of his office:

> I am not prepared in any way to abrogate the full freedom of the prerogative of mercy, or to attach to its exercise any obligation either to consult or to be bound by consultation.

Looking back, Churchill told Wilfrid Blunt:

> The power of the Home Secretary [is] absolute, either to quash [a] sentence or to confirm it. The Home Secretary can go into any prison and on his sole authority can order a release, which if once notified to a prisoner cannot be changed afterwards by any power in England.[13]

Churchill rejoiced in his authority, but he did not completely dominate his under-secretaries. He had to work with Sir Edward Troup and others, sometimes winning disputes, sometimes not.

Continuing his speech, Churchill declared that in his judicial interventions, 'in nearly every conceivable case' he consulted judges and magistrates. He had statistics:

> In 1909, before I was responsible for the administration of the Home Office, the prerogative of mercy was used in 436 cases. In twelve eases it was used on grounds affecting the original conviction; in seven cases on account of technical irregularities in conviction or sentence; in 160 cases on medical grounds; in thirty-one cases as a reward for information given or assistance rendered by prisoners; in 203 cases in simple mitigation of sentence; and in twenty other cases which cannot be tabulated.[14]

He did not have figures for his own period, but:

> I think I cannot be misleading the House when I say that I have not gone numerically beyond the limit of the use made of the prerogative by my immediate predecessor.

Cricketer Lyttelton did not know that his speech had provided Churchill with a ball with which his wicket would be spread-eagled. On Guisborough, he had slipped up on his homework. Winston told the Commons with some glee that:

> I was not directly responsible. My Noble Friend Lord Crewe was administering the Home Office during my absence from this country, and he decided the case in the ordinary and regular way. I am quite sure that if the Guisborough Bench had only known that the decision was not that of the wicked Home Secretary but that of the good Lord Crewe, we should not have had a word of controversy.

Evidently Crewe was one of the good-natured colleagues who stood in for Winston during his vacations abroad. He was Lord Privy Seal.

The problem with Churchill's judicial interventions was not their quantity, or nature, but their manner. He liked to publicize what he did. The impression was created of a large-scale dabbler in the province of magistrates and judges.

It appeared that there was not going to be a vote. But then, from the Conservative backbenches up popped Sir Frederick Banbury:

> I beg to move, "That [the money for the Home Office] be reduced by £500 in respect of the salary of the Home Secretary."

He explained that amid the criticism of the Home Office:

> No hon. Member has had the courage to move a reduction of the salary of the Home Secretary. I, therefore, move this Motion in order to testify to the disapprobation on this side of the House with the administration of the

Home Office by the right hon. Gentleman, and not only on this side of the House, but also on the other side.

Was there disapproval of Churchill on the Liberal side? Richard Holt, a Liverpool ship-owner, confided to his diary this month his disdain for the rising young minister:

> I don't like the clever Home Secretary, Winston Churchill. He has a bad face and is needlessly provocative to the Tories, which lengthens debate.[15]

The division bells sounded. The Ayes for reducing Churchill's salary and the Noes for preserving it filed through their lobbies. The result was: Ayes 143; Noes 175. It was tighter than it should have been.

The Conservatives voting to take a lump out of the WSC salary did not include F.E. Smith. Five days earlier the Home Secretary, writing to the King, had congratulated him on new appointments to the Privy Council:

> This honour conferred upon [F.E. Smith] by Your Majesty will give great satisfaction to the Tory working men who regard him with the utmost favour.[16]

It may be taken that Churchill canvassed the appointment. The station-climbing F.E. will have been gratified. Not so the higher echelons of the Conservative establishment. Arthur Balfour, Winston informed Clemmie, protested to the prime minister. Churchill called this 'an insight into the fatuous and arrogant mind of the Cecils and their refusal to share power with any able man of provincial origin'.[17]

Churchill enjoyed himself in reporting the debate to the King:

> Mr Lyttelton made a speech raking up a lot of old stories about Sidney Street, Tonypandy and the Dartmoor Shepherd, to which Mr Churchill endeavoured to reply – as was thought by his friends, not without some measure of success....The Opposition moved formally a reduction of £500 on the salary of the Home Secretary, and as the Irish members were away, half the Labour members absent, ministers at the gala [an opera at Covent Garden attended by the King and Queen] and holiday moods in the air, this flagitious proposal was rejected only by a majority of 32.[18]

It was perhaps fortunate for Churchill that the lead opposition speech did not sparkle. The charges against his manner of administration had some potential. WSC upset both individuals and institutions. An example is a row that blew up at this time.

A young woman Beatrice Carter was in Reading Jail. Her home address, The Cloisters, Palace Yard, Gloucester, spoke respectability. This was not the latest socially well-connected suffragette behind bars. The passion that landed this lady in prison was not the injustice of female exclusion from the vote, but lace dresses, silk slips and evening blouses, and silver cutlery. She had acquired a haul by taking away goods from shops on approval and not paying for or returning them. Travelling by rail and assuming identities such as rectory daughter, she made magpie trips around Bath, Stroud, Hereford, Worcester, Birmingham, Newport, Cardiff, and Bristol.

Gloucester's Conservative MP, Henry Terrell, was beseeched for help by Beatrice's mother. Terrell presented the Home Office with a newspaper cutting describing the conviction and sentencing by Reading magistrates. 'OVERSTUDY VICTIM' was the strange headline. Apparently, a well-bred young lady like Beatrice (who lived with her widowed mother and her brother) could not be a trickster. The newspaper explained that the young lady's mind must have gone into some sort of spin. The defence in court was a brain overwrought by too intensive a study of music. 'Frauds by lady who passed ten examinations', said the paper.[19]

Arrested at dawn, Beatrice was taken to Reading, where she was indicted on two deception and theft charges, the rest not being pressed. Her night in a police cell was described by her mother in a later letter to the King, asking for a pardon for her daughter: the cell was 'filthy, wretched and cold; she could not undress or lie down; everything was in a filthy state…she had no convenience to make herself tidy to appear in court.' Bessie's mother also complained that no food was offered to her daughter, though she had not eaten since the day before; in her week in custody before the trial there was 'not one word of sympathy or advice' for her. Sentenced to a month in the second division, she was removed from the dock 'sobbing bitterly'. Reading Jail with its four-turreted Gothic wall, where Oscar Wilde suffered, now held twenty-seven women on one of its five spokes-of-a-wheel wings. When the complaints on behalf of new inmate Beatrice Carter reached Winston Churchill, he had his staff send for reports from the magistrates – and from the medical officer at the prison, since the Gloucester MP was adamant that Bessie was insane. The doctor found no such signs. Ernley Blackwell considered the sentence 'a merciful one'. He saw no grounds for remission. Edward Troup agreed. Anyway, the woman was due for release very soon. But still Henry Terrell agitated, more than once visiting the Home Office. Blackwell thought he knew what was driving the campaign. If Miss Carter were released even three or four days early on the order of the Home Secretary, she and her family could point to wrongful conviction, preserving her chances of a career in music. Troup and Blackwell were against early release. Churchill agreed. He told Henry Terrell that he would not be interfering with the sentence.[20]

Beatrice was set to be released at 7.30 a.m. on 9 June. There was a twist. At 6.20 p.m. on 8 June a telegram arrived at the Home Office from the Chief Constable of Reading:

Hold warrant for Warwick police for Beatrice Marion Carter for false pretences. Please inform me by telegraph if warrant has to be executed.[21]

Beatrice's whistle-stop deceptions had included Leamington Spa: ordering goods in the name of well-known persons for collection at railway parcel-offices, claiming to be a clergyman's wife.

The family had picked up the news. Mrs Carter sent a personal telegram to Winston Churchill, urging him to prevent the re-arrest of her daughter at the prison gates: 'Mr Terrell will explain.' Gloucester Liberal Association (whose president was WSC) joined the pleas. Edward Troup wrote a memorandum. Whilst he thought that it would be wrong 'to go on prosecuting for offences of the same series', he had a word of caution:

> Strictly speaking you have no power to forbid the Police to execute the warrant. And it is just possible that the Justices who issued it may make some trouble.

The Home Office reply to the Reading Chief Constable was composed by Troup: because the offences committed under Warwick jurisdiction appeared to be of the same series as the others, the Home Secretary would 'strongly deprecate' the arrest of the woman on her release; if Warwick police still thought it necessary to prosecute, they should first report their reasons to the Home Office. A telephone call was made to Reading Prison. Beatrice would not be met at the gates with a warrant.

The Warwickshire police were shocked. Chief Constable John Brinkley wrote to the Home Office: the Leamington Spa offences were previously unknown, no mention being made at Carter's trial; no recompense had been made by the woman or her friends for the losses. 'I am consequently,' said the police chief, 'at a loss to understand the action of the Home Office in stopping the warrant.'

Churchill spluttered:

> What does he mean by using an expression of 'at a loss to understand H.O. action'? His tone appears disrespectful, and I am doubtful whether he should be answered.

A delicately worded reply, framed by Blackwell, was sent:

> The Secretary of State has observed with some surprise some of the expressions used in your letter, but has answered it on the assumption that the expressions were used accidentally and without intentional discourtesy.

That made matters worse. Warwickshire office-holders were affronted by the upbraiding of their Chief Constable, following upon the blocking of his warrant. At a meeting of a County Council sub-committee, a unanimous recommendation was passed that William Johnson, MP for Nuneaton, should be requested to pursue the matter in Parliament, asking for 'an explanation of the law governing the suspension of warrants legally issued'. The choice of a Labour MP is pertinent. Johnson was a former factory worker and miner. Individuals of the working classes did not have the connections to pull strings with ministers if they got into trouble. Churchill was intervening to save a middle-class woman from the full rigours of the law after she had been caught committing deception. The Recorder of Warwick, T.M. Colmore, saw it that:

> The Home Secretary has taken it upon himself to interfere with or override an Act of Parliament.[22]

Troup prepared Churchill for a likely parliamentary encounter, his line to be that:

> The Home Secretary did not suspend the warrant but expressed a strong opinion that it should not be executed for another offence of the same series.

He reassured that Home Office policy in this regard, as expressed in circulars, had the approval of judges. He cited an Appeal Court judgement. The permanent under-secretary's work earned a 'good' from WSC. Did it wash? Troup must have known that it did not. He was careful to cover himself with an asterisk footnote that the Home Office circulars related to 'cases tried on indictment', not the serving of warrants. He said, 'the principle is the same', but the ground looked shaky. Whilst the Home Office had not actually suspended the warrant, its advice was practically an instruction. The following day the *Daily Express* had a headline: 'ARRESTING THE LAW'.[23]

William Johnson put his question to Churchill, asking what prompted him 'without note to the justice who issued the warrant, the Mayor of Warwick, and the Warwick police, to interpose and prevent the execution of the warrant and due process of law?' He asked whether, 'it would not have been more courteous to have communicated with the Warwickshire authorities instead of writing them a sharp reprimand?'

Churchill replied:

> ... I had not, though much pressed, felt justified in reducing the sentence passed at Reading; but I had reason to think that to re-arrest her and take her back to prison at the moment she was returning to her home...would have been an act of useless cruelty. I wrote no sharp reprimand...but I took exception to some discourteous expressions, as I thought them.[24]

Johnson came back: 'The reply of the Home Secretary was very discourteous to the Warwickshire authorities.'

The ripples continued. In August a leading article in *Justices of the Peace* magazine declared that the Home Secretary's 'interference, with the object of preventing the execution of a warrant duly issued by a Warwickshire Justice, exemplifies a dangerous tendency of late.' The executive was assuming powers 'to override and make itself superior to the judiciary'.[25]

It is easy to understand why the Warwickshire Chief Constable was indignant that the law he policed had been pushed aside without reference to him, with the addition of insult to injury in the shape of a reprimand. The matter could have been solved by consultation. The bad feeling arose out of Churchill's neglect of the proper processes.

Mrs Carter was still trying for a pardon for her daughter. In her letter to the King, a mention of Bessie's experience in Reading Jail will have caught Winston Churchill's attention when it came to him:

> She worked fearfully hard, as she could not bear the dreadful solitude. Now she is a perfect wreck…[26]

Bessie does not seem to have been ruined. Fifteen years later she was a motor-car owner, reported in her local press as receiving a small fine from Gloucester magistrates for failing to display a licence.[27]

Home Office documents show the permanent staff striving to contain their ambitious and impulsive minister within departmental procedures, precedents, and conventions. We may imagine the likes of Troup and Blackwell (and Ruggles-Brise on the lower floor) being vexed by the rampaging young Secretary of State. But they seem to have enjoyed the stimulation. Troup in the *London Evening Standard* in 1925 spoke of his Churchill period as his most pleasant time at the Home Office. He recalled Charles Masterman having his office next to his and the connecting door often being open, allowing the pair to chat about 'the chief's latest exploit'. Then he would return to his papers 'with the feeling of having been out of doors on a breezy morning'. The reminiscence went on:

> Once a week or perhaps oftener, Mr Churchill came down to the office bringing with him some adventurous and impossible projects: but after half an hour's discussion something was evolved which was still adventurous, but no longer impossible.[28]

The picture of Churchill as the headstrong boy being talked out of well-meaning but impracticable schemes by his elders and then being allowed to proceed with more workable versions, has an element of truth. However, there was also Troup's penal conservatism versus Churchill's progressive approach. The Home Office papers disclose protracted tussles, with Churchill always conscious of his constitutional position, which set him above civil servants, even one as senior as Sir Edward Troup.

At the time Troup confided to the Mastermans:

> [Churchill] drives me crazy sometimes, but he's the first great Home Secretary we've had since Asquith. He brings ideas into the office.[29]

Previously, secretarial chiefs bringing matters to the minister, explained the usual practice as a preliminary to a signature for this to continue, this being usually forthcoming. Not so with Churchill, who asked, 'Why?'. It was, in Lucy Masterman's view, 'a wholesome discipline for any Government department'. This minister 'wanted to do things.'

Harold Butler's autobiography confirms that Home Office seniors were 'rather shocked by Churchill's impetuosity and unorthodoxy' – and disapproved when he played to the cameras. The memoir conveys the geography of 'that great Victorian quadrangle...the Home Office, India Office and Colonial Office: the innermost sanctuary of imperial government'. The Home Office spoke tradition and power: 'lofty, vaulted corridors, imposing high windows'. The Home Secretary's office was on the first floor. The secluded inner courtyard below may have reminded some of those working in the building of the Oxford and Cambridge colleges that had provided their route to the civil service. Forty-five years later Anthony Sampson's *Anatomy of Britain Today* would call the Home Office 'the most notoriously self-centred department', remarking that, 'its intense conservatism has trapped nearly every would-be reforming Home Secretary...the over-riding aim of the Home Office is to avoid trouble.' Churchill, with Napoleon on his desk, aimed to defeat the culture of caution. It made 1910 and 1911 quite interesting in this department.[30]

Chapter 20
Saving Mr Polly?

Winston Churchill at the Home Office introduced two major measures aimed at improving the conditions of British workers. One concerned safety in coal mines; the other addressed regulations for shops.

Britain had a million shop assistants. Hours were back-breaking. Pay was low. There was the special oppression of larger establishment 'living-in', a regime which saw many shop-girls being servants in all but name. Health suffered in the crowded, ill-ventilated, gas-lit buildings, consumption being one consequence. The cheaper drapery shops were notorious for their requirement of obsequiousness to customers. 1910 saw the publication of H.G. Wells's *History of Mr Polly*, to follow his earlier *Kipps*. These novels brought to the public the harshness of shop worker existence. Wells had been a drapery employee in his youth. The evocation in *Mr Polly* of 'scarce a gleam of rest or liberty between the toil' was topical. Churchill was a voracious Wells reader. He freely admitted to lifting lines from the works of the novelist and political thinker for his own speeches.

Recent years had seen the rise of shop assistants' trade unions, a famous female union pioneer being Margaret Bondfield, Assistant Secretary of the National Union of Shop Assistants. In 1910 the future first woman cabinet minister made a trip to the United States, under the auspices of the international labour movement. Whilst on a train out of Atlanta, she was shocked by the sight of prison chain-gangs working on the road, watched over by mounted armed-guards. In Britain, though prisoners' work (nearly all for government departments) had some financial value, there was never any question of labour exploitation of convicts, as in some southern USA states. Churchill would have been appalled had there been any suggestion of bringing convict slavery, which is what it was in effect, to Britain.[1]

The Shops Bill's chief aims were: a sixty hours per week maximum for shop-assistant work; an early-closing day each week; a statutory meal-break of reasonable length; Sunday closing; and the restriction of overtime. The bill was beset with conflicting interests, for example Jewish shops and Sunday closing. Also, shopkeepers were traditional supporters of the Liberal Party, a very strong interest. Some big stores, like Debenhams, supported the National Union of Shop Assistants. Masterman and Churchill received more than a hundred deputations and replied to a vast number of written representations. Churchill called his efforts at compromise between the interests, 'feeling my way along between Scylla and Charybdis every inch'.[2]

The second reading debate was opened by Charles Masterman on 31 March. Churchill's deputy knew about the desperate need for alleviation of the sufferings of shopworkers. His 1909 book *The Condition of England* drew on factory reports, including on living in for shopworkers:

> ...The daily rush from counter to dining-room and back, the unappetising food, the wearying sameness of the menu, the insufficiency of the food...[3]

The sleeping conditions could be horror: bug-infested beds crammed together in squashed accommodation that in the heat of summer smelt 'like a fowl house'. Masterman called his living-in chapter 'Prisoners'.

The rejection of the bill was moved by the maverick Liberal Horatio Bottomley (who in later years would do penal servitude at Maidstone for fraud). The ample-girthed showman objected to the bill's complications. He made sport of Sunday trading rules:

> ...You may buy smokers' requisites, but if a poor woman wanted a box of matches to light a fire with, she could not be served, unless she had a pipe in her mouth.[4]

Following Bottomley against the bill was Frederick Banbury. The Conservative stickler and the louche populist made for an odd alliance. Banbury likened Churchill's Shops Bill to his Miners' Eight Hours Bill:

> We were told that it was necessary to limit the amount of adult labour in mines because [miners] did not see the sky and the trees and the sun. Within a very short time similar legislation is being applied to people who do absolutely different work.

He moved on to the regular charge of Churchill as over-interventionist:

> Under this Bill the Home Secretary is a dictator...The greatness of England has been brought about because people were left free to do what they liked, and there were no Home Secretaries or anybody else to tell them what they might and what they might not do.

Banbury saw socialism in the 'enormous number of inspectors'. He set forth his political position:

> I am not either a Radical or a Democrat or a Socialist. Holding these views, I trust the House will have an interval of sanity and refuse to pass this very pernicious Bill.

He put Dublin Irish Nationalist J. J. Clancy in mind of the arguments used in Lord Shaftsbury's days for continuing to send little boys up chimneys.

The House heard Harry Lawson, newspaper magnate and Conservative Member for Mile End (he had been at Sidney Street) proclaiming compassion: 'Any man here must have a stony heart if he does not consider that great injury is done to the health of the women by the hours worked.' But he saw a plague of inspectors bothering the working classes. With a town house in Grosvenor Square and a country residence in Berkshire, Lawson was not the most obvious champion of the sons and daughters of toil. His speech caught the sentiment of a current book by three self-claimed working-class writers. *Seems So* was promoted by *The Times*. Its standpoint was 'akin to Old Tory': anti-the nouveau riche, who did not understand the working class as the old-time squires supposedly did, and calling for a New Toryism (or Nationalism). It castigated the Webbs' Minority Report, raising the spectre of busybody interference in working-class lives. The arguments were a sort of pre-echo of present-day protests about 'political correctness'. They were popular on the right of politics, the special phobia being inspectors.[5]

Winston Churchill was optimistic of some Conservative support. He had told the prime minister in December 1910:

> I am quite sure I can count upon a great deal of help from the younger and more advanced Tories in taking this measure through.[6]

Replying to the debate, Churchill frankly admitted the problems of conflicting interests around shops. An example was Manchester:

> There is the wealthy high-class trade in one part of the town, which always closes on Saturday afternoon. There is the trade which supplies the needs of the poorer populations, which does its principal business on Saturday afternoon.

He went on:

> My study has convinced me that all closing orders must carry with them local assent.

In the cases of very small family shops, kept by a husband and wife, or mother and son, or brother and sister, the second person would not be classed as an assistant, but a third family member would be. 'Of course, said Churchill, 'this does not deal with the case of a small child, who may keep the shop for an hour while its parents go out.' Across the chamber came a yell from Bottomley: 'What will happen in the case of twins?' This produced an election-style interruption-squasher from Churchill:

> Well, I hope they will meet with a better fortune than the twin brothers of obstruction, the hon. Member for South Hackney [Bottomley] and the hon. Baronet the Member for the City of London [Banbury].

It was time for Churchill's peroration:

> The lives of nearly a million shop assistants, many of them in the joyous years of youth, are under such a pressure of circumstances that they are lives of continual deprivation. What they ask for is that after the work is over there shall be a fair and reasonable opportunity for rest, for leisure, for recreation, for the pleasures of the country, for the pleasures of family life, and it is that demand that the House is asked to support. It is a Bill which will encounter opposition in many quarters. The powerful interests which it disturbs will not be friendly. The class it helps most is not strong in voting strength…We have been called in the past, tauntingly, scornfully, a nation of shopkeepers. We have never been much ashamed of that in former times, and when this Bill is upon the statute-book we shall have no reason to be ashamed of it in future times.[7]

The 'nation of shopkeepers' sneer was of course by the man whose bust adorned Churchill's Home Office desk.

The vote was on which type of committee would look at the bill: Grand or Select. Churchill wanted the former, since the latter would produce yet more evidence to add to the mountain. Bottomley, hostile to the Home Secretary's purpose, was for Select. He had little support, the vote going 261–21 for Grand.[8]

There were sixteen committee days, usually lasting until 4 a.m. The outcome was not determined until 30 November. *Whitaker's Almanack* records it grimly:

> Owing to the other business to be dealt with, the Prime Minister announced that the controversial portions of the Shops Bill would be dropped. Over half of the clauses were deleted, among them those for compulsory Sunday closing and for limiting the hours of work for shop assistants to 60 in a week…The clauses providing for a weekly half-holiday and for reasonable intervals between meals [and work] were retained, and the emasculated Bill was passed.[9]

At least, as was reported to Parliament by Sheffield Labour MP Joseph Pointer, there was satisfaction about the meal breaks provision:

> …I was told that a very great proportion of illness amongst shop assistants took the form of indigestion. I was given the instance of a big emporium in this city where the young lady assistants had to travel from the room in which they worked to the dining-room, 750 yards, there and back, of which distance half was up and down stairs, and it all had to be done in a twenty-five minutes' meal time.[10]

But Pointer lambasted the capitulation of Winston Churchill on its chief object, the limitation of the hours of shop assistants: 'He is giving us the husk instead of the kernel.'

His dismay was shared by some Conservatives, including Viscount Wolmer:

> It does seem very hard that this question should be put on the scrap-heap at the last moment. For [Churchill] to come down and draw his blue pencil through the Bill, and take out the kernel, appears to me to be nothing more nor less than sacrificing the Bill for political reasons.[11]

Churchill's fire for a better life for shop assistants seemed to have gone out. He said:

> The House is, I think, aware of the reduced character of the proposals which are now embodied in this Bill. If they are not, they may learn from glancing at the long succession of pages over which we went, inch by inch, in the Committee, and which are now relegated to the category of waste paper. It is quite impossible to go back on the question of the sixty hours week. That is gone.[12]

Eddie Marsh wrote mournfully to Lady Gladstone: 'I'm afraid poor Kipps and Mr Polly will have to wait some time now before they get their 60 hours week.' It would not be until the Shops Act of 1920 that measures of the sort that Churchill wanted were secured.[13]

The Coal Mines Safety Bill did better. Churchill delegated it to Charles Masterman, but he watched over it closely. Masterman told Parliament that on average every day four men or boys were brought up from the pits dead and five hundred seriously hurt. There were two terrible accidents in 1910: 136 lives lost at Whitehaven on 11 May; 344 at Lancaster on 21 December. Churchill took very seriously the improvement of safety in an industry employing 1.2 million men. He had to be versed in its detail to field questions in Parliament and for when TUC delegates came to the Home Office.[14]

The new legislation required mine-owners to establish rescue stations, with trained rescuers and appropriate equipment. Systematic checking of air pressure and gases became a requirement. In a modest but significant step in the direction of industrial democracy, power was established for miners to appoint their own inspectors to investigate conditions where accidents had occurred. A historian of coal-mining has identified the act as 'positivist legislation', promoting health and safety, the fullest example yet of this type of law-making.[15]

In this area the Whitehall engine-room was headed by a civil servant called Malcolm Delevingne. He is mentioned by Gladstone: 'extraordinarily accurate and zealous [but] thinks in Home Office papers, and has not seen quite enough of the world.' Delevingne's route into the Home Office had been the regular meritocratic one. This had been in place since the Northcote-Trevelyan Report of 1854 recommended that entry to the civil service should be solely on merit. (Previously, social connections and personal favour had considerably determined entry.) The Home Office, along with the rest of the civil service, had been transformed by the consequences of Northcote-Trevelyan. Delevingne had taken a first in classics at Trinity, Oxford. The classical education of men like Delevingne was seen to have the benefit, as Jill Pellew puts it, of producing civil servants 'highly effective at analyzing alternatives, at distinguishing points of value from irrelevancies, at ascertaining the best way of carrying out a policy, which excluded zeal for a cause or idea'. The issue of academic prowess versus practical knowledge was addressed by Winston Churchill in replying to a debate on mining accidents on 16 June 1910. It was a poignant occasion, a month after the Whitehaven disaster, with Keir Hardie and other Labour members participating. Churchill showed his readiness for working miners to be brought into the inspectorate:

> …I think it is undesirable that there should be a sharp line drawn so that it is not easy, almost not possible, for a man who begins life with manual labour at the face of the coal to rise to a position of responsibility in the inspectorate.[16]

The matter was raised in the Home Office Debate of 26 June. In a trenchant speech, Josiah Wedgwood compared the different ranks of inspector: the 'superior rank', which was recruited from the universities 'after a stiff examination', whose pay started at £300 per year; and the assistant inspectors, who had to pass an examination in factory legislation and started at £110 a year. He asked:

> Will it be believed that these assistant-inspectors, who have practical experience of factory life and know about the machinery are allowed to inspect every sort of building except that in which there is machinery, while the others who do not know a piston-rod from a pump-handle are the only people who are considered fit to inspect machinery?… It is not a matter of Latin and Greek. What is wanted is practical knowledge.

Wedgwood made a personal appeal to the Home Secretary who had so shaken up the conservative-minded Home Office:

> I do think that, with the democratic forces which we now have at the head of the Home Office, we might get a little more in the rank and file, and that we might make the first start by uniting the superior and the lower grades of inspector.[17]

If Wedgwood thought that he was knocking on an open door, he was correct.

Churchill made sure that the trade unions knew that they had his ear. The February 1911 visit of the Parliamentary Committee of the TUC to the Home Office was a big Labour occasion. Churchill had with him, as well as Charles Masterman and Sir Edward Troup, Chief Inspector of Factories Sir Arthur Whitelegge, David Shackleton now Labour Adviser to the Home Office, and Chief Inspector of Mines R.A.S Radmayne. The 1942 autobiography of Sir

Richard Redmayne has a striking impression of Churchill, as memoirs so often do. Redmayne, formerly a professor of mining-engineering at Birmingham University, was known as competent and hard-working. Still, on one occasion he found himself rebuked by Churchill. He had sent in a document late, with the plea of pressing business. On getting back from holiday, he was greeted by the return of the item – with a comment:

> The fact that the Chief Inspector of Mines is overworked is no excuse whatever for the delay in the circulation of this paper. W.S.C.[18]

Redmayne claimed not to have taken the scolding amiss, but his reminiscence describes Churchill as 'disturbing'. He will have been pleased that the Home Secretary arranged a deputy and an assistant secretary to relieve him of some of his burden. He called Churchill 'a driver and a demon for work', but:

> …Beneath a somewhat dogmatic and dictatorial manner he hid an affectionate heart and a kindly, generous nature. He was the nearest thing to genius that I have come across in the political world – not unaccompanied by a sense of humour.

There was humour at Churchill's meeting with the trade-unionists. The atmosphere seems to have been friendly. Churchill told his guests that the advent of David Shackleton had strengthened the Home Office staff. This will certainly have been the case. The Whitehall secretaries were upper middle-class: their attitudes reflected this. This is illustrated by a *Punch* cartoon of this time, entitled 'Improbable Scenes', of civil servants queueing at an Early Door. (*Punch* thought that civil servants were lazy.) The secretaries in the drawing are all top-hatted and finely tailored. By bringing in Shackleton, of working-class origin, Winston Churchill was making a start on broadening the social composition of the Home Office.[19]

The subject was raised of 'half-timers', meaning the practice of older children dividing their time between factory work and schooling. The delegation wanted an end to this. Churchill was vaguely supportive but warned that, 'the strong opinion of the textile operatives cannot be cast aside.' He said, as reported by *The Times*, that:

> We have in Mr Shackleton a proof that these hardships can be surmounted [laughter]. At any rate he has survived the hardship of being a half-timer [a voice: 'the exception proves the rule'].[20]

David Shackleton had been put to work in a cotton factory as a half-timer at the age of nine. He remembered not much daylight opportunity for cricket. In an industry with a terrible history of child labour and cruelty, the cotton unions had a record of voting against reform. The minimum working-age had gradually been raised to 12, each time the cotton union being out of step with general trade-union feeling. Churchill took the line of avoiding upsetting the textile industry.[21]

Shackleton, later knighted, would have a successful career. On the formation of the Ministry of Labour, he became its permanent secretary. He was the first working-class person to achieve a senior civil service position. His elevation was however ultimately clouded by hurt. He was twice demoted, first when a joint permanent secretary was put alongside him, and then when his position was re-designated. The social establishment re-asserted itself. That was for the future. In 1911 Winston Churchill, by giving working miners a say in the safety of their mines and by taking a former child loom worker into his department's assembly of ex-public schoolboys and university men, was showing himself to be an unusually democratic Home Secretary.[22]

Chapter 21

'Exactly Like Daisy Lord'

In July 1910 Winston Churchill was asked by Liberal Sir Howell Davies, leather merchant and Methodist, if 'in the interest of public decency', he could 'prohibit photographs of the recent prize fight in America being exhibited at cinematograph shows in this country.' Churchill replied that he had no powers in the matter. A nipped-in supplementary by Will Thorne sheds some light: did Churchill think that:

> ...if Jeffries had knocked out Johnson there would have been so much of this slobber talk?[1]

Jack Johnson, the heavyweight boxing champion, was black. James Jeffries, the challenger, had been dubbed 'the great white hope'. The fight had taken place before a large crowd in Nevada, filmed by a team of cameramen. Johnson had won by a knock-out. The film was banned in the southern United States. In 1911 a British event was arranged for Johnson: a fight against Englishman Bombardier Billy Wells, who had left the army to become a professional boxer and was British heavyweight boxing champion. It was scheduled for London's Earl's Court on 2 October. There was a campaign to ban it, on the grounds that a black-versus-white contest could spark race riots, as recently in America and the British Empire. Churchill touched on the controversy in a 24 September letter to Clementine: 'I have made up my mind to stop the Wells-Johnson contest. The terms are utterly unsporting and unfair.' He will have been thinking of the split of the £8,000 purse: seventy-five per cent for Johnson; twenty-five per cent for Wells. Winston – who during the last General Election declared that, 'the Tory party is knocked clean out of the ring' – will have been familiar with Jack Johnson's story. For years, racial discrimination had blocked him from competing for the world championship. Having gained it, he looked unbeatable. Presumably Churchill anticipated a battering for Wells.[2]

Did Churchill actually intervene? It appears that he did, though not with a direct ban. The sequence of events is slightly obscure. The campaign to stop the fight happening included the young Conservative politician Earl Stanhope (who would later have a long political career including First Lord of the Admiralty) writing to *The Times* on 23 September to protest about black against white prize-fighting, as being liable to cause a breach of the peace, perhaps sparking trouble in the British Empire. A memorial to Winston Churchill against the Wells-Johnson fight had been organized by the prominent London Baptist minister

F.B. Meyer, who predicted repercussions including in South Africa. Churchill promised to look carefully at the petition. A Home Office statement, which will certainly have been approved by him, appeared on 24 September, the day after Johnson's arrival in London. This called the fight 'illegal, as a breach of the peace'; and counter to the best interests of the nation and the Empire. Churchill did not himself impose a ban. If he had done (assuming this to have been legally possible) he would presumably have unleashed more charges that he was an over-mighty Home Secretary. Instead, he deflected the matter to the courts. The *Annual Register* states that, 'the principals and accessories were summoned at Bow Street Police Court on September 25.' The outcome was pre-empted by a high court injunction granted at the instance of the Metropolitan District Railway, the freeholder of the Earl's Court site. What exactly happened behind the scenes it is impossible to know. The fight did not take place.[3]

Churchill's intervention does not look good and reflects his already outdated attitude to race and the British Empire. The outcome provided a precedent for a British boxing colour bar, which lasted until 1947. Where was Churchill on race? During his life at various times, he made racially offensive statements. These were when he was in the company of cronies. But what he did, as opposed to what he said, was not racist. His attitudes followed his British imperial upbringing. He believed in European superiority, with the British leading. As Warren Dockter has demonstrated, he looked at cultural rather than biological differences. He was repelled by aggressive white supremacy like that of the Boers. His personality was not racist.[4]

On the projected Johnson-Wells contest, one may take it that as well as Churchill's sentiment regarding British soldiers (demonstrated in his use of penal discretion), he will have wanted to avoid disturbances.

Film censorship in Britain would not begin until 1912. Theatre was muzzled by the obligation to obtain the sanction of the Lord Chamberlain for the performance of plays. One of those pressing for liberation was Liberal MP Robert Harcourt. At parliamentary question time on 14 June 1910, Harcourt wanted to know what Churchill's attitude was to the Report of the Joint Committee on Stage Plays (Censorship), which recommended a single licence for both theatres and music-halls and an end to the Lord Chamberlain's role. Did Churchill, he inquired, propose to introduce legislation? The Home Secretary was not particularly encouraging: 'I can only reply at present that the Report is under my consideration.'[5]

On 17 July 1911 Harcourt followed up, entertaining the Commons as he asked Churchill:

> …whether he is aware that at the London Hippodrome a variety entertainment includes two items described as Velanche's Marvellous Football Dogs and Madame Réjane in "La Chance du Mari"; whether this place of entertainment has a licence for stage-plays, and, if not, whether the

first item is permissible whereas the second is an open defiance of the law; and whether, in view of these circumstances, he will at once cause Madame Réjane to appear before the police magistrate, to answer to the charge of a breach of good manners, decorum, and the public peace by the performance of an illegal play unlicensed by the Lord Chamberlain, with a view to confining her in future to activities within the legal ambit of the licence such as those of Velanche's Marvellous Football Dogs?[6]

La Chance Du Mari, a one-act comedy, was tucked in among a music-hall assortment. MPs enjoyed Harcourt's mischief, one Tory requesting highlights of the plot.[7]

Churchill played it with a straight bat:

> I suppose that my hon. Friend's object is to illustrate the desirability of alterations in the law rather than to press for the institution of proceedings. I can only say that in view of the number of more urgent matters before the House, I cannot hold out hope of legislation this year on this highly controversial subject.

Harcourt pertinently asked Churchill whether he was aware that:

> …a witness from the Home Office appeared before the Censorship Committee and expressly defended the policy of the present licensing discrimination?

Churchill was not inclined to interfere with censorship of the theatre by the Lord Chamberlain. It would continue until 1968.

Theatre was becoming increasingly political. In 1907 a ground-breaking production at the Savoy Theatre of Euripides' *Medea* in unexpurgated English translation had shocked audiences with its presentation of a woman so badly treated by a man that she feels she has to kill her children. The Australian-born academic and liberal progressive Gilbert Murray, a leading Euripides authority, thought that *Medea* 'might have been written for the women's movement'. The suffragettes agreed. *Medea* extracts featured in their events. *Medea* was put on by director Harley Granville-Barker, who is mentioned in Wilfrid Blunt's diary as a guest along with Winston Churchill at a weekend party at his Sussex home in April 1910. A brisk debate is described about suffragettes on hunger strike. Barker and Blunt likened force-feeding to the Spanish Inquisition; Churchill disagreed. In 1904 Churchill had been one of Granville-Barker's supporters in a campaign for a national theatre, to receive a state subsidy so that more ambitious productions might be possible. According to Blunt, Churchill had offered to 'get Barker a seat' at the next General Election. Barker approached Churchill several times to try to get theatre censorship relaxed.[8]

Churchill got to know well the plight of young mothers driven by social and economic circumstances to do away with their 'illegitimate' babies, sometimes attempting to kill themselves also. Two years before he came to the Home Office one case came to epitomize these women. A 22-years-old Surrey laundry worker, Daisy Lord, was convicted of infanticide, having strangled her new-born daughter. When arrested, she said, 'I thought I would put an end to it so that it should not have the trouble I had.' The judge was overcome when passing the mandatory death sentence. Herbert Gladstone routinely commuted. Churchill had been Home Secretary for a fortnight when, in the women's suffrage publication *The Vote*, Maud Arncliffe Sennett, owner of a confectionary-manufacturing business, explained that one reason she wanted the vote was:

> ...because Daisy Lord is being detained for the term of her natural life while the author of her agony is still at large – a voter, or a potential one.⁹

Daisy was in Aylesbury Prison. Campaigns for her release included a rally in Trafalgar Square. Gladstone had assured supporters that the woman would not be in jail for more than three years. In a Children Bill debate, the Lords considered what the papers called 'a Daisy Lord Clause'. In the case of women killing their children of under a year, this would give courts the option of passing penal servitude sentences instead of the death penalty. It was narrowly defeated (the bishops abstaining). Lord Coleridge felt that the 'solemn dread ceremony' served a purpose. During Churchill's Home Office tenure, he assumed the black cap five times. Churchill signed a licence on 13 June 1910 to see Daisy Lord out of prison: to 'such Home or Refuge as the Secretary of State may prescribe, for nine months'. She went to the House of Compassion, Pimlico.¹⁰

No woman had been executed for killing her baby since 1849. Bills attempting to end the passing of death sentences on women for killing their newly-born or young baby made no progress. The Home Office did not like a law based on the age of the infant. In 1910, reform activist Rev. W. G. Bowen arrived with a proposed bill. He had an MP ready to pilot it. Where infanticide was committed by a mother within four weeks of birth, sentence of death should not be pronounced: instead, there would be a penal servitude sentence of between three and ten years. Scrutiny fell to Harry Simpson, who recommended 'lay by', Home Office-ese for no action. Churchill had an idea of his own. A judge sentencing a woman who had killed her baby should be required to tell her that the death penalty would be commuted 'according to invariable practice' to three years' penal servitude. He suggested revival of the 1823 Judgment of Death Act. That legislation, at the time when the Bloody Code was on its way out, empowered judges to substitute a lesser penalty than death for offences other than murder or treason. Senior Home Office staff thought that Churchill's proposed use of it would make 'a mockery' of the sentence of death – and judges would resent having their wings trimmed. Winston backed down.¹¹

On 1 December 1910 Florence Boxall, a 24-year-old laundry worker, was sentenced to death at Guildford Assizes, having admitted to strangling her new-born baby in the water-closet of her lodgings. 'Exactly like Daisy Lord!', exclaimed the coroner. At Florence's trial, one juryman dissented from the Wilful Murder verdict, declaring that it should be manslaughter – and that the missing father should be held equally responsible. In *Common Cause*, the newspaper of the National Union of Women's Suffrage Societies, a letter called for women to sit on juries: 'It is our duty as women to see that the poor child Florence Boxall is saved from the abominable injustice of our man-made laws.' The Boxall jury strongly recommended mercy. Winston Churchill organized a reprieve before a hanging date could be set.[12]

June and July of 1911, with the country looking forward to the coronation, brought several infanticide cases. At Salisbury Assizes, 30-years-old Mary Ann Nash was sentenced to death for the murder of her illegitimate son. Stanley, aged five. had disappeared in 1907. Mary Ann had taken him supposedly to put in the care of an acquaintance and had returned alone. A child's body was discovered in a local well, fitting Stanley's profile, though not conclusively. The story had the familiar element of economic desperation. The mother had been told that she must take her son to the workhouse. Her trial for murder was presided over by Lord Coleridge, who remarked that, 'Unfortunately illegitimate children do not seem welcome anywhere.' The sort of economic plight suffered by the likes of Mary Ann engaged Churchill's eloquence: the previous year he shared with Wilfrid Blunt his indignation about 'a girl who had had a child and had put it in the workhouse, and who had been given two months' hard labour for deserting it.'[13]

The jury found Mary Ann guilty, with a recommendation of mercy. A local paper reported that she 'trembled and swayed' during sentence. The judge, in his correspondence with the Home Office, did not oppose commutation of the death sentence, but saw 'a bad case of murder'. Blackwell and Troup recommended: 'Respite and commute', commenting that the case was not as bad as a 'baby farmer'. (In 1896 Amelia Dyer was convicted and executed for taking money for the upkeep of babies but actually killing them.) Winston Churchill respited Nash but not as swiftly as in previous infanticide cases. He referred to the case in a letter to his wife: 'a very disagreeable Death Sentence, which will take me a good many hours'. Churchill's penal approach was mix-and-match between positivist and classical. The former school would look at rehabilitation of a woman driven by economic despair to kill her child; the latter at the most suitable tariff for a cruel and deliberately planned homicide. Winston told Clementine that the case was 'a woman who murdered her 2-year-old illegitimate child under very bad circumstances'. It must be Nash, but the age is wrong. Do we see a tweak in the telling? Diana Churchill was approaching her second birthday. Winston was buying toys, including a set of Noah's Ark animals – he worried about whether the paint could be licked off. He was proud of Diana. Lucy Masterman must be quoted:

Lloyd George and Churchill were on the bench together just after the birth of Winston's daughter. 'Is she a pretty child?' said George. 'The prettiest child ever seen', said Winston beaming. 'Like her mother, I suppose?' said George. 'No', said Winston still more gravely, 'she is exactly like me.'

Churchill wrote on the file that Mary Ann Nash should serve 'at least 10 years'. His sentiment was with the dead boy. Nash did serve (almost) ten years. After leaving Liverpool Prison on licence, she disappeared. The final entry in her file states: 'it would appear that the lady has flown.' Ticket-of-leave disappearances were commonplace. On 16 March 1911 Churchill was asked how many licence-holders had recently defaulted on reporting to the police. The Home Secretary's figure was: thirty-four in the Metropolitan Police area alone since the start of the year; twenty-four had so far evaded arrest.[14]

Another infanticide case at this time featured prominently in the women's suffrage press. Margaret Murphy, 38, was a Shoreditch flower-seller. She was far removed from George Bernard Shaw's perky stage creation of several years later. Separated from her husband, Murphy had five children. The family lived in two rooms, often short of food. Margaret's struggles were sketched by Sylvia Pankhurst in *Votes for Women* newspaper. When the woman gave birth to an illegitimate baby, an already difficult life turned into a nightmare. After one long and tiring day, the flower-seller lost her earnings on the way home. After a night of despair, she gave a fatal dose of salts to her baby and attempted to poison herself. *Humanitarian* called the Old Bailey death sentence on Murphy 'a disgrace to a civilised nation'.[15]

The trial judge, Charles Darling, had been in conversation with Winston Churchill on the day of the sentence, 30 June 1911. The occasion was as difficult for Darling as for everyone else. Sylvia Pankhurst described the delivery of 'the barbarous words', and the woman walking down the steps with her guard from the square wooden pen in the centre of the court to the cells beneath whilst in another part of the building her young daughters were hysterical. A later note from Darling indicates that he and the Home Secretary were agreed that Margaret should spend only a very short time in prison. WSC prepared his memorandum for the King almost immediately. With it he sent a note:

> This is a very sad case and although the sentence was only passed yesterday… Your Majesty will wish that it should be respited and commuted at the earliest moment in order that needless pain may be spared.[16]

He communicated to the King the jury's strong recommendation to mercy, 'warmly supported' by the judge. His recommendation was:

> …that [the sentence] be commuted to penal servitude for life…It will not be a long period.

Sylvia Pankhurst was preparing a request to the Home Office to have Margaret Murphy released to the care of someone willing to look after her. Sylvia's newspaper reflections about the negative effects of prison considerably accorded with Churchill's views:

> The prisoner, instead of being given the opportunity of learning to become a better citizen…is subjected to a soul-destroying monotony, and with the solitary, silent system, to a machine-like routine which steadily saps her courage, initiative, self-respect, nay her very womanhood.

The Pankhurst article reflects on the Murphy type of mother:

> …when they marry and children are born to them, they renounce any but reflected joys and cheerfully accept that whilst all others have their holidays and hours of leisure, their own work shall never be done.

It was very different from the life of the women in Winston's social circle, with nursemaids for their children, and abounding leisure. Diana Churchill had a brother in May. Randolph was nicknamed 'The Chumbolly', Farsi for a healthy new-born baby. Margaret Murphy's baby reportedly was less than a third of normal healthy weight.[17]

Women prepared to take on the care of Margaret appeared. What has to be the Murphy case turns up in a November 1911 entry in the diary of George Riddell. Charles Darling had told him that:

> …he had recently sentenced a young girl to death and that the suffragettes announced their intention of making a great stir in favour of a reprieve. He sent for Miss Pankhurst and told her that…if they would name a lady who would take charge of the girl this might be helpful. A prominent suffragette was named for this office and the girl was reprieved…but it subsequently transpired that in the interim the lady herself had been convicted for rioting and was then in prison so that the girl was being detained pending the release of her guardian – a somewhat Gilbertian situation which seemed to amuse the judge.[18]

The 'lady' in this highly distorted account must be Mrs E.K. Marshall, to whom Ernley Blackwell makes reference in a 7 July 1911 memo, remarking that, 'I doubt very much whether this is the sort of person who can be trusted to look after a prisoner.' Katherine (Kitty) Marshall was in her early 40s, married to a solicitor. She was an active member of the WSPU. Blackwell did not like the 'fuss': women would get it into their heads that poisoning the baby attracted sympathy. He gave instructions for a letter to Mrs Marshall to say that, '[the Home Secretary] regrets that he is unable at present to advise any further remission.' He thought that:

> …[Murphy] should serve a substantial term in prison and be quietly released under the supervision of the agencies connected with Aylesbury [Prison]. Consider after 12 months.

Edward Troup initialled. Winston Churchill followed suit.

On 24 July Sylvia Pankhurst wrote a long letter to Churchill:

> ...I shall never forget the pitiful and heartrending cries and pleading [of a Murphy daughter] that she might be taken to her mother and that the poor mother should be set free.

Blackwell was not budging. Churchill backed his adviser.

Kitty Marshall was arrested and imprisoned for suffragette activity around the time of the Riddell diary entry. On 24 November (by which time Churchill was out of the Home Office) Sylvia Pankhurst presented a petition signed by five thousand for Margaret Murphy's immediate release. Edward Troup judged July 1912 as the earliest possible release date, but as a matter of courtesy asked Sir Charles Darling if he had any observations. Darling did. The Home Office file records them:

> Mr Justice Darling states that he was under the impression that prisoner would not be detained for anything like the length of time now suggested. Thinks no harm would be done by releasing her before the close of the present year.

Darling had not forgotten his promise to Sylvia Pankhurst to watch over Margaret Murphy's interests. He mentioned his conversation with Winston Churchill after the trial. He enclosed a note from Lord Lytton suggesting a Mrs Webbe as a suitable person to take responsibility for Margaret. Blackwell caved in, penning a sulky memo:

> The judge was not very wise and I don't think the view he takes is a very sound one. But the prisoner had better be released as soon as satisfactory arrangements can be made.[19]

Mrs Webbe was a suffragist too, but the judge had to be obliged. Winston Churchill's original intention now saw Margaret Murphy out of jail.

Press concern about death sentences on young women who killed their illegitimate babies was not confined to the women's suffrage press. Towards the end of July 1911, the *Croydon Guardian* commented on a case at Guildford Assizes:

> Those who would harden their hearts against alteration [of the law] ought to witness the grim and awful solemnity of the passing of a sentence of death. The sight of the swooning girl in the dock at Guildford would have melted a heart of steel.[20]

In her early 20s, Kate Penrith was an unemployed domestic servant, 'pleasant-looking', the *Daily Mail* informed readers. She had booked herself out of an infirmary with the baby she had given birth to thirteen days earlier, saying that a friend had agreed to take it. Next morning the baby was found on waste ground dying from the effects of a poison substance. The jury strongly recommended mercy. The judge, Walter Phillimore, told the woman that he hoped she would have 'a long life in which to repent for your crime'.

He wrote to Winston Churchill in support of the jury's plea:

> The murder was a cold-blooded one, but the girl had borne previously a good character and was well spoken of in the infirmary.

Ernley Blackwell called the killing 'a cruel murder', but noted:

> The girl seems to have been fond of the child in a way as she cried bitterly as she nursed him before she took him out to kill him.

He recommended: 'Respite and commute', adding that: 'The case is a bad one in some of its aspects and she should serve a substantial term of p. s. At least 5 years I should say.'

The *Croydon Guardian* reported Kate Penrith's reprieve:

> Considering the usual leisureliness of the law, and the slow, creaking routine of the average state department, the fact is very noteworthy that only about four days elapsed from the passing of the sentence to the notification of the reprieve. In this matter, at any rate, Mr Winston Churchill figures in a very good light.

Churchill recommended that the woman 'should serve as for 5 years.' This meant that Kate would be released after three-and-a-third years, taking into account remission.

Next in the unhappy line was 22-year-old domestic servant, Mabel Blackmore. Mabel entered Neath Workhouse for the birth of her illegitimate baby. After five weeks, she left with her child wrapped in a workhouse shawl, travelling on a train to Port Talbot where she had been in service. Some boys playing near a pond noticed her no longer with the baby and looking wet. At Swansea Assizes Mabel's case was not helped by the attitude of Mr Justice Bray, who when a juryman asked whether there had been a search for the Mrs Jones to whom she claimed to have given the baby, invited the jury to use their 'common sense' on whether they believed in the lady's existence. Home Office procedure called for a 'good' newspaper account of major trials. A full-page on the Blackmore trial in the *Cambria Daily Leader* sits in the file with notes on Mabel (who had previous convictions for stealing a coat and two petticoats). Churchill will have observed that the prosecution was conducted by fellow Liberal MPs Llewelyn Williams and Clement Edwards. Both encouraged witnesses to agree that the accused looked 'strange'. The result was not in doubt. The jury strongly recommended mercy. The newspaper account described the scene between the sentencing judge and the woman:

The Judge having assumed the black cap, sentence of death was passed in the usual way. When his Lordship reached the words "and that you hang by the neck" prisoner shrieked "Never" and swooned in the arms of the wardress, and was removed below with the assistance of warders.[21]

On 1 August the *Daily News* reported that, 'large numbers of people in Swansea are signing the petition for the reprieve of the girl Mabel Blackmore.' The Home Secretary had already acted, communicating his memorandum to the King four days after the sentence:

> …The sentence of death has therefore been respited and it is recommended that it be commuted to penal servitude for life. The question of further mitigation of sentence is reserved for future consideration. An effective sentence should however in this case be served.[22]

Next in the procession was Cheltenham domestic servant Daisy Turner. *Votes for Women* reported in August that Daisy had been committed for trial, charged with the murder of her new-born illegitimate infant. The baby had apparently died of a head injury. Would another young woman face a death-capped judge? Not this time. The women's movement was fighting back. Daisy's defence was organized by the Women's Freedom League, backed by the Men's Committee for Justice to Women. A distinguished doctor backed the woman's claim that the baby had not lived after being born. The trial was halted and Daisy was acquitted. If she had been found guilty, her file would not have come to Winston Churchill. By the time of the trial, young women facing the gallows for infanticide were no longer his problem.[23]

Chapter 22

The Cad and the King

When the monarch had a speech to make on a visit, it was written by a Home Office under-secretary. The man with that job when Winston Churchill arrived was 'a past master of all the clichés', said Harold Butler. The drafts had to be signed off by the Home Secretary. Butler's memoir recalls that when a speech for King Edward came Churchill's way, he 'exploded when he saw the jejune oration.' The civil servant was relieved of this duty and Winston had a new outlet for his phrases. When the King gave a brisk address to the boys of Eton in the spring of 1910, they will have had no inkling of the Harrovian authorship of their pep talk.[1]

In 1898 the then Prince of Wales had advised Winston Churchill to hold back on entering Parliament. As King Edward, he watched without enthusiasm Winston's governmental progress (though he did give him a silver-headed stick as a wedding gift). He remarked to his son that Winston was 'almost more of a cad in office than in opposition'. There was frisson when Churchill tactlessly repeated a comment by the King, as Henry Asquith took power, that the new prime minister was 'not a gentleman'. Perhaps the King's antipathy towards the young dynamo was eased by the speech-writing assistance. But he took umbrage again when the Home Secretary invoked an alliance of Crown and Commons against the Peers.[2]

On King Edward's death, the Tory social ranks were swept by conspiracy gossip. It was said that Liberal Ministers, Churchill especially, by dragging the Crown into party politics, had damaged fatally the King's health. Eddie Marsh wrote to Lady Gladstone:

> The cock-and-bull stories going about as to the King having been killed by the Liberals are too amazing…Muriel Lady Helmsley assured Pauline as a fact that Winston had gone to the proclamation [of the new King] in a red tie!![3]

The excited tales were without basis (King Edward's over-eating will not have helped his health) but they had wide currency. A former Conservative MP with court connections, Cecil Manners, called Churchill 'without conscience or scruple'. He gossiped that when the Home Secretary came to the Palace as the King's health declined, he was snubbed by being left downstairs.[4]

Churchill's speech-shaping service continued for King George. On 16 May 1911 the King orated at the unveiling of the Victoria Memorial on the Mall. In a photograph Winston sports a tight, braided uniform, holding the book with the speeches. The King's private secretary, Sir Arthur Bigge, conveyed to WSC the monarch's commendation of his work. The newspapers called the royal address 'impressive'. Present was the German Emperor, the King's fellow grandson of Queen Victoria, who figured appropriately in Churchill's composition. The occasion provided a get-together opportunity for the royal cousins. Kaiser Wilhelm cleared with King George a prospective call by a German warship at the Moroccan port of Agadir on its way back from German South-West Africa. Unfortunately, the King failed to inform his government. A few weeks later a major international crisis would blow up, one effect of which would be to change the political course of Winston Churchill.[5]

Churchill was on speech production duty for the King for the year's big event, the coronation on 23 June 1911 at Westminster Abbey of George and Mary as King and Queen of Britain and its realms, and Emperor and Empress of India. Winston's wife was nursing the infant Randolph. The King provided Clementine with a seat in his private box and a royal brougham to convey her from Eccleston Square.

No glitter was spared. An extravaganza of coach processions occupied two days. Churchill's composition for King George was recited by the monarch at a stop-off on one of these, in front of the London County Council stand near Trafalgar Square. The press reported that:

> Just previously, Mr and Mrs Winston Churchill had driven up to the stand and the Home Secretary handed to the King the copy of the address from which his Majesty read, speaking with clarity and distinctly.[6]

Winston was thrilled by the ride, writing later to Clemmie that, 'Everyone admired the cat, the carriage, the horses and the tiger.' The 'cat' (that favourite Churchill image) was Clementine; the 'tiger' was a boy with striped livery. Churchill predicted that the memory would be handed down in the family.[7]

King George had followed King Edward in his poor view of Churchill, but that seemed to be changing. A couple of weeks before the coronation there was a suggestion of the King coming over to Eccleston Square to 'meet a few men'. It did not happen but the talk was an indicator of better relations. Churchill had some special credit with the King as a result of his assistance on a matter of a very personal nature. An old and persistent story claimed that the monarch had three children from a marriage contracted with the daughter of an admiral whilst he was serving with the Fleet in Malta, which would make him a bigamist. In November 1910 it was repeated by English journalist Edward Mylius in the French republican/anarchist paper *Liberator*. The situation was delicate. The King wanted to clear his name but for him to appear in court when the courts were in his name would have been indelicate. Winston Churchill took charge. He organized liaison of police, judiciary, the King himself, and the ministers who were privy. Mylius was tried on 1 February 1911 by the Lord Chief Justice before a special jury. He was convicted and received twelve months. Afterwards, the Liberal Chief Whip passed on to Churchill from the Palace the monarch's 'real gratitude for your exceeding care and sympathy'.[8]

Rapprochement between the King and the Home Secretary advanced. A week after the coronation, Winston wrote to Clemmie to tell her that he was: 'just back from a long day's drive with the King to the City and back through North London'. Keeping him company in the state coach, he said, were the Duchess of Devonshire and the Countess of Minto; these Tory ladies were upset when Winston was cheered but became happier when boos rang out from the section of the route around the Mansion House.[9]

King George's accession was proclaimed at Eton. Winston told Clemmie:

I have written a tart speech for the King to deliver to the Eton boys – putting these fashionable young cubs on their mettle.[10]

Churchill, of the second-ranked Harrovian tribe, will have enjoyed that.

On 13 July there was a royal event at which Churchill himself had to speak. George Riddell's diary mentions Winston practising the recitation of a 'long and involved' proclamation that he had to make at the Investiture of the Prince of Wales at Caernarfon. He was preparing intensively, trying out three or four different renderings of 'Know ye'. The ceremony had been devised by Lloyd George, with a special role for his political chum. Winston did not jib at being centre-stage.[11]

Two days before he performed, Churchill mentions in a letter to Clementine a woman in the family circle telling him about a doctor in Germany who completely cured her depression: 'I think this man might be useful to me – if my black dog returns. He seems quite away from me now. It is such a relief.' 'Black Dog' was the deep despond from which Churchill sometimes suffered. Whether it was clinical is disputed. How much his mental state was affected by his responsibility regarding death sentences, it is impossible to say. He would later recall the early period of his married life as one of 'terrifying, almost suicidal, depression when [I] carried out [my] duties mechanically.' That would fit the Home Office years.[12]

For the Investiture, Winston Churchill stayed at Penrhos on Anglesey, at one of the homes of Lord Sheffield. From here he was gathered by the Royal Yacht *Victoria and Albert*. On board he had a long talk with the King 'about the most important things', no doubt the House of Lords and the creation of new peers. At dinner, he sat next to the Queen, finding her, as he told his wife, 'rather alarming: her husband did most of the work.'[13]

At the Investiture, the King's 17-years-old son Edward knelt on a silk cushion in front of his father, as the monarch handed Letters Patent to the Home Secretary. Churchill's intonation of a battery of names and titles (including German ones) will have benefitted from his rehearsing. The King draped a mantle round Prince Edward's shoulders, hung a sword round his neck, and put a coronet on his head, a gold ring on his left hand and a golden rod into his other, as Churchill synchronized his declamation with each stage of this elaborate ritual. The intimate double-act between Sovereign and Home Secretary cannot but have deepened the relationship.[14]

Churchill retained happy memories of his royal duties when he composed his 1939 newspaper reminiscences:

> At the Coronation he plays a part which brings him in contact with all the most venerable and glittering traditions of our history. He is the adviser of the Sovereign in many grave and delicate matters.[15]

The article, entitled 'Sombre Memories of the Home Office', is dominated by the death sentences responsibility. The Investiture of the Prince of Wales was among Churchill's more pleasant Home Office recall. He reported to Clementine that the prince was 'a very nice boy – quite simple and terribly kept in order'. And Churchill thought that the new monarch had 'learned a lot'.[16]

Chapter 23
'Brilliant Lions'

The biographical detail that Winston Churchill founded a club is curious given his social eccentricity. It was a dining society. There was a precedent. In his early parliamentary days, Churchill, Hugh Cecil, and several other Tories gathered weekly at the House, calling themselves 'the Hooligans'. Churchill's new dining fraternity, called the Other Club, was a joint enterprise with F.E. Smith. The inaugural dinner was on 18 May 1911. The signatures on the card are collectively informative since they represent the world in which Churchill and Smith wanted their careers to bloom.[1]

It assembled fortnightly at the Savoy Hotel when Parliament was in session. Two-thirds of the original membership were twelve Liberals and twelve Conservatives. Among the Conservatives we find Tory Democrats ('advanced Tories') such as Edward Goulding. The non-party-political third was a collection of various, including press figures, one of whom was Churchill's golfing partner George Riddell. Among the signatures sits that of Charles Darling. Remarkably (but perhaps not) Churchill-baiter Lord Winterton was signed up. The membership bears the mark of Churchill's quest for Liberal-Conservative middle-of-the-road cooperation. The club membership was without a Labour or socialist presence.[2]

Among those invited to join was Arthur Ponsonby. The list of names presented to him included Lloyd George, Charles Masterman, and Rudyard Kipling. Ponsonby's diary confirms the politics around the club:

> I decided almost there and then No, but I said I would sleep over it. Talked it over with Ch. Masterman, who as a matter of fact had not yet been asked. He says there is a strong disposition on the part of Churchill and George to coalesce with the younger more prominent and progressive Tories. The plan is evidently connected with it. It is to be a collection of brilliant lions. I feel a growing hatred for the Tory attitude of mind, the exclusive select superior view adopted largely by Churchill...Winston Churchill spoke to me of it last night as I was standing at the Bar of the House. He and I have never seen eye to eye. I mistrust him. It is a pity when he is so brilliant.[3]

Lloyd George did not become a member, but he assisted the club's direction. Kipling did not join. Churchill presumably was not aware that the literary Imperialist regretted (in private correspondence) that among the Sidney Street bullets there had not been 'a shot where it would have done some good to the nation'.[4]

The Other Club would continue through Winston's life and beyond. Its place in history is as a WSC curiosity.

If the club is one piece of evidence of Winston Churchill being emotionally tugged back in the direction of Conservatives, another is a conversation around this time between Churchill and Lloyd George, passed on by LG to Charles Masterman, and recorded by Lucy:

> Late one evening when [Churchill] had become confidential he solemnly announced, 'The fact is, David [he always calls L.G. David when something portentous is coming], *I am a* Tory.'[5]

The heatwave of the summer of 1911 has passed into legend. Westminster tempers were hotting-up too, as the climax approached of Peers v People. 24 July was infamous in the annals of the House of Commons. Asquith attempted a statement on the Parliament Bill (to remove the Lords' power of Veto). Hansard records just two lines before he was halted:

> The PRIME MINISTER rose in his place to move "That the Lords Amendments be now considered," and was immediately assailed with Opposition cries of "Traitor".

Sustained bawling by Conservatives rendered Asquith inaudible, apart from single lines when the cacophony paused for breath. To the fore was Hugh Cecil. Of the shrieking of Churchill's best man little appears in Hansard except the phrase 'prostituted ordinary Parliamentary usage'. Looking down from above, Violet Asquith observed '[Cecil's] snow-white gibbering execrations, like a baboon, epileptic and suffragette rolled into one'.[6]

Asquith's ranks held their discipline to listen in silence to Arthur Balfour. But it was too much when F.E. Smith rose. He had been bellowing during Asquith's attempt to speak. Hansard records that Smith, 'was met with continued interruption during five minutes, and did not obtain a hearing.'

Churchill sent in his regular account to the King:

> The Prime Minister was this afternoon subjected to prolonged organised insult and interruption from a section of the Conservative Party, among whom Lord Hugh Cecil and Mr Goulding were most prominent. Mr F.E. Smith who had himself been very disorderly attempted to continue the debate but of course the House would not listen to him.[7]

How did Winston Churchill feel about the ragging of Asquith? He was sitting next to the standing figure of the prime minister amid the pandemonium, as a small *Punch* drawing on its Parliament page indicates. Unsurprisingly, there is an angry expression on Winston's face in the scene of a grim Asquith at the table, his papers on the brass-bound Dispatch Box, unable to get a word out, as shown by speech bubbles of interruptions with exclamation marks. Churchill, we may think, could have had mixed feelings. The House had a new Conservative Member, Leopold Amery, unopposed at a Birmingham by-election. Amery, a future cabinet minister, had been at Harrow with Churchill. A year older, he was of short stature. Once at school Churchill came upon him standing in front of a pool and took him for a younger pupil: he did what came naturally, pushing him into the water. This was a big mistake. The enraged boy who emerged seized Churchill and pitched him into the deepest part of the water. Peace was made uneasily, Winston informing Leo that, 'My father, who is a great man, is also small.' Was Churchill now in discreet awe of the audacious ambush of the prime minister by Tory colleagues of Leo with whom he had much in common?[8]

The behaviour of Churchill himself was not as expected from a Leader of the House. Winston could not resist schoolboy-type provocation of the opposition. On 20 April the House was deep into the night on the Parliament Bill, with Churchill on governmental duty. The ire of Earl Winterton was up. He made a protest to the presiding Deputy Speaker:

> When I rose to address the [House sitting as a committee] some of the right hon. Gentleman's [Churchill's] friends "barracked" me. They called out the name of an hon. Member – myself – by name instead of by the constituency he represents. Those cries were led by the right hon. Gentleman himself, the present Leader of the House of Commons, as I understand.[9]

By parliamentary etiquette Lord Winterton should have been referred to by his constituency (Horsham). The context of the teasing is not retrievable from Hansard, but the aggrieved victim saw Churchill as letting down his office by joining in the schoolboy-type japing. Churchill claimed innocence:

> I frankly admit that I called out the Noble Lord's name. That is not a disorderly interruption. It is not discourtesy.

Churchill's parliamentary letter to the King informed his Majesty that:

> The debate was dull and decorous, but at the very end after everything was settled there was a little ill-temper and Lord Winterton became conspicuous.[10]

In Hansard it looks like an uproarious night, with Harry Whitley in the Chair almost losing control. Irish Nationalist Michael Flavin decided that he was at an auction sale:

Mr FLAVIN
Going, going, gone.

Earl WINTERTON
Send for the Speaker—send for one who will keep order.

The CHAIRMAN
If the Noble Lord does not cease these cries, I shall have to deal with him.

Earl WINTERTON
I rise to a Point of Order. I desire to call your attention to the fact that there are continuous disorderly interruptions from hon. Gentlemen below the Gangway and by the Home Secretary, who is in charge of the House.

Mr CHURCHILL
I am sure I made no disorderly interruptions.

Earl WINTERTON
I most decidedly accuse the right hon. Gentleman of making most disorderly interruptions.[11]

Churchill wrote to Clementine that Winterton was 'a little pig...I have done with him. He showed real malignity – which I shall never forget.' Within months Winterton would be in Churchill's club.[12]

Churchill could be touchy. A George Riddell diary entry from March 1911 has:

Winston, L.G., and Neil Primrose were dining together. The evening was passing pleasantly when Neil Primrose said, in commenting upon some statement of Winston's, 'That's no argument!' Winston's face became over-clouded, and he at once called for the bill and broke up the party. LG said to him when they were driving home, 'What's wrong? What has happened?' Winston replied, 'I was annoyed that a boy like that should speak to me in that manner.'[13]

Strikingly good-looking and seriously wealthy, Primrose, 28, Liberal MP for Wisbech, was the second son of former Prime Minister Lord Rosebery. His set was known for its hedonistic lifestyle (turf, parties, dinners). He was a protégé of Churchill, who tried unsuccessfully to get him into Asquith's government. Eton-educated, president of the Bullingdon Club at Oxford, Primrose was the archetypal gilded youth. In *My Early Life* Churchill recollects lunching in his early days in Parliament with three title-bearers of this type who argued cleverly with him, leaving him frustrated. They were: 'young men only two or three years older than myself, all born with silver spoons in their mouths, all highly distinguished at Oxford or Cambridge...I felt I was the earthen pot among the brass.' Churchill's parents' marriage had been a union of American money (Jennie Jerome being a finance heiress) and a relatively impoverished branch of British aristocracy. Winston's battle with money was perpetual. He loved luxury and good living. His spending, which so worried his wife, ran to everything from his wines and cigars and foreign travel to his pink silk underwear. With his income not sufficient to cover the bills, debts were a regular problem. Neil Primrose lived the good life effortlessly. Churchill's prickliness, it should be noted, did not deny him a place in the Other Club.[14]

Primrose would die in 1917 on active service in Palestine. The hindsight of war casts a dark shadow over Parliament in this period. On 11 April 1911

Lord Ninian Crichton-Stuart, Conservative MP for Cardiff, had a question for Churchill, a fellow Harrow alumnus, on opium dens in London (used by Chinese seamen). Crichton-Stuart would die leading his men at the Battle of Loos in October 1915. There was also Lord Alexander Thynne, Conservative Member for Bath. Churchill speaks of Thynne in a 25 June letter to Clementine:

> I went for a long walk in the rain with Alex Thynne. He is just one of these young Tories who would have followed my father or me with perfect satisfaction. But now – without leaders or ideas or plan – they drift off into all sorts of foolish backwaters of thought.

Thynne would die in action in France in 1918, commanding his battalion.[15]

In scenes of Churchill and his political friends, we see a masculine world. Coming change was pressing hard. Winston continued to be bothered by the suffragettes and their male allies. At a National Liberal Club dinner for election-gain Liberal MPs (which he organized), *The Times* reported that:

> When Mr Churchill rose to speak, a man shouted out, "Mr Churchill, you ought to be thoroughly ashamed of yourself for the way you treated Miss __."[16]

On the votes-for-women front, nowhere was safe for Winston.

Chapter 24

Lorna Doone and a Cup of Tea

Soon, events would be moving Winston Churchill on from the Home Office. Before we consider his influence, it is worth observing that in July 1911 Churchill again differed from his advisers on reprieve. Ex-navy gardener George Pateman fatally attacked his girlfriend with a razor when she told him that she was leaving him. Troup and Blackwell were for no interference. Churchill saw absence of premeditation, and previous good character. He reprieved. Taking the capital sentences for which Churchill had responsibility, we have figures of: twenty reprieves; twenty-one non-interventions: roughly the Home Secretary average. Excluding the female cases, all infanticide, we have for Churchill thirteen reprieves out of thirty-four cases.[1]

He left capital punishment as he found it. In 1866 a Royal Commission had recommended that murders be classified into capital and non-capital, the latter for less heinous ones. Two months into Churchill's time at the Home Office, *Humanitarian* magazine expressed the hope that these proposals would at last be carried into effect. Had Churchill backed making a category of non-capital murder, he would have been opposed by the long-entrenched attitude of his department. The change would not come about until the Homicide Act of 1957, which established capital and non-capital murder categories, a division that proved difficult to work. Less than ten years from then the only effective solution would be adopted, namely the abolition of capital punishment for murder. Churchill was not drawn to any change in the law, except in the infanticide category.[2]

The summer of 1911 brought newspaper excitement over an attempted prison escape. Clementine wrote to Winston:

> Please be kind to the poor boy of 18 who jumped over the gaol wall at Bedford and swam twice across the Ouse followed by every policeman in the town and was finally caught when he fell down from exhaustion – it was in the Sunday papers.[3]

The youth, serving nine months for theft, got over the wall by way of a drainpipe. He was sighted running through the town in prison uniform. Sympathy bells must have jangled with Churchill with his memories of shinning over a Boer prison fence. With confinement tight, prison escapes were a rarity. There were just five in 1910–1911.[4]

1911 began with the seal-of-approval for Winston Churchill's prison reforms from a major penal figure. In *Nineteenth Century and After* magazine, Sir Edward

Clayton, ex-Secretary to the Prison Commission, pronounced that Churchill was moving the system 'in the right direction'. What did this Home Secretary achieve? The answer is a good deal. Certain aspects deserve particular notice. They are: education, libraries, entertainment, and aged prisoners.[5]

Within weeks of becoming Home Secretary, Churchill wrote to Ruggles-Brise:

> Will you kindly consider whether some regular system of lectures should not be introduced into the prisons?[6]

He invited the Prison Commission chief to make proposals. Brise was cautiously supportive. The lectures should have 'a moral and elevating purpose'. But he did not see how a lecture programme would work in local prisons, with their 'fugitive and ever-changing' population. Ninety-five per cent of prisoners were in for three months or less, the majority for two weeks or less. Most in local jails were at 'the penal stage', meaning solitary confinement. Sir Evelyn was keen to tell the Home Secretary of sermons given by Church Army, missionaries, chaplains, and 'suitable laymen'. This is scarcely what Churchill will have been thinking of. There had been a recent performance at a prison by celebrity concert singer Clara Butt. Here again it seems to have been a religious event. The Somerset Light Infantry band's jail rendition which Churchill flagged up in his parliamentary speech, was an Easter Day service (on the invitation of the Chaplain) rather than a concert. There is a Home Office file on 'addresses and lectures given to prisoners': these are religious. Churchill wanted lectures and entertainment.[7]

Brise proposed a prison event once a quarter for convict jails, expenses to be defrayed by the state: music (especially military) and 'lecturers, with illustrations, of a high class'. £500 would cover the programme. On local jails, the Commissioner was prepared to see something in the way of music and lectures on an ad hoc basis. Churchill agreed that it should be left to voluntary effort. On the convict jails, he said:

> Propose me a plan. Let an imaginary programme be worked out fully. Music especially and Magic Lanterns. Is there any reason why special classes should not be formed for the study of suitable subjects from among more educated convicts?

Brise produced a scheme. Each of the four male convict prisons would get either two lectures a year (Maidstone and Portland) or four (Parkhurst and Dartmoor). A Fleet Street firm had tendered for these: to be delivered by 'competent popular lecturers'. Magic lanterns would need to be purchased. An officer at each prison would be taught how to use them. The Commissioner proposed:

> Mr Richard Kerr, F.G.S, F.R.A.S. a well-known lecturer in popular science on such subjects as Halley and his Comet; Radium; Microscopic wonders in nature; Wireless Telegraphy etc, etc, and Mr Herbert Garrison, F.R.G.S.,

who lectures on foreign countries and Native races, on Pompeii and Herculaneum, the Eruption of Mont Pelée, etc…Experience at the Convict Prisons has shown that for an audience of such mixed education as the convicts, this sort of lecture is generally the most popular. The men like the lectures to be instructive as well as amusing.

Brise's choice was not innocent. Herbert Garrison was an Imperialist who toured the schools with his lantern slides under the aegis of the Royal Colonial Institute, promoting the glory of the British Empire. If the convicts listened attentively, some might after release sign up for imperial military service. This sort of lecture would sit well with the military rank of many prison governors.[8]

For the four convict jails, Churchill wanted altogether eighteen lectures plus eighteen concerts yearly. Ruggles-Brise wanted fewer. He warned of the hazards of convicts congregating in darkened rooms. He stressed the need to look out for 'the good order of prisons and the safety of officers'. The attention of convicts would need to be riveted by entertainment of 'rare quality', whilst they appreciated 'the great privilege and indulgence'. No inmate should be allowed to attend who had not been clear of report for six months. The Commissioner thought that, taking lectures and concerts together, each of the four convict jails should have one event per quarter. Churchill accepted the lower number, 'to begin with'. Brise wanted publicity held back until the Prison Commission's annual report. That was not the WSC way: 'I will consider further the question of publication', he told Sir Evelyn. The Commissioner bristled: he was not aware of 'any precedent for publication in any other form of matters relating to the interior economy of prison'. Churchill cut the ground from under him by announcing the principle of lectures and concerts in his speech to Parliament.[9]

The Treasury funding application was sent off by Harry Simpson: £84 a year for the lectures, £80 for the concerts, and £42 for a one-off purchase of magic lantern apparatus, along with a maximum of £50 per year for occasional lectures at local prisons and Borstals. The Treasury Commissioners signed off the sum, but not quite all: money for magic lanterns was rejected.

After Winston Churchill's departure from the Home Office, the file on convict prison lectures and entertainment is silent until the 1920s. However, the 1922 Hobhouse/Brockway report has some information:

> …Definite arrangements were made for two lectures and two musical entertainments at each Convict prison in the year. They have apparently been continued as regular quarterly events. Governors and chaplains have frequently testified to the benefit they have been to the prisoners.[10]

Churchill set about providing 'brain food' for prisoners. Integral was reform of the prison-libraries. These days most entering the prisons were literate, albeit in very varying degrees. The modern world required a good prison-library system.

As things stood, arrangements were rudimentary, with cataloguing irregular and distribution of books inefficient – and the libraries were restricted by the deprivation principles of the penal system.

A prison-library book features in the cell scene of *Justice*. A stage direction reads:

Falder's work (a shirt to which he is putting button-holes) is hung to a nail on the wall over a small wooden table, on which the novel "Lorna Doone" lies open.[11]

'Falder' must have been in prison for more than a month. In the first month of confinement a prisoner was allowed to have only 'books of instruction in addition to the usual religious books'. With the majority of sentences a month or less, many inmates would never have the chance to read a novel in prison. R.D. Blackmore's blood-and-thunder romance would not be permitted. Even for inmates entitled to read novels, the chaplain censored choice. There had been an internal debate about educational and recreational prison reading. Would the prospect for inmates of being able to read the *Strand Magazine* instead of Henry Hallam (a long-dead historian whose tomes were favoured by prison-libraries) be an incentive to good conduct? Churchill punctured the earnestness with a comment that, 'Some people would prefer Hallam to the *Strand*.' On libraries, he made an important move. With the agreement of the Prison Commissioners, he set up a committee to hold an inquiry and make recommendations.[12]

The recently founded Penal Reform League sent proposals to the Home Office. Prisoners, it said, should be allowed to read newspapers to encourage an interest in current events. That drew an under-secretary's comment that in practice the average prisoner was only interested in crime, prize fighting, and racing. The attitude of staff to the league's investigations was dismissive. The chief hope for wider in-prison reading experience lay with the Churchill Committee. In determining who sat on it, Churchill was creative. The members were: Rev C.B. Simpson, the Chaplain-Inspector; Mrs Olive Birrell (sister of Augustine), Lady Visitor at Holloway; Arthur Stanley, an ex-Liberal MP; Walter Raleigh, Professor of English Literature at Oxford University; and Basil Thompson, Secretary of the Prison Commission. Raleigh and Thompson were both known to be penally enlightened.[13]

The committee visited prisons, including Dartmoor, and interviewed inmates in their cells with their books. Its recommendations were modest but positive. Churchill wrote on the file, 'A good and thoughtful Report. Thank the committee.' Among the points was the need for sufficient financial support for prison-libraries. The Treasury was evidently impressed by the proposals, since capitation for books was increased. Among the organizational changes suggested were more frequent book exchanges and a more generous in-cell allowance. A prison-library feature familiar to later times that emerged from the committee was prisoner librarians. This humanizing detail was part of the Churchill wind of change that went through the system. Janet Fyfe, in *Books Behind Bars*, comments that the Churchill Committee's report (completed on 27 October 1910) was 'a signpost towards present day arrangements for library service in prisons'.[14]

A Churchill priority was the elderly in jail. One of the earliest cases he examined was a veteran convict sentenced at Middlesex sessions to eight years. George White's age was uncertain, perhaps seventy-one. The jury convicted him of receiving stolen jewellery. White had already spent a total of forty-three years in jail. The prisoner, as described in a newspaper clipping in the Home Office file, 'looked dazed' and said, 'I shall never be able to do it.' Churchill, plainly shocked, called for a special report. The man's convictions tracked back to 1865. In 1871, along with a fourteen-year sentence, he received thirty lashes. He had done previous stretches of penal servitude for larceny (twice), housebreaking (twice), robbery with violence, and keeping a brothel. The total of his sentences before remission was fifty-one and a half years.[15]

A report came in from the Medical Officer at Wormwood Scrubs that White was under treatment in the hospital, suffering from chronic bronchial catarrh and heart weakness. He would probably need to be kept in hospital during the winter months. The case brought out the difference in attitude to 'habitual' criminals as between the Home Secretary and his senior staff. Harry Simpson wrote on the file, '…not known ever to have done honest work…to be hoped that he may have served to discourage others from following his example'. Edward Troup saw: 'an absolutely worthless specimen of humanity'. Churchill's perspective was different. He saw 'the total failure even of the most terrible sentence of imprisonment to effect the slightest reform upon the criminal'. White was 'old, weak and failing': it was 'quite useless to keep him under punishment'. He wanted him put straightaway into the preventive detention category.

Under p. d. White would have a more comfortable time, in accommodation designed for incorrigible habituals. Troup reminded Churchill that the special prison was not yet ready. He said that under the 1908 Prevention of Crime Act the Home Secretary had no power to convert penal servitude to preventive detention until three years had been served. His memorandum bewailed the hopelessness of reforming 'moral imbeciles'. These were less than one in a thousand of the population, he said, but 'they all gravitate to the convict prisons': a prisoner of the White sort 'again and again reverts to a form of crime which is certain to bring him back to prison.' Troup thought that prisons could no more alter moral imbeciles than the elementary schools could 'teach hopeless imbeciles to read and write'.

Churchill came back sharply: 'What do you propose should be done with these old men under possible life sentences?' Troup thought that for White the only alternative to prison was release to the workhouse. He opposed this because the convict could have the 'excitement' of more housebreaking, an odd comment given White's physical condition. Sir Edward commented that prison would probably be preferable to the workhouse, being 'rather more comfortable with somewhat better medical attendance'. The suggestion that prison was easier than the workhouse was sometimes heard.

On George White and a similar case, Troup grudgingly gave a bit of ground:

> Perhaps the case might be noted for consideration after (say) two years when the prisoner may be no longer fit to commit even minor offences.

Churchill went along with this suggestion, but he saw an issue far beyond a couple of cases. He wanted more information: how many convicts were there with substantial periods to serve? He made a declaration of intent:

> It is clear that the ordinary prison rules require some modification in the case of those whom there is no chance to reform and no need to deter.

Troup was happy to let them rot. Churchill was not. The Home Secretary was short with the permanent under-secretary on his fear of prisoners getting an easier time than workhouse inmates. He told Troup: 'I am not concerned with any arguments relative to the treatment of aged paupers. They are not under my supervision. It is clearly our duty to suppress unnecessary and purposeless suffering.' He was determined to put in place a kinder regime for elderly long-term prisoners. On 8 May 1910 he asked Ruggles-Brise how mitigation could be achieved of the conditions of elderly recidivists who would probably not survive their sentences. He asked: 'Cannot a special class be formed?'[16]

Troup was tepid but Brise, after some foot-dragging, came aboard. He submitted a scheme for Churchill's consideration on 8 August 1910. An 'Old Guard' would have 'special relaxation and indulgencies'. He wanted them brought together at Parkhurst (or perhaps two centres). He found fifty-three convicts, currently in nine jails, fitting Churchill's specifications. They would live within the prison community. Their cells would have clear-glass windows, which could be opened widely, like those of tubercular convicts. They would have a hospital-type bedstead rather than the plank-bed, and a chair instead of a stool (with arms in some cases). Braces, and shoes (rather than boots) would be permitted, as would food in accordance with dietary arrangements to help them. They would have some useful occupation but the usual prison rules would be relaxed. They would be able to have as much exercise as they wanted. Seats would be available in a designated area. 'Excellent', Churchill wrote back on 17 August 1910: 'This carries out entirely my wishes.'[17]

Did the special regime actually happen? It did. It was instituted in time to be noted in the 1911 Annual Report of the Prison Commission (which came out in the spring), 'with a view of suppressing unnecessary and purposeless suffering'. The age qualification was 67, with younger prisoners with dementia included. The report describes the common room of this group:

> The aged convicts have a large, light association room with tables and chairs. No daily newspapers are allowed but magazines like the "Strand" and the "Grand" and journals like the "Church Family Newspaper" are permitted. A

door of this room leads out into a little garden brilliant with flowers, where the old men sit in the sun. They may talk, and although they have mail-bags to sew, no work is insisted upon. They quarrel occasionally, but not much.[18]

In 1922 Brise informed readers of *The English Prison System* that, 'Subject to good conduct, prison in the Aged Convicts Division is free, as far as possible, from all penal conditions.' Churchill as Home Secretary lived on in prison memory. Wilfred Macartney, who did ten years penal servitude in Parkhurst between the wars, was a communist. He hated Winston Churchill politically, but in his 1936 memoirs he called him 'the only Home Secretary who cut through the barriers erected by a stupid, cruel bureaucracy and helped the convict.' He thought that Churchill would have liked to do much more, but 'could not unstick the Home Office limpets.' He declared: 'Today many old lags of seventy to eighty bless his name, and often have these old fellows said to me: "...Winston was the only chap who ever helped the lag or did us any good."' Wilfred particularly approved of the provision for the elderly of 'a cup of tea at night in place of the filthy cocoa'.[19]

Macartney takes a few liberties with history (he thought it was Churchill who abolished the tread-wheel), but there was reality behind the legend of Winston who cared. Lucy Masterman put it thus:

[Churchill] was always accessible to the humanitarian appeal, and a number of mitigations, particularly of the lot of elderly "lags", were due to him.[20]

What about women prisoners as regards Churchill's reforms? The Aylesbury female convict prison certainly benefitted considerably. Lady Constance Battersea, a member of its board, writing to the Home Secretary on 20 December 1910, said: 'I want to tell you how much I appreciate the spirit of reform that is becoming apparent in prison management.' She commented approvingly on chairs in cells, plain-glass windows, lectures, and concerts. She endorsed the WSC approach: 'I must thank you for thinking so much of these unfortunate people: they are not entirely bad.' The Home Secretary scribbled: 'Send a nice letter of thanks.'[21]

Sir Edward Troup was considerably at cross-purposes with Winston Churchill regarding imprisonment. In a 9 February 1911 memorandum, Troup saw a damaging consequence of the shortening of sentences for crimes against property, in the habitual criminal having 'more frequent periods of liberty [which] give him more opportunities for committing crime'. He thought that an increase in burglary since 1898 was due to 'the great leniency in the carrying out of short sentences'. He and Harry Simpson thought that amelioration of prison conditions had gone too far. They were for beefing up deterrence by giving (some) prisoners a tougher time.[22]

Winston Churchill planned an Administration of Justice Act. The great reforms of the 1890s had sprung from the proposals of the Gladstone Committee. Churchill saw a similar route to the statute book. On 29 December 1910 he set up an Abatement of Imprisonment Committee, chaired by Ernley Blackwell. Its members included two Home Office and Prison Commission officials, two senior Metropolitan Police Officers, and a Metropolitan magistrate.[23]

The committee presented its report on 6 March 1911. On Winston Churchill's ideas, there were some heavy provisos, and rejection of certain of them, but a large degree of support for the general principles. The committee supported the Home Secretary on suspended sentences. It proposed that if the offender did not reoffend within a year, they should discharge their penalty, but if they did commit further offence, they should have to serve the original sentence plus a new one. It would be like 'binding over to keep the peace' but stronger. The committee did not like Churchill's idea of compulsory suspension of all sentences of up to a month. A totting-up system, it thought, would be abused and would bring the courts into disrepute. On Defaulters' Drill, the committee thought that medical clearance would be needed: there was the difference between 'a strong pit-boy and a newsboy of eighteen, ill-fed, over-smoked and underdeveloped'.

Churchill's 'time to pay' for fines was a reform that found clear favour with the committee, though one comment claimed that most fine defaulters were 'beggars, tramps and vagrants, not decent working men and women', and that a prison sentence would make them realize that the workhouse was preferable to jail.

A draft Administration of Justice Bill was published on 8 April 1911. It never received its parliamentary First Reading. It was still gathering comments in October when Churchill left the Home Office.[24]

Chapter 25
The Panther and the Mansion House

The much-predicted European war almost kicked off in 1911. Recent decades had seen the carve-up of Africa by five European powers in the 'Scramble for Africa'. Winston Churchill was not a jingo – not a WSC emotion – but he *was* an Imperialist. Britain's chief colonial rival used to be France. Now the French were Britain's partners; Germans were the invaders-in-waiting. The game was 'the Balance of Power': the Triple Alliance (Germany, Austria-Hungary, and Italy) versus the Triple Entente (France, Russia, and Britain). Within the latter arrangement was the Anglo-French Entente Cordiale. Britain's association with France was supposed to be a dispute resolution facility, not a military alliance. There were grave suspicions that it was the latter. In 1907 Richard Haldane had created the British Expeditionary Force of 160 thousand men. Many suspected that this oven-ready army was for the purpose of fighting alongside France in the continental war. No one had spelled out more powerfully the likely consequences of a full-blooded war between the European colonial rivals than Winston Churchill. In an early parliamentary speech, he warned that: 'A European war can only end in the ruin of the vanquished and scarcely less fatal commercial dislocation and exhaustion of the conquerors.'[1]

Invasion of Britain by Germany was still quite a strange idea. Germans and Britons were cousins. There were the shared language roots, Britain's use of German troops in its old European wars, Britain's Germanic Royal Family, Britain's many German residents, German restaurants, cultural visits to Germany by Britain's vacationing classes, and British use of German medics. And there was politics: Germany had its bombastic Kaiser Wilhelm II but, like Britain, it was part-way to democracy. In the German Reichstag the SPD (Social Democrats) had a strong presence. German social security had inspired Britain's ruling Liberals. But there was another side to Germany. Its 'Pan-German' imperialists wanted to challenge the dominance of the British Navy.

What was Churchill's current attitude? Peter de Mendelssohn in his 1961 book on the early Churchill, saw WSC's foreign policy doctrine in 1908–1909 as 'Radicalism, Pacifism, insularity, and Little Englanderism of the purest water'. In a speech in Swansea in August 1908 Winston mocked those who worked up a frenzy about Germany:

> How many people do you suppose there are in Germany who really want to make a marauding attack on this country? I do not suppose more than 10,000 would contemplate such a wicked crime.[2]

1908–09 was the high-water-mark of Churchill's peace promotion. There was no knowing when the Imperialist might re-emerge but in September 1910 Winston's thoughts, expressed in his mail to Edward Marsh from the Mediterranean, were about Anglo-German cooperation:

> The only view I have formed about this part of the world of ruined civilisations and systems is this – why can't England and Germany come together in strong action and for general advantage?[3]

Then came the Morocco crisis of 1911. That country was supposedly an independent state (ruled by its Sultan) but in reality, it was under the thumb of the French. Also with interests here were the British, the Spanish, and the Germans. It transpired that secret clauses of the Entente Cordiale embodied a Franco-British deal of French domination of Morocco in return for British sway over Egypt. A Moroccan crisis in 1905–6 had been resolved by the 'Act of Algeciras'. Now there was more trouble. Local tribes besieged the Sultan in Fez. France dispatched an expeditionary force, professedly to protect Europeans. Spanish soldiers showed up. There was much posturing. No European power actually wanted to go to war. The Germans were anxious to protect their commercial interests and to get compensation if France turned Morocco into a French protectorate: France was prepared to accommodate Germany.

Then, on 1 July 1911, the previously mentioned German warship made its Moroccan stop. The German government had told France that this boat was on the way to Agadir to look after German merchants during the crisis. It was gunboat diplomacy, but at a fairly low level. Similarly, the British had been prepared for the arrival of the *Panther* by the means of the Kaiser's conversation with George V at the Victoria Memorial event. Or so the Germans thought. But the British government did not receive the information. Now the crisis took a dangerous turn. At the British Foreign Office, senior clerk Sir Eyre Crowe saw Germany aiming at the subjection of France and the overthrow of the Balance of Power. Into the agitations now stepped a surprising new imperial drum-banger: David Lloyd George, closely encouraged by his political comrade Winston Churchill. Why would Churchill want to get into the Moroccan crisis? WSC was known for meddling. Lately he was watching foreign affairs intensely.[4]

According to the 1929 first volume of Churchill's *World Crisis*, with the *Panther*'s arrival 'all the alarm bells throughout Europe began immediately to quiver.' They did not – and in Britain the excitement in the backrooms of the British Foreign Office did not extend to the government generally. Some ministers did wonder whether a German port in Morocco facing the Atlantic might impact negatively on British naval trade and security, but the Admiralty was relaxed: its policy was to keep out of any European war and to use the Fleet as its shield to protect Britain and its Empire. It did not see a German Moroccan presence, if internationally agreed, as threatening. The majority of British ministers favoured caution. Not so the Foreign Office, which thought that Germany, and France too, should be told that Britain was not going to be excluded from any Moroccan helpings (or compensation). The imperialists in the cabinet, though outnumbered, were currently in the ascendancy. In this contest, Churchill would ordinarily have been placed on the peace-favouring side, but not now.[5]

The British background was the so-called 'Conversations' between senior French and British military staff on planning for Britain to send an expeditionary force to fight alongside the French in the event of war between France and Germany. The majority of ministers were kept in the dark. War Minister Lord Haldane wanted pre-arrangements for the Fleet to transport the British Expeditionary Force across the Channel at the start of any war between France and Germany. Looking for allies, he had let Churchill and Lloyd George into the secret of the Anglo-French military planning. By 1911 the pair were on his side. Haldane wanted pre-planning of the dispatch of the British Expeditionary Force, with coordination between the army and the navy. Coming up was Lloyd George's annual address to the bankers at their showpiece Mansion House dinner, on 21 July. He told Churchill that in his speech he intended to warn the Germans off Morocco. The pair saw eye-to-eye on the need for a tough British stand and readiness to fight a European war, including on land.[6]

Lloyd George delivered his purple passage. When it was reported, including by Conservative newspapers which greatly liked it, it was a sensation. The Chancellor's words were that:

> …If a situation were to be forced upon us in which peace could only be preserved by the surrender of the great and beneficent position Britain has won by centuries of heroism and achievement…then I say emphatically that peace at that price would be a humiliation intolerable for a great country like ours to endure.[7]

The opponent of the Boer War had turned sabre-rattling Imperialist. In *World Crisis* Churchill paints a picture of the Chancellor swaying for weeks, then making up his mind. Lloyd George's *War Memoirs* state that 'the initiative was my own.' Churchill's account implicitly scoops up some of the credit: he had been in George's ear ('numerous conversations' about Morocco), the suggestion being dangled that he was the inspiration.[8]

Lloyd George and Churchill could not make foreign policy. The declaration had been approved word-for-word by Grey and Asquith. France was addressed as well as Germany. Lloyd George delivered what the Foreign Secretary wanted. Sir Edward Grey was not warlike. The new Director of Military Operations at Army HQ, Brigadier-General Sir Henry Wilson, thought that Grey 'not only had no idea of what war means but…struck me as not wanting to know.' Grey took the diplomatic benefits of the conversations about a hypothetical war, whilst looking the other way from the implications of a gentleman's agreement to fight.[9]

A few days later Churchill and Lloyd George were walking by the fountains of Buckingham Palace. A messenger sped up: the Foreign Secretary wanted the Chancellor to see him at once. 'That's my speech', said George: 'The Germans may demand my resignation.' Churchill remarked: 'That will make you the most popular man in England.' The German government did indeed want the Chancellor dismissed, as a minister surely not representing the government line. That LG *was* speaking for the Foreign Office and the prime minister is shown by a comment in a letter of Winston to Clementine: 'The Germans sent their *Panther* to Agadir and we sent our little Panther to the Mansion House…' Lloyd George, called by some 'the little man', was five feet six inches. Lucy Masterman's diary records:

> …a visit from the German Ambassador to Sir Edward Grey, who was informed by him that the Germans could hold no communications with England unless that speech were disavowed and George left the Government!! The Ambassador began marching up and down the room and getting very excited.[10]

The Lloyd George pronouncement was seen by the German government as an insult to German honour – tinder-box territory. Asquith told Grey and Lloyd George that he had received a communication from the German Ambassador 'so stiff that the Fleet might be attacked at any moment'. He had warned First Lord of the Admiralty Reginald McKenna, who had put the Fleet on mobilization alert. The flare-up pitched Churchill into a flurry of enjoyably feverish war calculations. It happened that he was talking about the international situation to Sir Edward Henry at a Downing Street garden-party. Henry dropped in the information that the Metropolitan Police was responsible for a cordite store at some barracks in Kent. Churchill visualized armed German motorists overwhelming the constables. He dashed to the Home Office and telephoned the Admiralty. An unimpressed admiral declined to send marines. Winston phoned War Minister Haldane to arrange for a company of infantry to be added to the police guards. He was in comfortable territory.[11]

The Mansion House speech was a Churchill watershed. Henceforth he was with those who were up for war on the continent of Europe. His reminiscences saw it that:

> The accession of Mr Lloyd George in foreign policy to the opposite wing of the Government was decisive. We were able immediately to pursue a firm and coherent policy.[12]

No longer would Lloyd George and Churchill be with those who batted for the reduction of military spending and the maintenance of peace. A quiet compromise between Germany and Britain was not now possible. France could not now make its own deal with Germany. The Triple Entente, which had been in decline, had to be activated, with Britain put on a war footing. That would involve cabinet changes.[13]

For Churchill, a shift had occurred during the winter. Sidney Street had played a small but significant part. He now brooded over intelligence and the guarding of the nation against spies and aliens. The Churchill perspective was increasingly driven by military considerations. He looked back in *World Crisis*:

> Liberal politics, the People's Budget, Free Trade, Peace, Retrenchment and Reform – all the war-cries of our election struggles began to seem unreal in the presence of this new pre-occupation.[14]

The international crisis dragged on. It would not be resolved until November, when Germany accepted French ascendancy in Morocco in return for the transfer of some French Congo territory. The episode would turn Winston Churchill's career. His ministerial rise had started with Empire. Now he was returning to it.

Military security became a Churchill obsession. In April he had produced a set of clauses to sew into aliens legislation, including temporary detention of aliens in time of war or 'occasion of imminent national danger'. There is a study of Churchill at the Home Office on 20 April 1911, by society photographer Alexander Bassano. The papers before him appear to be maps. The desk looks more like that of a war or a naval minister than that of a Home Secretary. Though the Aliens Bill failed as a route to military security legislation, Churchill did get his way when, on 18 August 1911, a new Official Secrets Act was bundled through Parliament on a Friday afternoon almost without debate. It provided for prosecution of persons suspected of 'behaviour prejudicial to the safety or interests of the state', a sweeping formula. A backbench Liberal saw 'very unusual and extraordinary powers…which upset Magna Charta'. At that time rumours were circulating that the French-German negotiations on Morocco were breaking down. If war resulted, Britain would be pulled in. The Official Secrets Act's opponents included Labour's leader. It was supposed to be 'nothing novel' but when war came in 1914 socialists and peace campaigners were put under the same close surveillance as suspected German spies.[15]

If war was on the way, dangerous strikes would need to be settled – or squashed. Churchill's reputation as a Home Secretary acting against the working classes is built, unfairly, on Tonypandy 1910. A bigger industrial crisis was brewing in 1911.[16]

Chapter 26
'The Modern Nero'

A new novel was drawing attention. *Howard's End*, from the pen of Edward Marsh's friend E.M. Forster, had a gallery of characters teasing out the social currents. A metamorphosis appeared to be taking place. Virginia Woolf thought that, 'on or about December 1910 human character changed.' She was thinking of everything from the softening of the rigidity of servant and master/mistress relationships to the convulsions of industry and politics. 1910 and 1911 were pivotal years. Churchill at the Home Office was part of the process, but he was also resistant to it. Certainly, he was not with the sentiments of the Great Labour Unrest, the bubbles of which were getting angrier.[1]

The early months of 1911 brought a brief relative lull. Then conflict resumed. At the ports, there were stoppages by dockers and associated transport workers. It was threatening food supplies. The trouble jumped from Southampton to Cardiff and elsewhere, pulling in other sorts of workers. The term 'sympathy strike' came in. The Southampton seamen won higher wages, significant since seamen had poor remuneration and conditions. Other workers noted their victory. For the Home Office, a summer of industrial turmoil was going to put its confident and ambitious incumbent to his biggest test yet.[2]

On 19 July, *The Times* had: 'SERIOUS RIOTING IN CARDIFF... incendiarism and looting by strikers; police and rioters injured.' Reports were pasted into the Home Office's files, along with the representations reaching it. Troops remained in South Wales from the previous year. Were more needed for Cardiff? The Home Secretary wrote: 'No action at present.' So far there was no change in his cautious approach.[3]

In Parliament, Churchill defended the rights of trade unions. He declared: 'I consider that every workman is well advised to join a trade union.' He could not conceive how 'any man standing undefended against the powers that be could be so foolish...not to associate himself with an organization to protect the rights and interests of labour.' He used the imagery of an animal that fascinated him:

> Although it may be very difficult to define in law what is or what is not a trade union, most people know a trade union when they see one. It is like trying to define a rhinoceros: it is difficult enough but everyone can recognise it.[4]

Churchill ran into a storm when he spoke of legal action hampering the functioning of unions:

...Where class and party issues are involved, it is impossible to pretend that the courts command general confidence. On the contrary, a very large number of our population have been led to the opinion that they are, unconsciously, no doubt, biased. [HON MEMBERS: "No, no," and "Withdraw," and interruption.][5]

The Home Office received pleas for help from companies hit by the rioting. The China Trust took up the case of Chinese Laundry proprietors in Cardiff, who had lost £50,000. Among complaints of intimidation, the managing-director of a Fancy Biscuits and Cakes Company in Cardiff wrote emotionally to Winston Churchill. His workforce had never had any dispute but they had been so intimidated by threats at the gates that they were too frightened to start work. There was harassment of another sort. The mobile squads of Metropolitan Police were getting a reputation as brutes. A Cardiff Post Office employee reported that the police from London were 'assaulting peaceful pedestrians in all directions... filthy and obscene language...some under the influence of drink... more like a band of lunatics than protectors of the peace.' Churchill resisted calls for an independent inquiry into police conduct. In Parliament on 26 June, Labour's George Lansbury remarked that the Metropolitan Police, 'is ruled now as if it were part of the Army.' Edward Troup prepared a letter of reply to one objection to the use of imported police and the military:

...Their presence was absolutely necessary to prevent such outrages as would have brought discredit and disaster to the cause of the strikers.

Winston Churchill blocked this patronization. He wrote: 'Simple ack.t.' [acknowledgement only]. He held his line on troops: soldiers should not be called on until all the police resources were inadequate.[6]

Home Office strike files have a lengthy title-list: strike-breakers, public houses (suggested closure), picketing, fire dangers, torpedo boats, picket boats, 'messages from H.O. to H.M. [Churchill to the King]', compensation claims, police expenses, and injuries, food supply. Beneath the heading 'S. of S. [Churchill] and Magistrates', there is a note on: 'necessity of sharp punishment to offenders'. Magistrates were to be in readiness to read a proclamation under the Riot Act. This gave authority for a warning to be read out to a group of twelve or more, that it must disperse or face punitive action (soldiers opening fire). As the industrial trouble deepened, it became more political.[7]

Towards the end of July Churchill wrote a memorandum of deep foreboding:

...A new force has arisen in trade unionism, whereby the power of the old leaders has proved quite ineffective, and the sympathetic strike on a wide scale is prominent. Shipping, coal, railways, dockers etc etc are all uniting and breaking out at once. The 'general strike' policy is a factor which must be dealt with...control would be difficult if the railways went...[8]

He forecast that there would be 'great uncertainty, destruction of property, and probably loss of life'.

In late July the strike waves reached the capital. On 1 August the dock workers came out, for better pay, conditions, and union recognition. Speeches calling for a parade by the strikers and 'sweeping of the port' and 'downing the blacklegs' caused the Manager of the Shipping Federation to write to Churchill, asking him to issue reminders about the 1906 Trades Dispute Act. On the other side, Tower Hamlets MP (and Liberal Whip) William Wedgwood-Benn conveyed his constituents' unhappiness about police-boats being used to ferry blackleg loaders between barges. Churchill published rules on proper police behaviour: owners had the right to import labour in order to load and unload; strikers had the right 'to picket for the purpose of peacefully persuading labourers, but not in numbers sufficient to intimidate'.[9]

A letter was sent by the leader of the Dock, Wharf, Riverside, and General Workers, Ben Tillett, to Labour MPs, alerting them to the use of soldiers against strikers. Preserved in the Home Office file on 'Disturbances', it reported '… the ostentatious parading of military forces in the streets…a menace and an insult to workmen'. The 'Cossacking methods of the Government', said Tillett, were 'a great menace to the Labour movement'. The word, with its Russian association, was deliberately chosen. The Tsarist regime was hated by the British Labour movement.[10]

As the temperature in London nudged ninety-seven degrees Fahrenheit on 9 August, 20,000 troops were poised to travel from Aldershot and Woolwich to the docks to move supplies. The government debated whether the deed should be done. Winston Churchill's line appears in a letter from War Minister Haldane to his wife:

> Last night [10 August] I had our Home Secretary, the Chief of Police and some soldiers here. I resisted bringing the troops before the early morning – and I think I was right. It meant fixed bayonets and ball cartridge. The only justification could have been the danger of London starving.[11]

Churchill's caution had gone.

The climax of the dock strike was Friday, 11 August, a day of great heat, speeches on Tower Hill, and intense negotiations. The press reported 'penniless strikers', whose families did not know where the next meal was coming from. But there was a sense that the workers were winning. Tillett told those assembling that, 'as far as I understand we shall be able to settle this week.' The strikers were addressed by Keir Hardie:

> This is your opportunity. Your masters show you no mercy. They starve you; they sweat you: they oppress you. Pay them back in their own coin.

Churchill was among the visitors to the Board of Trade as negotiations proceeded. The outcome that night left no doubt. The *Daily News* hailed, 'VICTORY FOR THE MEN'. The paper pointed to the part played by working-class solidarity: 'the great mass of the working population was not only in sympathy with the strikers, but ready to suffer with them.'[12]

John Burns had been a severe disappointment as president of the local government board. He acted as a conservative upholder of the harsh Poor Law. He seems not to have understood the work of his department. Lucy Masterman wrote of his 'bluffing' to conceal his comprehension difficulty, a consequence of which was that he relied too much on his civil servants. One historian notes the social conservatism of the class from which Burns rose: 'not least in the artisan's contempt for the undeserving poor'. But Burns now came into his own. He knew the docklands and their people intimately from when he himself had been a leader of the great dock strike of 1889. That knowledge was needed. The strike settlement was threatening to come apart. Burns was down at the docks persuading the dockers to stick to their agreement. Tillett in a later recollection compared Burns and Churchill: 'Although the docks agitator was now a Cabinet Minister, he really forgot that at times, fussing like an old hen as he hovered about us; even Churchill couldn't forget he was Home Secretary.' Why 'even'? It is because Tillett, remarkably, thought that Winston's heart was with the workers.[13]

We need to move forward a week. The London situation was unstable. Lucy Masterman's diary states that: 'The Dock Strike had been settled with the ordinary Board of Trade machinery, but it had left a vast number of fringes in the shape of unsettled questions, on any one of which the men might have come out again.' One looked ominous. Mrs Masterman's account mentions trouble around a ship on the Thames called *The Highland Laddie*, loaded with chilled meat:

> Winston had promised her owners that she should be unloaded with police protection on Friday morning [18 August] and they were bringing a ship called the "Lady Jocelyn" full of blacklegs to unload her. The Commissioner of Police reported that if she were unloaded by the blacklegs, he could not guarantee without the aid of soldiers to keep clear the route along which the cargo must pass from Canning Town to Smithfield. The men's leaders declared that if the blacklegs were landed, there would be bloodshed.[14]

During the evening of 17 August Ben Tillett and his fellow union leaders decided to ask for a face-to-face meeting with the Home Secretary. By this time, Churchill was believed (correctly) to be a crush-the-strike hawk. Tillett knew that Churchill wanted to use troops. That had become obvious. But he thought that the Home Secretary was being used by others:

> ...The Right Hon. Winston Churchill had been used as a cudgel by the Board of Trade. This mighty young man was the terror; he had the soldiers;

he had given instructions: the men of gun and bullet and bayonet were ready primed...Winston was ready with puckered brow and angry mien to let loose the forces. Our Committee thought it best to see the ferocious man of blood and iron.[15]

They headed to the House of Commons. Lucy Masterman's diary identifies the Tillett group as 'a deputation of the National Union of Transport Workers'. As Tillett put it, they 'sent in for the Right Hon.' Churchill met them, accompanied by 'his henchman Mr Masterman'. An encounter took place, in Tillett's words, 'with the responsible person for the suppression by violence of our good fellows in all of the port fights – Liverpool, Bristol, London, Glasgow, Salford, Manchester, South Wales, Dublin and Cork'.

Tillett seems to have been entranced by Churchill:

Slightly bent, hesitant of speech, almost an apologetic manner, youth left in mobile features, ready for boyish fun, the cares of office sitting lightly on a good-sized brow, eyes that sparkle with a wistfulness almost sweet – this was the modern Nero whose terrible power had been threatened against us.[16]

The delegation's protests about the use of troops against strikers were met, says Tillett, by 'a look of astonishment and pain on the face of the Home Secretary'. By the end of the meeting blame was entirely shifted from the shoulders of Churchill. Ben became a Winston believer. He saw 'patience and courtesy'. The union leaders, Tillett at least, decided that military aggression against the workers was 'under the auspices of Lloyd George and Co'. As for Churchill: when 'the blood-lust had gone from the clubs of idlers to the seats of the editors, Winston had exercised great courage in refusing to murder and butcher the men we were fighting for...He turned a deaf ear to these clamours of the cowardly crew who would, under the name of law and order, have gloated over the killing of their fellow creatures.' The union leader thought that it was Churchill who kept 25,000 soldiers from marching into the docks to man the ships and clear the accumulation of merchandise; that the avoidance of a 'violent and bloody outbreak' was down to 'wiser counsels [which] prevailed at the Home Office, under the control of Mr Winston Churchill'.[17]

How do we square Lucy Masterman's perception of a Churchill child-like transparency with Winston's bamboozling of Tillett? The solution to the paradox must be that Churchill could dip into and out of his personae whilst staying inwardly detached. He could pursue with passion a career as a radical Liberal, whilst his inner purpose was the promotion of 'Tory democracy'.

Winston could observe a scene shrewdly. A.G. Gardiner wrote of this side of him, the compliment being double-edged:

No one absorbs the atmosphere of a situation more readily than he does, or exhales it with more intellectual conviction, or with a more assured grasp of underlying principles. But though he has a rare power of appeal to the popular mind, his sympathies are not engaged, and his interest in life is essentially the interest of the man of action and adventure.[18]

Winston was genuinely touched with compassion for aged convicts, juveniles in trouble, and military veterans – and was accused by his enemies of sentimentalism. But his feelings were not engaged by Tillett and his friends. He threw himself into his performance, apparently successfully, but his agenda was not theirs.

We must return to the *Lady Jocelyn*. That boat, once a sailing vessel, was a floating warehouse. There was the serious possibility that its transport of blackleg dockers could trigger a violent clash. The prospect of blood when the *Lady Jocelyn* reached the *Highland Laddie* caused frantic activity within the Home Office. Lucy Masterman relates:

> The members of the Ministry were up half the night getting soldiers into London…At about 2 o clock in the morning Winston and Charlie went out in a taxi to see the soldiers coming in.

She gives the outcome of the affair:

> Somehow or other the "Highland Laddie" was unloaded by normal dock men. Winston, on his own responsibility, had stopped the "Lady Jocelyn" and refused it admission up the river.[19]

So Tillett and his comrades got what they wanted from Winston Churchill. Tillett's positive view of Churchill was confirmed. But, as the next two days would show, WSC's halting of the *Lady Jocelyn* was his last act of conciliation of the strikers. He was about to let rip against them.

Chapter 27
'The Brink of Civil War'

The industrial shut-down was heaviest in Liverpool. Soldiers in the city totalled five thousand, along with two-and-a-half thousand police reinforcements from Birmingham. The dockers were out; their employers imposed a lockout. Power-station workers downed tools. Churchill told the King that there was 'a good deal of riotous disturbance'. On Sunday, 13 August there was a serious incident. At a mass meeting of transport workers, a fight broke out between demonstrators and police. A wave of fury swept the city, with 200 thousand people on the streets. Prison vans carrying sentenced rioters under military escort were stoned by protesting crowds. Troops fired at them. The violence that London escaped came to Liverpool.[1]

Of the representations reaching the Home Office, one stands out. Frederick O'Brien, editor of the *Liverpool Magazine*, sent Winston Churchill his personal account of what became known as Bloody Sunday:

> …The police turned their attention to the crowd listening to the speakers. Their baton-charges upon the quiet and orderly meeting were most brutal and savage…cruel blows upon the heads of men, women and children… dozens of bleeding and unconscious citizens upon the ground…

O'Brien wanted an early inquiry. Edward Troup's advice was: 'This will require attention if there is any inquiry into the conduct of the police. For the present: Put up.' Troup's inaction was endorsed by the Home Secretary's lack of contradiction of the file minute.[2]

Winston Churchill heard that the mayors of Liverpool and Birkenhead had lost control of the docks. He arranged for the passage to the Mersey of the warship *Antrim*. Here was another event from Churchill's tenure of the Home Office that would be embedded in collective memory. More than one vessel was involved. The press reported that *Antrim*'s sister, the *Warrior*, was off the Isle of Man, 'laden with foodstuffs'. Churchill was visited by Colonial Secretary Lewis (Loulou) Harcourt, who later wrote to his wife that the Home Secretary was 'mad': moving fifty thousand troops around the country to try to break the advancing railway strike.[3]

On 15 August Churchill reported to Parliament a telegram from Liverpool's Head Constable. A mob had lured police and troops into side-streets and had stoned them. Officers had fired revolver shots at house-tops. Cabinet minister Herbert Samuel wrote to his wife that Liverpool was 'verging on a state of revolution'. One of the reporters in the city was the *Daily Chronicle*'s Philip Gibbs. In his memoirs, Gibbs called the Liverpool turmoil 'the nearest thing to civil war I have seen in any English city'. The *Daily News* had reckoned during the London dock strike that Britain was on 'the brink of civil war'. Churchill was exhilarated by authority at such a time. He was the Home Office's commander in-chief. The Liberal press was queasy. The Tory papers were not. The *Daily Graphic* declared that 'the duty of the Home Secretary is obvious.' Churchill could expect the previously critical Conservative press to back him.[4]

As the railway strike spread, the Home Office became a field-headquarters. Churchill shifted troops around the conflict zones. He issued news updates to the press. The 'bulletins' became infamous. Lucy Masterman called them 'disastrous'. She recalled that of 11 August: 'Army Service Corps to have lorries in instant regiment and to be issued with ten rounds of ball ammunition.' Railway union official George Alcock had no doubt who was the government's hard-liner in chief. He recalled:

> The signs looked ominous of civil war, because of the Government's deeds, and especially those of Churchill.[5]

Churchill received a letter marked 'Secret' from the General Manager of the Midland Railway, Sir Guy Granet. One Bebel, previously a Glasgow waiter and said to be a German agent, and a trade-unionist, Joe Larkin, were claimed to be distributing 'money coming from abroad' among the strike leaders. The names of those said to be trousering the cash make a roll-call of some of the illustrious of the British Labour and Socialist movements. The tale gripped Churchill. Almeric Fitzroy's diary for 18 August has:

> Winston Churchill is said to be convinced that the whole trouble is fomented by German gold, and claims to have proof of it, which others regard as midsummer madness.[6]

'Others' were surely correct. The supposed information looks fanciful. It would be unsurprising if the name of August Bebel, chairman of the German Social Democratic Party, cropped up in the conversation of local Labour activists steeped in international workers' solidarity; similarly that of famous Irish trade-unionist (James) Larkin. Churchill took the story seriously. His brain teemed with coming continental war. Granet could not have written to a more receptively minded minister.

Churchill was also receiving communications from Lord Derby, former Balfour government minister. Presently in Harrogate, Derby had news from Liverpool's mayor. He told Churchill that his correspondent:

> ...is of opinion that a revolution is in progress. He fears that tonight there may be no light in the town and that looting will be wholesale.

The mayor thought that:

> if something is not done immediately...there can only be bloodshed on a large scale. The city is in a state of siege, the hospitals have but two days' supply, and in 48 hours the poor people will be face-to-face with starvation.[7]

There had been no progress with arbitration, since the employers would not recognize the unions. The widespread public view was that railway workers were poorly paid. Moral pressure was available for ministers to exert on the management. The employers could, if need be, be compelled by legislative instrument to recognize the unions. Churchill had no such perspective. He wanted to smash the strikes.

Strikers in Liverpool were digging trenches. It was reported that the police were to be issued with guns and swords, as the rioting spread to other cities. A national rail strike was declared, to start on 18 August, a Friday. Peaceful resolution looked hopeless. The General Manager of the Lancashire and Yorkshire Railway was heard to declare that he 'would rather the rails rust than parley.' The owners and shareholders, as one historian put it, 'remained intransigent, truculent, selfishly uncomprehending'. Whilst Lloyd George was critical of their attitude, Churchill appeared to be interested only in victory over the strikers.[8]

The trains were the nation's life-blood, vital for the transportation of post, merchandise and food. Train travel was getting safer as a result of government regulation, but the rail network was a hazardous workplace. Railways were the third most dangerous occupation (after mining and the navy), with over 500 fatalities each year. Fatigue contributed to the death-toll, with shifts of up to fourteen hours. The railway directors stubbornly resisted improvement of pay to meet rising living costs. The Conservative *Daily Mirror* said that railway shift lengths and pay rates were 'among the scandals of the labour world': the strikers' case had 'real justice'. Churchill's attitude put him on the wrong side of plain fairness.[9]

Following the news was an anxious King George. The monarch telegrammed Winston Churchill to urge that the employment of troops should 'not be half-hearted...They should be given a free hand and the mob made to fear them.' He need not have worried. WSC was sending troops to just about everywhere there was a railway-line of significance. Conservative MP Robert Sanders noted approvingly that 'Churchill took a firm attitude.' John Burns, who visited the Home Office, reported finding Churchill with a large map draped across the floor. Aboard it were model soldiers, which the Home Secretary was 'imaginatively moving'.[10]

In Parliament, Labour's John Ward asked the Home Secretary whether it was true that the government had promised to support the railway companies against the men. 'No, Sir', said Churchill crisply. But his rhetoric suggested that Ward was correct:

> ...It will be the duty of the Government in the event of the paralysis of the great railway lines upon which the life and food of the people depend, to secure to the persons engaged in working them full legal protection.

The *Daily News* voiced Liberal disquiet over Churchill's line:

> It is impossible to exaggerate the criticism which will overwhelm any Government that on the one hand calls out the military to protect non-union labour on the railways, without on the other hand compelling the directors, if necessary by Act of Parliament, to recognise the unions.

Lloyd George called it 'farce' that the employers would not meet the union leaders face-to-face. The Lloyd George and Churchill positions, usually so close, were diverging.[11]

Asquith offered a Royal Commission. The directors accepted. The unions declined. The prime minister told them that he would 'employ all the forces of the Crown to keep the railways open.' Asquith and Churchill were on the same page. With the start of the general railway strike set for midnight on Thursday, the 17th, the Labour Party put down a motion of censure against the government. Several months earlier Winston Churchill had been hoping to work with Labour's new leader. That was now out of the window. A book by Ramsay MacDonald six years later looked back on the railway conflict:

> When the railway strike broke out here in 1911, the Home Office, under Mr Winston Churchill, immediately put itself at the head of the military and in turn the military at the disposal of the railway directors. Troops were put in possession of the lines and were paraded fully armed in front of the men.[12]

Winston Churchill's telegrams to the King now went into cypher, reporting to the monarch on the signing up of special constables. The parliamentary correspondent of the *Daily News*, Philip Wilson, a recent Liberal colleague of Churchill in the House of Commons, wrote in his paper an 'inner history of the sensational story'. This included Churchill's behaviour on 17 August:

> On Thursday the Home Office [meaning Churchill] was pressing strongly for troops to be sent to the London Docks, where no suggestion of disorder had occurred. Happily, the Cabinet first sent Mr Burns to reconnoitre... His report saved East London from the presence of the military and a great error of judgement was narrowly averted.[13]

Lucy Masterman's diary account has:

> Winston was in a very excited state of mind. He has got rather a whiff-of-grapeshot attitude towards these matters; and he enjoyed intensely mapping the country and directing the movements of troops.[14]

With the Home Secretary now getting respectful nods from Conservatives, *The Times* signalled an editorial adjustment. The paper apportioned blame for the troubles to the 'spirit of "Syndicalism" [which] regards society as an enemy', and to 'the conspicuous incitements to class hatred by the CHANCELLOR OF THE EXCHEQUER and the coquetting of the HOME SECRETARY with disorder [presumably Tonypandy]', but on the other hand the paper told its readers that:

> Happily there are signs that the Government do not intend to yield...Mr CHURCHILL repeated in the House of Commons the assurance that the Government would take all necessary steps to ensure the supplies of food and other necessaries.

The paper had some reassuring news for its readers: at Fishguard, strikers had been driven back 'at the point of the bayonet'.[15]

Labour's prospective censure motion had a swift effect. Lloyd George met Ramsay MacDonald to get negotiations opened. The railway union executives visited the Board of Trade. MacDonald withdrew his motion. Positions were shifting. But the national rail strike would still go ahead.[16]

Churchill was getting a poor press in Labour circles. The *Labour Leader*, the house magazine of Labour politics, looked at his attitude to the behaviour of the police in Liverpool:

> The Home Secretary will support the Authorities through thick and thin. Although it is impossible for any unprejudiced person to read the description of the police bludgeoning at Liverpool except with horror, he will not hear of an enquiry. His theory that innocent people must keep themselves out of the way of policemen who have a fit of Berserker rage on them is absolutely indefensible. It is an amazing doctrine which will sooner or later bring Winston Churchill into collision with public opinion and wreck his career.[17]

A touch of sorrow may be noted. When Churchill became Home Secretary, some in the Labour movement had hopes for him. These were now fast dwindling. On Friday a rail strike leader declared, 'War has begun.' Churchill was content with that. The scheduled parliamentary recess was postponed.[18]

The government now offered the railway unions what Lucy Masterman described as 'a rapidly moving Committee'. A draft document was worked on. At the Home Office, Winston Churchill was scrutinizing intelligence on the movements of troops and police, along with the statistics coming in of how many employees were out and how many were working. The King's secretary wrote to Churchill to thank him for 'the many telegrams you have sent': His Majesty had 'appreciated authentic details of the strike.' Churchill told the King that, 'there seems little doubt that the railway strike will now be fought out.' In a Home

Office memorandum Churchill set out his view of the consequences should it succeed:

> The means by which the millions of people in this island get their daily livelihood are highly artificial and any serious breakdown no matter from what cause would lead to the starvation of great numbers of the poorer people.[19]

For the striking transport workers, there was a threat:

> It is a criminal offence to break a contract of employment where the effect will be to endanger life or to cause serious bodily injury.

Churchill claimed throughout to be protecting the vulnerable poor in the cities. The stance looks contrived. The consideration that if the railway owners were compelled to recognize the unions and negotiate with them, this would improve the lot of their downtrodden workers *and* save the cities from starvation, does not seem to have weighed with him. The *Daily News* report of dock strike-supporting working classes in London 'cheerfully starving' is an inconvenience for the WSC picture. But Churchill managed to be both a strike-breaking, owner-supporting minister *and* the champion of the poor. He estimated that fifty thousand railwaymen were on strike but that the majority were still working. He set about preparing the Home Office bulletin which would come out at 11.30 p.m., ready for the Saturday morning newspapers. He cannot have imagined the effect it would have.[20]

A central organization was set up for the dispatch of soldiers to protect strike-breaking workers. Churchill was much involved. Now companies no longer needed to make the case to magistrates and mayors that there was rioting and disorder. Railway owners and managers could have as many troops as were available. The *Daily News* warned of 'troops with ball, cartridge and naked bayonet virtually under the instructions of the companies'. The paper called the mass use of troops against the railway strikers 'unparalleled'. It reminded readers that the previous year French Prime Minister Aristide Briand had used troops to break a national rail strike: successfully but his government subsequently fell.[21]

On Saturday 19 August, the second day of the general rail strike, some tentative progress towards a settlement was being made. The railway owners still would not budge on meeting the union representatives face-to-face but the working document with its union and government input provided a basis for indirect negotiation. However, it was becoming apparent that the rank and file would not accept anything worked out through indirect contacts and the conciliation boards. Anything short of recognition of the unions by the companies would be unacceptable.

Saturday's *The Times* carried the new Home Office bulletin. This declared that, though the strike was causing partial dislocation in the railway services, 'considerably more than two-thirds of the railwaymen are remaining at their posts and numerous applications are being received by the railway companies for employment.' The communiqué added that:

> The military arrangements are being perfected. The enrolment of special constables has taken place where difficulty is experienced or disorder has occurred and if need be, very large numbers of citizens will be sworn in. The military authorities report that the situation is thoroughly under control.[22]

Churchill was addressing not railway workers but users of the railway. Landed gentlemen and industrial masters, reaching for their tray-presented papers, will have been relieved to read of the strikers being kept in their place by the Home Secretary. They may have been surprised. Was not Churchill that noisy radical minister? Perceptions were changing.

The Home Office bulletin was of course read also by the railway strikers. Hopes of peace were blown away. The *Daily News* reported 'profound indignation'. 'Defections' (to the strikers' side) was one instance of phraseology that outraged railway staff. The report of the state of the strike, said the *News*, was preposterously distorted:

> One sentence referred to the train services as being 'well maintained' when for days Manchester – to select one case – had been held up, and mines and factories were closing over large areas.

Churchill's blatant propaganda ended any chance of further progress with negotiation. The union executives dug in their heels. There would be no more discussion unless the managers sat down face-to-face with them.[23]

The companies were confident that with the army's guns and bayonets at their disposal, the trains would be kept running by strike-breakers. But the trade-unionists were now fired up and with army resources close to being exhausted, the logistics were turning in their favour. At a number of railway stations magistrates read the Riot Act and troops put crowds to flight. But the network was grinding to a halt over much of the country, as the army ran out of troops.

Philip Wilson's *Daily News* analysis was that, if the policy of 'batons, bayonets and bullets' continued over the weekend, the government 'would fall during the autumn [parliamentary] session.' The cabinet now changed tack. Instructions went out to the railway companies to sit down with the unions. Face-to-face talking began at midday Saturday. It was not what Winston Churchill wanted.[24]

On Saturday at 2 a.m. Churchill was composing a telegram for Chief Constables. He required by 11 a.m. detailed estimates of the proportions of strikers as against those remaining at work. At 6.20 a.m telegrams to mayors and others reminded them about enrolling special constables.[25]

During the morning Churchill, telegramming the King, was bullish:

Railway managers will give the Home Secretary a full report by this afternoon as to the general position on the railways and there is no doubt that in spite of a great deal of delay and inconvenience the whole railway system is working.[26]

By the afternoon, detailed statistics were coming in. They were bleak for Churchill. The strike had been fairly ineffective in the south but in the Midlands and the North the freight network was paralyzed. As Mrs Masterman's diary put it:

In a vast quadrilateral between Liverpool, Newcastle, Hull and Nottingham not a single goods-train had run for 24 hours.[27]

Churchill's latest bulletin had rallied many more workers behind the union action. An idea occurred to the Home Secretary. Where freight-trains were halted, some passenger-trains were still running. What about putting food and other essentials onto those trains? He put it to the company directors. They rejected the scheme, pointing out that practically every passenger-train was already packed with food. The diary continues: '"Yes", Winston flashed out, "food for the rich, who can afford to send parcels at passenger rates. I was speaking about food for the poor!"'[28]

He continued to believe in himself as a minister fighting for the disadvantaged. Mrs Masterman makes it plain that her husband's heart was not with the Home Secretary:

…Charlie was in a chair and Winston was marching up and down the room. Whenever a telegram came in announcing fresh men gone out, Charlie looked pleased and Winston looked furious and depressed.[29]

Charles Masterman knew first-hand about the struggles of the poor to put food on the table. He did not mind seeing the owner classes having their noses put out of joint a little. The strikes offered the chance of an adjustment of the wealth balance.[30]

During the evening Churchill's agitation turned to anguish:

The men have beaten us. We cannot keep the trains running. There is nothing we can do. We are done![31]

His strategy had fallen apart. Charles Masterman thought that he was unbalanced. He told Lucy that Churchill did things 'in an amazingly wrong way, issuing wild bulletins and longing for "blood".'[32]

At the end of the day news came that Lloyd George (who was famed as a negotiator) had pulled off his greatest conciliation triumph. The railway companies and the unions had agreed to settle. Churchill kicked his model soldiers across the room: 'Bloody hell!', he yelled. He telephoned LG to say: 'I'm very sorry to hear it. It would have been better to have gone on and given these men a good thrashing.' The yawning gap in the underlying politics of Churchill and Lloyd

George was exposed. Whilst the Home Secretary was fighting to yield not an inch of the social order, the Chancellor was prepared to see it re-arranged.[33]

The government's proposed Royal Commission now included senior Labour MP Arthur Henderson, who would be trusted on the union side. Importantly, all the sacked employees were reinstated (dismissal having been a major weapon on the owners' side). The unions spoke of 'a magnificent victory'. The *Daily News* agreed: 'the victory of the men is as complete as signed and attested documents can make it.' Churchill's bad temper about the settlement must cast doubt on his anxiety for the feeding of the poor as the determinant of what he did in the crisis.[34]

During the strikes, Churchill had communicated intensely with King George. When Lloyd George visited Balmoral Castle shortly afterwards, his impression was that the courtiers were civil to him 'as to a dangerous wild animal', and that the King was 'hostile to the bone to all who are working to lift the workmen out of the mire'. WSC liked Balmoral, writing to Clemmie from there in September that, 'Life is very quiet and easy.' The King talked to him a lot. The summer had drawn the pair closer.[35]

In the face of the Agadir crisis, the circumstance of Britain's standing Army being stretched around the railways had provided Lloyd George with an appeal to the patriotism of both sides in the industrial dispute. For Winston Churchill, his heightened interest this summer in Imperial politics, along with his agitation about German agents, may have charged his determination to break the strike. One way and another, the summer of 1911 saw a different Churchill from a year earlier.

Lucy Masterman's diary tells that on the Sunday after the settlement, 'Winston went off to golf.' Sunday was another day. Churchill's mood was never down for long. His mercurial spirits bounced back after his gloomy rages.[36]

Chapter 28

Saving the Jews

On the Monday after the conclusion of the strike (21 August), according to a cabinet report of Asquith to the King, Winston Churchill called for a public enquiry, perhaps chaired by the prime minister, into the 'menacing developments' of the recent strikes 'accompanied by a growing readiness to resort to violence'. He found agreement among his colleagues with his concerns but Asquith did not set up a general enquiry.[1]

The House of Commons debated the railway conflict on 22 August. To the fore were fatalities on the strike's last day at the South Wales town of Llanelli. After the demobilization of a railway engine by strikers, in the course of which the driver was injured, troops were clearing the line of stone-throwing crowds and a soldier was knocked down. A magistrate read the Riot Act. Troops fired half-a-dozen shots at intervals: a local man and a lodger were killed. Later in the day warehouses were pillaged and shops attacked; railway trucks were set on fire, causing explosions; there were four more deaths. Keir Hardie told Parliament that, 'there was no riot of serious consequence, no looting, no burning of railway wagons, until the soldiers had shot two men dead.' The Merthyr Tydfil MP pointed the finger at Winston Churchill:

> The calling out of troops has hitherto been very rare. A new regime began with the present Home Secretary. The Government has used all the forces of the Crown to intimidate the men [*The Times* reports 'Labour cheers'] … The men who have been shot down have been murdered by the Government in the interest of the capitalist system.[2]

For the government, Lloyd George supported Churchill. He asked Hardie whether, had he been Home Secretary, he would have 'allowed the law to be set at defiance, the whole food supply of the country to be paralysed, and a famine to be created?' The debate confirmed the breakdown of any chance of working relations between Ramsay MacDonald and Winston Churchill. MacDonald charged the Home Office with playing 'the most diabolical part in all this unrest'. He spoke of 'a new doctrine preached from that [Dispatch] Box'. He called Churchill's conduct 'blundering':

> If the Home Secretary had just a little bit more knowledge of how to handle masses of men, if he had a somewhat better instinct of what civil liberty means, and if he had a somewhat better capacity to use the powers which he has as Home Secretary, we should have had much less difficulty.

Other Labour MPs produced testimony of troops having been sent where they had not been asked for. The picture is confirmed by the Home Office's statistics. Soldiers were dispatched to twenty-nine places in response to applications; thirty-three without. Labour Member John Ward had found soldiers with fixed bayonets all over Clapham Junction Station. He told the government: 'Workers are considered "hooligans" when they strike but "great citizens of a glorious Empire" when you want their votes.'³

This would be Churchill's last House of Commons debate as Home Secretary. He said:

> The House should remember that the Llanelli rioters, left to themselves, with no intrusion of the police, and no assistance from the military, for some hours wrought in their drunken frenzy more havoc to life and limb, shed more blood, produced more serious injury among themselves, than all the 50,000 soldiers who have been employed on strike duty all over the country during the last few days.⁴

The troops figure is understated. There were already 58,000 troops around the railways before the general railway strike began. Churchill presented himself as having tried to meet the requirements of mayors and magistrates, as they put in requests for military aid to protect their areas from violence. He conceded however that there was, as he put it, 'a general scheme for the protection of the railways'.⁵

The Home Secretary defended the bulletins. Well or badly phrased, they were simply 'summarising information received from different parts of the country'. There was nothing unconstitutional in what the government did: a national railway strike threatening complete immobilization was without precedent. Had it succeeded:

> Every mill, every mine, every factory, must have closed. The wages for the household would have ceased…In a great many places to a total lack of employment would have been added absolute starvation.

Churchill recited a catalogue of mayhem and destruction: riots; attacks on railway stations and signal-boxes; attempts to damage the line, to wreck trains, or to tamper with points; 'almost innumerable' attempts to stop trains; telegraph and signal wires cut. These, he said, with his penal knowledge, were 'a class of offences punishable with penal servitude up to life'. He added: 'several instances of incendiarism, and in two cases in South Wales, of wholesale loot by persons previously of good record'.⁶

With the Conservatives endorsing the Home Secretary's use of troops against the strikers and some Liberals displaying unease, the composition of the regular parliamentary sketch in the leading Liberal daily paper cannot have been easy when it came to Churchill's speech. The *Daily News* was used to cheering on the Liberals against the Conservatives. Militarism was expected to be found on the Conservative side. The writer, probably Philip Wilson, picked his words judiciously:

> ...The argument that if soldiers are to be called out at all, the more the better, marks a momentous change in the established practice of the Home Office, the results of which in the future may be very serious. Mr Churchill took well deserved credit for not using the soldiers at Tonypandy. He must have valued the Liberal cheers that supported him more than the Tory cheers that punctuated his speech today.[7]

The paper's editor, A.G. Gardiner, commented elsewhere on 'Napoleonic posturing' at the Home Office.[8]

A Labour MP was reminded of Churchill's father in the House of Commons a generation earlier. In southern Ireland in 1887 when a tenant protest meeting turned into a fight, shots from a police barracks killed three men. Randolph Churchill pronounced that there was no right to resist the police: anyone with a complaint about them could take it to the courts. George Lansbury saw Winston Churchill taking the same line now:

> I would like to point out to the Home Secretary that if you sit in a garden or on a garden wall on a Saturday afternoon and your brains are blown out it is very poor consolation to your wife and children to know that the Courts are open.[9]

He thought that Churchill had 'practically handed over the country to generals.'

The Home Secretary's use of troops plainly found more favour with the Conservatives than with his own party. Liberal critics were appearing. Italian-born MP Chiozza Money – whose writings on economics had influenced Churchill when he crossed the floor of the House – asked whether there was any precedent for the close relationship between the Home Office and the War Office.

In early October 1911, with the railway strike fresh in the memory, Winston Churchill spoke to Liberals in Dundee. Questions were called out about the Royal Commission. Churchill made a remark which looks surprising:

> I said at the last election that I was in favour of the railways being nationalised. (Cheers).[10]

Really? (Dundee Liberals evidently liked the idea of railway nationalization.) Was Churchill an advocate three-and-a-half decades before its time of a nationalized rail system? Vocabulary should be noted. Churchill called railway workers 'servants', hardly a socialist or comradely term. And he said that nationalization would have to be in return for workers not being allowed to strike. Winston was not averse to the state taking the commanding heights. Government control of the railways would happen quite soon anyway – albeit temporarily – in a war in which ministers and their agents needed to be sure of supplies. At this meeting WSC lumped rail workers with those whom he had helped with his Sweated Trades Bill of 1909, that is those with 'no real power of collective bargaining', for whom special means were needed of fixing their wage rates. No audience cheer is recorded on this.

The diary of George Riddell for November 1911 reviewed Churchill and the strikes:

> ...His position at the Home Office was gradually becoming intolerable to him. It was obvious that he was setting his teeth, and being a soldier, he would be likely to act in a thorough and drastic manner in the event of further labour troubles.[11]

Churchill's essential soldier broke through the politics. Riddell saw Asquith and Lloyd George as 'very apprehensive'.

There was an ugly postscript to the troubles. Just before the railway strike ended, a separate set of riots began in South Wales. These were not directed at the railway owners, or the military, or the magistrates. The centre of the disturbances was Tredegar. The disturbances spread across a wide area of Monmouthshire. They were an anti-Jewish pogrom, something without precedent in Britain in modern times. The Home Office file on them opens with a report from Monmouthshire's police chief on an 'attack on Jews at Tredegar last night [19 August], eighteen shops looted, police hopelessly outnumbered, similar mischief likely tonight.' *The Times* reported that a mob of several thousand terrified the occupants of shops, smashing windows and looting, some carrying away jewels in their hats. There had been feeling against a Jewish landlord accused of charging excessive rents by splitting cottages into flats. The lawlessness around the railway strike provided an opportunity for settling scores. Winston Churchill backed local requests for troops. He asked the Chief Constable of Monmouthshire to keep in close touch with the commander of troops in South Wales. He called for full reports. Not all the shops attacked were Jewish.[12]

On 22 August the clerk to the justices reported that the riots had spread: the Riot Act had been read at Tredegar, Ebbw Vale, and Rhymney. He said that attacks were planned on Jews at more local towns. The following day *The Times* reported:

> Much frightened, the Jews are departing from Tredegar and the neighbouring town of Ebbw Vale by every train, leaving their homes undefended and uncared for.[13]

The outbreak got as far as the borders of Breconshire. One moment was particularly perilous:

> At Cwm…huge crowds assembled in the streets, and at one period their numbers could have been very little short of 10,000. The situation looked very dangerous…

The Home Secretary's coordination of the sending of local infantry and cavalry was crucially important. Rescue squads arrived by train in time to disperse the mobs. After several days of terror, the pogrom was squashed and order restored.

Recovered goods ranged from suits, boots, shirts, and ties to a football, pushcarts, and two teddy-bears. There were many prosecutions, with prison sentences of twenty-eight days or two months, one woman sarcastically calling her sentence 'my holiday'. The Home Office file has a number of representations for remission or reduction. Winston Churchill initialled a memorandum by a member of his staff who told petitioners that he could hold out no hope that the Home Secretary would interfere with any of the sentences.[14]

Churchill spoke of the Tredegar pogrom in the parliamentary debate:

> …a case of anti-Semitism: quite peculiar and quite unknown in this country before – persons hitherto respectable were seen going home with bundles of clothes which they had taken from shops as if they were not in the least ashamed of what they had done.[15]

If the Home Secretary was the villain of the mass sending of troops against the railway strike, he was the hero of the dispatch of the anti-pogrom troops.

Chapter 29
A Walk with Violet

Winston Churchill was increasingly fascinated by military intelligence. The ex-soldier who during the Boer War cycled behind enemy lines now assisted with the development of the Secret Service Bureau, forerunner of MI5 and MI6. He worked actively with the Bureau's head, Captain Vernon Kell. As Home Secretary, he had to sign warrants for the opening of mail. This, he later said, 'disclosed a regular and extensive system of German-paid British agents.' A signature was required for each item. Churchill instituted general mail interception warrants. His intelligence zeal bled easily into his increasing preoccupation with coming European war.[1]

The press generally was supportive of Lloyd George's summer 1911 Mansion House blast. *The Manchester Guardian* was an exception. Its editor C.P. Scott concluded that there had been an arrangement all along, behind the backs of MPs, for Britain to fight on the continent alongside France against Germany. The *Guardian* condemned the war gallop. But there was no great Liberal, or even Labour, outcry. One reason was the all-consuming industrial conflict. Another was that the climax of Peers versus People was approaching. On 10 August, amid intense drama, the Parliament Bill narrowly passed through the House of Lords. Until then radicals were reluctant to rock the foreign policy boat. As a result, the 'Continentalists', those who wanted commitment to Anglo-French European war against Germany, were getting their way, even though they were in a minority in the cabinet. They had the upper-hand over the 'Atlanticists', or 'isolationists', who wanted to keep Britain out of European land-wars, preferring a policy of securing Britain and its Empire by naval strength.[2]

In 1909 Churchill had met the Kaiser and watched German military manoeuvres. Sir Edward Grey's private secretary, Sir William Tyrell, reflecting on the tendency to vocal outpouring of both the Kaiser and Churchill, called Wilhelm 'the Winston of Germany'. Churchill, after viewing the German show, wrote to his wife his reflections:

> ... Much as war attracts me and fascinates my mind with its tremendous situations, I feel more deeply every year...what vile and wicked folly and barbarism it all is.[3]

Churchill's 1908 and 1909 'pacifist' period (the word then usually simply meaning peace-promoting) had been less than completely convincing, given his continuing love affair with matters military, but there had been some substance to it. That was now gone. WSC's anti-war rhetoric was in abeyance.

Now the behind-the-scenes understanding that, if the big war happened, the British Expeditionary Force would fight alongside the French army against Germany became real. Richard Haldane's concern to pre-plan the transport of British troops across the Channel became pressing. Haldane wanted a detailed combined army-navy plan. The First Lord of the Admiralty did not favour such preparations. Reginald McKenna's Fleet would play its part (and the Admiralty would promote economic warfare), but McKenna was against passage of the British Expeditionary Force to Europe at the start of the war. Given his attitude, Asquith decided that a cabinet change at the Admiralty was needed. Who would replace McKenna?[4]

Winston Churchill was often in the company of Edward Grey at this time. Grey recalled that in that summer of sweltering heat, Churchill's 'high-metalled spirit was exhilarated by the air of crisis and high events.' Winston made sure he was around the action. He regularly called on Sir Edward in the late afternoon to take him to the Royal Automobile Club, with its swimming pool. Grey's memoir recollects that, '[Churchill] would cool his ardour and I revive my spirits.' Grey was quiet and reserved. He disliked rows and scenes and populism. Nor, despite being on the Imperialist wing of the Liberal Party, did he like war. He was godfather to little Randolph. Affection between Winston and Edward seems to have been mutual. Winston wrote to Clementine:

> I am always hearing nice things [Grey] has said about me. He likes and wistfully admires our little circle.[5]

Lloyd George told Churchill that the chances of war were 'multiplying'. On 27 August, he wrote to Churchill about Belgium being ready to chip in with troops to fight alongside the French and the British. An Anglo-Belgian army could 'pivot on the great fort of Antwerp'. LG was now into the spirit of the European war-game. He wondered how much Russia would provide. He wanted the Triple Entente made into an alliance. Churchill took up his points, urging Grey that he should:

> ...Propose to France and Russia triple alliance to safeguard (*inter alia*) the independence of Belgium, Holland and Denmark. Tell Belgium that, if her neutrality is violated, we are prepared to come to her aid.

Germany's contingent war against France involved, on the regular modelling, passage of its army through Belgium. In 1914, defence of Belgian neutrality would be an attractive ethical argument for British participation in a Triple Entente versus Triple Alliance war. It would bring aboard many in the Liberal and Labour parties who had previously been against British involvement.[6]

Grey replied to Churchill tersely that Russia's promise of support in a French/British war against Germany was 'categorical'. Meanwhile Winston was expatiating to Lloyd George on the shape of the prospective war theatre, including a Belgian army that would hold the Liege-Namur line. Sounding more like a military minister with every day, he now picked the brains of Lord Kitchener (Sudan and Boer War) and General Sir William Nicholson, Chief of the Imperial General Staff, about the military capabilities of the French and the Belgians. Churchill saw in Nicholson a fellow Continentalist of 'extraordinary vision'. The two had served together on the Indian frontier in 1898. Churchill also turned his attention to the Admiralty. He did not like what he found, remarking to Lloyd George that Admiral Ottley (Secretary of the Committee of Imperial Defence) was 'full of cocksureness and deficient in imagination'.[7]

Around this time Churchill was invited to dine with the German Ambassador, Count Metternich. He recounted: 'We were alone and a famous Hoch from the Emperor's cellars was produced.' The conversation was friendly. The diners knew each other. The bones of contention between Germany and France were gone over, including the enduring French pain over the loss of Alsace-Lorraine to Germany in the Franco-Prussian War forty years earlier and the German feeling of being 'in a net' between Russia and France. Metternich articulated to Churchill the rationale behind Germany's aggressive policy: a proud, ambitious nation contained within the sandwich of the Triple Entente – to the east, Russia, to the west, France and (in recent years) Britain. The sense of strangulation had given rise to the longstanding 'Schlieffen Plan' for a lightning attack on France by way of Belgium, to grab territory and securities to relieve the pressure. Churchill hotly contested the perspective. Germany need not feel threatened: she had 'an alliance with two other first-class powers, Austria-Hungary and Italy'.[8]

That autumn a celebrity gossip piece appeared in the *Daily Mirror* about Winston building sand-castles with Clemmie and the children on the beach at Broadstairs. Little did the reporter know that Winston's spade-work was the 'first system' of fortification of Sébastien de Vauban, military engineer to Louis XIV. At Easter Churchill had stayed at Holyhead as a guest of Lord Sheffield. Edward Marsh reported to Lady Gladstone that Winston played the military board game *L'Attaque* (the old enemies England and France trying to capture each other's flag) with Sheffield's daughter Venetia much of the day. When Winston was not playing *L'Attaque*, he was digging dams on the sands. He had to leave that when viewers with opera-glasses assembled on the cliff-tops. Military calculating was never long absent from Churchill's brain.[9]

He put his European military assessment into a memorandum: MILITARY ASPECTS OF THE CONTINENTAL PROBLEM. The date, 13 August 1911, shows that the Home Secretary was working out continental war moves just as he was calculating anti-striker strategies with troops at home. His paper predicted the progress in the future European war of the British Expeditionary

Force. Its conclusions were that, if the Germans were not stopped in the early days, the outcome would be: after twenty days an allied retreat, with the Germans breaking through and besieging Paris; after forty days, as the German lines were extended, the advance halted; then 'a trial of strength'. Churchill would be almost precisely correct about the first forty days of the war in the west (the British retreat from Mons; the subsequent allied stabilization). The WSC crystal ball did not touch on the war mutating in its aims and objects, with an ever-expanding number of participants, and with the imperial aspirations of France, Britain, and Italy bulking large. The document was strictly a military college exposition.[10]

On 14 August, War Minister Haldane had dinner with Asquith, McKenna, Grey, and Churchill to put his colleagues in the military picture. European war might break out any time, he warned. A reference to this gathering is made by Director of Military Operations Henry Wilson: '[Haldane] told those d_ ignorant men something of war.' On the following day General Wilson and Winston Churchill met. Wilson's journal has: 'Winston had put in a ridiculous and fantastic paper on a war on the French and German frontier, which I was able to demolish.' At this stage, he does not seem actually to have read Churchill's paper. Meanwhile, Asquith decided to convene a meeting of the Committee of Imperial Defence.[11]

General Wilson, like Churchill a Boer War veteran, was formerly Commandant of the Staff College, Camberley, reputedly a spell-binding lecturer. He was a fervent Continentalist. He wanted Britain to be making active and detailed preparations for going into European war. Wilson's diary entry of the day before the CID conference shows that his dismissal of the Home Secretary as an ignorant dabbler in military matters, was changing. Churchill's European war projections had arrived for him to read. He was highly impressed, calling the composition 'a wonderful production'. But he added that it was 'not the equal of the 1st Sea Lord[']s'. The latter was First Sea Lord Admiral Sir Arthur Wilson, who would be batting for the Admiralty at the CID and did not favour the Fleet being used to transport the British Expeditionary Force to France at the start of the European War.[12]

The CID met on 23 August, chaired by the prime minister, with Grey, Haldane, Lloyd George, McKenna and Churchill, and top-rank army and navy officers present. Colonial Secretary Lewis Harcourt smelt a Continentalist stitch-up. Reginald McKenna was warned by Maurice Hankey, assistant secretary of the CID, that the meeting had been stacked: McKenna would be isolated. The suspicions were confirmed by Asquith's instruction to the conference to work out 'how to give armed aid to the French'.[13]

The event exposed the divide between the War Office and the Admiralty. On the army side, there was the Continentalist ardour of General Wilson, with which went a keen desire to introduce military conscription in Britain to match the monster armies available to France and Germany. The general's visual aids included an enormous map, which had to be specially transported: he presented detailed projection of the German invasion route through Belgium. Issues included how many troops the French and the Russians could muster. Wilson's diary account notes 'much questioning by Winston and Lloyd George especially'.

For the navy, Admiral Wilson apparently thought that the conference was just another round of the War Office trying to get better funding and provision. He was against deployment of the British Expeditionary Force upon the outbreak of war: the British Army would be inadequate for so big a war; the function of the British Fleet should be close blockade of the enemy's ports, with British troops aboard the ships making diversionary counter-stokes on the German coast. Asquith told Lord Haldane that he thought the navy scheme for diversionary landings in the Baltic 'puerile'. He was strengthened in his view that the Admiralty needed reorganization, with a cabinet change. McKenna had been coming round to setting up an army-type general staff, but he did not want Britain to fight a land war on the continent of Europe. Churchill would be very happy to plan for that. The odds were firming for Winston to reorganize the Admiralty and to prepare it to launch the army into Europe.[14]

Relations between Winston Churchill and General Wilson were warming. On 28 August, Wilson's diary recorded:

> After lunch Winston Churchill came to my room…I was rather pleased with Winston. He asked me to write him a letter, which he could show to Asquith and Lloyd George, of my opinion on: Policy; Value of Antwerp; Confining Germans south of Meuse; Strength of Russia.[15]

Music played between the two Continentalists. Wilson gushed:

> [Churchill] told me I had absolutely persuaded him that my paper laid before the CID last week was right and his was wrong. This was nice. He had written to thank me for my "valuable paper" which he was sending on to Lloyd George and Grey.[16]

Since Asquith and his circle were backing the army's General Wilson and given that Churchill was an army line enthusiast, a cabinet double-switch between the Home Office and the Admiralty would fit the needs, especially as it was known that WSC was keen on a move to the Admiralty. But there was a snag. Haldane made it clear that he himself wanted to be First Lord.[17]

Neither Churchill nor Haldane was shy about making his case to the prime minister. Haldane had the advantage of being a close friend and ally of Asquith. He was a long-term Imperialist, and having already reorganized the army, he would presumably be ideal to do likewise with the navy. But there were factors against him. Inconveniently, he sat in the Lords. At the same time, a WSC Admiralty appointment would solve a problem for the government by moving

Winston out of the Home Office where he was causing upsets, including of the Labour Party whose support the government needed.[18]

The CID conference did not create a definite policy of British participation in a land war on the continent. With a continuing majority against this in the cabinet, there was no clear decision. The drift went on, with no concrete British commitment – and certainly no public pledge – but with French expectations of British support in a European war. This state of affairs would continue until August 1914. Meanwhile the Sea Lord's botched performance at the CID had convinced Asquith that an Admiralty change was needed. Winston Churchill had demonstrated potential competence at the Admiralty. But his rival was set to battle hard for the post.

Archerfield House in East Lothian, an Adam-style mansion with its own golf course, was regularly lent to the Asquith family by a brother of Margot. Here Asquith migrated with his entourage in the annual late-summer migration from London. The Archerfield name derived from the ground occupied by the English King Edward I's bowmen six centuries earlier on their advance north to fight the Scots. Now war was again in the air at Archerfield, as Asquith prepared for conference with the two Admiralty contenders.

Churchill was at Archerfield for several days. Haldane made two shorter visits. Among the Asquith family in the house was H.H.'s daughter Violet. There was poignance when Violet and Winston were together. We need to go back three years. At that time a match between the pair was a serious possibility. Then there was a moment of Churchill decision: abrupt, decisive, hurtful.

The relentless self-focus of Winston Churchill made him awkward territory for women. Before Clementine, he had made marriage proposals, including to the daughter of a shipping tycoon. A WSC triumphantly fulfilled destiny would be enhanced by an admiration-drawing spouse, reflecting his glory – and keeping the follies that he acknowledged in check. Wooing in Churchill's earlier life seems to have been an odd mixture of grandstanding and gaucheness. But by 1908 there was a serious nuptial possibility, perhaps even an unspoken understanding.

WSC first made the acquaintance of Violet Asquith when her father was Chancellor of the Exchequer. Violet could take larger amounts of Winston waxing lyrical about Winston than most could. The friendship flourished at Ettie Desborough's Taplow Court gatherings. Violet was good for Winston. It was not just that she could listen to him for hours. She had a shrewd political brain. Was it more than mere chance that Winston should strike up with the daughter of a man who was plainly on his way to the top? Certainly, Churchill's progress was assisted by Violet. When Asquith became prime minister in April 1908, Violet urged him to, 'make the most of Winston'. Churchill did indeed advance to the cabinet. H.H. appreciated Winston's energy and talents, taking the WSC ego with a large pinch of salt. Both Asquith and his wife were social climbers: a ducally connected son-in-law would not come amiss. How did Violet feel about

Winston? Michael Shelden's biography of the young Winston sees Lady Violet Bonham Carter's Churchill memoir as 'clearly a story of unrequited love'. On the other hand, when Roy Jenkins looked at Violet's diary, he found 'little supporting evidence' for the Churchill-admirer having actually been in love with him. But whatever, in 1908 there was a *situation* between the two.[19]

In mid-August 1908 Winston accepted an invitation from Violet to stay with her family at the rented Slains Castle near Aberdeen. Things were moving. But there was another woman in Churchill's life. That was Clementine Hozier. Winston's passion for Clementine was real, insofar as it ever was for a woman. But Clemmie's previous interest in Winston had gone quiet. Then she read that he had leapt into his cousin's blazing house to rescue art and books at peril to his life. Miss Hozier's fondness was rekindled. Churchill's hopes were back on. But there was Violet's invitation – and the situation. Winston made his decision. Sending his excuses to the Asquiths, he set up the Blenheim invitation to Clementine that resulted in her acceptance of a marriage proposal. It was said that Violet fainted when the news reached her. Winston belatedly fulfilled the Slains invitation, thereby upsetting Clementine: it needed her brother to talk her out of breaking off the engagement. In a letter to her friend Venetia Stanley, Violet delivered herself of exquisite scorn: Clementine 'could never be more to Winston than an ornamental sideboard': he badly needed 'a critical, reformatory wife who would hold him back from blunders'. Churchill later confessed to Harry Rosebery (Neil Primrose's brother, later Earl of Rosebery): 'I behaved badly to Violet because I was practically engaged to her.' Quite remarkably, Violet's friendship with Winston continued.[20]

How was it for Clementine? We cannot really know. Winston was faithful and conventionally devoted. Roy Jenkins has waspishly written that he was 'probably the least dangerously sexed major politician on either side of the Atlantic, let alone across the Channel, since the Younger Pitt'. Clemmie, except for one flirting distraction during later years, would be at her husband's side through his vicissitudes. There is a sense however that she had to be a Stoic, since Winston's buzz came from men.[21]

Winston's sexual identity is as elusive as the rest of him. It has been claimed that he was a closet gay. It is easy to see why, but also why that hypothesis is wrong. Churchill was clearly heterosexual. He did however have a pronounced empathy with gay men. His long-time private secretary Edward Marsh, handsome with a thin falsetto voice, was homosexual and his style was camp. He said of Churchill: 'It was an understood thing that I was Ruth to his Naomi and that whither he went I should go.' Women were secondary in Winston's world, politically and emotionally. A revealing statement was made in 1917 by Lady Diana Manners: 'I talked to Winston a great deal about you [Duff Cooper, whom Diana later married] – which convinced me quite of his sod bias – he admires yr body.' A consequence of the 'bias' was that Churchill's wife never quite matched the electric charge that certain males generated in him. Venetia Stanley said that, '[Winston], I'm sure, yearns for fun and Clemmie gives him none. He's crazy about [Duff Cooper].'[22]

Winston's present buzz was ships. The salary for First Lord of the Admiralty was £4,500, slightly less than for Home Secretary. With it went Admiralty House in Whitehall, a uniform and the use of the 4,000-tonne yacht *Enchantress*, plus crew. The Admiralty residence needed twelve servants but Churchill already had a large domestic expense at Eccleston Square. Politically, a move to the Admiralty would be down a rung in cabinet seniority. These pros and cons did not weigh critically with Winston. His desire for the job ran deep.

The prime minister shut Churchill and Haldane in a room with him. It was already practically settled in his mind that Churchill should go to the Admiralty, but damage to governmental cohesion had to be avoided. Asquith let the two men make their cases. WSC was used to pitching to Asquith both in his numerous speeches in cabinet (the prime minister's habit was to sit quietly and let his ministers talk) and in his memoranda.[23]

Haldane attempted a negotiating ploy. Would Churchill let him go to the Admiralty for a year to put through the changes, during which time Churchill could be War Minister? Then he would return to the War Office and Churchill could move in at the Admiralty. Churchill was not interested. Asquith played a card of his own. Haldane was a distinguished lawyer with a known ambition for the Woolsack, the Lord Chancellor's seat in the House of Lords. It would soon be vacant, since Lord Loreburn whose contours presently graced it, was set to retire. Haldane was not tempted. One problem for Asquith was that however ideal Haldane was for reorganizing the Admiralty, it would be deadening to the Fleet's pride to have the army minister moving over to reshape it. The meeting could not end with a decision in favour of Haldane.[24]

It was Churchill who salvaged harmony. He confirmed to Haldane his wish to establish a War Staff for the Fleet and offered him the opportunity to come over to the Admiralty to help him set it up. Haldane readily accepted. The two men parted 'in a very friendly spirit', in Haldane's words. The outcome of the Asquith holiday-home conference moved Britain another notch towards participation in a European land war. For Churchill, it was a career-changer. And he and Clemmie would, in due course, be moving into a new house.[25]

Winston went away for a night on constituency business. When he returned to Archerfield on 30 September, he played golf. Previously his company on the links had been Violet and her father. This time it was just Asquith. Violet was finishing tea when Churchill and her father returned. She saw in Winston's face 'a radiance like the sun'. He asked to walk with her. When they were clear of the house, he said: 'I don't want tea – I don't want anything – anything in the world. Your father has just offered me the Admiralty.' Violet's diary for 1 October states that the Admiralty had 'long been [Churchill's] Mecca in the Cabinet.' He said to her: 'Look at the people I've had to deal with so far – judges and convicts – this is a big thing.' Penal reform had consumed him for a year-and-a-half, but no longer. His heart now was stirred by ships.[26]

It is worth winding back to 3 March 1911 and a dinner at Claridge's in connection with the 'pricking' of the sheriffs (whose appointment ritual involved the jab of a bodkin into a parchment). Almeric Fitzroy's diary records that the conversation was 'sparkling':

> Of course the lion's share fell to Winston. Certainly he is a wonderful talker, daring, not to say reckless, but always with a subcurrent of method, striking in phrase, vivid in colour, eloquent to the verge of romance, picturesquely vehement, and at the same time persuasive.

Under discussion was the recent Declaration of London, which outlawed 'general capture' on the seas of the goods of enemies, and protected the naval rights of neutral powers. (It was not ratified.) Churchill, says Fitzroy, 'denounced any restrictions on the right of British seamen to do as they liked.' Lord Crewe commented that Winston had 'all the spirit of the buccaneer and would have been in his element in the sixteenth century as a captain under Drake.' Fitzroy goes on:

> Samuel who was next to me, said dryly: 'He would prefer having Drake as a captain under him.'[27]

The existing First Lord of the Admiralty got a letter from the prime minister on 10 October. Asquith spoke of 'a certain amount of reconstruction' and of McKenna's 'legal training and large and tried administrative experience and capacity' suiting him for the Home Office. Reginald was shocked. His immediate impulse was to quit the government. He was talked out of this. He negotiated a delay of two months on the grounds of convalescence. Meanwhile Churchill wrote to Alick Murray to let him know as Liberal Chief Whip that the switch on his part would leave no administrative loose ends. He was willing to conduct the Shops Bill to its end, whilst Charles Masterman would see the Mines Bill through. Possibilities crossed the brain of the Chief Whip, as revealed in Fitzroy's diary. The departure of Churchill from the Home Office could 'afford good grounds for dropping the Mines Bill and the Shops Bill.' Even with the scheming pragmatism of a Chief Whip, this looks heartless for the miners and the shop assistants. Fitzroy saw in Murray the required qualities for a Whip: 'absorption in the calculations attaching to that office and their application without compunction or remorse'. Murray's calculation was that with two time-consuming bills out of the way, the National Insurance Bill could become law more quickly. The whip's plotting ('a Machiavelli and a wire-puller', Fitzroy called him) came to nothing.[28]

The delay in the cabinet switch had to be abandoned when the King raised the difficulty that it would mean that he could not present the Home Office seals to McKenna until February. McKenna travelled to Archerfield on 20 October. He argued in vain that he needed to stay put at a time of high international tension. He received congratulations but he saw no cause for celebration. Eddie Marsh was puzzled, writing to Lady Gladstone that McKenna had wanted to leave the Admiralty and particularly desired the Home Office. He thought that McKenna was friends with Churchill again. Other evidence suggests that this was wishful thinking.[29]

Mind McKenna certainly did. Early next year Violet Asquith sat next to him at a dinner. She wrote in her diary: 'McKenna ranted about Winston – to me of all people. He must be mad.' On 24 October, Almeric Fitzroy wrote that McKenna 'took a sardonic pleasure in the reflection that some days must elapse before the new Admiralty warrant was ready, during which he would draw two salaries, and I suppose Winston be without any.' Fitzroy saw fortuitous vengeance on the part of the Churchill family: 'It is not a little curious that poor Tweedmouth's nephew [WSC] should revenge upon McKenna the rude manner in which he [Lord Tweedmouth] was bundled out of the Admiralty for the other's benefit.' Of WSC's first four government posts, two of them – colonial under-secretary and First Lord of the Admiralty – were previously held by a relation. Fitzroy was at the Privy Council meeting that effected the cabinet changes. He commented that, 'Winston was evidently very pleased, receiving my congratulations with great cordiality.' Whilst Churchill danced on the clouds, there was acid in the heart of McKenna.[30]

The Gladstones were watching. Lady Gladstone, in her correspondence with Eddie Marsh, interpreted events as Winston being 'taken away from the Home Office because he was making a mess of it'. Departure in disgrace was vigorously contested by Eddie. Churchill, he said, had become 'quite the National hero' because of the railway strike. He passed over the Labour rage and Liberal embarrassment. National hero was for three decades later. The move of Churchill served a double purpose for Asquith, who was a man of operational subtlety. As Roy Jenkins neatly puts it, it was 'shake-up' at the Admiralty and 'calm-down' at the Home Office. Churchill's brilliance and energy made him excellent value, but up to a tipping-point when his hazards turned him into negative capital. That point was reached early at the Home Office.[31]

Around this time an interesting remark was made by Austen Chamberlain: 'Winston feels the Home Office is getting too hot for him.' The senior Conservative thought that Churchill had decided that he 'cannot rival Lloyd George as demagogue and will cultivate the role of statesman and strong man instead.' Chamberlain's observation is plausible. Churchill was never going to outdo Lloyd George in popular campaigning on the domestic front. Winston was swinging towards statecraft – and maybe war. The Admiralty was perfect for him.³²

Edward Marsh went with Winston Churchill to the Admiralty. Churchill took up his new cabinet post on 23 October 1911. Did he deliver effective reorganization? The answer is surprising. Richard Haldane's biographer finds that the Naval War Staff created under Churchill, 'fell far below the standards of its counterpart at the War Office.' R.C.K. Ensor calls it 'purely advisory and its role subordinate'.³³

Churchill's twenty months at the Home Office were over. Fifty years later Lucy Masterman recalled the complex feelings of the staff towards him:

> …a tinge of amused indulgence in his colleagues' attitude…the constant ebullitions in the press, which so much afflicted the Civil Service soul of Sir Edward Troup…[Troup's] indulgence towards "an extraordinarily gifted boy".³⁴

Mrs Masterman added, with retrospective foreboding:

> Few people were shrewd enough to realise the dangers of this prolonged boyishness, this clamour of a boy for the attention of his elders.

How did the staff react to Winston's departure? Eddie Marsh, an unreliable Churchill witness, reported to Lady Gladstone:

> The Office was most depressed at losing [Churchill]. He had of course annoyed some of the people at first, but I think everyone (including especially B[l]ackwell) had got to like him – [T]roup from the first, and more and more, and the King was more than pleased with him.³⁵

A dollop of salt is required, but we may find some truth: a difficult start, staff equilibrium disturbed by a brash young minister who disregarded convention and precedent, but in time warm regard. Edward Troup chatted with George Riddell a while after Churchill left. He said that he found Winston 'quite easy to get on with' and that he had 'inspired him with feelings of affection'. However, a Troup comparison of Churchill with the incoming McKenna is telling on industrial strikes: McKenna 'did not lose his head'. Lucy Masterman remembered Troup as 'deaf, disillusioned, kindly'. We may imagine the stress under which the bouncing Winston put him. It is hard to think that there was not some relief on Sir Edward's part when the more conventional McKenna (with his legal background) entered the portals, as Churchill with his child-like exuberance exited them.³⁶

No sadness was felt by the departing Churchill. At the end he cocked a final snook at the establishment. Wilfrid Blunt's diary records that:

> Just before leaving [Churchill] ordered a number of remissions of sentences, notwithstanding the protests of the judges in the cases.³⁷

The remissions were not reversible. That will have given Winston pleasure.

In Churchill's final Home Office days, there was a high profile suffragette case for him to deal with. Clemence Housman, sister of A.E., was prominent in the WSPU and the Women's Tax Resistance League. On 29 September 1911 she became the first woman to be jailed in the no-tax campaign. In Holloway, she was granted Churchill Rule status. Petitions for her release came to the Home Office. Suffragettes demonstrated outside the prison. Harry Simpson and Ernley Blackwell were firmly against letting Clemence go. Simpson was indignantly righteous: 'Miss Housman's imprisonment is due directly to the action of a government department in the discharge of its ordinary duty of collecting the taxes imposed by Parliament.' The women's case – that their sex was not represented in Parliament, and so they had every right to resist taxes – was lost on him. Blackwell thought Housman 'ought not to be let out until she has served a substantial term to deter others.' But Clemence was suddenly released. Her Home Office file offers no explanation, but we may see her as among the prisoners whom Churchill released just as he left the Home Office. The suffragettes had given him much trouble, but he did not bear grudges. And he liked the poetry of A.E. Housman. *Votes for Women* newspaper was jubilant. A 13 October cartoon had Chancellor of the Exchequer Lloyd George arguing with a police-uniformed Winston Churchill outside the prison about the cost of keeping Miss Housman and telling him that she would have to be let out. So came to an end the story of Winston, the Home Office, and the suffragettes.[38]

Churchill's Home Office tenure had been a bumpy ride. He upset South Wales, Liverpool, and the women's suffrage movement so severely that the bitterness rankles today. But he left great achievements. Most notable was what he did for prison inmates. In this most unusual of Home Secretaries, there was his personal experience of imprisonment, his sense of being an outsider, the chutzpa that nerved him to take on the conservative Whitehall establishment, his humanity, and his driving need to make a mark. For penal administration, it was a serendipitous combination.

Chapter 30

Civilization?

We leave our tracking of events as Winston Churchill leaves the Home Office. What remains is to look at how his flagship measures, his penal reforms, fared in the longer term.

We must visit briefly the week leading up to 4 August 1914, since it brought the big consequence of WSC's move to the Admiralty. Churchill's key action was moving the Fleet in the early hours of 29 July from Portland to its War Station at Scapa Flow. Most ministers opposed mobilization of the Fleet but Churchill persuaded Asquith into issuing an order. The effect was to push Russia towards fighting alongside its Slavic ally Serbia against Austria and Germany. France was committed by alliance to Russia and expected British support in the war. It was decided in cabinet on 2 August that the French ambassador should be told that the British Fleet would prevent the Germans from using the Channel. Churchill's voice was crucial. Anti-war Liberal MP Edmund Harvey wrote to his father during this week 'One dreads the influence of Churchill.'[1]

A Liberal MP, Francis Neilson, witnessed a scene between Churchill and Hugh Cecil in the House of Commons in the late afternoon of 3 August 1914. This was after Sir Edward Grey, in a famous speech, had announced, in effect, that Britain was going into the war. Neilson had arranged to meet Churchill in the Ayes lobby on some matter of journalism. He related in a 1952 American-published memoir:

> I saw Churchill enter from the other end. Suddenly a man rushed past me and flew towards him, took Churchill by the collar, shook him violently and cried, 'You did it! You did it!'. The next moment I could see that Churchill's assailant was Lord Hugh Cecil. He cast Churchill off and turned back the way he had come – a broken man, his face wet with tears.[2]

It was witnessed by another Liberal, Sir Stephen Furness. Cecil saw Churchill as personally responsible for plunging Britain into war.

War occupied Winston Churchill one way and another between 1911 and 1922. He was a soldier on the Western Front in 1915–1916. Having made the gesture, he was glad to take the chance of getting back quickly to Westminster; and in Parliament – unlike most soldier MPs – he did not wear military uniform. Here were the Churchill contradictions. When Winston was Home Secretary, he grabbed at any return to military life, but when he actually became a soldier again, he yearned to get back to his true vocation, namely being a politician, preferably at the heart of government. He admitted however in moments of candour that he loved war. The Winston the warrior stance which the *Panther* reignited in 1911 was around until the early 1920s. But there were always the different sides to Churchill, whether actual or latent. By the later 1920s when – following his father – he was (a Conservative) Chancellor of the Exchequer, trimming of military spending was again a virtue with him as it had been in 1908 and 1909. Back in 1911 Churchill's move from the Home Office to the Admiralty was noticed by Wallace Blake, governor of Lewes Jail, who chortled in his memoir:

> …[Churchill] gave us so much extra trouble that when I saw from the *Daily Mail* that he was leaving the Home Office for the Admiralty, I put in a special request to the chaplain for two hymns at morning prayers: 'Now Thank we all our God' and 'For Those in Peril on the Sea'.[3]

We may say that the inmates of Blake's prison, had they had access to newspapers, would have viewed it differently. Churchill deserves much credit for the civilizing of jails. There were gaps of course. Why did he not ease the painful restrictions on prisoners' correspondence; why did he not civilize the humiliating arrangements for visits to prisoners, and the dehumanizing address of inmates by number? He was at the Home Office for only a short time. He focussed on where he could make a change, as with the introduction of lectures and entertainment, and the institution of a kinder regime for elderly inmates. His ventilation of issues meant that his influence lasted long after his departure. He had to compromise on getting rid of solitary confinement but in 1922 the 'separate confinement' system was suspended and in 1931 it was abolished.[4]

Churchill's Abatement of Imprisonment bill lapsed on his departure, but in 1914 Reginald McKenna instituted an Administration of Justice Act which partly embodied it. A central plank was provision of time for the payment of fines. Ruggles-Brise's 1921 book *The English Prison System* has remarkable figures. In 1913–1914 the average daily prison population (local and convict) was 17,056: by 1918–1919 it was down to 8,302. The war of course had some effect, but it was the adoption of Churchill's policy on fines that was the chief reason for the spectacular drop. Brise reckoned it halved the jail population. And the lower figures were maintained. Winston's leading intention in penal reform was achieved.[5]

Churchill's discouragement of the use of preventive detention, which he showed to be arbitrary and unjust, had the consequence that it declined and withered.

We noted Churchill's attempt to end the passing of death sentences on women who killed their babies. The Infanticide Act of 1922 effectively abolished the death penalty for a woman who killed her new-born child. The 1938 Infanticide Act extended the provisions up to children of twelve months.[6]

Suspended sentences were an unfilled Churchill aspiration. They were not a novel idea. They existed in Europe (Belgium, France and Portugal for example), as well as in Australia. The fact that for the first time in Britain the idea became the subject of discussion in criminal justice circles was important: it was not forgotten. Suspended sentences came to Britain with the Criminal Justice Act of 1967.

It is clear that between the wars, following on the gusts of fresh air blown into the penal system by Winston Churchill, the culture of jails was changing. Reform quickened, along the lines charted by Churchill. Broad arrows and the 'convict crop' went. Prisoners met their visitors in a civilized room. Churchill's lectures and concerts were further developed. Handicrafts and gymnastics came in. A start was made on a prison adult education system. Socializing among inmates and between officers and inmates became more acceptable. Civilizing touches included shaving. From 1929, there were small cash payments to incentivize prisoner industry. Prison specialization developed. Before the Second World War paused the progress of reform, the open prison movement took its first steps. In terms of the effectiveness of the approach of Churchill and his successors, the statistics tell their tale. Between the wars the number of recorded homicides went down.[7]

There was still plenty of the old repressive regime. Dartmoor bubbled with pent-up resentment over poor living conditions and food, and excessive flogging. In 1932 prisoners seized control. Twenty-three men were sentenced collectively to nearly a hundred years imprisonment. On 19 November 1936, Churchill put a question to the then Home Secretary, Sir John Simon. Several MPs had been enquiring about remission for those still serving sentences consequent on the uprising. Simon promised a review. From the backbenches, Churchill asked:

> In making this review, will the right hon. Gentleman endeavour to take into consideration the individual guilt of the offenders rather than the far more serious aspect caused by the collective offence?[8]

It was the position that Winston Churchill had taken as Home Secretary. It was expressed in 1911 when he said in the reformatory scandal debate that: 'In matters of justice one ought not to give way to public opinion.' He thought that each mutineer should be treated on an individual justice basis, however shocking the event had been. He was against exemplary justice and panic-inspired sentencing.

After the Second World War, a major penal legislation landmark, the 1948 Criminal Justice Act, ended flogging, 'penal servitude', 'hard labour' and class divisions in prison. The act brought in 'preventative detention' of up to 14 years. This resulted in a recurrence of the intrinsic injustice about which Winston Churchill had been unhappy. New versions of the Dartmoor Shepherd were shocked to find themselves sent to the Crown Court to be sentenced to long stretches for relatively minor offences.

From the 1960s, the penal currents shifted. To say that the rehabilitative ideal had determined policy since the mid-1890s would be to oversimplify since there were always competing schools. But it did lead the thinking in penal administration for the first two-thirds of the twentieth century. Then rehabilitation went into retreat. Victor Bailey's study puts 'the high watermark of the treatment ethic' as early as 1959 – with Home Secretary R. A. 'Rab' Butler's White Paper, 'Penal Practice in a Changing Society'. By the mid-1970s, the direction had changed.[9]

In the last quarter of the twentieth century and the first quarter of the twenty-first, the punitive penal school has, in effect at least, re-asserted itself. The origins of the shift were in the 1950s, with what Victor Bailey calls 'the twin pincers of a growing crime rate and prison overcrowding', with two, sometimes three, prisoners having to share Victorian cells designed for one person. The number of prisoners serving a life sentence increased from 566 in 1970 to 10,600 in 2017, as 'sentence inflation' added to the prison population pressures. The figures for elderly prisoners increased markedly.[10]

The mass media's attitude to convicts has changed since Churchill's day. Then the tide of sentiment was with him. Vengeful sentiment was discouraged, as belonging to the bad old days. Now those days are back. It has become acceptable for newspapers to celebrate the 'caging' of a sentenced criminal. In contrast to the convention of Churchill's time when crime was kept out of party politics in order that justice should be dispassionate, crime sentencing has become political. When Churchill was at the Home Office even a brutal murderer like John Dickman received sympathy from the big readership *Daily Mail* as he faced the gallows. Now, sentencing is influenced by victim-impact statements, with the risk of individual justice being unbalanced by emotion. The rehabilitation aspect of imprisonment has suffered from insufficient provision of resources. (The reversal of the tracks on penal reform has been even more pronounced in the United States, with the total of the imprisoned there reaching two million, with a heavy racial skewing of incarceration.) The link between poverty and prison was something that Churchill tried hard to turn around. In 2022 screenwriter Jimmy McGovern, brought up in a deprived area of Liverpool, told a BBC Radio *Today* interviewer regarding his award-winning jail drama *Time*, that he could easily have ended up in prison himself. Churchill would have understood that.[11]

In Winston Churchill's first capital case, Joseph Wren was held in Manchester's Strangeways Prison. By the late twentieth century, conditions there had become intolerable. In April 1990 inmates wreaked fire and devastation. The horror lasted twenty-five days, and there were serious incidents at many other prisons. The QC Michael Mansfield, in his foreword to a 1995 book on the Strangeways Riot, had words that could have been Churchill's: 'Unless prisoners are treated as human beings and not disposable numbers; are given respect and dignity, and not treated as animals to be broken to the point of submission, there will be no progress into the next century.'[12]

The Woolf Report on the mutiny made many recommendations. Whilst action was awaited, one of the then Home Secretary's prison visits was recorded for posterity. This came about because one of the inmates of the jail would later become a *Guardian* columnist who wrote books about his experiences. Erwin James (Monahan), who grew up without a mother and with an alcoholic, violent father, served a sentence for murder between 1984 and 2004. The Home Secretary is unnamed in James's June 2001 newspaper account but it may be adduced from 'minister with a penchant for wearing brown suede shoes and smoking a large cigar with his pint', that this was Kenneth Clarke (1992–1993). The prison (not identified) was a progressive one, which held joint events with its local community. Clarke looked in on preparations for a charity half-marathon. Among the prisoners was 'a chronic self-harmer who rarely spoke to anyone'. He had the temerity to ask Clarke, 'the most powerful man in our lives', for a donation. An Oliver Twist workhouse moment could have been anticipated. Instead, the Home Secretary gave the inmate a five-pound note, wishing him 'Good luck with your run'. That moment was an inspiration, perhaps even life-changing, for the troubled prisoner. Irwin comments: 'I have seen with my own eyes what can be achieved with a little goodwill and encouragement.' The parallel between Ken Clarke's prison-visiting and that of Winston Churchill is inescapable. With both Home Secretaries, humanity shone through and good was clearly done.[13]

1993 brought the appointment of Michael Howard, who made the statement, 'Let us be clear. Prison works.' Lord Woolf's proposals were mothballed. The penal administration failings would continue. The evidence litters many a report. The definitive exposure is *Prisongate: The Shocking State of Britain's Prisons and the Need for Visionary Change* by David Ramsbotham (Lord Ramsbotham), ex-Chief Inspector of Prisons. This details the consequences of more and more prisoners being heaped into jails lacking the capability to manage them, with more crime thereby being bred, in a futile spiral: the opposite of Winston Churchill's vision.[14]

The advent in 1997 of New Labour did not bring a return to Churchill's ideal. Prison numbers rocketed further. As Joe Sim points out, Labour's Shadow Home Secretaries at the time of Michael Howard (Tony Blair and Jack Straw) were in broad agreement with Howard. In fact, as Sim puts it, Conservative ministers were 'dancing to New Labour's desperately corrosive law and order tune'. Ex-Home Secretary Douglas Hurd, speaking in the House of Commons on 4 November 1996, remarked:

> I am waiting for [Straw] to tell us before too long that…he has found the answer to prison overcrowding: to hang offenders outside the prison gate.[15]

Jeffrey Archer, a prisoner in 2001–2002, painted a bleak picture in his diary memoir. Reviewing it, Anthony Howard wrote: 'There is no member of the current Tory Opposition front bench to whom I would not recommend this book – but then the same would have to go for the majority of the government front bench and especially, perhaps, its Home Office team.'[16]

A central problem with which Churchill battled has continued: how to achieve protection of the public from those inclined to harmful conduct without doing injustice to individuals. 2005 saw the introduction of IPPs (Imprisonment for Public Protection). This system, like its preventive detention predecessors, raised the issues of individual unfairness that worried Churchill. It was abolished in 2012 (though existing prisoners on IPPs continued to be subject to them). We may say that Churchill's complaints about the inherent injustice of preventive detention were vindicated by the failure and abandonment of its successor systems.

Erwin James's jail experience was that, 'most of the prison system was geared to dehumanize.' A governor, told him: 'As a society we believe in rehabilitation for prisoners – but the truth is, we're not sure how rehabilitated we want them to be!' This expressed the outlook of a modicum of rehabilitation, but no more, so as not to offend those who thought that prisoners were having it soft. It may be contrasted with Churchill's approach of reforming and reintegrating all who possibly could be. Churchill would have agreed with prisoner James's sentiment: 'Rehabilitation is the best way to protect the public, Governor.'[17]

The direction of penal administration today would, we may guess, shock the Churchill of 1910–1911. Crowd-pleasing governmental pitches have marked it. A single example may serve to illustrate attitudes negative to rehabilitation: the ban in 2013–2014 by the then justice secretary on the sending of books into prisons for inmates, security concerns being cited. (It was quashed in 2014 by the high court.) The contrast with the efforts made by Churchill to make books more readily available to prisoners is a defining one.[18]

When Churchill was at the Home Office, he searched for ways of avoiding sending people to jail. His initiatives generated much success. Defaulters' Drill was one idea that did not get off the ground, but an alternative later did, and considerably so. In 1966 Roy Jenkins, in some senses a new Churchill at the Home Office, took a leaf out of Churchill's reform playbook by setting up a committee: the Advisory Council on the Penal System. Its non-custodial and semi-custodial sub-committee was chaired by the inspirational Baroness Barbara Wootton. One result, which was developed in the 1970s, was community service. Money was saved and the reoffending rate among participants significantly reduced. However, recent times have seen stigmatization of community service participants, as in the compulsory wearing of tabards emblazoned with the words 'Community Payback' for offenders doing public space work. Deprivation of dignity was the opposite of Churchill's aim. Public 'shaming' as a part of governmental policy would have appalled him. Churchill's policy was to rid from penal administration this unlovely strand, going back as it does to the stocks, ducking-stools, public executions, and gibbets. Lately, it has reappeared. The shift in penal attitudes since about 1970 has been visible in various ways. The shackling of prisoners to guards in public hospitals (witnessed by this writer on a visit to a ward) is one reflection of a change of direction since Churchill and his successors. If humiliation of prisoners is one indicator, the privatization of prison services is another. This would have been unthinkable to Churchill.[19]

The tension between punishment/deterrence and rehabilitation/reintegration has never been resolved. There have always been those, variously described as 'pathological', 'habitual', 'incorrigible', 'morally imbecile', who would not be susceptible to even the most imaginative and well-resourced training and education, and who would continue to commit crimes when given the chance. Winston Churchill knew this. He was not an all-out 'positivist'. He was not opposed to the punitive side to sentencing. He was a believer in personal responsibility, meaning that sentences needed to reflect the crime and the degree of culpability. He thought that serious crime should incur long imprisonment. And he was firm on the need to protect society from those with anti-social and dangerous emotions. But he tried to strike a fair balance in punish-versus-reform. It is worth revisiting Churchill's declaration to Parliament on 20 July 1910, when he spoke of the need in a civilized society for:

> A calm and dispassionate recognition of the rights of the accused against the State, and even of convicted criminals against the State, a constant heart-searching by all charged with the duty of punishment, a desire and eagerness to rehabilitate in the world of industry all those who have paid their dues in the hard coinage of punishment.

Here is the balance that has been missing in recent times when penal policy-making has followed media sensation and looked to popularity. Churchill's message is as apt surely today as it was in 1910. It has not completely been forgotten. The brief tenure of Michael Gove at the Justice Ministry (2015–2016) saw again a spirit of care for prisoners, exemplified by the cancellation of the limit on the number of books permitted for prisoners. Gove had plans for education and training and was developing alternatives to custody for women. One may also point to the mission statement of the present-day Dartmoor, which declares that, '[prisoners] are not here to be punished; their punishment is loss of liberty tempered by help towards reform and rehabilitation.' That was Churchill's policy. The stabilization of prison figures in recent years perhaps affords some hope (but see Chapter 30: note 26). Prisons like modern Dartmoor, and thoughtful 'restorative justice' initiatives, and development of the open prison sector, show that Churchill's spirit and imagination in penal administration are still alive.[20]

If one thing is agreed about Winston Churchill, it is that in 1940 he was the person for the moment. We may say that had it not been Churchill as prime minister in 1940, Britain would have come to terms with the Nazis (with the then still neutral Italy mediating) and would have become a fascist client state. Churchill was a gambler. This element was required in his 1940 decision. The later participation in the war against Germany of both Russia and the United States could not then have been predicted. In the event it was a close-run thing but Churchill was vindicated. In his leadership of the British war effort, defending the Empire but also Britain's liberal democracy, his phrase-making came into its own. Unfortunately, a distorted impression of the maker of those speeches has recently taken shape. In liberal reform versus conservative traditionalism, a spurious Churchill has become the talisman of the latter side. It is highly damaging to the chances of Churchill's record as a penal reformer being taken seriously and being part of the mix in today's thinking. He is seen as an aristocratic (and racist) oppressor of the disadvantaged – the man of the statue, statues being bitter politics and Churchill's being in the reactionary camp in this conflict.

Admittedly, Churchill is to some extent the author of his own misfortune. In 1910, female suffrage campaigner H.N. Brailsford accused him of being 'treacherous' because he had said something to him which he had taken as a promise of support for the Conciliation Bill. An aggrieved Churchill wrote to him that he 'ought not to repeat for public purposes private conversation or such fragments of it as you can remember, or think you can remember…rather a well-known rule'. Herein lay the Churchill problem. He said many things, many of them contradictory. Asquith's charge that he 'thinks with his mouth' was about the Winston habit of blurting out off-the-cuff comments and remarks that he had not thought through. By cherry-picking from Churchill's unguarded utterances, hagiographies, and hatchet-jobs may equally easily be constructed. The WSC fame means that words off his cuff as well his brain have often ended up on the record.[21]

Geoffrey Wheatcroft in his *Churchill's Shadow* has an interesting point regarding the highly vexed question of what Winston Churchill's sentiments really were. Churchill has incurred well deserved opprobrium for his reactionary statements in the 1930s regarding India. But what did he actually think about India? Lord Wolmer, who pursued WSC in 1911 over the Sidney Street affair, was one of the diehards against Indian devolution. So *apparently* was Winston Churchill. But *was* he really? This was a time when Churchill was out in the cold and he wanted whatever help he could get. Wheatcroft quotes Wolmer on Churchill and India: 'He *discredits* us. *We* are acting from conviction but everybody knows Winston has no convictions; he has only joined us for what he can get out of it.'.[22]

Winston Churchill's recent years afterlife has been as a figure of (ultimate) supreme wisdom. The popular *Churchill Factor* by Boris Johnson and Andrew Roberts's more nuanced *Churchill: Walking with Destiny* have been followed, especially by politics' right-wing, which has adopted this Churchill figure. This development has significantly damaged WSC's chances of being taken seriously as a politician and a thinker. Geoffrey Wheatcroft's presentation of the litany of ways in which this has occurred includes a look at the decidedly bizarre spectral appearance of Churchill the Brexiteer. In reality, whilst WSC's utterances on Europe are, like everything about him, contradictory, the balance is on the side of his having favoured integration of Britain and continental Europe. We should remember that in 1940 Churchill, with the great-heartedness that was such an appealing side of him, offered to unite Britain and France. But the Churchill landscape is dominated lately by films and books that leave the kind of patriotic glow in which Winston shimmers forth as the standard-bearer of old-fashioned values. This process has naturally produced a reaction. Tariq Ali's *Winston Churchill: His Times, His Crimes* urges that Churchill nostalgia should be 'scrubbed off' *HMS Britain*'s hull. But this would be Soviet-style history air-brushing. Churchill as the builder of part of the foundation of the welfare state and Churchill the penal reformer would be lost in the process, along with Churchill the prime minister whose 1940 decision saved British democracy.[23]

Was Winston Churchill's struggle to create a modern Home Office successful? The simple answer must be No, if for no other reason than that he was not in the post long enough. But Churchill's twenty months had profound and lasting effects, not fully overthrown until the 1990s. He did not expel the H.O. stuffiness and conservatism but his gales of fresh air were felt long afterwards. He set in train in the department a positive attitude towards penal reform. As this account concludes, it is worth taking a glance at the Home Office Churchill in the context of modern times.

There has been discussion in recent times about the fall, whose inception may be dated from around 1980, of the liberal-outlook Home Office establishment, previously dominant since the middle years of the twentieth century. This was, it should be said, far from completely ousted in the 1980s. There were Home Secretaries in that decade, most notably William Whitelaw (1979–1983) and Douglas Hurd (1985–1989), who, to an extent at least, maintained liberal values, whilst around them a new philosophy swept in, a socially uncaring one, led by Prime Minister Margaret Thatcher, who famously in promoting the politics of individual and family aspiration said that she did not recognize 'society'. The changed outlook caught up with criminal administration. The attitudes that now prevailed had been a fringe in Winston Churchill's Home Office days, in the shape of those rising middle-class members who in the defence of their wealth wanted criminal elements kicked hard without interference from penal-reforming do-gooders. The years from the 1990s have seen a sort of Old Tory-New Labour penal consensus under which policy has been shaped by a populist bidding war, making for a climate of hyperactive legislation, in which patient and open-minded governmental research has been pushed aside in the face of electorally purposed 'focus groups'.[24]

There was no Home Office liberal-values elite in 1910. Churchill was the advanced Liberal arrival. Generally, the senior secretaries – the likes of Edward Troup, Harry Simpson, and Ernley Blackwell – did not like his approach. Nor did juniors like those who grumbled in the minutes book about public rejoicing over Churchill's rescue of a coal-pilfering boy from seven years in a reformatory. Civil Service memoranda show that the backroom chiefs regarded their new minister as 'soft' – though in time they warmed to him. The later rehabilitative establishment at the Home Office was to a significant degree the creation of Churchill. Not unreasonably, there is no desire today for a return to penal administration elitism. Elitism was certainly not Churchill's intention. His humane and constructive legacy needs to be rescued, but in a more democratic and accessible shape than the way in which it later developed. Churchill's personal 1910–1911 history can help here. He was the outsider when he entered the Home Office: the man who had not been to university and was of part-American breeding. We saw that Churchill identified with the Britain of industrial muscle; we saw his put-down of the Eton boys as 'fashionable young cubs'; his scorn at the refusal of the Cecils to share power with 'any able man of provincial origin'; his opening of the coal-mines inspectorate to men from the coal-face; the approving comment of radical Liberal Josiah Wedgwood on 'the democratic forces which we now have at the head of the Home Office'. It may be added that Churchill felt strongly about the class-based inequality of British education. In 1942 he told a Labour politician that he wanted about two-thirds of pupils of the great public schools to be not fee-payers but scholarship-holders. Francis Green and David Kynaston's book *Engines of Privilege* mentions that in November 1939 Conservative MP Robert Boothby thought Churchill the only politician with sufficient imagination to sweep away 'our "caste" system of education'. Churchill also wanted continuing education for all up to 18, as he told trade-unionists visiting the Home Office in 1911.[25]

The Winston Churchill of 1910–1911 was a democratically based penal reformer. In making his great speech to Parliament on 20 July 1910 about criminal justice he was addressing the nation. This was not the not-in-front-of-the children Home Office liberal penal establishment of later times. Nowadays his and his successors' penal philosophy and reforms have been superseded by a harsh and thoughtless populism. For their rehabilitative legacy to be recovered, Churchill himself is in urgent need of rescue from the now long sterile saint-versus-monster debate. The Churchill 1940 reputation is probably safe; not so his penal reforms of 1910–1911.

Winston Churchill did not in the end succeed in his struggle to change the stuffiness and conservatism of the Home Department into something more modern. No one could have done that. But Churchill the Liberal put through major reform, which included large progress towards making the prisons more humane, and the penal system more rational and effective. The later Churchill's 'Fight on the beaches' and 'We shall never surrender' will endure. But will the earlier Winston Churchill's maxim that the way authority deals with offenders is 'an unfailing test of the civilization of any country'? Time will tell. Arguably it is needed more than ever today.[26]

Notes

For abbreviations list, see page vii.

Chapter 1
1. *Westminster Gazette*, 1 February 1910.
2. Roy Jenkins, *Churchill*, 106; Alan S. Baxendale, *Winston Leonard Spencer-Churchill, Penal Reformer*, 2.
3. Bentley B. Gilbert, *The Evolution of National Insurance in Great Britain*, 248–251.
4. Hansard, 5: 484.
5. *News of the World*, 7 May 1939.
6. CV, II:2, 1133–1134; David Lough, *No More Champagne: Churchill and His Money*.
7. British Library Sound and Moving Image Catalogue, 1LL0007079 (Winston Churchill and Anthony Asquith Speech Made for Budget League 1909); HCS II, 1387–1400.
8. Robert Rhodes James, *Churchill A Study in Failure 1900 – 1939*, 24; Martin Gilbert, *Churchill A Life*, 78–84.
9. Piers Brendon, *Winston Churchill*, 47–49; Sonia Purnell, *First Lady*, 50–51; Jenkins, 149.
10. Martin Gilbert, 102.
11. L. A. Atherley-Jones, *Looking Back*, 122; Paul Addison, Churchill the unexpected hero, 33–35.
12. Colin Clifford, *The Asquiths*, 164–165; Richard Toye, *Lloyd George & Churchill*, 63–65.
13. Clifford, 163.
14. *Punch*, 23 February 1910; *News of the World*, 7 May 1939.
15. *News of the World*, 7 May 1939; Jill Pellew, *The Home Office 1848–1914*, 1–4; Sir Edward Troup, *The Home Office, passim*; Charles Mallet, *Herbert Gladstone*, 202–227; Roy Jenkins, *A Life at the Centre*, 179.
16. Murrays of Elibank, *Master and Brother*, 40; *Inside Asquith's Cabinet*: Charles Hobhouse Diaries, edited by Edward David, 73–76.
17. CV II: 2, 1138–1140; R and H, 714.
18. Sir Harold Scott, *Your Obedient Servant*, 28.
19. Pellew, 90.
20. CFG, 109; YS, 341; A.J.P. Taylor, *British Prime Ministers and Other Essays*, 119.
21. CV II:2, 1137–1138.

Chapter 2
1. CV II:2, 1069; Jacob F. Field, *The Eccentric Mr Churchill*, 59; HF, 112–113; Samuel Hynes, *The Edwardian Turn of Mind*, 129–131; Winston S. Churchill, *The Boer War*, 71.
2. *The Plays of John Galsworthy* (Duckworth), 260–261.
3. H.V. Marrot, *Life and Letters of John Galsworthy*, 257–258; Fenner Brockway, *Towards Tomorrow*, 54.
4. Gerold Clayton, *The Wall is Strong*, 24–27.
5. Wilfrid Scawen Blunt, *My Diaries* II, 271; CV II:2, 1144–1148.
6. Victor Bailey, 'English Prisons, Penal Culture and the Abatement of Imprisonment, 1895–1922', in *Journal of British Studies*, 36 (July 1977), 320.
7. *Vanity Fair*, 10 February 1910; Shane Leslie, *Sir Evelyn Ruggles-Brise*, passim; Pellew, 211.

8. Marrot, 261–262.
9. Victor Bailey, 'English Prisons, Penal Culture and the Abatement of Imprisonment, 1895 – 1922', in *Journal of British Studies 36* (July 1977), 318; Forsythe, *passim*.
10. *Daily News*, 22 July 1910.
11. Gordon Rose, *The Struggle for Penal Reform*, 11–12; Geoffrey Pearson, *Hooligan: A History of Respectable Fears*, 121–150.
12. Lionel W. Fox, *The English Prison and Borstal Systems*, 48–49; Bailey (*English Prisons*) 285–289; R and H, 573–583.
13. R and H, 594–595; Bailey (*English Prisons*), *passim*; Martin J. Wiener, *Reconstructing the Criminal: Culture, Law and Policy in England, 1830–1914*, *passim*; David Garland, *Punishment and Welfare: A History of Penal Strategies*, *passim*.

Chapter 3
1. 1909–1910 Report of Commissioner of Prisons (Cd 5360), 1910, Parliamentary Papers 1910, vol. 45, 290–291, cited by R and H.
2. Harold Butler, *Confident Morning*, 78.
3. R and H, 594–595; Ruggles-Brise, *The English Prison System*, 7–8.
4. CHAR 12/4/13.
5. W. Sydney Robinson, *Muckraker: The Scandalous Life and Times of W.T. Stead*, 246.
6. R and H, 595; CV II:2, 1150; Baxendale, 60.
7. *Humanitarian*, November 1910.
8. CV II: 2, 1141.
9. R and H, 744 – 745.
10. J.A. Thomas, *The House of Commons 1906–1911*, 39.
11. HF, 114–116; R and H, 652–653.
12. *The Times*, 27 July 1910.
13. Baxendale, 101–104; HO 144/18869.
14. HO 144/18869; Baxendale, 104–109.
15. CHAR 12/4/50–61 (9 February 1911).
16. Arthur Paterson, *Our Prisons*, 10–11, 46–50, 59.
17. Victor Bailey, *The Rise and Fall of the Rehabilitative Ideal*, 107.
18. H and B, 95; 369.
19. *Shields Daily News*, 29 September 1910; *Durham Advertiser*, 29 July 1910.
20. *Daily Express*, 12 April 1910.
21. Hansard, 16: 1077; Lucy Masterman, *History Today*, 1964, 827.
22. HO 144/1072/191394/32.
23. HO 144/1072/191394; R and H, 208–210.
24. *Daily News*, 13 April 1910.
25. HO 144/1072/191394/32.
26. Hansard, 16: 1419.
27. HO 144/1072/191394/32.
28. *Daily News*, 15 April 1910.
29. CV II: 2, 1293.
30. *Punch*, 4 May 1910.
31. HO 144/1018/157273; HO 144/18869.
32. HO 144/938/A59031; *Birmingham Gazette*, 27 January 1910.
33. Pellew, 61, 211.
34. HO 144/18869.
35. R and H, 275–277.
36. Hansard, 19: 1352 (20 July 1910); HO 144/1002/134165.
37. LMD, 12 October 1910, 8; HO 144/18869.
38. HO 144/1087/194478.

Notes 243

39. HO 144/1649/175716.
40. HO 144/1649/175716; R and H, 284.
41. HO 144/1009/143484.
42. Philip Priestley, *Victorian Prison Lives*, 239–240, 292; CV II:2, 1143–1144.
43. *CV*, II: 2, 1202.
44. Forsythe, 68.
45. HO 144/1087/194175; Christopher Hassall, *Edward Marsh*, 121.
46. HO 144/1045/184808.
47. *CV* II: 2, 1139; Scott, 61–62.

Chapter 4
1. Mallet, 222; Hansard, 14: 561 (28 February 1910).
2. HCS II, 1368 (4 December 1909); Anne Fernihough, *Freewomen and Supermen*, 8–10.
3. Troup (*Home Office*), 119–120; William Murphy, *Political Imprisonment and the Irish*, 12–13.
4. Constance Lytton, *Prisons and Prisoners – Some Personal Experiences*, 205–267.
5. HF, 130–131.
6. R.C.K. Ensor, *England 1870–1914*, 459; Paul Foot, *The Vote*, 210–212; Martin Pugh, *The Pankhursts*, 208–209; *CV*, II: 3, 1431–1434.
7. Alan S. Baxendale, *Winston Leonard Spencer-Churchill, Penal Reformer*, 42–45; HF, 131–132.
8. Hansard, 15: 177
9. CHAR 12/4/17.
10. Lytton, 267.
11. Lytton, 251–254; H and B, 206–207.
12. Kenneth D. Brown, *The Unknown Gladstone*, 121–122; *CV*, II:2, 1156–1157.
13. Peter Rowland, *The Last Liberal Governments: The Promised Land, 1905–1910*, 355–357.
14. Murrays of Elibank, 46.
15. Hansard, 15: 1457 (31 March 1910).
16. Ross M. Martin, *The Lancashire Giant*.
17. Scott, 25.
18. *Whitaker's Almanack* 1910, 186, 397.
19. LMD, 12 October 1910, 10; *HCS*, II, 1387 (6 December 1909).
20. F.M. Leventhal, *The Last Dissenter*, 73–77.
21. LMD, 12 October 1910, 10; Hynes, 57–73.
22. LMD, 12 October 1910.
23. LMD, 12 October 1910, 10.
24. John Campbell, *F.E. Smith*, 177.
25. Conciliation Bill debate: Hansard, 19: 41–150; 207–333.
26. LMD, 12 October 1910.
27. *Punch*, 20 July 1910.
28. CV II:3, 1447.
29. Hassall, 120; Edward Marsh, *A Number of People*, 171–173; David Freeman, 'Great Contemporaries – Eddie Marsh: A profile' in *Finest Hour* 131 (Summer 2006); Michael Bloch, *Closet Queens*, 82–83 and 93; Richard Davenport-Hines, *Ettie*, 115; Piers Brendon, *Winston Churchill*, 37; Peter Clarke, *Mr Churchill's Profession*, 73–74.
30. *Dundee Evening Telegraph*, 1 December 1910; Andrew Liddle, *Cheers, Mr Churchill! Winston in Scotland*, 82–84.
31. Martin, 90–107; Harry Taylor, *Victor Grayson*, 63.

Chapter 5
1. Blunt, 302–303; Jenkins (*Asquith*), 212; YS, 426–431; Jenkins (*Churchill*), 172–173.
2. Rowland, 301; Leslie, 152–153.

3. CV II: 2, 1183–1186; CHAR 12/4/26–35; H and B, 110–119.
4. CV II:2, 1186.
5. Baxendale, 75–83.
6. Hansard, 18: 1916W. Cecil's point on the missing comma is well demonstrated by Lynn Truss's *Eats Shoots and Leaves*.
7. A. G. Gardiner, *Prophets, Priests and Kings*, 232.
8. A.G. Gardiner, *Pillars of Society*, 153–158.
9. Prisons debate: Hansard, 19: 1326–1357.
10. J.E. Thomas, *The English Prison Officer Since 1850: A Study in Conflict*, 130–131; H and B, 222–224.
11. HO 144/18869
12. William Nester, *Winston Churchill and the Art of Leadership*, 30.
13. R and H, 774.
14. Ian Packer (Ed.), *The Letters of Arnold Stephenson Rowntree to Mary Katherine Rowntree*, 40–41.
15. H and B; CHAR 12/4/24; 12/4/36–7; 12/4/48.
16. *Daily Mail*, 11 August 1910; *Daily News*, 22 July 1910.
17. *Daily News*, 22 July 1910; CHAR 12/4/23.
18. *Humanitarian*, September 1910.
19. *The Times*, 23 July 1910; *Humanitarian*, September 1910.
20. *Blackwood's Magazine*, September 1910.
21. HO 144/18869.

Chapter 6
1. *Daily News*, 1 August 1910; Jenkins (*Churchill*) 186–188; *Western Daily Press*, 4 August 1910; *Dundee Courier*, 4 August 1910; *Londonderry Sentinel*, 20 September 1910.
2. *Illustrated Police News*, 23 July 1910; *Nation*, 23 July 1910.
3. Troup, 55–71; Fenton Bresler, *Reprieve*, 123.
4. Celia Lee, *Jean, Lady Hamilton*, 197.
5. HO 144/1058/188656; Bresler, 227.
6. HO 144/1058/188656; *Manchester Evening News*, 4, 22 February 1910; *Manchester Evening Chronicle*, 4 February 1910; *Daily Dispatch*, 5 February 1910.
7. CHAR 12/2.
8. CHAR 12/13; *News of the World*, 7 May 1939; Lucy Masterman, *History Today*, 1964, 823; Scott, 22.
9. *CV* II: 2, 1139.
10. Baxendale, 14–15; CV II:2, 1139–1140; Mallet, 206.
11. Jenkins (*Asquith*), 19.
12. Brian Bailey, *Hangmen of England*, 61.
13. HO 144/1086/194114.
14. P COM 8/196; *Guardian*, 24 February 2001.
15. Victor Bailey (*English Prisons*), 160; P COM 8/196
16. P COM 8/196; HO/144/1086/194114.
17. HO 45/24605.
18. HO 45/24605.
19. HO 144/1093/195751: Churchill to Grey, 1 August 1910.
20. HO 45/24605; *CV* II: 2, 1021.
21. HO 144/1093/195751 (Churchill to Grey, 1 August 1910); *Leeds Mercury*, 21 July 1910, *Yorkshire Post*, 22 July 1910.
22. *Scotsman*, 1 August 1910.
23. HO/45/24605.

24. *Staffordshire Advertiser*, 16 July 1910; HO 144/1090/195342; CHAR 12/13/2; H and B, 337–338.
25. Hansard, 19: 852.
26. HO 144/1092/195705; CHAR 12/13/2; *Liverpool Echo*, 20 July 1910; *Exeter and Plymouth Gazette*, 21 July 1910.
27. *Chester Courant*, 20 July 1910; HO 144/8554; CHAR 12/13/2; *The Times*, 29 July 1910; *Daily Telegraph*, 29 July 1910.
28. HO 45/24605 (3 September 1910).
29. Hansard, 453: 1438 (15 July 1948).
30. Butler, 79–80.
31. HO 144/4202; *The Trial of John Alexander Dickman* (transcript), Ed. S.O. Rowan-Hamilton; Diane Janes, *Edwardian Murder*, *CV* II:3 1191–1196.
32. Rowan-Hamilton, preface.
33. *News of the World*, 7 May 1939.
34. HO 144/4202; Janes, 20, 130–131.
35. *New Age*, 28 July 1910; letters of Orage to Churchill: HO 144/4202, 28, 29 July 1910.
36. *Daily News*, 1 and 5 August 1910; Blackwell letters to Grey: HO 144/4202, 3, 7 August 1910.
37. *Daily Mail*, 11 August 1910.
38. HO 144/4202.
39. Lucy Masterman, *History Today*, 1964, 823; *Newcastle Illustrated Chronicle*, 10 August 1910; Hobhouse/Brockway, 210–211; 249.
40. *Northern Whig*, 10 August 1910; YS, 416–417.
41. *The Manchester Guardian*, 29 November 1954; Lucy Masterman, *History Today*, 1964, 823.
42. LMD, 12 October 1910, 12.
43. Butler, 72–73; *News of the World*, 7 May 1939.
44. *Nottingham Evening News*, 25 October 1910.
45. HO 144/1718/195492; Filson Young (Editor), *The Trial of Hawley Harvey Crippen*, 190–211.
46. HO 144/1718/195492.
47. HO 144/1718/195492; Bresler, 129.
48. Blunt, 322.
49. Hobhouse/Brockway, 249; Oscar Wilde, *The Ballad of Reading Jail*, I
50. Blunt, 399 (20 October 1912); R and H, 676–681.
51. HO 144/937/A58585; Molly Whittington-Egan, *Murder on the Bluff*; Butler, 72–73.
52. Whittington-Egan, 10–11; HO 144/937/A58585.
53. Butler, 80–81; HO 144/937/A58585.
54. Whittington-Egan, 197–199.

Chapter 7
1. Forsythe, 33–39.
2. HO 144/18869.
3. HO 144/18869; Victor Bailey, 'Churchill as Home Secretary', *History Today*, 3 March 1985.
4. CV II: 2, 1196.
5. CV II: 2, 1197; Hansard, 25: 423 (3 May 1911).
6. HO 144/18869.
7. CV II: 2, 1196–1197; Baxendale, 129–132; H and B, 210–212.
8. CV II: 2, 1196–1197; Baxendale, 129–132.
9. HO 144/18869; Blunt, 321 (14 October 1910).
10. CV II: 2, 1198–1203.
11. Baxendale, 195, n. 52.

12. M. A. Crowther, *The Workhouse System*, 54–57; Peter Clarke, *Hope and Glory Britain 1900–2000*, 58–61.
13. Baxendell, 199, n.8.
14. Bodleian Library: CAB 37/103/53; Garland,135.
15. Gareth Stedman Jones, *Outcast London*, 334–335.
16. CV II:2, 1179 – 1182.
17. J.E. Thomas, 141–142; Winston S. Churchill, *My Early Life*, 14.
18. J. E. Thomas, 142–144; Hansard, 21: 1239.
19. Hansard, 21: 1239 (16 February 1911); 21: 1735 (21 February 1911); J. E. Thomas, 47–50.

Chapter 8
1. Bodleian Library: H.H. Asquith Papers 12: 222–228 (Churchill to Asquith, December 1910).
2. CV II, 1037; Martin Gilbert, 'Leading Churchill Myths: "Churchill's campaign against the 'feeble-minded' was deliberately omitted by his biographers"', in *Finest Hour* 152, Autumn 2011.
3. HO 144/1098/197900; Paul Addison, 'Churchill and the Sterilisation Issue', in *Finest Hour*, 131 (Summer 2006); Martin Gilbert, in *Finest Hour*,152.
4. Hansard, 17: 1166W; HO 144/1098/197900.
5. HCS II, 1588; Paul Addison in *Finest Hour*, 131; G. R. Searle, *Eugenics and Politics in Britain*, 108 (citing *Eugenics Review* 2, 1910–1911, 163-4).
6. Searle, passim.
7. HO 144/1088/194663.
8. HO 144/1098/197900.
9. HO 144/4202; Ruggles-Brise, 198–215.
10. CHAR 12/1/2.
11. CHAR 12/1/3.
12. CHAR 12/1/3; Martin Gilbert (*Finest Hour*, 152).
13. LMD, 12 October 1910, 14.
14. CHAR 12/9/2.
15. Hansard, 22:177W; 24:1350; 26:39; 26:1073.
16. Simon Heffer, *The Age of Decadence*, 427; Blunt, 399–340.
17. Searle, 106 – 111.
18. R and H, 333 n.
19. Lucy Masterman, *History Today*, 1964, 823–824.

Chapter 9
1. Ensor, 437–440; Peter De Mendelssohn, *The Age of Churchill*, 495.
2. YS, 367–373
3. British Library, Fitzroy Papers: Add MS 48,376: 54.
4. Troup (*The Home Office*), 53.
5. R. Page Arnot, *South Wales Miners*, 1898–1914, 174–222; Kenneth Morgan, *Rebirth of a Nation*, 145–148; HF, 141–145.
6. Hansard: 959: 693 (30 November 1978); Morgan (*Rebirth*), p. 147.
7. CV II:2, 1207, Heffer, 671.
8. HF, 141–144; Churchill to King George V: draft quoted in YS, 373–375.
9. CV II:2, 1207–1210; YS, 375–378; *Daily Express*, 9 November 1910; *The Times*, 9 November 1910; *The Manchester Guardian*, 10 November 1910.
10. Heffer, 671–676; Morgan, *Rebirth*, 147.
11. *News of the World*, 7 May 1939.
12. CHAR 12/4/58; Morgan (*Rebirth*), 146–149; HF, 141–144.

13. Lord Askwith, *Industrial Problems and Disputes*, 146–147.
14. Heffer, 675.

Chapter 10
1. *Daily Telegraph*, 25 October 1910: HF, 135; Clive Ponting, *Churchill*, 110–111.
2. HO 144/1102/199183.
3. *Daily Telegraph*, 25 October 1910; *Daily News*, 25 October 1910; HO 144/1102/199183.
4. Andrew Rosen, *Rise Up, Women!* 138–140.
5. CV II: 3, 1457; Rosen, 138–140; Pugh (*Pankhursts*), 218–219; HF, 137.
6. Emmeline Pankhurst, *My Own Story*, Book 3, Ch. 2; Rosen, 140–141.
7. Hansard, 22: 1834W.
8. E Sylvia Pankhurst, *The Suffragette Movement*, 463.
9. CHAR 12/3/62–64; Hansard, 22:1034 (7 March 1911); CV II: 3, 1457–1464; YS, 400; Rosen, 143–144.
10. *CV* II: 3, 1467; Roy Jenkins, *The Chancellors*, 365; Lord Riddell, *More Pages from My Diary*, 37.
11. Trevor Wilson, *The Political Diaries of C.P. Scott*, 35–37 (2 February 1911); *CV* II: 3, 1468.
12. Hansard, 22; 1834W; *CV* II: 3, 1464–1465.
13. *The Times*, 2, 3 March 1910; CV II:3, 1468–1470; Rosen, 134–144.

Chapter 11
1. *Daily News*, 21 September 1910; Brendon, 55.
2. LBM: 'Reminiscences of the 1909 Budget' [composed during 1910], 20–21.
3. *Londonderry Sentinel*, 20 September 1910; *The Times*, 17 September 1910.
4. Warren Dockter, *Churchill and the Islamic World*, 49–51, 189ff; Blunt, 322; *Sevenoaks Chronicle*, 9 September 1910.
5. *Punch*, 2 November 1910.
6. LMD, Reminiscences of the 1909 Budget, 14.
7. Lucy Masterman, LP 8/2, 36; Jenkins (*Asquith*) 214–215; YS, 340–341; *War Memoirs of David Lloyd George*, Vol. 1, 20–24; Jenkins (*Churchill*), 189–191.
8. British Library: Lord Riddell Diaries, Add MSS 62956, 145; Robert Farquharson and J.S. Sargent, *The House of Commons From Within*, 207; Robert Lloyd George, *David & Winston*, facing p. 80.
9. CV II: 2, 1024–1025.
10. LMD, 12 October 1910, 5.
11. Beatrice Webb, *Our Partnership*, 466–467; Rose, 70; CFG, 129; Ted Morgan, *Churchill: Young Man in a Hurry*, 274; Toye, 71.
12. LMD, 12 October 1910, 6.
13. Taylor, 119.
14. Lucy Masterman Papers, at Lucy Cavendish College, Cambridge, LP 8/2, 18–20.
15. Lucy Masterman Papers, LP 8/2, 18–20.
16. LMD, 12 October 1910, 6.
17. LMD, Reminiscences of the 1909 Budget, 22.
18. Shulbrede Archives: Arthur Ponsonby Diary, 13 May 1911; Paul Addison, 'Churchill and the Working Class', 45, in Jay Winter (ed.), *The Working Class in Modern British History*.
19. Lucy Masterman Papers, LP 8/2, 37.
20. Lucy Masterman Papers LP 8/2, 27.
21. LMD, 8 December 1910, 8.
22. LMD, 8 December 1910, 9.
23. *The Manchester Guardian*, 29 November 1954.
24. Toye, 71.
25. LMD, 8 December 1910, 10.

26. *Punch*, 16 November 1910.
27. Coal Strike debate: Hansard, 20: 406–434.
28. *Votes for Women*, 23 September 1910.
29. *The Times*, 20 January 1910.
30. Douglas J. Hall, 'Churchill's Elections', in *Finest Hour*, 103; HCS II, 1651–1657.
31. YS, 244; Liddle, 191.
32. HCS, 1657–1659.
33. CV, II: 2, 1029.
34. LMD, Reminiscences of the 1909 Budget, 20; Lucy Masterman, *History Today*, 1964, 820.
35. HCS, 1660.

Chapter 12
1. Scott, 22.
2. Scott, 24.
3. CHAR 12; Michael Shelden, *Young Titan*, 206; Stefan Buczacki, *Churchill & Chartwell*, 45; Lough, 92–95.
4. Census of England and Wales, 1911; Winston S. Churchill, *Thoughts and Adventures*, 43–44.
5. Donald Rumbelow, *The Houndsditch Murders*, 15–31 and 105–123; Colin Rogers, *The Battle of Stepney*, 101–108; Churchill (*Thoughts*), 41–48.
6. HO 144/19780.
7. *Reynold's Newspaper*, 8 January 1911; Rogers, 98; Churchill (*Thoughts*), 45- 46; *Evening News*, 3 January 1911; Butler, 79.
8. Sir Melville MacNaghten, *Days of My Years*, 260; HO 144/19780; Rumbelow, 118–119. *Daily Chronicle*, 4 January 1911.
9. Blunt, 296.
10. *Illustrated London News*, 7 January 1911; Rogers, facing p. 96.
11. *Daily Chronicle*, 4 January 1911; Rogers, 98–99.
12. Sir William Nott-Bower, *Fifty-two Years A Policeman*, facing p. 234; Churchill (*Thoughts*), 44.
13. Fitzroy Papers, Add MS 48,376: 156; Rogers, 106–112; Churchill (*Thoughts*), 46.
14. Mary Soames, *Clementine Churchill*, 83–84.
15. CV II: 2, 1032–1033.
16. CHAR, 12/11/3.
17. CV II: 2, 1033.
18. Churchill (*Thoughts*), 46–47; Churchill (*My Early Life*), 198–200; Shelden, 240.
19. *Daily Chronicle*, 4 January 1911.
20. The Siege of Sidney Street Gunfight, British Pathé (consulted 20 October 2020); Huntley Archives, Film 160 (consulted 20 October 2020).
21. Hassall, 171.
22. Hassall, 171.
23. *Daily Chronicle*, 4 January 1911.
24. Rogers, 113; CHAR 12/11/3.
25. Churchill (*Thoughts*), 47–48.
26. Churchill (*Thoughts*), 45.
27. LMD, 12 October 1910, 9.
28. Rogers, 129–137.
29. *Reynold's Newspaper*, 8 Jan 1911.
30. Geoffrey Wheatcroft, *Churchill's Shadow*, 151.
31. *The Times*, 12 January 1911.
32. Rogers, 134.
33. *Daily News*, 19 January 1911; *Reynold's Newspaper*, 8 January 1911.
34. YS, 408.

35. Rowland, 48; Hansard, 21: 44, 52; *CV*, II: 2, 1114.
36. Hansard, 21: 55.
37. Churchill (*Thoughts*), 48; Hansard, 22: 66.
38. Rogers, 130; Hansard, 21: 696; 21: 843W; 24: 1043; 1971; *Daily Chronicle*, 4 January 1911; Gary Mason, *The Official History of the Metropolitan Police*, 16–17.
39. Gardiner (*Pillars*), 153.
40. Roberts, 47; Riddell Diaries, Add 62955, 18–19 (November 1911, no date, 1910) and 62956, 39 (November 1911, no date).
41. *Daily News*, 21 January 1911.

Chapter 13
1. HO 144/1720/200372; HO 144/4206.
2. HO 144/1720/200372; Dictionary of National Biography; Leslie, 168.
3. HO 144/106/200426.
4. CHAR 12/13/3; *Islington Gazette*, 21 November 1910.
5. HO 144/1114/202916.
6. HO 144/1114/202916; *Morning Advertiser*, 14 January 1911; H and B, 208–210.
7. HO 144/1114/202916; HO 144/18869.
8. *Reynold's Newspaper*, 8 January 1911.
9. Butler, 78; Hansard, 23: 39; 29:928W; Eric Linklater, *The Corpse on Clapham Common*, 172–178.
10. Hansard, 29: 2103.
11. H. Fletcher Moulton (editor), *The Trial of Steinie Morrison*.
12. Butler, 78.
13. Hansard, 24: 621.
14. Derek Walker-Smith, *The Life of Lord Darling* 148.
15. Walker-Smith, 149.
16. HO 45/22268; Bailey (*Rise and Fall*), photograph f. 248.
17. *Humanitarian*, May 1911.
18. *News of the World*, 7 May 1939.
19. CHAR 12/7; https://www.lancashirepolfed.org.uk/about/history.htm, consulted 14 October, 2020; Hansard, 448: 1552 (11 March 1948); *Shoreditch Observer*, 8 July 1911.
20. *The Times*, 19 June 1911; Linklater, 173–178.
21. CV II: 2, 1095, 1097.

Chapter 14
1. Linklater, 189.
2. Bernard Porter, 'The British Government and Political Refugees, c. 1880–1914' in *From the Other Shore*, ed. John Slater, 23–29; John A. Garrard, *The English and Immigration*, 41–42; CV II: 1, 354–356.
3. Martin Gilbert, *Churchill & The Jews*, 9–15, 18–19; Michael J. Cohen, *Churchill and the Jews*, 22–23, 35–39; Garrard, 43; Bernard Gainer, *The Alien Invasion*, 189–190.
4. CV, II:2, 1230.
5. HO 144/19780; CHAR 12/14/5; Philip Ruff, *A Towering Flame*; Gainer, 205; Rumbelow, 15–31; Rogers, 23–37; Porter, 24–26.
6. CV II: 1, 385 – 386; Winston Churchill *(My Early Life)*, 162–163.
7. Hansard, 19: 1311.
8. Hansard, 19: 1320; Cohen, 23–24; 39; Garrard, 132–133.
9. Hassall, 170–171; CV II: 2, 1033.
10. CV II:2, p. 1239.
11. CAB 37/105, 1911: 2; CHAR 12/14/5 and 12/14/6.
12. Gainer, 205; Cohen, 40–41; Rogers, 124–126.

250 Churchill, the Liberal Reformer

13. Porter, 26; CHAR 12/14/1–2; 28/117/59; 28/117/60; 12/14/6; CV II:2, 1140.
14. Hansard, 18: 686; 24: 623; Lucy Masterman, *History Today*, 1964, 823; Hansard, 24: 623.
15. HO 45/10641/206332.
16. Hansard, 24: 2106.
17. Hansard, 24: 2124.
18. Hansard, 24: 2133.
19. Hansard, 24: 2144.
20. Hansard, 24: 2170.
21. Hansard, 24: 2185.
22. Hansard, 24: 2139.
23. Hansard, 25: 6.
24. CHAR 12/14/11,12.

Chapter 15
1. *The Times*, 25 March 1910; *Dundee Evening Telegraph*, 25 March 1910; *Nottingham Journal*, 26 March 1910; Forsythe, 63.
2. HO 144/18869 (prison capacity census, 1910); Geoffrey Howse, *A History of London's Prisons*, 107–108; R and H, 490–492.
3. *Dundee Courier*, 4 October 1910; Hansard, 21: 1851.
4. LMD, 12 October 1910, 12–13.
5. Hansard, 21: 1851–1859.
6. A.G. Gardiner, *The War Lords*, 65.
7. Butler, 79; *The Times*, 24, 25 October 1910.
8. Robert Graves, *Goodbye to All That*, 168.
9. *The Scotsman*, 26 November 1910.
10. *Daily News*, 24 November 1910.
11. *The Times*, 7 January 1911.
12. *The Times*, 11, 12 January 1911.
13. *The Times*, 16 January 1911.
14. *The Times*, 19 January 1911; Forsythe, 21–23.
15. *The Times*, 21 January 1911; R and H, 698.
16. *The Times*, 27, 30 January 1911.
17. *Daily News*, 2 February 1911; HO 144/18869; Hansard, 21: 291; 22: 366; 25: 206; *Scotsman*, 9 February 1911; *The Times*, 8 February 1911.
18. Garland, 212–213; Victor Bailey, 'Churchill as Home Secretary', *History Today*, 3 March 1985; Ruggles-Brise, 156–157.
19. Hansard, 21: 55.
20. Hansard, 21: 1535.
21. *The Times*, 5, 14 April 1911.
22. Hansard, 24: 877.
23. A Scriven, *The Dartmoor Shepherd*, 76; Toye, 70.
24. *Annual Register*, 1911, 5; *Northern Whig*, 4 April 1929; William Wallace Blake, *Quod*, 132.

Chapter 16
1. Hansard, 23: 40.
2. *Birmingham Gazette and Express*, 15 March 1911.
3. HO 45/10428/A52980.
4. *Birmingham Gazette and Express*, 15 March 1911.
5. Hansard, 19: 1314 (20 June 1910).
6. *Dundee Courier*, 18 October 1910.
7. Hassall, 130–131; *Northern Daily Telegraph*, 19 October 1910; *Hull Daily Mail*, 19 October 1910; HO 144/18869.

8. Purnell, 52.
9. HO 144/1148/210238.
10. Hansard, 15: 734W.
11. HO 144/1148/210238.
12. HO 144/1148/210238.
13. *Observer*, 25 July 1914.

Chapter 17
1. *The Times*, 31 January 1911.
2. SFT, 41 (19 December 1910); Lough, 95–96.
3. Winston S. Churchill, *The People's Rights*, 126–130; Stephen Ridgwell, "'The Mangold's Champion", in *Journal of Liberal History*, 105, 2019–2020; Shulbrede Archives: Arthur Ponsonby Diary, 27 February 1911.
4. LMD, 8 December 1910, 10; Soames, 113.
5. Ridgwell, 22.
6. *Northampton Daily Echo*, 5 April 1911.
7. HO 144/1134/207057; *Morning Leader*, 10 April 1911
8. Hansard, 24: 1583; *Northampton Daily Echo*, 26 April 1911.
9. HO 144/1134/207057.
10. Baxendale, 155–156.
11. Hansard, 25: 422.
12. HO 144/1134/207057.
13. HO 144/18869.
14. Hansard, 25: 609.
15. Clarke (*Hope and Glory*), 58–61; Hansard, 26: 508; Liddle, 88.

Chapter 18
1. Hansard, 22: 2581W (16 March 1911); Riddell diary, 24 (November 1911); YS, 231–232; Richard Toye, *Churchill's Empire*, 108 ff.
2. Hansard, 29: 571 (3 August 1911).
3. *Leeds Mercury*, 28 October 1911.
4. R and H, 689–719.
5. Hansard 14: 340 (24 February 1910).
6. Hansard, 16: 2063W; Churchill (*My Early Life*), 19–20; Alex Renton, *Stiff Upper Lip*, 28–29.
7. Hansard, 20: 293.
8. *CV* II: 2, 1195–1196.
9. Hansard, 29: 2103.
10. R and H, 699.
11. *Humanitarian*, March 1911.
12. *Humanitarian*, August 1911.
13. Hansard, 21: 2159–2202; *CV* II:2, 1051; *The Manchester Guardian*, 29 November 1954.
14. Hansard, 21: 2197.
15. Hassall, 169.
16. CFG, 190–191.

Chapter 19
1. Hansard, 22: 1422–1708; *Daily Mirror*, 11 March 1911. *Daily News*, 11 March 1911; Shelden, 243–244.
2. Churchill quoted in Christopher Silvester, *Pimlico Companion to Parliament*, 426–427.
3. Hansard, 22: 1611.
4. *Daily Mirror*, 11 March 1911; Hansard, 22; 1614.

5. *CV* II:2, 1057.
6. *Daily Mirror*, 11 March 1911.
7. Shelden, 244.
8. Home Office debate: Hansard, 27: 238–305; Jeanne MacKenzie, *The Children of the Souls*, 69.
9. Hansard, 23: 2384W; 26: 1082.
10. Hansard, 27: 245.
11. Hansard, 27: 250.
12. *Liverpool Daily Post*, 13 May 1911.
13. Blunt, 399 (20 October 1912).
14. Hansard, 27: 252.
15. David J. Dutton (Ed.), *Odyssey of an Edwardian Liberal: The Political Diary of Richard Durning Holt*, 22 (5 June 1911).
16. *CV* II:2, 1090–1091.
17. SFT, 46–47.
18. CV II:2, 1094.
19. HO 144/1144/209195; *Gloucester Journal*, 3 May 1911; *Gloucester Citizen*, 10 May 1911; *Reading Mercury*, 13 May 1911.
20. HO 144/18869; HO 144/1144/209195.
21. HO 144/1144/209195.
22. *The Times*, 10 July 1911.
23. *Daily Express*, 11 July 1911.
24. Hansard, 28: 1024; *The Times*, 21 July 1911.
25. *Justices of the Peace*, 19 August 1911.
26. HO 144/1144/209195.
27. *Gloucester Journal*, 13 February 1926.
28. *London Evening Standard*, 22 April 1925, quoted in Baxendale, 39 and CFG, 135.
29. *The Manchester Guardian*, 29 November 1954.
30. Butler, 79; Anthony Sampson, *Anatomy of Britain Today*, 267–268; Bresler, 65–67, 115.

Chapter 20
1. Tony Judge, *Margaret Bondfield*, 63; Michael Winstanley, *The Shopkeeper's World, 1880–1914*, 70, 96; H and B, 110.
2. Hansard, 23: 1685–1761; Winstanley, 72; Jenkins (*Churchill*), 178.
3. Charles Masterman, *The Condition of England*, 129.
4. Hansard, 23: 1699; Alan Hyman, *The Rise and Fall of Horatio Bottomley*.
5. Stephen Reynolds, *Seems So*, 298–335.
6. Bodleian Library: H.H. Asquith Papers 12: 222–228: Churchill to Asquith, December 1910.
7. Hansard, 23: 1753.
8. Hansard, 23: 1761.
9. *Whitaker's Almanack* 1913, 179.
10. Hansard, 32: 1784.
11. Hansard, 32: 1788.
12. Hansard, 32: 1776.
13. YS, 425; Jenkins (*Churchill*), 178; Hassall, 175–176.
14. Eric Hopkins, *Charles Masterman*, 118–119; John Grigg, *Lloyd George: The People's Champion, 1902 – 1911*, 190–217.
15. Arnot, 343–344; *CV* II: 2, 1296.
16. CV II:2, 1140, 1197; Arnot, 339; Pellew, 90; Hansard, 17: 1512.
17. Hansard, 27: 292.
18. *The Times*, 17 February 1911; Sir Richard A.S. Redmayne, *Men, Mines and Memories*, 143.
19. *Punch*, 28 September 1910.

20. *The Times*, 17 February 1911.
21. Martin, 92–93.
22. Martin, 130–133.

Chapter 21
1. Hansard, 19: 19.
2. CV, II:2, 1128; HCS II, 1557.
3. Richard M. Langworth (https://richardlangworth.Com/Boxing-1911), 16 June 1911.
4. Dockter, 42–43.
5. CV II: 2, 1138; Hansard, 17: 1185; HCS, 1447.
6. Hansard, 28: 666.
7. *Westminster Gazette*, 30 June 1911; *Christchurch Times*, 3 July 1911; *Music Hall and Theatre Review*, 3 July 1911.
8. Edith Hall, 'Medea and British legislation before the First World War', *Greece and Rome*, Vol. 46, 1 (April 1999); Heffer, 136; Blunt, 296–298.
9. *Croydon Chronicle*, 25 July 1908; *The Vote*, 26 February 1910.
10. HO 45/10573/176819; Hansard, House of Lords, 194: 1143 (21 October 1908); 196: 484 (12 November 1908); *Daily News*, 12, 14 September 1908, 13 November 1908; HO 144/1026/167981.
11. HO 45/10573/176819; Troup, 65; R and H, 670–671.
12. HO 144/3148; CHAR 12/13/3; *Croydon Chronicle*, 22 October 1910; *Common Cause*, 17 November 1910; *The Times*, 2 December 1910; *West Sussex Gazette*, 8 December 1910.
13. HO 144/7056; Blunt, 321–322.
14. SFT, 50 and 53 (Winston to Clementine, 29 June 1911; 11 July 1911); LMD, Reminiscences of the 1909 Budget, 21; HO 144/7056; CHAR 12/13/4; *Salisbury and Winchester Journal*, 3 June 1911; *Western Daily Press*, 9 June 1911; *Wiltshire Times*, 24 June 1911; Hansard, 22: 2581W.
15. *Western Gazette*, 7 July 1911; *Votes for Women*, 18 August 1911; Pankhurst (*The Suffragette Movement*) 223; *Humanitarian*, August 1911.
16. HO 144/1150/210777.
17. YS, 294; Roberts, 153; *Votes for Women*, 18 August 1911.
18. Riddell Diaries: Add MSS 62956, 53–54.
19. HO 144/1150/210777.
20. *Croydon Guardian*, 29 July 1911.
21. *Cambria Daily Leader*, 27 July 1911; CHAR 12/13/5; HO 144/1155/212030.
22. *Daily News*, 1 August 1911; HO 144/1155/212030.
23. *Votes for Women*, 18 August 1911; *Gloucester Examiner*, 2 November 1911; *Gloucester Journal*, 4 November 1911.

Chapter 22
1. Butler, 79.
2. Churchill (*My Early Life*), 162–163; *The Times*, 21 February 1910; Jane Ridley, *George V*, 146–147.
3. Hassall, 156.
4. Shelden, 225.
5. *CV* II:2, 1257–1260; *Western Daily Press*, 17 May 1911; *Sheffield Daily Telegraph*, 17 May 1911; Clifton Society, 18 May 1911; LMD, 11 September 1911, 1.
6. *Coventry Evening Telegraph*, 23 June 1911.
7. Roberts, 153; YS, 355 – 356; *CV* II:2, 1093; *Daily News*, 23 June 1911; Buczacki, 46; SFT, 48–49.
8. Shelden, 226; YS, 418–423; Ridley, 167–168.
9. SFT, 50.

10. SFT, 49.
11. Riddell, 19.
12. SFT, 53.
13. SFT, 53–55.
14. *Belfast News Letter*, 14 July 1911.
15. *News of the World*, 7 May 1939.
16. SFT, 54.

Chapter 23
1. Churchill (*My Early Life*), 376; Colin Coote, *The Other Club*, 10, 21.
2. Coote, 21; Roberts, 150–153; Alfred F. Havighurst, *Radical Journalist: H.W. Massingham*, 186.
3. Shulbrede Archives: Ponsonby Diary, 8 May 1911.
4. Shelden, 242.
5. Lucy Masterman, 'Winston Churchill The Liberal Phase', Part Two, *History Today*, 1964, 827.
6. Hansard, 28: 1467–1484; Rowland, 49–52; *Punch*, 'Essence of Parliament', 2 August 1911; Lady Violet Bonham Carter, *Lantern Slides: The Diaries and Letters of Violet Bonham-Carter*, 274; Shelden, 248–250.
7. *CV* II:2, 1101 – 1102.
8. Bonham Carter (*Lantern Slides*), 274; David Faber, *Speaking for England*, 18–19; Churchill (*My Early Life*), 25–26; *Punch*, 2 August 1911.
9. Hansard, 24: 1231.
10. CV II: 2, 1067.
11. Hansard, 24: 1228.
12. CV II: 2, 1069.
13. Riddell Diaries: Add MSS 62956, 33.
14. Martin Gibson, *A Primrose Path*, 94, 115, 150 and *passim*; Churchill (*My Early Life*), 206–207.
15. Hansard, 24: 420W; *CV* II: 2, 1093.
16. *The Times*, 11 March 1911.

Chapter 24
1. HO 144/1829; CHAR 12/13.
2. *Humanitarian*, April 1910; R and H, 661–665; Victor Bailey (*Rise and Fall*), 342–376.
3. SFT, 46.
4. *Northampton Mercury*, 9 June 1911; J.E. Thomas, 172.
5. YS, 390.
6. HO 45/16483/192637.
7. HO 45/16483/192637.
8. Andrew Thompson, *The British Empire Strikes Back?*, 113–114.
9. Baxendale, 89; HO 45/16483/192637.
10. H and B, 172.
11. Duckworth Galsworthy plays, 261.
12. Baxendale, 90–93.
13. Janet Fyfe, *Books Behind Bars*, 41.
14. Baxendale, 94–99, Fyfe, xii.
15. HO 144/1067/189934.
16. Baxendale, 67.
17. Baxendale, 67–70.
18. Prison Commission Report, 1910–1911 (quoted in H and B, 332).
19. Wilfred Macartney, *Walls Have Mouths*, 261–262; Ruggles-Brise, 41.
20. *The Manchester Guardian*, 29 November 1954.

21. CHAR 12/4/49; R and H, 283.
22. CHAR 12/4/50–61.
23. Baxendale, 145–146.
24. Baxendale, 153.

Chapter 25
1. Hansard, Fourth Series, 93:1572 (13 May 1901); David Owen, *The Hidden Perspective*, 2.
2. *HSC*: II, 1085.
3. De Mendelssohn, 405; CV II:2, 23.
4. LMD, 11 September 1911, 1; A.J. A. Morris, *The Scaremongers*, 288.
5. Winston S. Churchill, *The World Crisis 1911–1918*, 28–34; A.J.P. Taylor, *The Mastery of Europe, 1848–1918*, 466–471. A.J. Anthony Morris, *Radicalism Against War 1906–1914*, 236–241; Trevor Wilson (Scott Diaries), 44–45.
6. John W. Coogan and Peter F. Coogan, 'The British Cabinet and the Anglo-French Staff Talks, 1905–1914: Who Knew What and When Did He Know It', *Journal of British Studies*, 24: 1 (Jan 1985), 120–124.
7. Grigg, 309.
8. Lloyd George, *War Memoirs*, Vol. I, 26–27; Churchill (*World Crisis*), 32.
9. Coogan and Coogan, 122; Keith Wilson, 'The Agadir Crisis, the Mansion House Speech, and the Double-Edgedness of Agreements', *Historical Journal*,15:3, September 1972; Martin Farr, *Reginald McKenna*, 210; Rowland, 110–116.
10. CV II:2, 1109 (WSC to Clementine, 6 August 1911); LMD, 11 September 1911, 1.
11. Churchill (*World Crisis*), 34–35.
12. Churchill (*World Crisis*), 32.
13. Trevor Wilson (Scott Diaries), 46–52; Churchill (*World Crisis*), 32–34; A.J. A. Morris (*Scaremongers*), 288; Taylor (*Struggle for Mastery*), 467–473.
14. Churchill (*World Crisis*), 31–36.
15. Bernard Porter, *The Origins of the Vigilant State*, 168–169; A.J.A. Morris, *The Scaremongers*, 288.
16. CAB 37/106, 1911: 50; CHAR 12/1/8; *The Times*, 19 August 1911; Hansard, 29: 2254.

Chapter 26
1. Hassall, 168 – 169; Peter Stansky, *On or About December 1910: Early Bloomsbury and its Intimate World*, 1–3.
2. Ensor, 440–441.
3. HO 45/10649/210615; *The Times*, 19, 20, 21 July 1911.
4. Hansard, 26:1024, cited by Chris Wrigley, 'Churchill and the Trade Unions', in *Winston Churchill in the Twenty-First Century*, ed. David Cannadine and Ronald Quinault, 55.
5. Hansard, 26: 1014.
6. HO 45/10649/210615; Hansard, 27: 296.
7. HO 144/1157/212342.
8. CVII:2, 1263–1264; Jane Morgan, *Conflict and Order*, 49–50.
9. HO 45/10649/210615.
10. HO 45/10649/210615.
11. John Douglas Pratten, The Reaction to Working Class Unrest, 1911–1914, 124, Sheffield University PhD. thesis (1975), citing Haldane Papers; Jenkins (*Asquith*), 234.
12. *Daily News*, 12 August 1911; *Sheffield Daily Telegraph*, 12 August 1911.
13. LMD, 11 September 1911, 5–6; British Library, John Burns MSS: 46333, Vol. LIII (15–22 August 1911); William Kent, *John Burns*, 220–221; Ben Tillett, *History of the London Transport Strike*, in *Social Tracts* 1902–1912, 37; Ensor, 516–518; Clarke (*Hope and Glory*), 59.
14. LMD, 11 September 1911, 4.

15. Tillett, 34.
16. Tillett, 35.
17. Ben Tillett, *Memories and Reflections*, 242–243.
18. Gardiner (*War Lords*).
19. LMD, 11 September 1911, 8.

Chapter 27
1. C.V. II: 2, 1268–1269; *Annual Register*, 1911, 204–207.
2. HO 45/10649/210615.
3. Shelden, 252, citing Harcourt Papers: Lewis Harcourt to Mary (Molly) Harcourt, 16, 17 August 1911; *Liverpool Evening Express*, 18 August 1911.
4. C.V. II: 2, 1270–1271; *Daily News*, 21 August 1911; Pratten, 125–128; Hansard, 29: 1756; *Daily Graphic*, 10 August 1911.
5. Lucy Masterman, *History Today*, 1964, 825; LMD, 11 September 1911, 7; George W. Alcock, *Fifty Years of Railway Trade Unionism*, 429.
6. Fitzroy Papers: Add MS 48,376: 242; CV II:2, 1271 – 1272.
7. C.V. II:2, 1274.
8. *Daily News*, 16, 17 August 1911; Gregory Blaxland, *J.H. Thomas*, 68; A.J.A. Morris (editor), *Edwardian Radicalism*, 143.
9. 'Locomotion', BBC Productions 2013, consulted September 2020; *Daily Mirror*, 21 August 1911; LMD, 11 September 1911, 11.
10. John Ramsden, ed., *Real Old Tory Politics: The Political Diaries of Sir Robert Sanders, Lord Bayford*, 33; Kent, 220–221; YS, 382–383; Brendon, 58–59.
11. Hansard, 29: 199; *Daily News*, 16, 17 August 1911.
12. *Daily News*, 21 August 1911; Sir Almeric Fitzroy, *Memoirs*, Vol. II, 462; Ramsay MacDonald, *National Defence: A Study in Militarism*, 103–104.
13. Jane Morgan, 54; *Daily News*, 21 August 1911.
14. LMD, 11 September 1911, 5.
15. *The Times*, 19 August 1911.
16. CV II:2, 1279; Sanders, 33.
17. *Labour Leader*, 18 August 1911.
18. *Daily News*, 23 August 1911; Morris (*Scaremongers*), 292.
19. LMD, 11 September 1911, 3; CV II:2, 1281–1282.
20. CV II:2, 1281.
21. Jane Morgan, 52,170; *Daily News*, 21 August 1911.
22. *The Times*, 19 August 1911.
23. *The Times*, 19 August 1911; *Daily News*, 21 August 1911; Jane Morgan, 171.
24. *Daily News*, 21 August 1911.
25. CV, II:2, 1283–1285.
26. CV II:2, 1286–1287.
27. LMD, 11 September 1911, 9.
28. LMD, 11 September 1911, 10.
29. LMD, 11 September 1911, 8.
30. *Daily News*, 12 August 1911.
31. LMD, 11 September 1911, 10.
32. LMD, 11 September 1911, 5.
33. LMD, 11 September 1911, 11; Brendon, 59.
34. *Daily News*, 21 August 1911.
35. Grigg, 305; SFT, 55–56 (WSC letter, 24 September 1911).
36. LMD, 11 September 1911, 11.

Chapter 28
1. Wrigley, in Cannadine and Quinault, 58.
2. John Edwards, *Remembrance of a Riot*, *South Wales Gazette*, 25 August 1911; *National Register*, 1911, 210; Hansard, 29: 2282–2378; *The Times*, 23 August 1911.
3. Hansard, 29: 2282–2378; *The Times* 23 August 1911; LMD, 11 September 1911, 8; Jane Morgan, 54.
4. Hansard, 29: 2332.
5. Jane Morgan, 52; Roberts, 13.
6. Hansard, 29: 2329.
7. *Daily News*, 23 August 1911.
8. Norman Rose, *Churchill: An Unruly Life*, 79.
9. Hansard, 29: 2369.
10. HSC: II, 1881.
11. John McEwen, ed., *The Riddell Diaries*, 25.
12. HO 144/1160/212987; *The Times*, 21 August 1911.
13. *The Times*, 23 August 1911.
14. *Merthyr Express*, 9 September 1911.
15. Hansard, 29: 2329.

Chapter 29
1. Christopher Andrew, *The Defence of the Realm: The Authorized History of MI5*, 1–37; CHAR 13/1/25; Porter, 168; Churchill (*World Crisis*), 36.
2. Morris (*Scaremongers*), 290–292; Morris (*Radicalism*), 241–243; Keith Wilson, *The Policy of the Entente*, 27–28.
3. T.G. Otte, *The Foreign Office Mind*, 351; SFT, 30 (Winston to Clementine, 15 September 1909).
4. Farr, 152–154; Especially valuable on the Anglo-French 'Military Conversations' is *The Hidden Perspective* by David Owen (Foreign Secretary, 1977–1979).
5. Morris (*Scaremongers*), 295; Viscount Grey of Fallodon, *Twenty-five Years*: Vol. I, 238; YS, 357.
6. Churchill (*World Crisis* I, 47); Owen, 212–213; CV II: 2, 1116–1117.
7. CV II: 2, 1118–1126.
8. Churchill (*World Crisis* I), 37–38; Michael Howard, *The First World War*, 25–29, 35–37.
9. Hassall, 172–174; Shelden, 245, 258; *Daily Mirror*, 5 September 1911.
10. Churchill (*World Crisis* I), 42–46; YS, 526–528.
11. Imperial War Museum Archives: Diaries of Henry Hughes Wilson, 1911 (Volume 15), August.
12. Wilson Diary, 22 August 1911.
13. Farr, 211–212: T.G. Otte, *Statesman of Europe: A Life of Sir Edward Grey*, 418–420.
14. Churchill (*World Crisis* I), 38–42; C.E. Callwell, *Field-Marshal Sir Henry Wilson*, Vol I, 99–103; Allan Mallinson, *Too Important for the Generals*, 24–29; Nicholas Lambert, *Planning Armageddon*, 152–154; Coogan and Coogan, 120–124; Farr, 211–222.
15. Wilson Diary, 28 August 1911.
16. Wilson Diary, 31 August 1911.
17. Churchill (*World Crisis* I), 38–42; Richard Burdon Haldane, *An Autobiography*, 225–228; Farr, 211–213.
17. Jenkins (*Asquith*), 240–242, 360–362; Andrew Roberts, *Churchill: Walking with Destiny*, 155; Haldane, 226–230; Otte (*Statesman*), 418–420; John Campbell, *Haldane*, 274–275.
18. Stephen Wynn, *Churchill's Flawed Decisions*, 10–12; Earl of Birkenhead, *Churchill 1874–1922*, 112–113 and 177; Violet Bonham Carter, *Winston Churchill as I Knew Him*, 4, 186; Shelden, 104–107; 149–191; Davenport-Hines, 161–162; Jenkins Foreword to Bonham-Carter and Pottle, xxv.

20. Shelden, 180–185; Bonham Carter, 172–173; Bonham Carter and Pottle, 161–162 (Violet Asquith to Venetia Stanley, 14 August 1908); Birkenhead, 112.
21. Jenkins (*Churchill*), 448.
22. Brendon, 47–49; Purnell, 50–51; Roberts, 385–387; Jenkins (*Churchill*), 448; Bloch, 78–83; Marsh (*People*) 171–173; Stefan Buczacki, *Darling Mr Asquith*, 48–49, 203: Buczacki provides the 'sod' reference in a passage in a Diana to Duff Cooper letter which she omitted from her quotation of it in her memoirs.
23. Haldane, 230–232; Jenkins (*Asquith*), 241–242; *Whitaker's Almanack* (1911), 210, 224; Roberts, 161.
24. Haldane, 230–232; CV II: 2, 1295.
25. Haldane, 231–232.
26. Campbell, 275–276; Bonham Carter, 188–189; Bonham Carter and Pottle, 285.
27. Fitzroy Papers: Add MS 48,376: 436–437.
28. Fitzroy Papers: Add MS 48,376: 248, 130; CV II:2, 1295–1296.
29. Farr, 212; Hassall, 175.
30. CHAR 2/39/124 (Lord Morley to Winston Churchill, 27 December 1909); Bonham Carter and Pottle, 306 (Violet Asquith Diary, 8 February 1912); Fitzroy, 466–467.
31. Hassall, 175; Jenkins (*Churchill*), 205–206.
32. V.G. Trukhanovsky, *Winston Churchill*, 101–102.
33. Campbell, 276; Ensor, 436.
34. *The Manchester Guardian*, 29 November 1954.
35. Hassall, 175.
36. Riddell Diary, Add MSS 62956, 58; *The Manchester Guardian*, 29 November 1954; Baxendale, 39.
37. Blunt, 399 (20 October 1912).
38. HO 144/1169/214572; Jill Liddington, *Vanishing for the Vote: Suffrage, Citizenship and the Battle for the Census*, 67–70, 204–206.

Chapter 30
1. SFT, 96; CV, II: 3, 1990–1991; Churchill (*World Crisis*), 160–172; Douglas Newton, *The Darkest Days*, 51–54; Nester, 46; Duncan Marlor, *Fatal Fortnight*, 78–79; Cameron Hazlehurst, *Politicians at War*, 39.
2. Francis Neilson, *My Life in Two Worlds*, 324–325.
3. Blake, 132–133.
4. Baxendale, 171.
5. Baxendale, 168–169; Ruggles-Brise, 223; Bailey (*Rise and Fall*), 82–85.
6. Victor Bailey (*Rise and Fall*), 97.
7. Victor Bailey (*Rise and Fall*), 106; Fox, 66–70 and 98; Home Office: Trends and drivers of homicide Research Report 113, (https:// assets.publishing.service.gov.uk) p. 4; UK Prison Population Statistics - House of Commons Library (parliament.uk), consulted, 5.1.2022.
8. History of Dartmoor Prison (dartmoor-prison.co.uk), consulted, 5.1. 2022; Hansard, 317: 1899.
9. Victor Bailey (*Rise and Fall*), 277; David Garland, *The Culture of Control*, 54.
10. Professor Nicola Padfield, University of Cambridge, 'Parole: Reflections and Possibilities', A discussion paper, published by the Howard League for Penal Reform, 2018; Bailey (*Rise and Fall*), 496–503.
11. Garland (*Culture*), 8–12; McGovern interview: *Today*, 11 May 2022.
12. Nicki Jameson, Eric Allison, *Strangeways 1990*.
13. Erwin James, *A Life Inside*, 94–96.
14. David Ramsbotham, *Prisongate* (2003).

15. Bailey (*Rise and Fall*), 496–503; Joe Sim, *Punishment and Prisons: Power and the Carceral State*, 66–67; Hansard, 933: 284.
16. Jeffrey Archer, *A Prison Diary*: Anthony Howard (*Sunday Times*) review quoted in blurb.
17. Erwin James, *Redeemable*, 326–331.
18. *Guardian*, 30 March 2014, 5 December 2014.
19. *Guardian*, 8 January 2013; Harold Mozley: letter to *Financial Times* reprinted in *The Week*, 12 February 2022; Garland (*Culture*), 9.
20. Gemma Birkett, *Media, Politics and Penal Reform*, 21–22; History of Dartmoor Prison (dartmoor-prison.co.uk), consulted, 5.1. 2022.
21. *CV* II: 3, 1434, 1440–1444.
22. Geoffrey Wheatcroft, *Churchill's Shadow*, 522.
23. Boris Johnson, *The Churchill Factor: How One Man Made History*; Tariq Ali, *Winston Churchill: His Times, His Crimes*, 417; Wheatcroft, 520–522.
24. For a valuable analysis, see Ian Loader, '"Platonic Guardians": Liberalism, Criminology and Political Responses to Crime in England and Wales', in *British Journal of Criminology*, September 2006.
25. Francis Green and David Kynaston, *Engines of Privilege*, 30–32; *The Times*, 17 February 1911.
26. As this book is completed the *Guardian* of 8 September 2023 reports, in an article by deputy political editor Peter Walker, that the current prisoner population for England and Wales stands at just over 87,000, fewer than 1,000 below absolute maximum capacity; also that prison sentences are more than 50 per cent longer on average in the decade to 2022. It may be argued that these facts, going with insufficient prison resources and heavy overcrowding, underline the urgency of the need for reform in the spirit of Winston Churchill in 1910–1911.

Bibliography

SOURCES

Primary Sources
British National Archives, Kew
Home Office and Prison Commission Papers

Churchill College, Cambridge
Chartwell Trust Papers, 1874–1945

Lucy Cavendish College, Cambridge
Lucy Masterman Papers

Cadbury Research Library, Birmingham University
Lucy Masterman Diary

British Library
Sir Almeric Fitzroy diary
Lord Riddell diary
John Burns diary
Sound and Moving Image collection: Winston Churchill speech of 1909

Imperial War Museum
Henry Hughes Wilson Diary

Bodleian Library, Oxford
H.H. Asquith Papers

Shulbrede Archives, Sussex
Arthur Ponsonby Diary

Hansard: House of Commons Parliamentary Debates

Addison, Paul *Churchill on the Home Front, 1900–1955*
Addison, Paul 'Churchill and the Sterilisation Issue', in *Finest Hour*, 131 (Summer 2006)
Addison, Paul *Churchill the Unexpected Hero*
Addison, Paul 'Churchill and the Working Class', 45, in Jay Winter (ed.), *The Working Class in Modern British History*
Alcock, George W. *Fifty Years of Railway Trade Unionism*
Andrew, Christopher *The Defence of the Realm: The Authorized History of MI5*
Archer, Jeffrey *A Prison Diary*
Arnot, R. Page *South Wales Miners*, 1898–1914
Askwith, George *Industrial Problems and Disputes*
Atherley-Jones, L.A. *Looking Back*

Bailey, Victor *The Rise and Fall of the Rehabilitative Ideal*
Bailey, Victor 'English Prisons, Penal Culture and the Abatement of Imprisonment, 1895–1922', in *Journal of British Studies*, 36 (July 1977)

Bailey, Victor 'Churchill as Home Secretary', *History Today*, 3 March 1985
Baxendale, Alan S. *Winston Leonard Spencer-Churchill, Penal Reformer*
Blake, William Wallace *Quod*
Blaxland, Gregory *J.H. Thomas*
Bloch, Michael *Closet Queens*
Blunt, Wilfrid Scawen *My Diaries*
Bonham Carter, Lady Violet *Winston Churchill as I Knew Him*
Bonham Carter, Lady Violet *Lantern Slides: The Diaries and Letters of Violet Bonham Carter*
Brendon, Piers *Winston Churchill*
Brockway, Fenner *Towards Tomorrow*
Brown Kenneth D. *The Unknown Gladstone*
Buczacki, Stefan *Churchill & Chartwell*
Buczacki, Stefan *Darling Mr Asquith*
Butler, Harold *Confident Morning*

Callwell, C.E. *Field-Marshal Sir Henry Wilson*
Campbell, John *F.E. Smith*
Campbell, John *Haldane*
Churchill, Randolph S. *Winston S. Churchill, Volume II, Young Statesman 1901–1914*
Churchill, Randolph S. *Winston S. Churchill Companion Volume II, Parts 1,2 and 3*
Cohen, Michael J. *Churchill and the Jews*
Churchill, Winston S. *Thoughts and Adventures*
Churchill, Winston S. *The Boer War*
Churchill, Winston S. *My Early Life*
Churchill, Winston S. *The People's Rights*
Churchill Winston S. *The World Crisis 1911–1918*
Clarke, Peter *Hope and Glory Britain 1900–2000*
Clayton, Gerold *The Wall is Strong*
Clifford, Colin *The Asquiths*
Coogan, John W. and Coogan, Peter F. 'The British Cabinet and the Anglo-French Staff Talks, 1905–1914: Who Knew What and When Did He Know It', *Journal of British Studies*, 24: 1 (Jan 1985)
Crowther, M.A. *The Workhouse System*

David, Edward *Inside Asquith's Cabinet*
Davenport-Hines, Richard *Ettie*
De Mendelssohn, Peter *The Age of Churchill*
Dockter, Warren *Churchill and the Islamic World*
Dutton, David J. (ed.) *Odyssey of an Edwardian Liberal: The Political Diary of Richard Durning Holt*

Earl of Birkenhead *Churchill 1874–1922*
Edwards, John *Remembrance of a Riot*
Ensor, R.C.K. *England 1870–1914*

Faber, David *Speaking for England*
Farquharson, Robert and Sargent, J.S. *The House of Commons From Within*
Farr, Martin *Reginald McKenna*
Fernihough, Anne *Freewomen and Supermen*
Field, Jacob F. *The Eccentric Mr Churchill*
Foot, Paul *The Vote*
Forsythe, W.J. *Penal Discipline, Reformatory Projects and the English Prison Commission 1895–1939*

Fox, Lionel W. *The English Prison and Borstal Systems*
Freeman, David 'Great Contemporaries – Eddie Marsh: A Profile' in *Finest Hour* 131 (Summer 2006)
Fyfe, Janet *Books Behind Bars*

Gainer, Bernard *The Alien Invasion*
Galsworthy, John The Plays of (Duckworth)
Gardiner, A.G. *Pillars of Society*
Gardiner, A.G. *Prophets, Priests and Kings*
Gardiner, A.G. *The War Lords*
Garland, David *Punishment and Welfare: A History of Penal Strategies*
Garland, David *The Culture of Control*
Garrard, John A. *The English and Immigration*
Gibson, Martin *A Primrose Path*
Gilbert, Bentley B. *The Evolution of National Insurance in Great Britain*
Gilbert, Martin *Churchill A Life*
Gilbert, Martin 'Leading Churchill Myths: "Churchill's campaign against the 'feeble-minded' was deliberately omitted by his biographers"', *Finest Hour* 152, Autumn 2011
Gilbert, Martin *Churchill & The Jews*
Graves, Robert *Goodbye to All That*
Grigg, John *Lloyd George: The People's Champion, 1902 – 1911*

Haldane, Richard Burdon *An Autobiography*
Hall, Douglas J. 'Churchill's Elections', in *Finest Hour*, 103
Hall, Edith 'Medea and British legislation before the First World War', *Greece and Rome*, Vol. 46, 1 (April 1999)
Hassall, Christopher *Edward Marsh*
Hazlehurst, Cameron *Politicians at War*
Heffer, Simon *The Age of Decadence*
Hobhouse, Stephen and Brockway, Fenner *English Prisons Today: Being the Report of the Prison System Enquiry Committee*
Hopkins, Eric *Charles Masterman*
Howard, Michael *The First World War*
Howse, Geoffrey *A History of London's Prisons*
Hyman, Alan *The Rise and Fall of Horatio Bottomley*
Hynes, Samuel *The Edwardian Turn of Mind*

James, Erwin *A Life Inside*
James, Erwin *Redeemable*
James, Robert Rhodes *Churchill A Study in Failure 1900–1939*
Jameson, Nicki, Allison, Eric *Strangeways 1990*
Janes, Diane *Edwardian Murder*
Jenkins, Roy *Churchill*
Jenkins, Roy *The Chancellors*
Jenkins, Roy *A Life at the Centre*
Johnson, Boris *The Churchill Factor*
Johnson, Paul *Churchill*
Jones, Gareth Stedman *Outcast London*
Judge, Tony *Margaret Bondfield*

Kent, William *John Burns*

Lambert, Nicholas *Planning Armageddon*
Leslie, Shane *Sir Evelyn Ruggles-Brise*
Leventhal, F.M. *The Last Dissenter*
Liddington, Jill *Vanishing for the Vote: Suffrage, Citizenship and the Battle for the Census*
Liddle, Andrew *Cheers, Mr Churchill! Winston in Scotland*
Linklater, Eric *The Corpse on Clapham Common*
Lough, David *No More Champagne: Churchill and His Money*
Lloyd George, David *War Memoirs*
Lloyd George, Robert *David & Winston*
Lytton, Constance *Prisons and Prisoners – Some Personal Experiences*

Macartney, Wilfred *Walls Have Mouths*
MacDonald, Ramsay *National Defence*
Marlor, Duncan *Fatal Fortnight*
Mallet, Charles *Herbert Gladstone*
Marrot, H.V. *Life and Letters of John Galsworthy*
Marsh, Edward *A Number of People*
Martin, Ross M. *The Lancashire Giant*
MacKenzie, Jeanne *The Children of the Souls*
MacNaghten, Sir Melville *Days of My Years*
Mallinson, Allan *Too Important for the Generals*
McEwen, John (ed.) *The Riddell Diaries*
Mason, Gary *The Official History of the Metropolitan Police*
Masterman, Charles *The Condition of England*
Masterman, Lucy *C.F.G. Masterman*
Masterman, Lucy *History Today*, 1964
Morgan, Jane *Conflict and Order*
Morgan, Kenneth *Rebirth of a Nation*
Morgan, Ted *Churchill: Young Man in a Hurry*
Morris, A.J.A. *The Scaremongers*
Morris, A.J.A. *Radicalism Against War 1906–1914*
Morris, A.J.A. (ed.), *Edwardian Radicalism*
Moulton, H. Fletcher (ed.), *The Trial of Steinie Morrison*
Murphy, William *Political Imprisonment and the Irish*
Murrays of Elibank *Master and Brother*

Neilson, Francis *My Life in Two Worlds*
Nester, William *Winston Churchill and the Art of Leadership*
Newton, Douglas *The Darkest Days*
Nott-Bower, Sir William *Fifty-two Years A Policeman*

Otte, T.G. *Statesman of Europe: A Life of Sir Edward Grey*
Otte, T.G. *The Foreign Office Mind*
Owen, David *The Hidden Perspective*

Packer, Ian (ed.) *The Letters of Arnold Stephenson Rowntree to Mary Katherine Rowntree*
Padfield, Professor Nicola 'Parole: Reflections and Possibilities', A discussion paper, published by the Howard League for Penal Reform
Pankhurst, Emmeline *My Own Story*
Pankhurst, E. Sylvia *The Suffragette Movement*
Paterson Arthur *Our Prisons*
Pearson, Geoffrey *Hooligan: A History of Respectable Fears*

Pellew, Jill *The Home Office 1848–1914*
Porter, Bernard 'The British Government and Political Refugees, c. 1880–1914' in *From the Other Shore*, ed. John Slater
Porter, Bernard *The Origins of the Vigilant State*
Pratten, John Douglas 'The Reaction to Working Class Unrest, 1911–1914', 124, Sheffield University PhD. thesis
Priestley, Philip *Victorian Prison Lives*
Pugh, Martin *The Pankhursts*
Purnell, Sonia *First Lady*

Radzinowicz, Leon and Hood, Roger *The Emergence of Penal Policy in Victorian and Edwardian England*
Ramsden, John (ed.) *Real Old Tory Politics: The Political Diaries of Sir Robert Sanders, Lord Bayford*
Redmayne, Sir Richard A.S. *Men, Mines and Memories*
Renton, Alex *Stiff Upper Lip*
Reynolds, Stephen *Seems So*
Ramsbotham, David *Prisongate*
Riddell, Fern *Death in Ten Minutes*
Riddell, George *More Pages from My Diary*
Ridgwell, Stephen 'The Mangold's Champion', in *Journal of Liberal History*, 105, 2019–2020
Roberts, Andrew *Churchill: Walking with Destiny*
Rogers, Colin *The Battle of Stepney*
Rose, Gordon *The Struggle for Penal Reform*
Rose, Norman *Churchill: An Unruly Life*
Rosen, Andrew *Rise Up, Women!*
Rowan-Hamilton, S.O (ed.) *The Trial of John Alexander Dickman*
Rowland, Peter *The Last Liberal Governments: The Promised Land, 1905–1910*
Ruff, Philip *A Towering Flame*
Ruggles-Brise, Sir Evelyn *The English Prison System*
Rumbelow, Donald *The Houndsditch Murders*

Sampson, Anthony *The Anatomy of Britain Today*
Scott, Sir Harold, *Your Obedient Servant*
Searle, G.R. *Eugenics and Politics in Britain*
Shelden, Michael *Young Titan*
Silvester, Christopher *Pimlico Companion to Parliament*
Sim, Joe *Punishment and Prisons: Power and the Carceral State*
Soames, Mary *Clementine Churchill*
Soames, Mary (ed.) *Speaking for Themselves: The Personal Letters of Winston and Clementine Churchill*
Stansky, Peter *On or About December 1910: Early Bloomsbury and its Intimate World*

Taylor, A.J.P. *The Mastery of Europe, 1848–1918*
Taylor, A.J.P. *British Prime Ministers and Other Essays*
Taylor, Harry, *Victor Grayson*
Thomas, J.A. *The House of Commons 1906–1911*
Thomas, J.E. *The English Prison Officer Since 1850: A Study in Conflict*
Tillett, Ben *Memories and Reflections*
Tillett, Ben *History of the London Transport Strike*, in *Social Tracts 1902–1912*
Toye, Richard *Lloyd George & Churchill*
Toye, Richard *Churchill's Empire*

Troup, Sir Edward *The Home Office*
Trukhanovsky, V.G. *Winston Churchill*

Walker-Smith, Derek *The Life of Lord Darling*
Webb, Beatrice *Our Partnership*
Wheatcroft, Geoffrey *Churchill's Shadow*
Wiener, Martin J. *Reconstructing the Criminal: Culture, Law and Policy in England, 1830–1914*
Wheatcroft, Geoffrey *Churchill's Shadow*
Whittington-Egan, Molly *Murder on the Bluff*
Wilde, Oscar *The Ballad of Reading Jail*
Wilson, Keith *The Policy of the Entente*
Wilson, Keith 'The Agadir Crisis, the Mansion House Speech, and the Double-Edgedness of Agreements', *Historical Journal*, 15:3, September 1972
Wilson, Trevor *The Political Diaries of C.P. Scott*
Winstanley, Michael *The Shopkeeper's World, 1880–1914*
Wrigley, Chris 'Churchill and the Trade Unions', in *Winston Churchill in the Twenty-First Century*, ed. David Cannadine and Ronald Quinault
Wynn, Stephen *Churchill's Flawed Decisions*

Index

Abatement of Imprisonment Committee, 193
Administration of Justice Bill of 1911, 192
Administration of Justice Act of 1914, 232
Agadir Crisis, 195–197
Akbar Reformatory scandal, 145–46
Akers-Douglas, Aretas, 116–17
Aliens Act (1905), 115
Alverstone, Lord, 59
Anglo French 'Conversations', 196
Amery, Leopold, 183
Anderson, Sir Robert, 118
Archer, Jeffrey, 235
Askwith, George, 78, 80
Asquith, Herbert Henry, 9, 37, 49, 65, 71–2, 89, 91–2, 99, 103–104, 147, 157, 177, 184, 196–7, 208, 214, 216, 222–26, 227–228, 231
   becomes Prime Minister, 1
   appoints Churchill as Home Secretary, 2
   says that Churchill 'thinks with his mouth', 6
   is shouted down in Parliament, 182
   decides cabinet change at the Admiralty needed, 220
   interviews Churchill and Lord Haldane regarding Admiralty cabinet post, 224–26
Asquith, Margot, 3–4, 35, 224
Asquith, Violet (later Lady Violet Bonham-Carter), 182, 228
   unspoken understanding with Churchill, 224–26
Aylesbury Prison, 61, 65,170, 173,192

Balance of Power, 194
Balfour, Arthur, 36, 37, 90, 92, 116, 129, 147, 150–51, 153, 182, 206
   mocks Churchill, 103–104
Banbury, Sir Frederick, 152
   blocks Churchill's Aliens Bill, 121–22
   opposes Churchill's Shops Bill, 160–61
Barnes, George, 93
Battersea, Lady Constance, 192
'Battle of Downing Street', 82–4
'Battle of Sidney Street', 97–106
Bentinck, Lord Henry, 83
Beron, Leon, 109
Betting and Gaming, 135
Beveridge, William, 66–7

Bigge, Sir Arthur, 178
Birrell, Augustine, 36, 84, 189
Birrell, Mrs Olive, 189
'Black Friday', 82–5, 135
Blackmore, Mabel, 175–76
Blackwell, Ernley (afterwards Sir Ernley Blackwell), 18, 23–6, 50–3, 56–7, 59, 60–1, 97, 107–108, 111, 134, 145, 154–55, 157, 171, 173–75, 186, 230
   unusual as a First Division civil servant not a university graduate, 49
   unhappy about Churchill's reprieve of Edward Woodcock, 51–2
   sceptical about Churchill's penal reform plans, 64–6
   chairs Abatement of Imprisonment Committee, 193
   attitude to Churchill as Home Secretary, 239
Blair, Anthony (afterwards Sir Anthony) Charles Lynton (Tony), 235
Blake, Major Wallace, 131–32, 232
'Bloody Code', 8, 25, 170
Blunt, Wilfrid Scawen, 30, 60, 65, 76, 87, 151, 169, 171, 229
   advises Churchill about prison reform, 8
Boer War, xii, 7, 107, 168, 186, 219
Boilermakers' Union, 78
Bondfield, Margaret, 159
Booth, Handel, 120
Boothby, Robert, 240
Borstal system, 5, 13–14, 40, 65, 124, 188
Bottomley, Horatio
   opposes Churchill's Shops Bill 160–2
Bowen, Rev W. G., 170
Boxall, Florence, 170–1
Brailsford, Henry, 29, 33
   accuses Churchill of treachery, 238
Briand, Aristide, 210
Bridgeman, William, 130
British Expeditionary Force, 194, 196, 220–23
Broadmoor Asylum, 65, 74, 114
Brockway, Fenner, 7, 15
Bulbeck, Charles, 16–17, 26
Burns, John, 34, 72, 207–208
   compared by Ben Tillett with Winston Churchill, 202

Butcher, John, 35
Butler, Harold, 59, 61, 109–110, 125–126, 177
  on Churchill as Home Secretary, 11, 54, 97, 158
Butler, Richard Austen ('Rab'), later Lord Butler, 234
Byles, William, 41–2, 142–45
Byrne, William, 49, 139

Callaghan, Leonard James (Jim), later Lord Callaghan, 78
Cambrian Combine, 78
Camp Hill Prison 20, 123
Capital Punishment, 47–61, 107–12, 169–76, 186
  not questioned as an institution by Churchill, 60
Capital Punishment Act (1868), 60
Carew, Edith, 61–2
Carter, Beatrice, 153–57
Castlereagh, Lord, 148–49
Cave, Sir George, 109
Cecil, Lord Hugh, 40–1, 125, 148, 181–82
  clashes with Churchill on the eve of war, 231
Censorship of stage, 168–69
Chamberlain, Austen, 149–150
  claims that Churchill finding the Home Office 'too hot' for him, 228
Chapman, Cecil, 135–36
Chelmsford Prison, 49, 108
Children Act (1908), 5, 42, 124
Churchill, Clementine Ogilvy Spencer-Churchill (née Hosier; later Baroness Spencer-Churchill)), 1, 97, 99, 113, 127, 131, 134–35, 137–38, 153, 167, 171, 178–80, 184–85, 186, 197, 213, 220–21, 224–26
  marriage to Churchill 3, 225
  as a radical Liberal 88
  makes election speeches 135
  dislikes Churchill's cousin, the Duke of Marlborough 138
Churchill, Diana Spencer- (later Churchill), 27, 97, 171, 173
Churchill, Jeanette (Jennie) Spencer- (née Jerome), known as Lady Randolph Spencer-Churchill, 7
  marriage as a union of American money and British aristocracy 184
Churchill, Lord Randolph 7, 12, 71, 216
  as Chancellor of the Exchequer 3
  promotes 'Tory democracy' 3
  scorn for his son Winston 31–32
Churchill, Randolph Frederick Edward Spencer- (son of Winston), 173
Churchill, Winston Leonard Spencer-, later Sir Winston Churchill, 4, 37, 56, 59, 98, 112

BOOKS AND JOURNALISM
  income from writing important to Churchill in maintaining his lifestyle, 2
  articles and books largely dictated, 3
MILTARY CAREER
  fights in the Boer War and is captured, xi–xii, 7, 186
  military side engaged by the Siege of Sidney Street, 97–106
  tells George Riddell that in the event of Britian being in a land war he would resign as Home Secretary and go to the front, 95–6
  tells Clementine that he is confident in himself as a military tactician, 99
POLITICAL CAREER
  Parliamentary Under-Secretary at the Colonial Office, 1, 6, 31, 37, 89, 142, 228
  President of the Board of Trade, 1–2, 6, 19, 66, 92, 140, 217
  First Lord of the Admiralty, 229, 31
  Chancellor of the Exchequer, 232
  Prime Minister 237–38
  accused of being self-advertising and overriding rules and procedure, 150–51, 155–57
  helps Lloyd George with the National Insurance Bill, 140
  as Leader of the House, standing in for Asquith, 147–50
AT THE HOME OFFICE
  appointed Home Secretary, 1–4
  learns of his decision-making responsibility regarding death sentences, 4
  resolves to reduce prison numbers, 8
  shocks Home Office traditionalists, 11, 158
  investigates sentencing with a view to 'Abatement of Imprisonment', 12–15
  reduces 'separate confinement', 12
  makes plans for 'Defaulters' Drill, 12–13
  deals with petitions and approaches regarding sentences, 15–29
  ameliorates conditions for political prisoners with 'Churchill Rule' 30–2
  plans to improve aid to discharged convicts, 40
  sets out to Parliament his prison reform programme, 42–4
  aims to abolish imprisonment for debt, 63
  plans to make prisons specialised, 63
  plans for prison sentences for minor offences to be suspended, 65
  aims for a unified sentencing system, 66
  opposition to prison officer trade unionism, 68–9
  enthusiasm for eugenics, 70–6

attitude to syndicalism and 'The Great
  Unrest' 78–80
tries to bring in new Aliens
  legislation, 117–22
visits Parkhurst Prison, 123
visits Pentonville Prison and interviews
  prisoners, releasing some, 123–25
Visits Dartmoor Prison, 125–26
and the 'Dartmoor Shepherd' Affair, 126–32
visits Lambeth Police Court, 134
defends his record during the June 1911
  Home Office Debate, 150–53
hosts the Parliamentary Committee of the
  Trades Union Congress at the Home
  Office (February 1911), 164–66
democratic approach to staff
  recruitment, 166
attempts to bring in automatic commutation
  of death sentences on women killing their
  babies, 170
composes speeches for the King (Edward
  VII, then George V) to deliver,
  39, 177–79
brings in prison reforms regarding lectures
  and entertainment, libraries and gentler
  conditions for elderly inmates, 187–192
defends the rights of trade unions, 199–200
sets up a committee with a view to an
  Administration of Justice Act, 192–93
holds to his line on conciliation in the early
  stages of the 1911 strikes, 200
drops caution and moderation as the wave
  of strikes reach London in July 1911, 201
takes a militant anti-striker line in the
  August 1911 national rail strike, using the
  Home Office to coordinate the dispatch
  of troops, 205–213
organises the sending of troops to suppress
  an anti-Jewish pogrom in South Wales in
  August 1911, 217–18
orders remissions regarding a number of
  prison sentences shortly before leaving
  the Home Office (October 1911), 229–30
POLITICAL VIEWS AND OUTLOOK
attitude to female suffrage, 28–38, 81–5
elusiveness of his political identity, 86
political differences with Lloyd George, 87
attitude to moves for a Liberal-Conservative
  coalition, 88–90
many-sidedness and shifting positions, 91
yo-yo political behaviour, 91
his rhetoric as leading his policy, 91
as a 'Tory Democrat' 91, 182
dislike of plans to remove the veto powers of
  the House of Lords 90–1
clashes in Parliament with Keir
  Hardie, 92–3

as a New Liberal, 92–3
electoral value to the Liberals, 93–5
lack of interest in the campaign to improve
  the status and conditions of the police
  rank-and-file, 114
allies with Manchester's Jewish
  community, 115
acknowledges class bias in the jury
  system, 133–34
ambivalence regarding land reform,
  138, 140–41
not minded to abolish flogging, 142–145
not a racist but makes racially offensive
  remarks at various times, 168
middle-of-the-road politics, 181
peace promotion and anti-militarism
  (chiefly 1908, 1909) 194–95, 219–20
and the 1911 Agadir Crisis, being no longer
  anti-war as his interest in potential
  British involvement in European war
  deepens, 195–98
writes an assessment of the likely course
  of Brtish involvement in a European
  war, 221–22
increasingly absorbed in military security
  and intelligence, 198, 219
attends a meeting of the Committee of
  Imperial Defence on 23 August 1911 on
  the subject of a British Expeditionary
  Force in a European war, 222–23
interviewed with Lord Haldane at Asquith's
  East Lothian holiday home in September
  1911 regarding the post of First Lord of
  the Admiralty, 224, 226–27
CHARACTERISICS AND
PERSONAL LIFE
personal appearance, 2
accent and manner of speech, 2
high energy rate, 1, 11, 12, 40–41, 65, 67,
  131, 224, 228
reputation for scooping the credit of others
  31–2, 89
talkative in cabinet, 5, 226
humanity and compassion for prisoners
  and accusations against him of
  'sentimentality', 10, 45, 101, 204
not of the all-work-no-play school, 78
attracted to the Islamic world, 86
liking for parvenus, 87
brain process as viewed by Charles
  Masterman, 76
self-promotion and bombast, 90
unable to resist the limelight, 102
accusations of intriguing, 90
said by Lloyd George to lack humour, 89
has Napoleon as his hero, 89, 105
addiction to gambling, 3, 51, 106, 135

his Ecclestone Square house, 96
extravagant lifestyle, 96–97, 184
risky investments and heavy borrowing, 96–7, 184
rapport with crowds, 125
sense of being excluded from wealth and privilege, 184
'practically engaged' to Violet Asquith, 225
marriage to Clementine, 225–26
changeability of his causes and alliances, 90
Lady Diana Manners on his 'sod bias', 225–26 and Chapter 29, note.22.
Churchill, Winston Spencer- (grandson of Winston Churchill), 78
'Churchill Rule', 41, 81, 230
CID: *see* Committee of Imperial Defence
Clancy, J.J., 160
Clarke, Kenneth, 235
Clayton, Sir Edward, 186–87
Clunas, Lila, 37
Coal Mines Safety Bill 163–64, 227
Cobden-Sanderson, Anne, 83, 95
Coleridge, Lord 50–1, 170–71
Committee of Imperial Defence, 221, 222–24
Common Cause, 171
Community Service, 236
Conciliation Bill, 29–38, 82, 238
Connolly, Annie 25–7
Cooper, Duff 225–26
Coronation of King George V, 171, 178–80
Coulson, John, 51, 56, 58
Crackenthorpe, Montague, 72
Crewe, Lord, 152, 227
Crichton-Stuart, Lord Ninian, 185
Crippen, Hawley, 47, 58–9, 60, 111–12
Crowe, Sir Eyre, 195
Cunynghame, Sir Henry, 49

Daily Chronicle, 98, 100, 206
Daily Express, 16, 44, 79, 118, 156
Daily Mail, 45, 57, 98, 118, 174, 234
Daily Mirror, 148–49, 207, 221
Daily News, 6, 9, 16–17, 45, 47, 79, 103, 106, 147–48, 176, 202, 206, 208, 210–11, 213, 215
Daily Telegraph, 118–19
Dalziel, Sir Henry, 102, 111, 130
Darling, Sir Charles, 24–5, 107, 109–11, 113, 172–74, 181
Dartmoor Prison, 14, 43, 64, 123, 125–27, 130, 187, 189, 237
Dartmoor Riot 233
Davies, David ('The Dartmoor Shepherd'), 126–32
Davies, Sir Howell, 167
'Defaulters' Drill', 12–13, 42, 46, 65, 193, 236
De Forest, Baron Maurice, 47, 86, 115

Delevingne, Malcolm, 163–64
Derby, Lord, 206–207
Derrick, Alfred, 53
Desborough, Lady, 37, 224
Dew, Inspector, 47
Dickman, Annie, 57
Dickman, John 55–60, 74, 112
Disraeli, Benjamin, 87, 120
Donkin, Sir Bryan, 72–3
Du Cane, Sir Edmund, 9–10
Dugdale, John, 20
Duval, Victor, 81
Dyer, Amelia, 171

Earl, Mary Frances, 84
Edwards, Clement, 175
Education Act (1902), 90
Eight Hours Act (1908), 6, 65, 77–8, 93, 160
Elgin, Ninth Earl of (Victor Alexander Bruce), 1
Ellis, John, 50, 108
Entente Cordiale, 194
Eugenics Society, 72
Euripides, 169
Executioners, 49, 123

Fitzroy, Sir Almeric, 77, 99, 206, 227–28
Flavin, Michael, 183
Flogging, 45, 142–45, 233
Foreman, Frederick, 49
Forster, E.M., 199
Franklin, Hugh, 83
Free Pardons, 139

Galsworthy, John, 7–10, 11, 45
Gardiner, A.G., 6, 41, 105, 125, 203, 216
Garibaldi, Margherita, 52
Garrison, Herbert, 187–88
Gatty, Katherine, 81
General Election of 1906, 12, 115
General Election of January 1910, 1, 2, 28, 90, 167
General Election of December 1910, 93–5, 126. 137
Gibbs, Philip, 98, 206
Gill, Ernest, 24–5
Ginnell, Lawrence, 17, 81
Gladstone, Herbert, 4–5, 9–12, 27, 30–2, 34, 48–9, 66, 71–2, 119, 163, 170
  sketches the breadth of a Home Secretary's responsibilities, 4
  indignant that Churchill has appropriated credit from him, 31
Gladstone, Lady Dorothy (wife of Herbert), 100, 117, 146, 163, 177, 221, 228–29
Goulding, Edward, 119–22, 181–2
Gove, Michael, 237

Granet, Sir Guy, 206
Grantham, Sir William, 108, 128–29
Grant-Wilson, Wemyss, 40
Granville-Barker, Harley, 169
Graves, Robert, 126
Great Unrest, The, 77, 199
Greaves, Constable George, 109, 112–13
Greenwood, George 142, 144
Grey, Sir Edward, 36, 56–60, 144, 196–97, 219–23, 231
  is disturbed by the experience of taking over Churchill's discretion duty (during his absence abroad) regarding hanging or reprieve, 58
  often visited by Churchill during the Agadir crisis, 220

Haldane, Lord Richard 36, 78, 194, 196–97, 220, 222–24, 226
  resolves industrial crisis at Newport while Churchill is away on holiday, 77
  resists Churchill's wish to send troops to the London docks, 201
  concedes to Churchill in a friendly spirit regarding the Admiralty cabinet post, 226
Hamilton, Jean, 47
Harcourt, Lewis (Loulou or Lulu), later Lord Harcourt, 205, 222
Harcourt, Robert, 168–69
Hardie, Keir, 33, 36, 79, 120, 164, 201
  confrontation in Parliament with Winston Churchill, 92–3
  blames Churchill for violence and deaths in the railway strike, 214
'Hard Labour', 22, 233
Harvey, Edmund, 231
Heaton, John, 44
Helmsley, Viscount, later Earl of Feversham, 137, 148
Henderson, Arthur, 213
Henry, Sir Edward, 82, 113, 135, 197
Hobhouse, Charles, later Sir Charles, 5, 39–40
Hobhouse, Stephen, 15
Holloway Prison, 189, 230
Holt, Richard 153
Homicide Act (1957), 186
Hopwood, Sir Francis, later Lord Hopwood, 6
House of Lords and its veto power, 3, 39, 90–2, 94–5, 182
Housman, Clemence, 230
Houston, Robert, 75
Howard, Michael, later Lord Howard, 235
Hughes, Spencer, 138
Hull Prison, 73
Humanitarian League, 5, 10, 12, 81, 112, 142, 144, 172, 186
  encouraged by Churchill's actions at the Home Office, 45
Hurd, Douglas, later Lord Hurd, 235, 239

Illustrated London News, 98
Infanticide Acts (1922 and 1938), 232
Investiture of the Prince of Wales (later King Edward VIII), 179–80
Irish Home Rule, 16, 39, 88

Jackson, Elizabeth, 97
Jacobs, George, 81
James, Erwin, 235–36
Jeffries, James, 167
Jenkins, Roy, later Lord Jenkins, 225, 228, 236
John Bull, 145
Johnson, Jack, 167
Johnson, William, 155–56
Judgement of Death Act (1823), 170

Kell, Captain Vernon, 219
Kellaway, Frederick, 138–39
Kerrigan, Margaret, 129
King Edward VII (formerly Prince of Wales), 7, 39, 71, 177–78
King George V, 43, 77, 79, 92, 116–17, 177–79, 200, 205, 207–209, 213–14, 228–29
  upset by Churchill's 'very socialistic views', 71
  offended by Churchill's invocation of an alliance of Crown and Commons against the Peers, 177
  urges Churchill that troops should be given 'a free hand' against strikers and 'the mob made to fear them', 207
Kinloch-Cooke, Sir Clement, 75
Kipling, Rudyard, 181
Kitchener, Lord, 221
Knollys, Lord, 71

Lambert, Richard, 94
Land Reform, 88, 137–41
Lane, Thomas, 20–21
Lansbury, George, 200, 216
Laski, Nathan, 115
Law, Andrew Bonar, 88
Lawson, Harry (Harry Lawson Webster Levy-Lawson), later Lord Burnham, 161
Le Neve, Ethel, 47, 58–60, 111
Leveson, Edward, 18–19
Liverpool Prison (Walton Jail), 28, 53, 172
Llanelli Riot (1911), 214–15
Lloyd George, David, 3, 4, 36, 81, 87–92, 93, 125–27, 129–31, 138, 172, 179, 181–82, 203, 207–209, 212–14, 217, 219–23, 228, 230
  political differences with Churchill regarding 'the social order', 87

proposes Liberal-Conservative coalition to Churchill, 88
uses the 'Dartmoor Shepherd' as election propaganda 126, 131
speaks at the Mansion House about the Agadir Crisis 195–98
Lloyd, Seymour, 93
Lombroso, Cesare, 10
London Evening Standard, 157
Lord Chamberlain (office), 168–69
Lord, Daisy 170–71
Lyttelton, Alfred, 124, 150–53
Lytton, Lady Constance, 29–31
Lytton, Second Earl of, 29, 37, 174

Macartney, Wilfred, 192
MacDonald, Ramsay, 36, 113, 120, 146, 208–209, 214
MacVeagh, Jeremiah, 148
Maidstone Prison, 18, 65, 123, 160, 187
Manchester Guardian/Guardian, 79, 86, 135, 219, 235
Manners, Diana, 134, 225
Mansfield, Michael, 234
Marlborough, Ninth Duke of (Charles Spencer-Churchill), 91, 138
Marsden, Dora, 28
Marsh, Edward, 26, 37, 51, 64, 89, 96–7, 100, 117, 134, 146, 150, 163, 177, 195, 221, 225, 228–29
as Churchill's secretary through a succession of ministries, 37
takes Churchill to task for his Sidney Street self-advertisement, 99
Marshall, Katherine (Kitty), 173–74
Martin, Selina, 28
Masefield, John, 7
Masterman, Charles, 6, 21, 33–5, 40, 63, 65, 74–5, 90–1, 99, 101, 119, 123, 131, 134, 138, 157, 159–60, 180–82, 203, 212, 227
deeply moral social perspective, 33
dissuades Churchill from supporting Conciliation Bill with its aim of enfranchising some women, 33–4
handed eugenics bill by Churchill, 75
heads Akbar Reformatory investigation team, 145–46
in charge of Coal Mines Safety Bill, 163
Masterman, Lucy, 6, 16, 33–4, 36, 58, 63, 74–6, 86–91, 94, 123, 150, 157–58, 171, 192, 197, 202–204, 206, 208, 212–13, 229
reads Churchill's Home Office minutes, finding 'a tendency to the rhetorical', 21
view of Churchill's Home Office approach as 'a wholesome discipline', 158
calls Churchill's Home Office 'bulletins' during the 1911 rail strike 'disastrous', 206

Matthews, Sir Charles, 18, 23, 84
McClaren, Lady Laura, 36
McGovern, Jimmy, 234
McKenna, Reginald, 197, 220, 222–23, 227–29
1914 Administration of Justice Act, 232
Mental Deficiency Act (1914), 76
Merxplas (Merksplas) Labour Colony 25, 65
Metropolitan Police, 81–2, 84, 92, 102, 105, 197
as Churchill's responsibility, 47
used by Churchill in South Wales during the mining disputes, 78–80, 92, 200
Metternich, Count (German Ambassador), 197, 221
Meyer, F.B,. 168
Money, Chiozza, 216
Morgan, Hay, 144
Morning Leader, 16, 79, 138
Moroccan Crisis of 1905–1906, 195
Morrison, Stinie (or Steinie), 109–112, 115
Morrison, William, 127
Muldoon, John, 16, 143
Mulvaney, Detective Superintendent, 97
Murphy, Margaret, 172–74
Murray, Alick (Master of Elibank), 5, 31, 79, 227
Murray, Gilbert, 169
Mylius, Edward, 178–79

Napoleon Bonaparte, 89, 105, 158, 216
Nash, Mary Ann, 171
National Insurance Act (1911), 87, 140, 227
National Liberal Club, 185
National Union of Police and Prison Officers, 114
National Union of Women's Suffrage Societies, 171
Neilson, Francis, 231
Neville, Reginald, 133
New Age, 56
Newcastle Illustrated Chronicle, 57–8
Newcastle Prison 56–8
Newgate Prison, 49
Newport, 77, 154
News of the World, 2, 4, 56, 59, 102, 112
Newton, George, 108–109
Nicholson, General Sir William, 221
Nineteenth Century and After, 118, 186–87
Nisbet, John, 54–5
Norman, C.H., 56
Northcliffe, Lord, 119
Northcote-Trevelyan Report, 163–64

O'Brien, Frederick, 205
O'Connor, John, 30, 32
Other Club, The, 181–82, 184
Ottley, Admiral, 221
Oxtoby, Alfred, 73–4

Pall Mall Gazette, 118
Pankhurst, Christabel, 84
Pankhurst, Sylvia, 13, 83, 172–74
Parkhurst Prison, 65, 85, 112, 123, 187, 191–92
Parliament Bill, 182–83, 219
Pateman, George, 186
Paterson, Arthur, 14
Pease, Sir Alfred, 150
Pedder, John, 119
Penny Illustrated Paper, 129
Penrith, Kate, 174–75
Pentonville Prison, 60, 81, 107, 123–25, 131, 150
People's Budget (1909), 3, 89, 126, 198
Perry, George, 49
'Peter the Painter', 97, 101
Pethick-Lawrence, Emmeline, 84
Phillimore, Walter, 175
Pickersgill, Edward, 64, 102, 128
Pierrepoint, Henry, 49–50
Plowden, Pamela, 29
Poaching 137–140
Poaching Prevention Act (1862), 138–40
Pointer, Joseph, 162
Poland, Sir Harry, 102
Ponsonby, Arthur, 90, 137, 181
Porch, Montague, 61
Preventative Detention, 233
Prevention of Crime Act (1908), 5, 19, 22, 25, 127, 190
Preventive Detention, 19–24, 43, 46, 66, 123, 126–28, 190, 236
  disliked by Churchill, 22–4
  use of discouraged by Churchill, 232
Primrose, Neil, 184, 225
Prince Edward (son of George V), 179–80
Prinscep, Alfred, 22
Prison conditions, 9–10, 14–15, 31
Prisoner divisions, 10, 28, 30
Prison escapes, 186
Prison industries 39–40
Prison lectures and entertainment 187–88
Prison libraries 188–190
Prison Officers 8, 15, 67–9, 144
Prison Officers' Magazine, 69
Privy Council, 77, 102, 153, 228
Punch, 4, 17, 36, 46, 87, 92, 165, 182

Queen Mary (wife of George V), 179

Raleigh, Walter, 189
Reading Prison, 64, 153–57
Redmayne, Richard (later Sir Richard), 164–5
Reynold's Newspaper, 102
Rhondda, The, 79
Riddell, Sir George, 83, 88, 142, 173–74, 179–80, 184, 217, 229

provides Churchill with close insights during their golf rounds, 105
Riot Act (1715), 200, 211, 214
Roberts, Charles, 120
Rosebery, Harry, 225
Rowlands, Jimmy, 94
Rowntree, Arnold, 44
Royal Commission on Capital Punishment (1866), 186
Royal Commission on the Feeble-Minded (1908), 72, 74
Royal Commission on the Poor Law (1905), 65–6
  Minority Report 66, 161
Ruggles-Brise, Sir Evelyn, 7–9, 11–15, 39–40, 46, 63–7, 109, 129, 150, 157, 187–88, 232
  at variance with Churchill on Borstal, 13–14
  opposed to Churchill's plans for a category of political prisoners, 30
  close follower of international penal developments, 63
  considers Churchill's ideas for prison specialisation too ambitious, 66
  supports Churchill on more comfortable conditions for elderly prisoners, 191
Runciman, Walter, 70
Rutter, Frank 81

Samuel, Herbert, 83, 205, 227
Schlieffen Plan, 221
Scott, C.P., 84, 219
Scott, Harold, 5, 27, 32, 48, 96
Scramble for Africa, 194
Secret Service Bureau, 219
Sennett, Maud Arncliffe, 170
'Separate Confinement', 7–12, 43, 232
Shackleton, David, later Sir David, 32–4, 38, 134, 164–66
Sharp, Dr 72
Shaw, George Bernard, 172
Sheriffs, 50, 58–9, 227
Shipbuilding Employers' Federation, 77
Shops Bill (1911), 159–63, 227
'Siege of Sidney Street': *see* 'Battle of Sidney Street'
'Silent System' (prisons), 8, 11, 173
Simon, Sir John, 84, 233
Simpson, C.B., 189
Simpson, H.B. (Harry), 19–22, 24–7, 61, 150–51, 170, 188–90, 192, 230
  penal traditionalist, 19
  strongly in favour of preventive detention, 22
  called by Harold Scott 'capricious' 27
  as Home Office's chief crime statistician, 49
  dislike of Churchill's Home Office approach, 239

Smith, F.E., 3, 34, 47, 59, 86–7, 153, 181–82
Smith, Oliver, 107
Snowden, Philip, 35–6, 68, 80
Solitary confinement: *see* separate confinement
Solomon, Mrs Saul, 84
SPD (German Social Democrats), 194, 206
Stafford Prison, 52
Stanley, Arthur, 189
Stead, William 11
Strand Magazine, 189
Strangeways Prison, Manchester, 41, 48, 64, 234
    Strangeways Riot 234
Straw, John Whitaker (Jack), 235
Suffragettes, 28–38, 106, 184, 230
Sultan of Morocco, 195
Sultan of Turkey, 86
Suspended sentences, 193, 222–23
Syme, ex-Inspector John 112–14
Syndicalism, 77, 209

Thatcher, Margaret, 239
Theatre Censorship, 168–169
The Vote newspaper, 170
Thomas, D.A., later Lord Rhondda, 80
Thompson, Basil, 189
Thorne, Will, 17, 109–10, 167
Thynne, Lord Alexander, 185
Ticket of Leave, 43, 172
Tillett, Ben 38, 201–204
Times, 11, 13, 29, 44–45, 79, 84, 99, 101–102, 105, 115, 117–18, 126–28, 130, 137, 161, 165, 167, 185, 199, 209–10, 214, 217
Tonypandy, 78–80
Townsend, George 138–140
Trade Boards Act (1909), 21
Trade Union Congress, 133–34, 163–64
Tread-wheel and crank in prisons, 11
Tredegar anti-Semitic pogrom (1911), 217–18
Tredgold, Dr A.F. 74–75
Triple Alliance 194, 220
Triple Entente, 194, 197, 220–221
Troup, Sir Edward, 5, 17–28, 30, 40, 46, 49–54, 56, 61–3, 65–7, 72, 80–81, 84, 108, 111, 113, 135–36, 139–40, 155–57, 164, 171, 174, 185, 190–91, 200, 205, 239
    believes in the need for separate confinement, 11–12
    sceptical about the need to make prisoner conditions more humane, 14
    disputes with Churchill, 151
    calls Churchill 'the first great Home Secretary since Asquith, 157
    discusses with Reginald Mckenna the experience of working with Churchill at the Home Office, 229
Turkey, 86–7
Turner, Daisy, 176
Tweedmouth, Lord (Second Baron), 228
Tyrell, Sir William, 219

Vagrancy Act (1824), 135, 142
Vanity Fair, 7, 50
Votes for Women newspaper, 29, 83, 93, 172, 230

Waller, Maurice, 13–14, 65–6
Wandsworth Prison, 42, 64, 127, 135
Ward, John, 52, 139, 207, 215
Webb, Beatrice and Sidney, 66, 89, 161
Wedgwood, Josiah (Commander Wedgwood), 117, 143, 164, 240
Wedgwood-Benn, William, 201
Wells, Bombardier Billy, 167
Wells, H.G., 159
Welsh Church Disestablishment, 88
Whitelaw, William, later Lord Whitelaw, 239
Whitley, Harry, 147, 149, 183
Wilde, Oscar 60, 64, 127–28, 154
Wilhelm II, Kaiser, 178, 194, 196, 219
Wilkie, Alexander, 93
Wilkins, Henry, 19–20
Williams, Llewelyn, 175
Willis, Sir Alfred, 127
Wilson, Admiral Sir Arthur, 222–23
Wilson, General Sir Henry, 196, 222–23
Wilson, Henry Joseph, 122
Winterton, Sixth Earl of, 35, 124, 148–49, 181, 183–84
Wolmer, Viscount, 105, 130, 163, 238
Women's Social and Political Union (WSPU), 1, 2, 15, 29, 34, 82, 84, 173, 230
    targets Churchill, 13
    accused by Churchill of generating 'a copious fountain of mendacity', 82
    anger Churchill with their accusations, 84
Woodcock, Edward, 50–52, 54
Woolf, Noah 107–108
Woolf Report 234–35
Wormwood Scrubs Prison, 144
Wren, Joseph 48, 234
Wright, James 22–3

Young Turks, 86
Yoxall, Sir James, 75